MICRONESIA 1944-1974

A BIBLIOGRAPHY OF ANTHROPOLOGICAL AND RELATED SOURCE MATERIALS

by
Mac Marshall and James D. Nason

HRAF PRESS

New Haven
1975

INTERNATIONAL STANDARD BOOK NUMBER: 0-87536-215-x
LIBRARY OF CONGRESS NUMBER: 75-28587
© 1975
HUMAN RELATIONS AREA FILES, INC.

TABLE OF CONTENTS

TABLE OF CONTENTS

ACKNOWLEDGMENTS

This work has taken shape over the span of a decade. It began
in 1966 as a card file to aid in locating and organizing the anthropological literature on Micronesia as we prepared to undertake field
research in the islands while we were both graduate students at the
University of Washington. From 1969 to 1972, it lay dormant while
we completed our studies and embarked on our academic careers. During a long conversation in December, 1972, while attending a conference in Honolulu, we agreed that a comprehensive, systematic, easy-
to-use bibliography of the ever-increasing anthropological literature published on the Trust Territory of the Pacific Islands and
Guam since the end of World War II was long overdue. This idea was
nurtured by our shared experience that available bibliographic
resources for this region were either hopelessly outdated, too
limited in scope, or simply inadequate. With the lack of up-to-date,
useful bibliographic materials for anthropologists interested in
Micronesia as our initial stimulus, then, we undertook this work
not only as a service to our colleagues in anthropology, but also
to Micronesians curious to discover what others have written about
them and to scholars in related disciplines working in the area.

A work such as this inevitably owes a great deal to many other
people. We can only draw attention here to those whose input has
been direct and significant to the completion of the project. The
specific bibliographic format we have used derives from a computer
program written by Karen A. Mullen for a similar bibliography prepared by June Helm on Subarctic Athapaskans. We are most grateful
for the advice and encouragement provided by both of these persons,
and particularly to Karen Mullen for direct assistance in helping
us to modify the program to fit our own needs. Our hearty thanks
go to Mark Borthwick, Andrea Fisher Maril, and Stephan Pisarik,
Research Assistants in the Department of Anthropology, University
of Iowa, who uncomplainingly submitted to the drudgery involved in
verifying citations. A special note of gratitude must go to Mark
Borthwick who, in addition to his duties as a Research Assistant,
voluntarily helped us coax an often recalcitrant computer into
doing our bidding. Leslie B. Marshall has provided valuable edi-
torial assistance at several points along the way, and Emilie G.
Johnston and Renee Heyum have aided our endeavor by checking
obscure references.

Funds for this project have come entirely from the University
of Iowa. The Department of Anthropology paid the salaries of the
Research Assistants, and the Graduate College generously provided
money for computer time through an allocation to the Department
of Anthropology. We are genuinely appreciative of this support.

Timothy J. O'Leary, Director of File Research at the Human
Relations Area Files, offered encouragement at an early stage in
the project, and it was he who suggested HRAF Press as a potential
publisher of the completed manuscript. Elizabeth P. Swift, Man-
aging Editor of HRAF Press, has also been helpful, particularly
as the manuscript neared completion.

-1-

To the countless others who have checked references for us, drawn our attention to works of which we were unaware, or who have provided us with fuller information on their own publications, we offer our gratitude.

Mac Marshall
Iowa City, Iowa

James D. Nason
Seattle, Washington

FOREWORD

It must be emphasized at the outset that this is a bibliography of <u>anthropological</u> and related source materials. As such, it is not meant to be a compilation of <u>all</u> publications that have appeared concerning Micronesia in the post-World War II era. We are confident, however, that this bibliography covers all significant anthropological research on Micronesia published during the period from 1944 to 1974. In addition, it includes references to many papers read by anthropologists at professional meetings and to some anthropological sources published in 1975 or known to be in press. In all, over 1900 individual sources are included.

In determining the scope of "related source materials," we have relied on our own judgment, but in every case we have interpreted this phrase in a broad sense. Thus one will find reference to sources in a great many fields below besides the obviously related disciplines of sociology, political science, psychology, linguistics, economics and history. While we have sought to include all pertinent materials that primarily concern the Trust Territory of the Pacific Islands and Guam, we have also listed a few sources of interest that deal more generally with the Pacific region.

The decision to incorporate published research from other disciplines has been guided by our view of anthropological research as an inherently eclectic enterprise. Like the work of many of our colleagues, our own work has benefitted from a consideration of data collected by scholars in a variety of fields, including the natural and physical sciences as well as the social sciences and the humanities. The desirability of having reference information assembled within an interdisciplinary framework is brought home when dealing with small island environments. The point has been made many times that on small islands human and environmental interactions are clearly and closely intertwined. We have incorporated work from other disciplines wherever that work appears to have possible application to problems that arise in anthropological inquiry on Micronesia's "small islands." By the same token, we suggest that non-anthropologists also may benefit from an examination of anthropological materials that may bear on their own research concerns.

There are bound to be some items that others may feel we should have included which we did not, or items of relevance published in related disciplines that simply escaped our attention. Since this bibliography is stored on computer tape, it will prove quite easy to make additions in future updated versions, and we shall be grateful to users of this bibliography for bringing new items to our attention.

Readers familiar with the literature on Micronesia will note that this bibliography dovetails with an earlier bibliography compiled by Huzio Utinomi. Utinomi's work covers the literature from the earliest published sources on Micronesia up through 1944. Since his bibliography can be consulted for the pre-World War II sources, we have made no effort to duplicate his effort here.

-3-

We have added a number of features to this bibliography that are not often found in such works. Wherever we are aware that a source has been reviewed, the citation for the review is given along with the original source. Where several articles and replies have been published concerning a single controversy, we have provided cross-references to the related sources (see, e.g., Raulet 1959). Reference to papers read at professional meetings has been included only in instances where these papers are known not to have been subsequently published. Other unpublished papers and materials pertaining to the area have not been included. All foreign language titles are followed by an English translation. In a limited number of cases, books and articles of central interest to Micronesian anthropology that are known to be in the final stages of preparation are cited as no date (n.d.). The order numbers for Ph.D. Dissertations completed at universities in the United States which cooperate with Xerox University Microfilms have been provided. Such materials may be ordered either in microfilm or in bound xerographic copy directly from: Xerox University Microfilms, 300 North Zeeb Road, Ann Arbor, Michigan, U.S.A., 48106. Finally, books and other materials that are available in reprinted editions are so noted; generally, we have not cited reprints of works originally published pre-1944.

Scholars just embarking on research in Micronesian studies should be apprized that major collections of published and unpublished source materials on Micronesia may be found in the libraries of the following institutions: (a) Bernice Pauahi Bishop Museum, Honolulu, Hawaii; (b) Micronesian Area Research Center (MARC), University of Guam, Agana, Guam; and (c) University of Hawaii at Manoa, Honolulu, Hawaii.

Many different kinds of sources have been consulted in compiling this bibliography. We have combed the literature for other bibliographies containing Micronesian references, from which we have extracted those citations pertinent to our purposes. In addition to bibliographies, we have systematically searched all of the major anthropological journals that regularly carry articles on Micronesia: Journal of Pacific History, Journal of the Polynesian Society, Micronesica and Oceania. Major anthropological journals both in this country and abroad, e.g., American Anthropologist, Anthropos, Current Anthropology, Journal of Anthropological Research [formerly called Southwestern Journal of Anthropology], and Man have been similarly scrutinized. Many other periodicals have been perused in preparing this work; a complete list of all journals cited in the bibliography may be found below.

We have avoided the use of abbreviations for journals and other sources in the bibliography with four major exceptions:
  (1) ASAO: Association for Social Anthropology in Oceania.
  (2) CIMA: Coordinated Investigation of Micronesian Anthropology.
  (3) PALI: Pacific and Asian Linguistics Institute, University of Hawaii.
  (4) SIM : Scientific Investigations in Micronesia.
Both the CIMA and SIM investigations were sponsored by the Pacific Science Board, National Research Council, National Academy of

Sciences, Washington, D.C., U.S.A.

There is one notable and purposeful limitation to this bibliography: we have not included governmental reports and publications
issued by the Congress of Micronesia, the Trust Territory Government, the Government of Guam, the U.S. Government, or the United
Nations, except in those few cases where such publications directly
relate to anthropological research concerns in the area. Users
wishing to obtain references to such materials will have to look
elsewhere. A beginning may be made by consulting Wright (1969;
cited below in the bibliography).

A final word is in order regarding our use of the term
Micronesia. The earliest meaning of this geographic place name
included the Caroline, Gilbert, Mariana and Marshall Island groups.
Because of the post-World War II incorporation of the Trust Territory of the Pacific Islands with the Territory of Guam as areas
administered by the United States, it is now common to find these
areas--excluding the British-controlled Gilbert Islands--referred
to as Micronesia. This, combined with the internal consistency of
most reported research, much of which is related to the contemporary political map, has led us to exclude the Gilbert Islands
from our purview.

LIST OF SERIAL PUBLICATIONS CONSULTED OR CITED

Academy of Political Science, Proceedings [New York, New York]
Acta Genetica et Statistica Medica [now called Human Heredity; Basel,
    Switzerland]
American Anthropologist [Washington, D.C.]
American Association of University Professors Bulletin [Washington,
    D.C.]
American Historical Review [Washington, D.C.]
American Journal of Clinical Nutrition [Bethesda, Maryland]
American Journal of Epidemiology [formerly called American Journal
    of Hygiene; Baltimore, Maryland]
American Journal of Human Genetics [Chicago, Illinois]
American Journal of Ophthalmology [Chicago, Illinois]
American Journal of Physical Anthropology [Philadelphia, Pennsylvania]
American Journal of Public Health [Washington, D.C.]
American Journal of Sociology [Chicago, Illinois]
American Journal of Tropical Medicine and Hygiene [Lawrence, Kansas]
American Museum of Natural History Bulletin [New York, New York]
American Neptune [Salem, Massachusetts]
American Neurological Association, Transactions [New York, New York]
American Political Science Review [Washington, D.C.]
American Society of International Law, Proceedings [Washington, D.C.]
Annals of the American Academy of Political and Social Science
    [Philadelphia, Pennsylvania]
Annals of the Association of American Geographers [Washington, D.C.]
Annals of Internal Medicine [Philadelphia, Pennsylvania]
Annals of the New York Academy of Sciences [New York, New York]
Anthropologica [new series; Ottawa, Canada]
Anthropological Forum [Perth, Australia]
Anthropological Linguistics [Bloomington, Indiana]
Anthropology UCLA [Los Angeles, California]
Anthropos [Fribourg, Switzerland]
Antiquity [Cambridge, England]
Anuario de Estudios Americanos [Seville, Spain]
Applied Anthropology [now called Human Organization; Boulder, Colorado]
Archaeological Society of New Jersey Bulletin
Archaeological Society of New Jersey Newsletter
Archaeology [New York, New York]
Archaeology and Physical Anthropology in Oceania [Sydney, Australia]
Archiv für Völkerkunde [Vienna, Austria]
Archives of Neurology [Chicago, Illinois]
Archives of Ophthalmology [Chicago, Illinois]
Arthritis and Rheumatism [Hagerstown, Maryland]
Asia [New York, New York]
Asia and the Americas [New York, New York]
Asian Folklore Studies [Tokyo and Nagoya, Japan]
Asian Perspectives [Honolulu, Hawaii]
Asian Studies [Quezon City, Philippines]
Asian Survey [Berkeley, California]
Association for Anthropology in Micronesia Newsletter [Agana, Guam]
Atlantic Monthly [Boston, Massachusetts]
Atoll Research Bulletin [Washington, D.C.]
Auckland Institute and Museum, Records [Auckland, New Zealand]

Australian Foreign Affairs Record [Canberra, Australia]
Australian Journal of Science, The [now called Search; Sydney,
    Australia]
Australian National University Historical Journal, The [Canberra,
    Australia]
Australian Zoologist [Sydney, Australia]

Bernice Pauahi Bishop Museum Bulletin [Honolulu, Hawaii]
Bernice Pauahi Bishop Museum, Occasional Papers [Honolulu, Hawaii]
Bibliographical Society of America, Papers [New York, New York]
Brain [London, England]
Bulletin of the Institute of Ethnology, Academia Sinica [Taipei,
    Taiwan]
Bulletin of the History of Medicine [Baltimore, Maryland]
Bureau of American Ethnology Bulletin [Washington, D.C.]

California Medicine [San Francisco, California]
California Western International Law Journal [San Diego, California]
Canadian Journal of Zoology [Ottawa, Canada]
Central States Anthropological Society Bulletin [Central States
    Bulletin; Cincinnati, Ohio]
Chicago Natural History Museum Bulletin [now called Field Museum
    of Natural History Bulletin; Chicago, Illinois]
Clearinghouse Bulletin of Research in Human Organization [Boulder,
    Colorado]
Comparative Studies in Society and History [New York, New York]
Condor, The [Journal of the Cooper Ornithological Society; Edgewater,
    Maryland]
Contemporary Review [London, England]
Current Anthropology [Chicago, Illinois]
Current History [Philadelphia, Pennsylvania]

Dance Perspectives [New York, New York]

East-West Center Magazine [Honolulu, Hawaii]
East-West Culture Learning Institute, Working Papers [Honolulu, Hawaii]
Ecological Monographs [Durham, North Carolina]
Ecology [Durham, North Carolina]
Economic Botany [Bronx, New York]
Economic Geography [Worcester, Massachusetts]
Educational Forum, The [Toronto, Canada]
Educational Leadership [Washington, D.C.]
Ethnohistory [Tucson, Arizona]
Ethnologica [Köln, West Germany]
Ethnology [Pittsburgh, Pennsylvania]
Ethnomusicology [Middletown, Connecticut]
Ethnos [Stockholm, Sweden]
Expedition [Philadelphia, Pennsylvania]
Explorations [Berkeley, California]

Far Eastern Economic Review [Hong Kong]

Far Eastern Quarterly [now called Journal of Asian Studies; Ann Arbor,
    Michigan]
Far Eastern Survey [New York, New York]
Foreign Affairs [New York, New York]
Foreign Agriculture [U.S. Department of Agriculture; Washington, D.C.]
Foreign Service Journal [Washington, D.C.]
Friends of Micronesia Newsletter [Berkeley, California]

Gengo Kenkyu [Tokyo, Japan]
Geographica [Kuala Lumpur, Malaysia]
Geographical Journal, The [London, England]
Geographical Review, The [New York, New York]
Geography [London, England]
Geological Society of America Bulletin [Boulder, Colorado]
Growth and Change [Lexington, Kentucky]
Guam Recorder [new series; Agana, Guam]

Harper's Magazine [New York, New York]
Hawaiian Academy of Science, Proceedings [Honolulu, Hawaii]
Hawaiian Historical Society, Annual Reports [Honolulu, Hawaii]
Hawaii Institute of Pacific Relations, Notes [Honolulu, Hawaii]
Honolulu Advertiser, The [Honolulu, Hawaii]
Hospital Corps Quarterly, The [supplement to the U.S. Naval
    Medical Bulletin; Washington, D.C.]
Human Biology [Detroit, Michigan]
Human Biology in Oceania [Sydney, Australia]
Human Organization [formerly called Applied Anthropology; Boulder,
    Colorado]
Humanities-Cahiers de l'Institut de Science Economique Appliquee
    [Paris, France]

Imago Mundi [The Hague, Netherlands]
Indiana Academy of Science, Proceedings [Indianapolis, Indiana]
Institute of Ethnic Affairs Newsletter
International and Comparative Law Quarterly [London, England]
International Bulletin [Osaka, Japan]
International Journal of American Linguistics [Chicago, Illinois]
International Journal of Comparative Sociology [Leiden, Netherlands]
International Journal of Epidemiology [Oxford, England]
International Journal of Leprosy [Honolulu, Hawaii]
International Journal of Social Psychiatry [London, England]

Jahrbuch des Museum für Völkerkunde zu Leipzig [Leipzig, East Germany
    (D.D.R.)]
Jesuit Missions
Jesuit, The [Baltimore, Maryland]
Jinruigaku Kenkyu [Japan]
Jinruigaku Zassi [Tokyo, Japan]
Journal de la Societe des Oceanistes [Paris, France]
Journal of Abnormal and Social Psychology [now called Journal of
    Abnormal Psychology; Washington, D.C.]
Journal of American Folklore [Austin, Texas]

Journal of Anthropological Research [formerly called Southwestern
    Journal of Anthropology; Albuquerque, New Mexico]
Journal of Asian Studies [formerly called Far Eastern Quarterly;
    Ann Arbor, Michigan]
Journal of Clinical Pathology [London, England]
Journal of Conflict Resolution [Beverly Hills, California]
Journal of Cross-Cultural Psychology [Bellingham, Washington]
Journal of East Asiatic Studies [Manila, Philippines]
Journal of Ecology of Food and Nutrition
Journal of Food Science [Chicago, Illinois]
Journal of Geography [Coral Gables, Florida]
Journal of Land and Public Utility Economics [Chicago, Illinois]
Journal of Nervous and Mental Disease [Baltimore, Maryland]
Journal of Pacific History [Canberra, Australia]
Journal of Parasitology [Lawrence, Kansas]
Journal of Social Issues [Ann Arbor, Michigan]
Journal of Studies on Alcohol [formerly called Quarterly Journal
    of Studies on Alcohol; New Brunswick, New Jersey]
Journal of the American Dental Association [Chicago, Illinois]
Journal of the American Dietetic Association [Chicago, Illinois]
Journal of the American Medical Association [Chicago, Illinois]
Journal of the Folklore Institute [Bloomington, Indiana]
Journal of the New York Botanical Garden [Bronx, New York]
Journal of the Polynesian Society [Wellington, New Zealand]
Journal of the Siam Society [Bangkok, Thailand]
Journal of the Society for Ethnomusicology [Ann Arbor, Michigan]

Kindlers Literatur Lexicon [Zurich, Switzerland]
Kodaigaku: Palaelogica [Japan]
Kokogaku Zassi [Tokyo, Japan]
Kroeber Anthropological Society Papers [Berkeley, California]

Lancet [London, England]
Language [Arlington, Virginia]
Language Learning [Ann Arbor, Michigan]
Languages and Linguistics
L'anthropologie [Paris, France]
Life Magazine [New York, New York]
Lingua [Amsterdam, Netherlands]
Living Wilderness, The [Washington, D.C.]
Lore [Milwaukee, Wisconsin]
Lud [Warsaw, Poland]

Man [new series; London, England]
Man in the Pacific [Honolulu, Hawaii]
Mankind [Sydney, Australia]
Marianas Variety News and Views [Saipan, Mariana Islands]
Marine Corps Gazette [Quantico, Virginia]
Mariner's Weather Log [Washington, D.C.]
Mayo Clinic, Proceedings of the Staff Meetings [Rochester, Minnesota]
Medical Journal of Australia [Glebe, N.S.W., Australia]
Michigan Law Review [Ann Arbor, Michigan]
Micronesian Independent [formerly called Micronitor; Majuro, Marshall

Islands]
Micronesian Monthly [now called Micronesian Reporter; Saipan,
    Mariana Islands]
Micronesian Program Bulletin [Honolulu, Hawaii]
Micronesian Reporter [formerly called Micronesian Monthly; Saipan,
    Mariana Islands]
Micronesica [Agana, Guam]
Micronitor [now called Micronesian Independent; Majuro, Marshall
    Islands]
Military Review [Fort Leavenworth, Kansas]
Minzogaku-Kenkyu [Tokyo, Japan]

Nation, The [New York, New York]
National Geographic [National Geographic Magazine; Washingtcn, D.C.]
National War College Forum, The [Washington, D.C.]
Natural History [New York, New York]
Nature [Lcndon, England]
Naval War College Review [Newport, Rhode Island]
Navigation [Journal of the Australian Institute of Navigaticn;
    Sydney, Australia]
Navigation [Journal of the Institute of Navigation; Washington,
    D.C.]
Neurology [Minneapolis, Minnesota]
New England Journal of Medicine [Boston, Massachusetts]
New Guinea [Sydney, Australia]
New York Academy of Sciences, Transactions [New York, New Ycrk]
New York Law Forum [New York, New York]
New York University Center for International Studies Policy Papers
    [New York, New York]
New Yorker Magazine [New York, New York]
New World Antiquity [Brighton, England]
Newsweek [New York, New York]
New Zealand Geographical Society, Proceedings [Christchurch, New
    Zealand]
New Zealand Geographer [Christchurch, New Zealand]
Not Man Apart [San Francisco, California]

Oceania [Sydney, Australia]
Oceanic Linguistics [Honolulu, Hawaii]
Oceans [Menlo Park, California]
Oral Surgery, Oral Medicine, and Oral Pathology [St. Louis,
    Missouri]

Pacific Affairs [Vancouver, Canada]
Pacific Asian Studies [Agana, Guam]
Pacific Daily News [Agana, Guam]
Pacific Discovery [San Francisco, California]
Pacific Historical Review [Los Angeles, California]
Pacific Islands Monthly [Sydney, Australia]
Pacific Perspective [Suva, Fiji]
Pacific Profile [Agana, Guam]
Pacific Science [Honolulu, Hawaii]
Pacific Science Association Bulletin [Honolulu, Hawaii]

Pacific Science Congress, Proceedings
Pacific Travel News [San Francisco, California]
Pacific Viewpoint [Wellington, New Zealand]
Papua and New Guinea Volunteer [Port Moresby, Papua-New Guinea]
Papua-New Guinea Journal of Education [Konedobu, Papua-New Guinea]
Paradise of the Pacific [now called Honolulu Magazine; Honolulu,
    Hawaii]
Pediatrics [Evanston, Illinois]
Philippine Journal of Public Administration [Manila, Philippines]
Phonetica [Basel, Switzerland]
Plant Disease Reporter [U.S. Department of Agriculture, Washington,
    D.C.]
Political Research: Organization and Design
Political Science Quarterly [New York, New York]
Population Index [Princeton, New Jersey]
Population Studies [London, England]
Practical Anthropology [now called Missiology; New Canaan,
    Connecticut]
Progressive, The [Madison, Wisconsin]
Psychiatry [Washington, D.C.]
Public Administration Review [Washington, D.C.]
Public Health Reports [now called Health Service Reports;
    Washington, D.C.]

Radiocarbon [published by the American Journal of Science, Yale
    University, New Haven, Connecticut]
Reader's Digest [Pleasantville, New York]
Research Reviews [Office of Naval Research, Washington, D.C.]
Reviews in Anthropology [Westport, Connecticut]
Revista de Indias [Madrid, Spain]

Saturday Evening Post, The [Indianapolis, Indiana]
Saturday Review [New York, New York]
Science [Washington, D.C.]
Scientific Monthly, The [Washington, D.C.]
Sea Frontiers [Miami, Florida]
Sea Power [Washington, D.C.]
Smithsonian Journal of History, The [Washington, D.C.]
Social Forces [Chapel Hill, North Carolina]
Sociologus, Zeitschrift für Empirische Soziologie, Sozialpsycholo-
    gische und Ethnologische Forschung [Berlin, West Germany]
Sociology and Social Research [Los Angeles, California]
Soil Science [Baltimore, Maryland]
South Pacific [Australia]
South Pacific Bulletin [Noumea, New Caledonia]
South Sea Sciences [Japan]
Southwestern Journal of Anthropology [now called Journal of
    Anthropological Research; Albuquerque, New Mexico]
State Government [Lexington, Kentucky]
Summer Institute of Linguistics, Working Papers [Fargo, North
    Dakota]

Texas International Law Forum [now called Texas International

Law Journal; Austin, Texas]
The School in Rose Valley Parents' Bulletin [Pennsylvania]
Think [New York, New York]
Travaux du Cercle Linguistiques de Prague [Prague, Czechoslovakia]
Travel [Floral Park, New York]

United Nations Review [now called United Nations Monthly Chronicle;
    New York, New York]
United States Armed Forces Medical Journal [Washington, D.C.]
United States Department of State Bulletin [Washington, D.C.]
United States Naval Institute Proceedings [Annapolis, Maryland]
United States Naval Medical Bulletin [Washington, D.C.]

Venture
Virginia Quarterly Review, The [Charlottesville, Virginia]
Vital Issues [Washington, Connecticut]

War/Peace Report [New York, New York]
Washington Monthly [Washington, D.C.]
Wissenschaftliche Zeitschrift der Universität Leipzig [Leipzig,
    East Germany (D.D.R.)]
Word [Worcester, Massachusetts]
Working Papers in Linguistics [Department of Linguistics,
    University of Hawaii, Honolulu, Hawaii]
World Mission [now called Enterprise; London, England]
World Politics [Princeton, New Jersey]

Zeitschrift für Ethnologie [Braunschweig, West Germany]
Zeitschrift für Morphologie und Anthropologie [Stuttgart, West
    Germany]
Zeitschrift für vergleichende Rechtswissenschaft [Stuttgart,
    West Germany]
Zygon, Journal of Religion and Science [Chicago, Illinois]

EXPLANATION OF THE BIBLIOGRAPHY CODE

Each entry in this bibliography is followed by both a geographical and a topical code designation. The index into which these
codes are organized directs the user's attention to those works
dealing with a particular district or island and to research that
has been published on major topics of interest. Thus, the codes
provide a rapid means of locating published sources relevant to the
user's research. The code index follows the main bibliography,
which is organized alphabetically by the last name of the author.

The code index is very simple to use. For example, to locate
those sources dealing with Micronesian archaeology, one need only
turn to the portion of the index entitled, "Archaeology and Culture
History." There will be found a listing of all relevant sources by
author, date, and a portion of the first line of the publication
title, together with an indication of the geographic area to which
the sources pertain. Complete bibliographic information may then
be had by turning back to the main bibliography. To locate published material for a particular island or island group, the user
must run through each topic code looking for the name of the island
in question among the geographic headings. In this way, a single
index does double duty as a source of both topical and geographical
information.

GEOGRAPHICAL CODE DESIGNATIONS

Four different degrees of areal coverage are represented by the
geographical code designations. The most inclusive are the two
regional designations: P for general Pacific, and M for Micronesia.
While Micronesia is the largest primary areal focus for the bibliography, many works that deal with Micronesia in the broader context
of the Pacific region have been included. The second level of the
geographic code is that of major island group: Mr for Mariana
Islands, C for Caroline Islands, and Ms for Marshall Islands. Since
the Mariana and Marshall Island groups are also political districts
of the Trust Territory (excepting Guam in the Marianas), these
island groups correspondingly entered at the third or district
level along with the four districts that comprise the Caroline
Islands: Y for Yap District, T for Truk District, PL for Palau
District, and Pn for Ponape District. The island of Kusaie, in
what is now Ponape District, soon will achieve separate district
status within the Trust Territory Government, and we have coded it
accordingly. The final and most specific geographical code designation is at the individual island or atoll level. Each inhabited
island (or island cluster, such as Truk Lagoon or the Palau Islands),
as well as those uninhabited islands on which relevant research has
been conducted, has been given a numerical code following the district or island group letter designation (e.g., T10= Namoluk Atoll
in Truk District). In all, a total of seventy-six separate islands
and atolls have been so coded.

Two other types of areal codes have been created in order to
deal accurately with references found in the bibliography. First,

the geographical code W stands for "the Woleai"--that group of
atolls to the east of Yap that formerly were a part of the so-
called Yapese Empire--extending from Ulithi in the west to the
Satawal-Puluwat area in the east (see, e.g., Lessa 1950). Second,
two small island groups located in Truk District have received
special designations. Although part of the Caroline Islands, both
of these multi-atoll groups commonly are referred to by their group
names: the Hall Islands, made up of Murilo and Nomwin Atolls, and
the Mortlock Islands, made up of Etal, Lukunor and Satawan Atolls.

Some individual bibliographic items pertain to more than one
area. Where this is the case, more than one code designation has
been given to the item, and the item may be found classified under
each of these areas in the index. For example, a publication dealing with both Truk Lagoon and Ponape Island would be coded T1 and
Pn1 (see, e.g., Fischer 1956).

TOPICAL CODE DESIGNATIONS

A total of nineteen major topic headings has been established
in order to code references according to the primary subject area
of each one. These Roman numeral codes are organized alphabetically from I for Agriculture through XIX for Zoology. As indicated
in the listing of the code headings below, no attempt has been made
to establish any detailed breakdown of entries outside of the field
of anthropology. For the general heading II, Anthropology, ten
additional subdivisions have been provided which encompass the
major subdisciplinary and theoretical interests within sociocultural
anthropology. In addition, anthropological materials are coded in
four other categories: III, Archaeology and Culture History; VIII,
Folklore and Oral Literature; XIII, Linguistics; and XVI, Physical
Anthropology. An examination of the subjects subsumed under other
topical headings will reveal other areas where anthropological works
may be found in the appropriate context. For example, research on
native medicine might be found in XIV, Medical, and research on
traditional horticulture might be located in I, Agriculture.

No easy-to-use system of organizing materials by subject can
sort research that is related to several fields of endeavor into
mutually exclusive categories. For this reason, there are neces-
sarily some areas of overlap in this bibliography. To illustrate,
studies of a political nature may be found coded as XVII, Political
Science, as well as II3, Anthropology-Political Organization. A
similar situation prevails for studies in economics, history, psychology (especially culture and personality studies), and other
fields. The guiding factors determining the coding of studies that
overlap traditional academic boundaries were the primary scholarly
identification of the author, the intent or perspective of the work,
and the place of publication (i.e., the intended readership).
Studies of a political nature that have been coded XVII, Political
Science, for example, are those that characteristically deal with
the subject from a territorial or international perspective, or
with a focus on the non-traditional political systems of the area.
By contrast, political studies that have been coded II3, Anthropology-Political Organization, are those that deal mainly with
traditional political behavior or with the interaction of tradi-

tional and introduced political units at the more restricted levels
of district, island, or local community. There may be some cases
where scholars with a particular specialization will question the
placement of their area of research. This is unavoidable in this
type of "lumping" system and is defensible only insofar as the
categorizations used seem to offer the greatest informational
benefits to most users.

As with the geographical codes, some references deal with
materials in more than one subject area. Where this occurs, the
reference has been given both of the appropriate topic code designations (see, e.g., Nishi 1968).

Finally, it should be noted that we have been unable to locate
complete information for a few sources contained herein. In these
cases we have employed our best judgment on the basis of available
information in providing geographical and topical codes. Where we
may have erred, we shall be indebted to our users for pointing out
necessary corrections to us.

LIST OF GEOGRAPHICAL AND TOPICAL CODES

GEOGRAPHICAL CODES

Code	Area of Reference
P	Pacific Islands
M	Micronesia (U.S.T.T.P.I.)
Mr	Mariana Islands/Mariana District
Mr1	Guam
Mr2	Saipan
Mr3	Rota
Mr4	Tinian
Mr5	Pagan
Mr6	Anatahan
C	Caroline Islands
PL	Palau District
PL1	Palau Islands
PL2	Pulo Anna
PL3	Tobi
PL4	Sonsorol
PL5	Merir
Y	Yap District
Y1	Yap Islands
Y2	Ngulu
Y3	Ulithi
Y4	Fais
Y5	Sorol
Y6	Woleai
Y7	Faraulep
Y8	Elato
Y9	Lamotrek
Y10	Satawal
Y11	Ifaluk
Y12	Eauripik
Y13	Gaferut
W	"The Woleai"
T	Truk District
T1	Truk Islands (Truk Lagoon)
T2	Hall Islands
T2a	Murilo
T2b	Nomwin
T3	Namonuito
T4	Puluwat
T5	Pulap
T6	Pulusuk
T7	Kuop
T8	Losap

-16-

```
T9                      Nama
T10                     Namoluk
T11                     Mortlock Islands
T11a                    Etal
T11b                    Lukunor
T11c                    Satawan

Pn                      Ponape District
Pn1                     Ponape Island
Pn2                     Oroluk
Pn3                     Pakin
Pn4                     Ant
Pn5                     Ngatik
Pn6                     Mokil
Pn7                     Pingelap
Pn8                     Nukuoro
Pn9                     Kapingamarangi

K                       Kusaie

Ms                      Marshall Islands/Marshalls District
Ms1                     Utirik
Ms2                     Mejit
Ms3                     Ailuk
Ms4                     Likiep
Ms5                     Wotje
Ms6                     Maloelap
Ms7                     Aur
Ms8                     Majuro
Ms9                     Arno
Ms10                    Mili
Ms11                    Enewetok
Ms12                    Ujelang
Ms13                    Bikini
Ms14                    Rongerik
Ms15                    Rongelap
Ms16                    Wotho
Ms17                    Ujae
Ms18                    Lae
Ms19                    Kwajalein
Ms20                    Lib
Ms21                    Namu
Ms22                    Ailingalapalap
Ms23                    Jaluit
Ms24                    Kili
Ms25                    Namorik
Ms26                    Ebon
Ms27                    Taongi
```

TOPICAL CODES

Code   Primary Subject and Subtopics

I   Agriculture
                          -agricultural development
                          -conservation

-17-

	-forestry -traditional horticulture
II	Anthropology [General Ethnographic and Ethnologic Studies; Newsletters]
II1	-social organization; social structure; kinship; land tenure
II2	-religion; ethics; values; magic; sorcery; foreign missions; divination
II3	-political organization; political development and change; law
II4	-material culture; technology and technological change; handicrafts
II5	-cultural ecclogy; resource analysis; man-land relationships
II6	-culture and personality studies; cognition
II7	-culture change; modernization; cultural evolution; urbanization; acculturation; community development; disaster studies; Peace Corps
II8	-applied anthrcpology; anthropological ethics
II9	-ethnohistory; folk history; historical
II10	-anthropological economics; economic change
III	Archaeology and Culture History -cultural reconstructions -prehistoric artifact analyses -radiocarbon dates and dating -site surveys and reports
IV	Art -dance -graphic arts -music -recreational activities (sports and games)
V	Botany -ethnobotanical studies -floral description and classification
VI	Economics -economic development -financial and business studies -manpower and manpower training studies
VII	Education -child training

```
                              -educational administration
                              -educational literature
                              -libraries and librarianship

VIII                    Folklore and Oral Literature
                              -myths and legends
                              -omens
                              -proverbs

IX                      General and Popular Literature
                              -bibliographies
                              -cookbooks
                              -fiction works
                              -general periodical literature
                              -newsletters
                              -photographic essays
                              -travel literature

X                       Geography
                              -atlases
                              -cartography
                              -conservation studies
                              -cultural geography
                              -ecological studies
                              -native navigation and astronomy
                              -physical geography
                              -transportation studies

XI                      Geology
                              -geomorphology
                              -island hydrology and formation
                              -mineralology
                              -soil studies

XII                     History
                              -historical documents (translations)
                              -pre-1900 historical studies
                              -post-1900 historical studies (World Wars I and
                               II and post-World War II studies)

XIII                    Linguistics
                              -dictionaries and grammars
                              -language studies
                              -word lists

XIV                     Medical
                              -epidemiology
                              -medical anthropology
                              -native medicine (ethnomedicine)
                              -nutrition studies
                              -public health and public health administration

XV                      Military
                              -foreign military activities
                              -military security studies
                              -military weapons testing
```

```
                              -native warfare and martial arts
                              -World Wars I and II

XVI                      Physical Anthropology
                              -human genetics
                              -population (demographic) studies

XVII                     Political Science
                              -colonization and decolonization studies
                              -community development
                              -government and administration
                              -international relations
                              -law
                              -political development and change
                              -trusteeship studies

XVIII                    Psychology
                              -culture and personality studies
                              -intelligence testing and evaluation
                              -psychiatry and mental health

XIX                      Zoology
                              -ethnozoological studies
                              -island faunal studies
                              -marine biology and ecology
                              -zoological description and classification
```

INTRODUCTION

A long-standing premise in the conduct of anthropological
inquiry has been that region-specific research would provide the
data base required for theoretical advancement. This position is
most widely known as the effort to conduct studies in "controlled
comparison" (Eggan 1954). Eggan has advocated

> ...the utilization of the comparative method on a
> smaller scale [than that of world-wide comparisons]
> and with as much control over the frame of compar-
> ison as it is possible to secure. It has seemed
> natural to utilize regions of relatively homogeneous
> culture or to work within social or cultural types,
> and to further control the ecology and the historical
> factors so far as it is possible to do so (1954:747).

The importance of areal specialization in anthropology continues to
the present, as may be seen from the common identification of
anthropologists as specialists in a particular geographical region.
Such areal specialization stems from several interrelated sources.
First, there is simply the romantic intrigue of different geographical regions which appeals to persons of varied temperaments
and backgrounds. Often this is what initially attracts scholars
to a particular area. Once fieldwork has been carried out in a
region, the anthropologist has made a substantial investment in
language training, background study, and emotional commitment that
makes it somewhat difficult to relinquish this areal specialization.
Finally, the information explosion of the post-World War II era is
obviously also related. The outpouring of publications on all of
the world's major regions has made it increasingly difficult for
anthropologists and other scholars to keep abreast of, let alone
to command, the burgeoning literature on more than one geographical
area. Thus it appears that the importance of regional studies
indicated in two recent evaluations of the discipline will remain
secure in the years ahead (Murdock 1972; Spoehr 1966).

From the beginnings of systematic anthropology, the division
of the world into geographical culture areas served as an organ-
izational device that promoted the accumulation and comparison of
data based on in-depth field research. A trend to establish scholarly societies defined by a common interest in one region was
already well underway when anthropology emerged as a formal discipline. This trend has continued to the present day in Oceania
with the addition of comparatively new groups like the Association
for Social Anthropology in Oceania to older organizations such as
the Polynesian Society and the Pacific Science Association. Finally, large-scale regional research projects initiated in this
century have been very important to the development of anthropology.
In Oceania, the most notable of these have been the Hamburg South
Sea Expedition, the Cambridge Torres Strait Expedition, the pre-
World War II survey of Polynesia undertaken by the Bishop Museum,
and several post-World War II projects in Melanesia and Micronesia.

The continuing interest in and completion of research in specific areas of the world also has given rise--particularly in recent decades--to a need to develop new informational tools that can assist in the formulation and conduct of further research. This book provides one such informational source for the contemporary work that has been done in Micronesia. In this essay, we offer a modest review of this research. We hope that this will establish a better understanding of what already has been done and, more importantly, of what remains to be accomplished.

PRE-WORLD WAR II RESEARCH

Unlike many areas of the world, Micronesia only recently has come into its own in the anthropological literature. That this is so after more than 450 years have passed since the first Western contact is not unduly surprising. First, although these small islands are scattered over an area as large as that of the continental United States, they add up to less than 2590 square kilometers of dry land area. Thus Micronesia represented an isolated and fragmented island region that was not easily assayed from the usually sporadic and fleeting reports of the explorers, whalers, traders and missionaries who came into the area during the sixteenth through the nineteenth centuries (see Lessa 1962, for an evaluation of these early reports). Second, significant foreign governmental interest, which frequently had been an early and important precursor to research activity in other parts of the world, did not come about in Micronesia (except in the Marianas) until the late 1800s, with the initiation of Spanish, German and American foreign policies, and with international conflicts over the ownership and commercial development of the islands.

Systematic anthropological research in Micronesia began in 1868 with the work of the Polish ethnographer, Johann S. Kubary, who conducted investigations in the Caroline Islands on behalf of the Museum Godeffroy in Hamburg. Until the Spanish period at the end of the nineteenth century, most of the reports on Micronesia came from only a handful of individuals, men like the American missionary, Luther H. Gulick, German scholars such as Bastian, Finsch and Hernsheim, and English researchers like Christian. Nearly all of the limited number of inquiries carried out during this period were focused on the larger islands of Micronesia, most of which already were established as ports-of-call for commercial and governmental shipping.

The years of German occupation, from 1898 to 1914, ushered in a new level of anthropological endeavor in Micronesia with the South Sea Expedition of 1908-1910, carried out for the Ethnological Museum in Hamburg. This project resulted in a set of eleven volumes on Micronesia published between 1914 and 1938, presenting the work of eight German scholars under the leadership of Georg Thilenius. These volumes contain data on the physical anthropology, language, material culture, folklore, social structure and political organization of some thirty-four islands in the Carolines and the Marshalls. Profusely illustrated, the more than 6400 combined pages of this series remained the most reliable and available source of information about Micronesia until the post-World War II period, and even now these volumes are regularly consulted by many researchers. To this set of monographs may be added the works of some two score other German scholars published up to the time of the Japanese takeover of the islands, including men such as Bollig, Born, Erdland, Girschner and Hahl.

The Japanese period, from 1914 to 1945, was one of intensified cultural change for the peoples of Micronesia. It was also a period during which a significant amount of Japanese anthropological research on Micronesia was published. Unfortunately, the bulk of this material remains little known outside of Japan, largely as a result of problems of availability, the language barrier, and to some extent the destruction of copies during World War II. We can, however, gain some appreciation for the amount of Japanese research that was carried out by reference to Utinomi's bibliography (1952). Utinomi lists 273 Micronesian references by Japanese scholars published between 1890 and 1945 on the ethnology, archaeology, physical anthropology and linguistics of the area. While this constituted a signal increase in the quantity of reports concerning Micronesia, almost three-fourths of these were relatively brief journal articles that dealt with matters of only general ethnographic interest. Moreover, the total amount of anthropological research published by Japanese scholars made up only about 14 percent of all the pre-World War II Japanese scientific work carried out in Micronesia.

RESEARCH DURING WORLD WAR II

American interest in Micronesia revived as a consequence of military operations in the islands during World War II. During the period of the Japanese occupation of the territory, Westerners were rarely permitted in the area either as casual visitors or for purposes of scientific inquiry. This lack of recent contact led to a major effort to acquire and analyze existing reports as a part of the intelligence gathering activities that preceded American combat activities and military administration in Micronesia.

At the Institute of Human Relations at Yale University, cross-cultural materials were utilized to prepare a bibliography of Micronesia and, in cooperation with the Smithsonian Institution, a series of Strategic Bulletins of Oceania, four of which dealt with Micronesia. Of greater importance, though, were the Civil Affairs Handbooks that were prepared for the Occupied Areas Section of the Office of the Chief of Naval Operations. This scientific research, carried out under the general supervision of George P. Murdock, resulted in four volumes published in 1943-1944, with one on the Marshall Islands, one on the Mariana Islands, and two on the Caroline Islands. These four reports encapsulated almost the whole of what was known about Micronesia in the West at that time, covering an impressive range of data from geography, basic resources, history of the native cultures and of foreign contacts, government and law, and health and sanitation, to education, communications, public safety, transportation, public utilities, food production and industry. A corollary effort was made by British scientists under the direction of H. C. Darby for the Naval Intelligence Division of the British Admiralty, and one of these four volumes dealt in part with Micronesia. While field research, as such, was clearly out of

-23-

the question, the research that went into the preparation of these
military intelligence and administration studies not only gct
Western anthropologists and other scientists back into the investigation cf Micronesia, but it also demonstrated the utility of
such research for pragmatic concerns.

POST-WAR RESEARCH

Considering what occurred in the immediate post-war pericd,
the wartime cooperation among military and scientific personnel
concerned with Micronesia must have been satisfactory. In 1946,
three projects were developed that were to prove of major importance in the American effort to make up for lost time and lost
opportunities for research in Micronesia. One of these was the
School of Naval Administration (SONA), begun at the Hoover Institute at Stanford University to train naval officers in the actual
administrative tasks they were to have in the territory. Drawing
on the earlier Civil Affairs Handbooks, military and civilian
staff at SONA developed one new general and six new regional handbooks that corrected, up-dated, and otherwise expanded the earlier
research, particularly by adding information on post-war conditions.

The production of these new SONA materials was assisted by data
then being collected as a part of two scientific projects. An economic survey of Micronesia was undertaken in 1946 by a team of
twenty-four scientists, including four anthropologists, for the
U.S. Commercial Company, an arm of the wartime Foreign Econcmic
Administration. This research team, under the direction of Douglas
L. Oliver, traveled throughout the territory, its work culminating
in a twenty volume report that unfortunately has never been published in full.

Finally, the Pacific Science Board of the National Research
Council was established in 1946. Beginning in 1947, the Board
sponsored the first large-scale anthropological research effort
conducted in Micronesia since the German South Sea Expediticn at
the turn of the century. Assisted by funding from the Office of
Naval Research, this project--the Coordinated Investigation of
Micronesian Anthropology (CIMA)--resulted in field research by
some thirty-five anthropologists (among a total of forty-two
scientists) working under the overall supervision of George P.
Murdock. The twofold objectives of the CIMA were to compile basic
scientific information on the islands and to provide data relevant
to the practical problems of administering the area and its peoples.
By 1949, thirty-two final reports on the ethnography, linguistics,
cultural geography, physical anthropology, ethnobotany, and culture
and personality of fourteen islands had been completed.

But mention of the final reports does not convey the full
impact of the CIMA project on ccntemporary Micronesian anthropology.
The final CIMA bibliography, compiled in 1963, lists an additional
100 publications that were based cn CIMA supported research (Bowen
1963). Altogether then, this single three year project generated
close to one-half the number of all published materials that had
appeared on Micronesia during the preceding thirty-five year period
from 1910-1945. Although not all of the CIMA researchers maintained

their interest in Micronesia, those who did became the teachers of succeeding generations of anthropologists who have furthered anthropological investigations in the area (for details on this, see Mason 1969).

As the CIMA drew to a close in 1949, the Pacific Science Board began another large-scale research project with funding from the Office of Naval Research: Scientific Investigations in Micronesia (SIM). SIM involved forty-nine scientists (including anthropologists) in work upon selected islands, and had as its primary emphasis the Coral Atoll Program--an intensive examination of tropical island ecology. SIM also extended the CIMA objective by contributing additional data to assist in administrative planning in the territory. Three of the five major expeditions of the Coral Atoll Program went to Arno, Ifaluk, and Kapingamarangi, and an anthropologist participated in each of these expeditions. By the time it was phased out in 1966, SIM-sponsored research had added another 160 scientific publications to the literature on Micronesia (Coolidge 1966).

There were several other important results of the CIMA and SIM projects, two of which deserve mention in this brief account. First, some of the CIMA and SIM investigators continued to be active in the on-going affairs of Micronesia as staff and district anthropologists with the Trust Territory Government. From 1950 until most of the positions were vacated in the early 1960s, a total of thirteen anthropologists organized and carried out basic research in the field and provided advisory information for the administration of the territory (see Barnett 1956, for a full account of this period). Some of the results of their work were published between 1957 and 1961 as the Anthropological Working Papers Series, under the general editorship of John E. de Young. This series dealt with topics such as Micronesian horticultural practices, the use of names, and land tenure. Second, the volume of research produced by the CIMA and SIM projects led to the establishment of the Atoll Research Bulletin, a publication originally issued by the Pacific Science Board with Office of Naval Research backing, and now continued as an outlet for current research by the Smithsonian Institution.

Three other significant group projects in the postwar period have involved the efforts of anthropologists in Micronesia. The first of these was the five year Study of Displaced Communities in the Pacific, directed by Homer G. Barnett at the University of Oregon with a grant from the National Science Foundation. Begun in 1962, this program was intended to analyze the changes that had occurred when whole or part-island communities had been uprooted and relocated. Four Trust Territory communities were involved in this study: the Ex-Bikini Marshallese on Kili, the Ex-Enewetok Marshallese on Ujelang, the Kapingamarangi colonists on Ponape, and the Lib Marshallese who had been relocated temporarily on Kwajalein.

The second major research effort was the Tri-Instituticnal Pacific Program (TRIPP), initiated in 1963 under the supervision of anthropologists at the University of Hawaii, the Bishop Museum, and Yale University, with support from the Carnegie Corporation in New York. By the time it ended in 1964, TRIPP had sponsored the work of some thirty social scientists studying cultural change in Pacific Island communities, with seven individual projects focusing on Micronesian islands.

The final research project, conducted by the Pacific and Asian Linguistics Institute (PALI) at the University of Hawaii, was begun in 1967 to study thirteen Trust Territory languages with a grant from the Peace Corps. The objective of the project was to develop dictionaries, grammars and teaching materials for the languages spoken in the following areas: the Marshall Islands, Kusaie, Ponape, Truk, Kapingamarangi, Pulap, Puluwat, Ulithi, Woleai, Yap, Palau, Saipan (Carolinian), and the Marianas (Chamorro).

AN OVERALL REVIEW OF CONTEMPORARY RESEARCH

With the exceptions noted above, contemporary anthropological research in Micronesia has been conducted by individual researchers rather than by the research teams that characterized the early post-World War II period. As subsequent data will show, this research activity has differed in other ways as well, particularly by expanding the number of communities studied.

In order to come to a crude quantitative assessment of the research conducted in Micronesia since 1944, a sample of over three-fourths of the entries in this bibliography has been examined. The results of this examination are summarized in table 1, in which several trends are apparent. First, almost two and one-half times as many published materials have appeared in the 1964-1974 decade than appeared in either of the two preceding decades. More than anything else, this indicates the increased scholarly interest in Micronesia and, by extension, the growing number of scientists who share this interest. Second, it is noteworthy that the level of general and comparative research published (as indicated by area codes P, M, C, and W in table 1) has remained fairly constant since 1944. Approximately one-half of all research published in the 1944-1953 decade was at this level, compared with 35 percent in the 1954-1963 decade, and 45 percent in the 1964-1974 period. Third, an examination of those publications that deal only with district center islands also indicates a surprising uniformity. Forty-eight percent of all published research dealt only with district center communities in 1944-1953, with 58 percent and 46 percent being the corresponding figures for each succeeding decade. It has always been the case that problems of logistic supply, medical treatment, communication and transportation have made district centers the most convenient choice of field site for many researchers. It is also true that district centers offer the best opportunities for useful inquiries into many research problems, e.g., urbanization, educational change and political development. At the same time, the relative consistency of attention paid to district centers has been contrary to the informally expressed feelings of some scholars that more research is needed on the much more numerous outer islands (for an up-to-date review of some of these issues, see Mason 1975).

For Truk and Ponape Districts, a shift to the outer islands

-26-

Table 1. Summary of published research by decade and by geographical area, presented as a percentage of the total published research completed in that decade.*

Geographical Area	Decade		
	1944-1953	1954-1963	1964-1974
P - Pacific Islands	4.6	9.5	8.4
M - Micronesia	39.0	22.6	33.3
C - Caroline Islands	3.7	2.2	3.2
W - "the Woleai"	0	0.5	0.4
Mr - Mariana District	4.6	7.0	5.8
Mr1 - Guam	5.1	4.1	6.3
Mr2 - Saipan	2.0	1.4	0.1
PL - Palau District	0.3	0	0.6
FL1 - Palau Islands	4.3	9.2	5.1
Y - Yap District	4.8	6.0	2.7
Y1 - Yap Islands	3.0	6.8	3.9
T - Truk District	1.1	2.2	4.6
T1 - Truk Islands	4.3	8.4	5.5
Pn - Ponape District	4.6	1.6	4.9
Pn1 - Ponape Island	6.0	5.2	6.4
K - Kusaie Island	0.3	0	1.7
Ms - Marshalls District	12.0	13.0	7.0
Ms8 - Majuro Atoll	0.3	0.3	0.1
TOTAL PERCENT	100.0	100.0	100.0
N =	351	368	894

*District figures (e.g., Truk District) include all studies published for that district that do not concern the district center island(s) (e.g., that do not concern T1).

has occurred in the research reported between 1944 and 1974. This shift accounts in part for the overall increase in the number of Micronesian outer islands where anthropological and related research has been conducted: in the 1944-1953 period, only twelve outer islands served as field sites, as compared to nineteen in the 1954-1963 period, and twenty-eight in the 1964-1974 period. The data for the Mariana, Palau and Yap Districts show a continuing significant level of interest in district center rather than outer island areas as research sites (including Guam with Saipan for the Mariana data). However, research on Majuro, the Marshall Islands' District center, never has constituted more than 2 percent of all research carried out in that district. Two factors seem to explain this: first, the negligible physical advantages of research on Majuro Atoll as compared to other Marshallese atolls, and second, the very significant amount of research that has been conducted in association with U.S. military operations involving the populations of Bikini, Enewetok, Kwajalein, Kili, Ujelang, Lib, Rongerik and Rongelap.

Further insight into the characteristics of contemporary Micronesian research can be gained from an examination of anthropological and linguistic publications alone. The data in table 2 indicate that the total amount of anthropological and linguistic research has remained relatively constant over the thirty year period 1944-1974, when viewed as a percent of the total published research contained in this bibliography. Notable increases have occurred only in investigations of the linguistics and physical anthropology of the area. Although within each decade the total amount of anthropological research has remained constant in comparison with other research, the actual number of published reports has increased dramatically in the 1964-1974 decade when compared with either preceding decade. Publications in linguistics have tripled, those in physical anthropology have grown nearly fivefold, and citations in archaeology, folklore and oral literature, and general and sociocultural anthropology all have doubled in the last decade.

Finally, even though the total number of outer islands that have been studied either anthropologically or linguistically between 1944 and 1974 has increased significantly, nearly forty islands remain to be investigated by anthropologists or linguists in the post-World War II era. These islands are listed in table 3 by district.

SUMMARY

There are many areas of specific anthropological investigation that remain to be adequately researched in Micronesia, not to mention work that needs to be done in related disciplines. Indeed, one might infer from the current situation that the rapidly changing social and political conditions both on Guam and in the Trust Territory, coupled with ever-changing theoretical concerns and perspectives in anthropology, mean that the future will suffer no dearth of interesting anthropological research problems. While no two reviewers of the current state of research in Micronesia would be likely to agree completely upon areas requiring further investigation, several lines of study

Table 2. Number and percentage of published sources in anthropology and linguistics, with the percentage representing the portion of all published research for that decade in all fields.

	Decade					
Topic Code	1944-1953		1954-1963		1964-1974	
II - General and Socio-cultural Anthropology	105	30%	133	36%	286	32%
III - Archaeology	14	4%	26	7%	45	5%
VIII - Folklore and Oral Literature	10	3%	11	3%	27	3%
XIII - Linguistics	21	6%	29	8%	98	11%
XVI - Physical Anthropology	18	5%	11	3%	54	6%
TOTAL	168	48%	190	57%	510	57%

Table 3. Inhabited Micronesian islands and atolls that have not been
researched anthropologically or linguistically during the
period 1944-1974 by district.

Administrative District	Island and Atoll Names
Mariana District	Agrihan
	Alamagan
	Anatahan
	Pagan
Palau District	Pulo Anna
Yap District	Fais
	Faraulep
	Ngulu
	Sorol
Truk District	Dublon (Tonowas)
	Fanapanges
	Fefan
	Murilo
	Nama
	Nomwin
	Param
	Pulap
	Pulusuk
	Satawan
	Tol
	Tsis
	Udot
Ponape District	Ngatik
Marshalls District	Ailingalapalap
	Ailuk
	Aur
	Ebon
	Jaluit
	Kwajalein
	Lae
	Likiep
	Maloelap
	Mejit
	Mili
	Namorik
	Ujae
	Utirik
	Wotho
	Wotje
TOTAL ISLANDS AND ATOLLS=	39

strike us as particularly deserving of immediate attention. First, and perhaps too obvious, is the point that research on islands and communities presently unreported in the literature would be most welcome, although this observation is not meant to detract from the importance of restudies of communities that already have received anthropological attention. Truk and the Marshalls stand out as the two districts with the largest remaining number of unstudied islands (see table 3). With the exception of the high islands of Palau, Yap and the Marianas, another clear lacuna in our knowledge of Micronesia is in the area of archaeological research. This is most notable for the high islands of Truk Lagoon, and the islands of Ponape and Kusaie, although virtually nothing is known of the prehistory of the coral atolls in Micronesia (Nukuoro being a single important exception). Also underrepresented in research completed to date are investigations into the oral literature, ethnohistory, art, and material culture of Micronesia. This listing simply indicates the most clear-cut examples of areas of inquiry that need greater attention from future workers. Perhaps by the end of the next decade of anthropological research in Micronesia, we may be able to look back on our labors and conclude that we have closed the most glaring gaps in our knowledge of the islands. To that end, we hope that this bibliography will prove of assistance.

REFERENCES CITED

Barnett, Homer G.
    1956   Anthropology in Administration.   Evanston: Row,
            Peterson and Co.

Bowen, R. N.
    1963   Bibliography of the Coordinated Investigation of
            Micronesian Anthropology (CIMA).   Honolulu: Pacific
            Scientific Information Center, Bishop Museum.

Coolidge, Harold J.
    1966   Scientific Investigations in Micronesia: Final
            Report.   Washington, D.C.: Pacific Science Board,
            National Research Council.

Eggan, Fred
    1954   Social anthropology and the method of controlled
            Comparison.   American Anthropologist, 56(5), Part 1:
            743-763.

Lessa, William A.
    1962   An evaluation of early descriptions of Carolinian
            Culture.   Ethnohistory, 9(4):313-403.

Mason, Leonard E.
    1969   Anthropological research in Micronesia, 1954-1968.
            Anthropologica, n.s., 11(1):85-115.

    1975   The many faces of Micronesia: District Center and
            Outer Island Culture.   Pacific Asian Studies [Uni-
            versity of Guam], 1(1):5-37.

Murdock, George P.
    1972   Anthropology's Mythology.   Proceedings of the Royal
            Anthropological Institute of Great Britain and
            Ireland for 1971, pp. 17-24.

Spoehr, Alexander
    1966   The part and the whole: Reflections on the study
            of a Region.   American Anthropologist, 68(3):629-640.

Utinomi, Huzio (compiler)
    1952   Bibliography of Micronesia, translated and revised
            by O.A. Bushnell, et al.   Honolulu: University of
            Hawaii Press.

MAIN BIBLIOGRAPHY

Listed Alphabetically by Author's Last Name

MAIN BIBLIOGRAPHY

Abraham, Isamu
1974   Kusaie's quest for separate district Status.   Micronesian
        Reporter, 22(4):16-19.
        K XVII

Adam, Thomas R.
1967   Western Interests in the Pacific Realm.   New York: Random
        House.   246 pp.
        P XVII

Adams, Col. Lawrence E.
1972   American involvement in Perspective.   IN National Security
        and International Trusteeship in the Pacific, W.R. Louis,
        ed.   Annapolis: Naval Institute Press.   pp. 80-96.
        M XV XVII

Adels, B. R. and D. C. Gajdusek
1963   Survey of measles patterns in New Guinea, Micronesia,
        and Australia.   With a report of new virgin soil
        epidemics and the demonstration of susceptible primitive
        populations by Serology.   American Journal of Hygiene [now
        called American Journal of Epidemiology], 77(3):317-343.
        M XIV

Aderkroi, David M.
1965   Palau's imported Festivity.   Pacific Profile, 3(10):15-17.
        PL1 II

Ae'a, Hezekiah
1947   The history of Ebon, translated from the Hawaiian by Mary
        Kawena Pukui.   Fifty-sixth Annual Report of the Hawaiian
        Historical Society, pp. 6-19.
        Ms26 XII

Agthe, Johanna
1969   Die Abbildungen in Reiseberichten aus Ozeanien als Quellen
        für die Völkerkunde (16.-18. Jahrhundert).   [Illustrations
        in the reports of travelers from Oceania as sources for
        ethnology (16th-18th Centuries)].   Ph.D. Dissertation,
        University of Göttingen, Göttingen.   Published 1969.
        Arbeiten aus dem Institut für Völkerkunde der Universität
        zu Göttingen, Band 2.   München: Klaus Renner.   220 pp.
        P XII

Akerblom, Kjell
1968   Astronomy and Navigation in Polynesia and Micronesia.   A
        Survey.   Publication No. 14, Monograph Series.   Stockholm:
        Etnografiska Museet.   171 pp.   Reviewed: 1970 by Ben R.
        Finney, American Anthropologist, 72(1):134-135; 1972 by
        Leith Duncan, Journal of the Polynesian Society, 81(2):
        272-273.
        M X

MAIN BIBLIOGRAPHY

Alden, J. E.
     1944 Press in paradise: The beginnings of printing in Micronesia.
           Papers of the Bibliographical Society of America, 38(3):
           269-283.
           M XII

Alicata, Joseph E.
     1946 Helminthic infection among natives of the islands of Ponape
           and Truk, Eastern Carolines. Journal of Parasitology, 32(1):
           12-13.
           Pn1 T1 XIV

Alicata, Joseph E.
     1947 Science spotlights mysteries of Ponape. Paradise of the
           Pacific [now called Honolulu Magazine], 59:23-25.
           Pn1 III

Alicata, Joseph E.
     1965 Notes and observations on murine angiostrongylus and
           eosinophilic meningitis in Micronesia. Canadian
           Journal of Zoology, 43(5):667-672.
           M XIV

Alkire, William H.
     1959 Residence, economy, and habitat in the Caroline Islands: A
           study in ecologic Adaptation. M.A. Thesis, University
           of Hawaii, Honolulu.
           C II5

Alkire, William H.
     1960 Cultural adaptation in the Caroline Islands. Journal of
           the Polynesian Society, 69(2):123-150.
           C II5

Alkire, William H.
     1965 Lamotrek Atoll and Inter-Island Socioeconomic Ties. Ph.D.
           Dissertation, University of Illinois, Champaign-Urbana.
           Published 1965. Illinois Studies in Anthropology, No. 5.
           Urbana: University of Illinois Press. 180 pp. Reviewed:
           1966 by F. Raymond Fosberg, Atoll Research Bulletin, 117:
           7-8; 1966 by William A. Lessa, American Anthropologist,
           68(5):1274-1275; 1966 by J.S. Uberoi, Man, n.s., 1(3):426;
           1969 by D.P. Sinha, Oceania, 40(1):82.
           Y9 II1

Alkire, William H.
     1968 An atoll environment and Ethnogeography. Geographica
           [Geographical Society, University of Malaya, Kuala Lumpur],
           4:54-59.
           Y9 X

MAIN BIBLIOGRAPHY

Alkire, William H.
    1968 Porpoises and Taro. Ethnology, 7(3):280-289.
          Y6 II2

Alkire, William H.
    1968 Review of Saul H. Riesenberg, The Native Polity of Ponape.
          Anthropos, 63/64:1039-1040.
          Pn1 II3

Alkire, William H.
    1970 Systems of measurement on Woleai Atoll, Caroline Islands.
          Anthropos, 65:1-73.
          Y6 II4

Alkire, William H.
    1972 An introduction to the peoples and cultures of Micronesia.
          Addison-Wesley Module, No. 18. Reading, Massachusetts:
          Addison-Wesley Publishing Co. 56 pp.
          M II

Alkire, William H.
    1972 Concepts of order in Southeast Asia and Micronesia.
          Comparative Studies in Society and History, 14(4):484-493.
          M II

Alkire, William H.
    1972 Population dynamics of Woleai and Lamotrek Atolls. Paper
          read at the Conference on Pacific Atoll Populations, East-
          West Center Population Institute, Honolulu, Hawaii, 27-30
          December, 1972.
          Y6 Y9 XVI

Alkire, William H.
    1974 Land tenure in the Woleai. IN Land Tenure in Oceania, Henry
          P. Lundsgaarde, ed. ASAO Monograph No. 2. Honolulu: Uni-
          versity Press of Hawaii. pp. 39-69.
          W II1

Alkire, William H.
    1974 Native classification of flora on Woleai Atoll.
          Micronesica, 10(1):1-5.
          Y6 V

Alkire, William H.
    1974 Review of Roland W. Force and Maryanne Force, Just One
          House: A Description and Analysis of Kinship in the Palau
          Islands. Journal of the Polynesian Society, 83(3):379-381.
          PL1 II1

MAIN BIBLIOGRAPHY

Alpers, Antony
1970 The eitu who went as a man's Wife. IN Legends of the
South Seas, Antony Alpers, ed. New York: Thomas Y.
Crowell Co. pp. 311-313.
Pn9 VIII

Alpers, Antony
1970 The lobster and the Flounder. IN Legends of the South
Seas, Antony Alpers, ed. New York: Thomas Y. Crowell
Co. p. 314.
Pn9 VIII

Alpert, Elmer
1946 Nutrition and Dietary Patterns of Micronesia. IN U.S. Commercial Company's Economic Survey of Micronesia, Report No.
18. Honolulu: U.S. Commercial Company. Mimeographed. 23 pp.
M XIV

American Factors Associates
1970 Feasibility and Study for Establishment of a Large Scale
Commercial Rice Production, Island of Ponape, Trust Terri-
tory of the Pacific Islands. Honolulu: American Factors
Associates.
Pn1 VI

Amerson, A. Binion, Jr.
1969 Ornithology of the Marshall and Gilbert Islands.
Atoll Research Bulletin, No. 127. 348 pp.
Ms XIX

Anonymous
1947 Anthropological research and related research in Micronesia.
Oceania, 18(1):87.
M II

Anonymous
1947 Micronesian expedition of University of Hawaii summer of
1946. Pacific Science, 1(1):60-62.
M XIV XIX

Anonymous
1949 The Trust Territory: Its 2,130 islands form a new
U.S. domain in the Pacific. A photographic essay with
pictures by Eliot Elisofon. Life Magazine, 26(17):97-
110. [April 25, 1949].
M IX

Anonymous
1954 Islanders appeal to the United Nations on bomb tests in
Pacific Trust Area. United Nations Review [now called
United Nations Monthly Chronicle], 1(3):14-16.
Ms XVII

-37-

MAIN BIBLIOGRAPHY

Anonymous
    1956   Modernizing without uprooting: The challenge of the Pacific?
            United Nations Review [now called United Nations Monthly
            Chronicle], 3(2):46-52.
            M XVII

Anonymous
    1966   The amyotrophic lateral sclerosis of Guam.   Medical Journal
            of Australia [53rd year], 2(1):31.
            Mr1 XIV

Anonymous
    1968   Notes on Micronesian Art. A working paper in conjunction
            with the first Micronesian art exhibition at the Univer-
            sity of Guam, April 1968. Micronesian Working Papers,
            No. 1. Agana: University of Guam, Gallery of Art.   14 pp.
            M IV

Anonymous
    1969   Micronesia--America's 'South Seas'. Venture, 5:54-63.
            M IX

Anonymous
    1973   Micronesia: Strategic Trust Territory.   Australian
            Foreign Affairs Record, 44(8):514-519.
            M XVII

Anttila, Elizabeth K.
    1965   A history of the people of the Trust Territory of the
            Pacific Islands and their Education.   Ph.D. Dissertation,
            University of Texas, Austin. Available from University
            Microfilms, Ann Arbor: No. 65-10706.
            M VII XII

Apple, Russell A.
    1972   Historic Properties Policy and Program in Micronesia (Trust
            Territory of the Pacific Islands): Report, Recommendations,
            and Examples. Prepared in cooperation with the Branch of
            Land Resources, Division of Lands and Surveys, Dept. of
            Resources and Development, Trust Territory of the Pacific
            Islands. Saipan: Trust Territory of the Pacific Islands
            Publications Office. 88 pp.
            M I II9 X

Arai, Soji
    1953   Anthropometric research on the Micronesians. Proceedings of
            the 7th Pacific Science Congress, 2 February-4 March, 1949,
            Auckland, New Zealand, 7:218-220.
            M XVI

MAIN BIBLIOGRAPHY

Arnold, Arthur, Donald C. Edgren, and Vincent S. Paladino
     1953   Amyotrophic lateral sclerosis: Fifty cases observed on Guam.
            Journal of Nervous and Mental Disease, 117(2):135-139.
            Mr1 XIV

Arnold, Edwin G.
     1947   Self government in United States Territories. Foreign
            Affairs, 25(4):655-666.
            M XVII

Ashman, C. M.
     1970   Native money of Palau. Micronesian Reporter, 18(3):39-40.
            PL1 II4

Association for Anthropology in Micronesia
     1972   to 1974. Newsletter Vol. 1, Nos. 1-3; Vol. 2, Nos. 1-3.
            [no longer published].
            M II

Association for Social Anthropology in Oceania
     1967   to present. Newsletter Nos. 1-16 issued through 1974.
            P II

Azuma, Aloysius Y.
     1969   Survey and Development of Managerial Resources in
            Micronesia. Boulder, Colorado: Economic Development
            Internship Program, Western Interstate Commission for
            Higher Education. 29 pp.
            M VI

Bailey, Charles-James N.
     1967   Transformational outline of Marshallese Syntax.
            M.A. Thesis, University of Chicago, Chicago.
            Ms XIII

Bailey, K. H.
     1946   Dependent areas of the Pacific. Foreign Affairs, 24(3):
            494-512.
            P XVII

Baird, J. Henry
     1954   The Guam Museum. Journal of the Polynesian Society,
            63(3&4):253-254.
            Mr1 II4

Baird, J. Henry
     1968   The purpose of the Mariana "Latte." Journal of East Asiatic
            Studies [University of Manila], 12:1-21.
            Mr III

Baker, Rollin H.
    1946 Some effects of the war on the wildlife of Micronesia.
          Transactions of the 11th North American Wildlife Conference,
          11-13 March, 1946, New York, Ethel M. Quee, ed. Washington,
          D.C.: American Wildlife Institute. pp. 205-213.
          M XIX

Baker, Rollin H.
    1951 The Avifauna of Micronesia, Its Origin, Evolution and
          Distribution. University of Kansas Publications, Museum
          of Natural History, 3(1):1-359.
          M XIX

Ballendorf, Dirk
    1970 Mutiny on the whaleship Globe.   Micronesian Reporter,
          18(1):24-30; 18(2):14-20.
          Ms10 XII

Ballendorf, Dirk
    1972 Americans/Palauans--their first Encounter. Micronesian
          Reporter, 20(3):36-45.
          PL XII

Ballendorf, Dirk
    1973 The confidential Micronesian Reporter. Micronesian Reporter,
          21(3):14-18.
          Mr II XV

Ballendorf, Dirk
    1974 The violent first Encounters. Guam Recorder, n.s., 4(1):
          37-40.
          M XII

Ballendorf, Dirk
    1975 The Micronesian Ellis Mystery. Guam Recorder, n.s., 5(1):
          35-48.
          M XII

Balos, Ataji
    1965 Christmas song contest in the Marshalls. Pacific Profile,
          3(10):11, 16.
          Ms IV

Banner, Albert H.
    1961 Fish poisoning in the tropical Pacific. South Pacific
          Bulletin, 11(4):18-21, 65.
          P XIV XIX

MAIN BIBLIOGRAPHY

Bargmann, A.
    1955 A. Erdland's Grammatik und Wörterbuch der Marshall-Sprache
          in Mikronesien. [Grammar and Dictionary of the Marshallese
          Language in Micronesia]. Anthropos, 50:931-934.
          Ms XIII

Barnett, Homer G.
    1949 Palauan Society, A Study of Contemporary Native Life in the
          Palau Islands. CIMA Report, No. 20. 223 pp. Reprinted n.d.
          Eugene: Department of Anthropology, University of Oregon.
          Reviewed: 1950 by Joseph Weckler, American Anthropologist,
          52(4), Part 1:538-539.
          PL1 II

Barnett, Homer G.
    1953 The Koror Community Center. South Pacific Commission
          Technical Paper, No. 46. Noumea: South Pacific Commis-
          sion. 21 pp.
          PL1 II3

Barnett, Homer G.
    1956 Anthropology in Administration. Evanston, Illincis: Row,
          Peterson. 196 pp. Reviewed: 1957 by Cyril S. Belshaw,
          American Anthropologist, 59(2):381-382; 1957 by Arthur Capell,
          Oceania, 27(3):245-246; 1958 by Ralph Piddington, Journal of
          the Polynesian Society, 67(4):427-429.
          M II8

Barnett, Homer G.
    1960 Being A Palauan. New York: Holt, Rinehart and Winston.
          87 pp. Reviewed: 1960 by Mervyn J. Meggitt, Oceania, 31(1):
          83; 1961 by Edward M. Bruner, American Anthropologist, 63(1):
          141-143; 1962 by Ernest Beaglehole, Journal of the Polynesian
          Society, 71(1):129-130.
          PL1 II

Barnett, Homer G.
    1960 Review of Roland W. Force, Leadership and Cultural Change
          in Palau. American Anthropologist, 62(6):1099-1101.
          PL1 II7

Barnett, Homer G.
    1966 Review cf Roland W. Force, ed., Induced Political Change in
          the Pacific: A Symposium. American Anthropologist, 68(2),
          Part 1:540-542.
          P II3

Barnett, Homer G.
    1970 Palauan Journal. IN Being an Anthropologist, George D.
          Spindler, ed. New York: Holt, Rinehart and Winston.
          pp. 1-31.
          PL1 II

Barras de Aragon, Francisco de las
    1949   Las islas Palaos. [The Palau Islands]. Anuario de
           Estudios Americanos, 3:1062-1095.
           PL1 II

Barrau, Jacques
    1960   Plant exploration and introduction in Micronesia.
           South Pacific Bulletin, 10(1):44-47.
           M V

Barrau, Jacques
    1961   Subsistence agriculture in Polynesia and Micronesia. B.P.
           Bishop Museum Bulletin, No. 223. Honolulu: Bishop Museum
           Press. 94 pp. Reviewed: 1962 by William H. Davenport,
           American Anthropologist, 64(2):406; 1962 by Douglas E.
           Yen, Journal of the Polynesian Society, 71(4):350-351.
           M I

Barrau, Jacques
    1965   Histoire et prehistoire horticoles de l'Oceanie Tropicale.
           [Horticultural history and prehistory of tropical Oceania].
           Journal de la Societe des Oceanistes, 21(21):55-78.
           P V

Bartlett, Cdr. D.
    1970   Vice Admiral Chuichi Hara: Unforgettable Foe. U.S. Naval
           Institute Proceedings, 69(10):51-56.
           T1 XV

Bascom, Willard R.
    1946   Ponape: A Pacific Economy in Transition. IN U.S. Commercial
           Company's Economic Survey of Micronesia, Report No. 8. Hono-
           lulu: U.S. Commercial Company. Mimeographed. 287 pp. Re-
           printed 1965. University of California Anthropological Rec-
           ords, Vol. 22. Berkeley: University of California Press.
           149 pp. Reviewed: 1967 by Richard G. Emerick, American
           Anthropologist, 69(2):250; 1969 by Harry H. Jackman,
           Oceania, 39(4):312-315.
           Pn1 II10

Bascom, Willard R.
    1946   U.S. Commercial Company Survey on Micronesia. Central
           States Bulletin, 1:1,3,5.
           M VI

MAIN BIBLIOGRAPHY

Bascom, Willard R.
    1948 Ponapean prestige Economy. Southwestern Journal of Anthro-
         pology [now called Journal of Anthropological Research],
         4(3):211-221. Reprinted 1970. IN Cultures of the Pacific:
         Selected Readings, Thomas G. Harding and Ben J. Wallace, eds.
         New York: Free Press. pp. 85-93.
         Pn1 II10

Bascom, Willard R.
    1949 Subsistence farming cn Ponape. New Zealand Geographer,
         5(2):115-129.
         Pn1 I

Bascom, Willard R.
    1950 Ponape, the cycle of Empire. The Scientific Monthly,
         70(3):141-150.
         Pn1 II3

Bascom, Willard R.
    1950 Ponape, the tradition of Retaliation. Far Eastern
         Quarterly [now called Journal of Asian Studies], 10(1):
         56-62.
         Pn1 XII XV

Bascom, Willard R.
    1953 Ponapean subsistence Farming. Proceedings of the 7th Pacific
         Science Congress, 2 February-4 March, 1949, Auckland, New
         Zealand, 7:158. [abstract].
         Pn1 I

Bates, Marston
    1956 Ifalik, lonely paradise of the South Seas. National
         Geographic Magazine, 109(4):546-571.
         Y11 II

Bates, Marston and Donald P. Abbott
    1958 Coral Island, Portrait of an Atoll. New York: Charles
         Scribner's Sons. 254 pp. Reprinted 1959. Ifaluk: Portrait
         of a Coral Island. London: Museum Press. 287 pp. Reviewed:
         1959 by Joseph Weckler, American Anthropologist, 61(4):707-
         708; 1962 by Andrew P. Vayda, Journal of the Polynesian
         Society, 71(1):130.
         Y11 IX

Bauer, F. H.
    1960 Kwajalein Atoll Geography and Facilities. Pacific Missile
         Range Technical Memorandum PMR-TM-60-4. Point Mugu,
         California.
         Ms19 X

MAIN BIBLIOGRAPHY

Bayard, Donn T.
   1966   The cultural relationships of the Polynesian Outliers.
          M.A. Thesis, University of Hawaii, Honolulu.
          Pn8 Pn9 II

Beaglehole, Ernest
   1952   Review of Alice Joseph and Veronica Murray, Chamcrros
          and Carclinians of Saipan.   American Anthropologist,
          54(4):547-548.
          Mr2 II6

Beaglehole, Ernest
   1962   Review of Homer Barnett, Being a Palauan.   Journal of the
          Polynesian Society, 71(1):129-130.
          PL1 II

Beardsley, Charles
   1964   Guam: Past and Present.   Tokyo: Charles E. Tuttle Co.
          262 pp.
          Mr1 XII

Beaty, Janice J.
   1962   Mystery of the Marianas latte Stones.   Pacific Discovery,
          15(1):8-12.
          Mr III

Beaty, Janice J.
   1967   Discovering Guam: A Guide to Its Towns, Trails, and
          Tenants.   Tokyo: Faith Bookstore.   142 pp.
          Mr1 IX

Beauclair, Inez de
   1960   Notes on pottery of Yap, Micronesia.   Journal of East Asian
          Studies [University of Manila], 9(2&3):64-67.
          Y1 II4

Beauclair, Inez de
   1961   Bericht aus Yap, Mikronesien.   [Report from Yap, Micronesia].
          Sociologus, Zeitschrift für Empirische Soziologie, Sozialpsy-
          chologische und Ethnologische Forschung, 12(1):72-76.
          Y1 II

Beauclair, Inez de
   1961   Ken-Pai, a glass bracelet from Yap.   Asian Perspectives,
          5(1):113-115.
          Y1 II4

Beauclair, Inez de
   1962   Addenda to "Ken-Fai": A glass bracelet from Yap.   Asian
          Perspectives, 6(2):232-235.
          Y1 II4

Beauclair, Inez de
1963   The stone money of Yap Island. Bulletin of the Insti-
       tute of Ethnology, Academia Sinica, 16:147-160.
       Y1 II4

Beauclair, Inez de
1963   Black magic on Ifaluk. American Anthropologist, 65(2):388-
       389. [see Lessa 1961; Spiro 1961].
       Y11 II2

Beauclair, Inez de
1963   Some ancient beads of Yap and Palau. Journal of the Poly-
       nesian Society, 72(1):1-10.
       Y1 PL1 II4

Beauclair, Inez de
1963   Ueber Religion und Magie auf Yap. [About religion and magic
       in Yap]. Sociologus, Zeitschrift für Empirische Soziologie,
       Sozialpsychologische und Ethnologische Forschung, 13(1):68-84.
       Y1 II2

Beauclair, Inez de
1966   On pottery in Micronesia, Palauan lamps and Mediterranean
       lamps in the Far East. Bulletin of the Institute cf Ethno-
       logy, Academia Sinica, 21:197-214. Partially reprinted 1967.
       Micronesian Reporter, 15(1):18-21.
       PL1 II4

Beauclair, Inez de
1967   Infant burial in earthenware pots and the pyramidal grave on
       Yap. Bulletin of the Institute of Ethnology, Academia
       Sinica, 24:35-40.
       Y1 II2

Beauclair, Inez de
1967   On religion and mythology of Yap Island, Micronesia.
       Bulletin of the Institute of Ethnology, Academia Sinica,
       23:23-37.
       Y1 II2

Beauclair, Inez de
1968   On the religion of Yap Island, Micronesia. IN Folk Religion
       and the Worldview in the Southwestern Pacific (A Symposium of
       the 11th Pacific Science Congress, 1966), N. Matsumoto and
       T. Mabuchi, eds. Tokyo: Keio Institute of Cultural and
       Linguistic Studies, Keio University. pp. 7-11.
       Y1 II2

MAIN BIBLIOGRAPHY

Beauclair, Inez de
1968   Social stratification in Micronesia: The low caste people
        of Yap. Bulletin of the Institute of Ethnology, Academia
        Sinica, 25:45-52.
        Y1 II1

Beckett, Jeremy
1961   Review of Roland Force, Leadership and Cultural Change in
        Palau. Oceania, 32(2):155-156.
        PL1 II7

Belknap, R. L. and Norma K. Lopes
1969   The United States Weather Bureau in Micronesia. South
        Pacific Bulletin, 19(1):27-30.
        M X

Belshaw, Cyril S.
1957   Review of Homer Barnett, Anthropology in Administration.
        American Anthropologist, 59(2):381-382.
        M II8

Benavente, Ignacic V.
1952   Land tenure in the Northern Marianas. Micronesian Monthly
        [now called Micronesian Reporter], 1(7):12.
        Mr II1

Bender, Byron W.
n.d.   Marshallese Reference Grammar. Honolulu: University
        Press of Hawaii, forthcoming.
        Ms XIII

Bender, Byron W.
1963   A linguistic analysis cf the place-names of the Marshall
        Islands. Ph.D. Dissertation, Indiana University, Bloom-
        ington. Mimeographed 1963. 152 pp. Reviewed: 1964 by
        Aarne A. Koskinen, Journal of the Polynesian Society, 73(1):
        92-94. Available from University Microfilms, Ann Arbor:
        No. 64-445.
        Ms XIII

Bender, Byron W.
1963   Marshallese phonemics: Labialization or Palatalization?
        Word, 19(3):335-341.
        Ms XIII

Bender, Byron W.
1966   Towards a systematic phonemicization of Marshallese. Paper
        read at the 41st Annual Meeting of the Linguistic Society of
        America, 28-30 December, New York City.
        Ms XIII

MAIN BIBLIOGRAPHY

Bender, Byron W.
    1968   Marshallese Phonology.   Oceanic Linguistics, 7(1):16-35.
           Ms XIII

Bender, Byron W.
    1969   An Oceanic place-name Study.   Working Papers in Linguistics,
           1(11):43-74.   Honolulu: Department of Linguistics, University
           of Hawaii.   Reprinted 1970.   IN Pacific Linguistic Studies in
           Honour of Arthur Capell, S.A. Wurm and D.C. Laycock, eds.
           Pacific Linguistics Series C, No. 13.   Canberra: Linguistic
           Circle of Canberra, Australian National University Press.
           pp. 165-188.
           Ms XIII

Bender, Byron W.
    1969   Spoken Marshallese.   An Intensive Language Course with
           Grammatical Notes and Glossary.   PALI Language Texts:
           Micronesia.   Honolulu: University of Hawaii Press.   438 pp.
           Reviewed: 1971 by Arthur Capell, Oceania, 41(4):314-315;
           1971 by John L. Fischer, Language, 47(3):734-736; 1971 by
           Robert C. Kiste, American Anthropologist, 73(2):407-408.
           Ms XIII

Bender, Byron W.
    1969   Vowel dissimilation in Marshallese.   Working Papers
           in Linguistics, 1(1):88-96.   Honolulu: Department of
           Linguistics, University of Hawaii.
           Ms XIII

Bender, Byron W.
    1971   Micronesian Languages.   IN Current Trends in Linguistics,
           Thomas A. Sebeok, ed.   Volume 8, Part 1, Linguistics in
           Oceania.   The Hague: Mouton.   pp. 426-465.
           M XIII

Bender, Byron W.
    1973   Parallelisms in the morphophonemics of several Micronesian
           Languages.   Working Papers in Linguistics, 5(8):1-16.   Hono-
           lulu: Department of Linguistics, University of Hawaii.
           M XIII

Bender, Byron W. and Tony de Brum
    1966   Lessons in Marshallese.   Honolulu: University of Hawaii Peace
           Corps Training Center.   Mimeographed.
           Ms XIII

Bender, Byron W.; Takaji Abo; Alfred Capelle; and Tony de Brum
    n.d.   Marshallese-English Dictionary.   Honolulu: University
           Press of Hawaii, forthcoming.
           Ms XIII

MAIN BIBLIOGRAPHY

Benton, Richard A.
    1968   Numeral and attributive classifiers in Trukese.
           Oceanic Linguistics, 7(2):104-146.
           T XIII

Benton, Richard A.
    1968   Substitutes and classifiers in Trukese.   M.A. Thesis,
           University of Hawaii, Honolulu.
           T XIII

Benton, Richard A., assisted by Sokichi Stephen
    1967   Trukese; An Introduction to the Trukese Language for
           Speakers of English. Honolulu: Pacific and Asian Linguistics
           Institute, University cf Hawaii. 2 vols. 607 pp.
           T XIII

Bentzen, Conrad
    1949   Land and Livelihood cn Mokil, an Atoll in the Eastern
           Carolines. CIMA Report, No. 25, Part 2 [Part 1 ty Joseph E.
           Weckler]. Washington, D.C.: Pacific Science Board. 188 pp.
           Pn6 II

Bentzen, Conrad, in collaboration with Mel Sloan
    1948   Mokil. 16 mm. documentary film with narration and music in
           Color. 61 minutes. Distributed by: Special Purpose Films,
           26740 Latigo Shore Drive, Malibu, California, 90265.
           Reviewed: 1974 by Robert C. Kiste and Paul D. Schaefer,
           American Anthropologist, 76(3):715-717.
           Pn6 II

Bergbauer, Cdr. Harry W., Jr.
    1970   A review of the political status of the Trust Territory
           of the Pacific. Naval War College Review, 22(7):43-51.
           M XVII

Berger, Rainer and W. F. Libby
    1968   UCLA radiocarbon dates VIII. Radiocarbon, 10(2):402-416.
           [published by the American Journal of Science, Yale University;
           dates for Guam series collected by Fred M. Reinman on p. 407].
           Mr1 III

Berland, Joseph and Stephen Boggs
    1969   The distribution of focd and money in Moen, Truk. IN The
           Truk Report, Stephen Boggs, ed. Honolulu: Department
           of Anthropology, University of Hawaii. 21 pp.
           T1 II10

MAIN BIBLIOGRAPHY

Bieber, Patricia
1973   Translation from the Spanish of Rafael Garcia y Parejo,
       Considerations on the Rights of Spain over the Caroline
       Islands. Madrid: Establecimiento Tipographico de Gregorio
       Juste. 1885. With an Introduction. Honolulu: Pacific Is-
       lands Program, University of Hawaii, Miscellaneous Work
       Papers, 1973:1.
       C XVII

Biggs, Bruce
1961   Review of Saul H. Riesenberg and Shigeru Kaneshiro,
       A Caroline Islands Script. Journal of the Polynesian
       Society, 70(2):254-255.
       W T1 XIII

Bikajle, Tion
1960   Taro culture as practised by the Marshallese. IN Taro Cul-
       tivation Practices and Beliefs, Part II (The Eastern Caro-
       lines and the Marshall Islands), John E. de Young, ed.
       Anthropological Working Papers, No. 6. Guam: Office of the
       Staff Anthropologist, Trust Territory of the Pacific Islands.
       pp. 133-140.
       Ms I

Bikajle, Tion and John E. de Young
1958   Marshallese Names. IN The Use of Names in Micronesia, John
       E. de Young, ed. Anthropological Working Papers, No. 3.
       Guam: Office of the Staff Anthropologist, Trust Territory of
       the Pacific Islands. pp. 99-111.
       Ms II

Black, Peter
1975   Some vicissitudes of Roman Catholic dogma on Tobi Island.
       Paper read at the 4th Annual Meeting of the Association for
       Social Anthropology in Oceania, 26-30 March, Stuart, Florida.
       PL3 II2

Blackburn, Thomas
1967   Some examples of Ponapean Folklore. Journal of American
       Folklore, 80(317):247-254.
       Pn1 VIII

Blackwood, Beatrice
1951   Review of Te Rangi Hirca, Material Culture of Kapingama-
       rangi. American Anthropologist, 53(4), Part 1:549-550.
       Pn9 II4

Blake, N. M.; K. Omoto; R. L. Kirk; and D. C. Gajdusek
1973   Variation in red cell enzyme groups among populations of
       the Western Caroline Islands, Micronesia. American
       Journal of Human Genetics, 25(4):413-421.
       C XIV

Blaz, Vicente T. and Samuel S. H. Lee
    1971 The Cross of Micronesia. Naval War College Review,
          23(10):59-89.
          M XVII

Blumenstock, David I.
    1958 Typhoon effects at Jaluit Atoll in the Marshall Islands.
          Nature, 182(4645):1267-1269.
          Ms23 X

Blumenstock, David I.
    1958 Typhoon Ophelia at Jaluit Atoll. Mariner's Weather Log,
          2(6):182-183.
          Ms23 X

Blumenstock, David I., ed.
    1961 A report on typhoon effects upon Jaluit Atoll. Atoll
          Research Bulletin, No. 75. 105 pp.
          Ms23 X

Blumenstock, David I., F. Raymond Fosberg, and Charles G. Johnson
    1961 The re-survey of typhoon effects on Jaluit Atoll in the
          Marshall Islands. Nature, 189(4765):618-620.
          Ms23 X

Blumenstock, David I. and Daniel F. Rex
    1960 Microclimatic observations at Eniwetok, with a special
          section on vegetation by Irwin E. Lane. Atoll Research
          Bulletin, No. 71. 158 pp.
          Ms11 X

Bogan, Eugene F.
    1950 Government of the Trust Territory of the Pacific Islands.
          Annals of the American Academy of Political and Social
          Science, 267:164-174.
          M XVII

Boggs, Stephen T., ed.
    1969 The Truk Report: A Report on Field Training in Truk.
          Honolulu: Department of Anthropology, University of
          Hawaii. 140 pp.
          T1 II

Borden, Charles A.
    1945 The far flung islands of Micronesia. Travel, 85(4):4-9, 30.
          M IX

Bornemann, Fritz
    1956   P. W. Schmidt's Studien über den Totemismus in Asien und
            Ozeanien. [P. W. Schmidt's studies concerning tctemism in
            Asia and Oceania]. Anthropos, 51:595-734.
            P II2

Bowden, Elbert V.
    1970   Micronesia--A laboratory model of growth and Change.
            Growth and Change, 1(3):27-31.
            M II7

Bowden, Elbert V., James R. Leonard, and J. Raymond Carpenter
    1966   Economic Development Plan for the Trust Territory of the
            Pacific Islands. Submitted to the High Commissioner.
            Prepared by Robert R. Nathan Associates, Trust Territory
            Economic Development Team. Parts I-IV. Saipan: Nathan
            Associates. Mimeographed. 736 pp.
            M VI

Bowen, R. N. (compiler)
    1963   Bibliography of the Coordinated Investigation of Micro-
            nesian Anthrcpology (CIMA). Honolulu: Pacific Scientific
            Information Center, Bishop Museum. Mimecgraphed. 12 pp.
            M IX

Bowen, R. N. (compiler)
    1964   Bibliography of the Scientific Investigation of Micronesia
            (SIM). Honolulu: Pacific Scientific Infcrmation Center,
            Bishop Museum. Mimecgraphed. 14 pp.
            M IX

Bowers, Neal M.
    1950   Problems of resettlement on Saipan, Tinian, and Rota,
            Mariana Islands. Ph.D. Dissertation, University of
            Michigan, Ann Arbor. Published 1950. CIMA Report,
            No. 31. Washington, D.C.: Pacific Science Board. 258 pp.
            Mr II7

Bowers, Neal M.
    1951   The Mariana, Volcano, and Bonin Islands. IN Gecgraphy
            of the Pacific, Otis W. Freeman, ed. New York: John
            Wiley and Sons. pp. 205-235.
            Mr X

Boyd, Mary
    1971   The southwest Pacific in the 1970s. IN Asia and
            the Pacific in the 1970s, Bruce Brown, ed. Canberra:
            Australian National University Press. pp. 61-85.
            M XVII

MAIN BIBLIOGRAPHY

Boyer, David S.
    1967   Micronesia: The Americanization of Eden.   National
           Geographic, 131(5):702-744.
           M II7

Boykin, J.
    1963   The voyage of the Ulithians.   Micronesian Reporter,
           11(2):18-20.
           Y3 X

Bradley, David
    1948   No Place to Hide. Boston: Little, Brown.   182 pp.
           Ms XV

Bradley, W. P.
    1967   The history of the Marianas, Caroline, Peleu and Marshall
           Islands to the year 1922. M.A. Thesis, University of
           Southern California, Los Angeles.
           M XII

Brady, Ivan A.
    1973   Review of Vern Carroll, ed., Adoption in Eastern
           Oceania. American Anthropologist, 75(2):436-439.
           P II1

Brandt, John H.
    1962   Nan Matol: Ancient Venice of Micronesia.   Archaeology,
           15(2):99-107.
           Pn1 III

Brandt, John H.
    1962   Nests and eggs of the birds of the Truk Islands.   The Condor
           [Journal of the Cooper Ornithological Society], 64(5):416-437.
           T1 XIX

Brandt, John H.
    1963   By dunung and bouj: Water movements, stick charts
           and magic help natives stay on Course. Natural History,
           72(7):26-29.
           Ms X

Bridge, Josiah and William D. Mark
    1946   Mineral Resources of Micronesia. IN U.S. Commercial Com-
           pany's Economic Survey of Micronesia, Report No. 3.   Hono-
           lulu: U.S. Commercial Company. Mimeographed.   104 pp.
           M XI

Brislin, Richard W.
    1970   Back-translation for cross-cultural Research.   Journal of
           Cross-Cultural Psychology, 1(3):185-216.
           M XVIII

MAIN BIBLIOGRAPHY

Brislin, Richard W.
    1974   The Ponzo illusion: Additional cues, age, orientation,
           and Culture. Journal cf Cross-Cultural Psychology, 5(2):
           139-161.
           M XVIII

Brislin, Richard W. and Walter Scott Wilson
    1971   Perception of similarities and differences among ethnic
           groups at the University of Guam. Micronesica, 7(1&2):
           19-26.
           M II6

Broadbent, William A.
    1970   A Profile of Chamcrro and Statesider Attitudes Toward Edu-
           cation and Educationally Related Values. Prepared for and
           in cooperation with Dr. Thomas Bell and Dr. James Hale.
           Guam: Northwest Regional Educational Laboratory. 115 pp.
           Mr VII

Brody, Jacob A., Thomas N. Chase, and E. K. Gordon
    1970   Catabolite levels in cerebrospinal fluid of patients
           with Parkinsonism dementia of Guam. New England
           Journal of Medicine, 282(17):947-950.
           Mr1 XIV

Brody, Jacob A. and Kwang-Ming Chen
    1969   Changing epidemiology patterns of amyotrophic lateral
           sclerosis and Parkinsonism-dementia on Guam. IN Motor
           Neuron Diseases: Research on Amyotrophic Lateral Scle-
           rosis and Related Disorders, Volume 2, F.H. Norris, Jr.
           and Leonard T. Kurland, eds. New York: Grune and Strat-
           ton. pp. 61-79.
           Mr1 XIV XVI

Brody, Jacob A., Asao Hirano, and R. M. Scott
    1971   Recent neuropathologic observations in amyotrophic lateral
           sclerosis and Parkinsonism dementia of Guam. Neurclogy,
           21(5):528-536.
           Mr1 XIV

Brody, Jacob A.; I. E. Hussels; Edward Brink; and Jcse M. Tcrres
    1970   Hereditary blindness among Pingelapese people of Eastern
           Caroline Islands. Lancet, 1(7659):1253-1257.
           Pn7 XIV

Brody, Jacob A. and Leonard T. Kurland
    1973   Amyotrophic lateral sclerosis and Parkinsonism-dementia
           in Guam. IN Tropical Neurology, J. Spillane, ed. New
           York: Oxford University Press. pp. 355-375.
           Mr1 XIV XVI

MAIN BIBLIOGRAPHY

Brower, Kenneth
    1974 With Their Islands Around Them. New York: Holt, Rinehart
          and Winston. 216 pp.
          PL1 IX

Brown, Bruce, ed.
    1971 Asia and the Pacific in the 1970s: The Roles of the United
          States, Australia, and New Zealand. Canberra: Australian
          National University Press. 253 pp.
          P XVII

Brown, Carroll
    1953 A survey of United States administration of the Trust
          Territory of the Pacific Islands. M.A. Thesis, Columbia
          University, New York.
          M XVII

Brown, Paul, Mint Basnight, and D. C. Gajdusek
    1965 Response to live attenuated measles vaccine in susceptible
          island populations in Micronesia. American Journal of
          Epidemiology, 82(2):115-122.
          M XIV

Brown, Paul and D. C. Gajdusek
    1970 Disease patterns and vaccine-response studies in
          isolated Micronesian Populations. American Journal of
          Tropical Medicine and Hygiene, 19(1):170-175.
          Y XIV

Brown, Paul, D. C. Gajdusek, and J. Anthony Morris
    1966 Epidemic A2 influenza in isolated Pacific Island populations
          without pre-epidemic antibody to influenza virus types A
          and B, and the discovery of still unexpected Populations.
          American Journal of Epidemiology, 83(1):176-188.
          Y XIV

Brown, Paul, D. C. Gajdusek, and T. Tsai
    1969 Persistance of measles antibody in the absence of
          circulating natural virus five years after immunization
          of an isolated virgin population with Edmonston B Vaccine.
          American Journal of Epidemiology, 90(6):514-518.
          Y3 XIV

Brown, Paula
    1960 Review of Roland Force, Leadership and Cultural Change in
          Palau. Journal of the Polynesian Society, 69(3):297-298.
          PL1 II7

Brownell, Jean
    1968 Papers of Ephraim and Myra Roberts of Ponape. Journal of
          Pacific History, 3:177.
          Pn1 XII

Browning, Mary A.
    1968 The sailing of the Rurick. Micronesian Reporter, 16(1):17-25.
          Ms XII

Browning, Mary A.
    1970 Micronesian Heritage. Dance Perspectives, No. 43. New
          York: Dance Perspectives Foundation. 49 pp. Reviewed: 1972
          by Mervyn McLean, Journal of the Polynesian Society, 81(2):
          279-282.
          M IV

Browning, Mary A.
    1972 Traders in the Marshalls. Micronesian Reporter, 20(1):32-38.
          Ms VI XII

Browning, Mary A.
    1972 Walab im Medo: Canoes and navigation in the Marshalls.
          Oceans, 5(1):25-37. Reprinted 1973. Micronesian
          Reporter, 21(1):25-31.
          Ms X

Browning, Mary A.
    1973 Stick Charting. Sea Frontiers, 19(1):34-44.
          Ms X

Brum, Oscar de and Henry Rutz
    1967 Political succession and intra-group organization in Laura
          Village. IN The Laura Report, Leonard Mason, ed. Honolulu:
          Department of Anthropology, University of Hawaii. 68 pp.
          Ms8 II3

Bruner, Edward M.
    1961 Review of Homer G. Barnett, Being a Palauan.
          American Anthropologist, 63(1):141-143.
          PL1 II

Bryan, Edwin H., Jr.
    1946 Geographic Summary of Micronesia. Climate of Micronesia.
          Gazetteer of Micronesia. Atlas of Micronesia. IN U.S.
          Commercial Company's Economic Survey of Micronesia,
          Report No. 2. Honolulu: U.S. Commercial Company.
          Mimeographed.
          M X

Bryan, Edwin H., Jr.
    1950 Check list of Atolls. Atoll Research Bulletin, No. 19. 38 pp.
          P X

Bryan, Edwin H., Jr.
    1965 Life in Micronesia. Kwajalein, Marshall Islands: Hourglass
          Special Publications. Mimeographed. 63 pp. folio.
          M II

Bryan, Edwin H., Jr.
    1971 Guide to Place Names in the Trust Territory of the
          Pacific Islands (the Marshall, Caroline and Mariana
          Islands). Honolulu: Pacific Scientific Information
          Center, Bishop Museum. 406 pp.; 114 maps.
          M X

Bryan, Edwin H., Jr.
    1971 Notes on the ancient culture of Guam. Guam Recorder, n.s.,
          1(1):6.
          Mr1 III

Bryan, Edwin H., Jr.
    1972 Life in the Marshall Islands. Honolulu: Pacific Scientific
          Information Center, Bishop Museum. 237 pp.
          Ms II

Bryan, Edwin H., Jr.
    1972 Notes on the ancient culture of Guam Pottery. Guam Recorder,
          n.s., 2(1):13-14.
          Mr1 III

Bryan, Edwin H., Jr.
    1975 Review of Benjamin C. Stone, The flora of Guam. Atoll
          Research Bulletin, No. 185:27-28.
          Mr1 V

Bryan, Edwin H., Jr. and staff
    1970 Land in Micronesia and its Resources: An Annotated Biblio-
          graphy. Honolulu: Pacific Scientific Information Center,
          Bishop Museum. 119 pp.
          M IX

Buck, Sir Peter [see Te Rangi Hiroa]

Burns, Richard D.
    1968 Inspection of the Mandates, 1919-1941. Pacific
          Historical Review, 37(4):445-462.
          M XVII

Burridge, K. O. L.
    1967 Review of William A. Lessa, Ulithi: A Micronesian Design for
          Living. Man, n.s., 2(1):155.
          Y3 II

Burris, E. J.
    1954 Sanvitores' grammar and catechism in the Mariana (or
          Chamorro) Language (1668). Anthropos, 49:934-960.
          Mr XIII

Burrows, Edwin Grant
    1952 From value to ethos on Ifaluk Atoll. Southwestern Journal
          of Anthropology [now called Journal of Anthropological
          Research], 8(1):13-35.
          Y11 II2

Burrows, Edwin Grant
    1958 Music on Ifaluk Atoll in the Caroline Islands.
          Ethnomusicology, 2(1):9-22.
          Y11 IV

Burrows, Edwin Grant
    1963 Flower in My Ear, Arts and Ethos of Ifaluk Atoll.
          University of Washington Publications in Anthropology,
          Volume 14. Seattle: University of Washington Press. 439 pp.
          Reviewed: 1963 by Ernest S. Dodge, Ethnohistory, 10(3):306-
          307; 1963 by Katharine Luomala, Pacific Historical Review,
          32(4):419-420; 1964 by Samuel H. Elbert, Journal of the
          Polynesian Society, 73(1):90-92; 1964 by John L. Fischer,
          American Anthropologist, 66(2):460-461.
          Y11 VIII

Burrows, Edwin Grant and Melford E. Spiro
    1953 An Atoll Culture, Ethnography of Ifaluk in the Central
          Carolines. Behavior Science Monographs. New Haven: HRAF
          Press. 355 pp. [CIMA Reports, Nos. 16 and 18]. Reprinted
          1970. Westport, Connecticut: Greenwood Press. Reviewed:
          1955 by William A. Lessa, American Anthropologist, 57(5):
          1090; 1955 by William A. Lessa, Journal of the Polynesian
          Society, 64(1):171.
          Y11 II

Bushnell, G. H. S.
    1955 Review of Erik K. Reed, Archaeology and the History of
          Guam. Antiquity, 29(113):56-57.
          Mr1 III

Cabranes, Jose A.
    1973 The evolution of the 'American Empire'. Proceedings of the
          American Society of International Law, 67(5):1-7.
          M XVII

Caldwell, John C.
    1969 Let's Visit Micronesia; Guam (USA) and the Trust Territory of
          the Pacific Islands. New York: John Day. 95 pp.
          M Mr1 IX

MAIN BIBLIOGRAPHY

Cammack, Floyd M. and Shiro Saito
    1962 Pacific Island Bibliography. New York: The Scarecrow Press.
          421 pp.
          P IX

Cammack, Floyd M. and Donald M. Topping
    1965 University of Hawaii Peace Corps Language Training Program.
          Language Learning, 15(1&2):29-42.
          M XIII

Capell, Arthur
    1947 Review of, "Books on Micronesian Linguistics." Oceania,
          18(1):91-93.
          M XIII

Capell, Arthur
    1948 Palau-English Dictionary; English-Palau Dictionary; A
          Grammar of the Language of Palau; Palau First Reader;
          Palau Number Book and Introduction to Arithmetic. CIMA
          Report, No. 6. Washington, D.C.: Pacific Science Board.
          241 pp.
          PL1 XIII

Capell, Arthur
    1950 Education for Pacific People: Education in Micronesia.
          The Educational Forum, 16(1):79-91.
          M VII

Capell, Arthur
    1950 Grammar and Vocabulary of the Language of Sonsorol-Tobi.
          CIMA Report, No. 30. Washington, D.C.: Pacific Science
          Board. 152 pp. Reprinted 1969. Oceania Linguistic Mono-
          graph No. 12. Sydney: University of Sydney Press. 224 pp.
          Reviewed: 1969 by A.G. Haudricourt, Journal de la Societe
          des Oceanistes, 25:404; 1971 by J.A. Z'graggen, Anthropos,
          66:292.
          PL3 PL4 XIII

Capell, Arthur
    1954 Review of Erhard Schlesier, Die Erscheinungsformen des
          Männerhauses und das Klubwesen in Mikronesien. [The charac-
          teristic forms taken by men's houses and the nature of club
          life in Micronesia]. Oceania, 25(1&2):133-135.
          M II1 II4

Capell, Arthur
    1957 Palau possessives and problems in morpheme Identification.
          Oceania, 27(4):273-282.
          PL1 XIII

Capell, Arthur
    1957 Review of Homer Barnett, Anthropology in Administration.
           Oceania, 27(3):245-246.
           M II8

Capell, Arthur
    1962 Oceanic linguistics Today. Current Anthropology, 3(4):
           371-428.
           P XIII

Capell, Arthur
    1971 Review of Donald M. Topping, Spoken Chamorro, and Byron
           Bender, Spoken Marshallese. Oceania, 41(4):314-315.
           M XIII

Carano, Paul
    1972 Ancient Chamorro Leaders. Guam Recorder, n.s., 2(4):7-8.
           Mr II3 XII

Carano, Paul
    1972 Development of representative self-government in Guam.
           Guam Recorder, n.s., 2(4):51-56.
           Mr1 XVII

Carano, Paul
    1974 British privateers visit Guam. Guam Recorder, n.s.,
           4(3):25-30.
           Mr1 XII

Carano, Paul
    1975 Who's who--in Guam History. Guam Recorder, n.s., 5(1):
           3-15.
           Mr1 XII

Carano, Paul and Pedro C. Sanchez
    1964 A Complete History of Guam. Rutland, Vermont: Charles
           E. Tuttle Co. 452 pp. Reviewed: 1966 by H.E. Maude,
           Journal of Pacific History, 1:243-245.
           Mr1 XII

Carlson, Clayton H.
    1967 Lessons in Palauan. Honolulu: University of Hawaii Peace
           Corps Training Center. Mimeographed.
           PL1 XIII

Carlson, Clayton H.
    1968 Palauan Phonology. M.A. Thesis, University of Hawaii,
           Honolulu.
           PL1 XIII

MAIN BIBLIOGRAPHY

Carr, Denzel
    1945 Notes on Marshallese consonant Phonemes. Language,
          21(4):267-270.
          Ms XIII

Carr, Ronald E., Newton E. Morton, and Irwin M. Siegel
    1971 Achromatopsia in Pingelap islanders: Study of a genetic
          Isolate. American Journal of Ophthalmology, 72(4):746-756.
          Pn7 XIV XVI

Carroll, Vern
    n.d. Communities and non-communities: The Nukuoro on Ponape.
          IN Exiles and Migrants in Oceania, Michael D. Lieber, ed.
          ASAO Monograph Series. Honolulu: University Press of
          Hawaii, forthcoming.
          Pn8 Pn1 II1

Carroll, Vern
    n.d. Incest on Nukuoro. IN Incest Prohibitions in Polynesia
          and Micronesia, Vern Carroll, ed. ASAO Monograph Series.
          Honolulu: University Press of Hawaii, forthcoming.
          Pn8 II1

Carroll, Vern, ed.
    n.d. Incest Prohibitions in Polynesia and Micronesia. ASAO
          Monograph Series. Honolulu: University Press of
          Hawaii, forthcoming.
          P II1

Carroll, Vern
    1964 Place names on Nukuoro Atoll. Atoll Research Bulletin,
          No. 107. 13 pp.
          Pn8 X

Carroll, Vern
    1965 An outline of the structure of the language of Nukuoro.
          Part 1, Journal of the Polynesian Society, 74(2):192-226;
          Part 2, Journal of the Polynesian Society, 74(4):451-472.
          Reprinted 1965. Polynesian Society Reprint Series, No. 10.
          56 pp.
          Pn8 XIII

Carroll, Vern
    1966 Generative elicitation techniques in Polynesian
          Lexicography. Oceanic Linguistics, 5(2):59-70.
          Pn8 XIII

Carroll, Vern
    1966 Nukuoro Kinship. Ph.D. Dissertation, University of
          Chicago, Chicago.
          Pn8 II1

Carroll, Vern
    1968 Nukuoro kinship Terms. Paper read at the 67th Annual
          Meeting of the American Anthropological Association, 21-24
          November, Seattle.
          Pn8 II1

Carroll, Vern, ed.
    1970 Adoption in Eastern Cceania. ASAO Monograph No. 1.
          Honolulu: University of Hawaii Press. 422 pp. Reviewed:
          1971 by Ian Hogbin, Mankind, 8(1):76-77; 1971 by Joan Metge,
          Man, n.s., 6(3):518; 1971 by Martine Segalen, L'anthropologie,
          15(5&6):515-516; 1971 by Walter Scott Wilson, Micronesica,
          7(1&2):244-245; 1972 by Stephen Foster, Journal cf the Poly-
          nesian Society, 81(2):268-270; 1972 by I.S. Mitchell, Practi-
          cal Anthropology, 19(6):237-238; 1973 by Ivan A. Brady,
          American Anthropologist, 75(2):436-439; 1973 by Robert
          McKinley, Journal of Asian Studies, 734-37.
          P II1

Carroll, Vern
    1970 Adoption on Nukuoro. IN Adoption in Eastern Oceania,
          Vern Carroll, ed. ASAO Monograph No. 1. Honolulu:
          University of Hawaii Press. pp. 121-157.
          Pn8 II1

Carroll, Vern
    1971 Review cf Norman Meller with the assistance of Terza
          Meller, The Congress of Micronesia: Development cf
          the Legislative Process in the Trust Territory of the
          Pacific Islands. American Anthropologist, 73(4):884-885.
          M XVII

Carroll, Vern
    1972 The Nukuoro notion of 'Person'. Paper read at the 71st
          Annual Meeting of the American Anthropological Association,
          29 November-3 December, Torontc.
          Pn8 II1

Carroll, Vern
    1973 'Rape' on Nukuorc. Paper read at the 2nd Annual Meeting
          of the Association fcr Social Anthropolcgy in Oceania,
          21-25 March, Orcas Island, Washington.
          Pn8 II1

Carroll, Vern
    1975 The population cf Nukucro in historical Perspective. IN
          Pacific Atoll Populations, Vern Carroll, ed. ASAO
          Monograph No. 3. Honolulu: University Press of Hawaii.
          pp. 344-416.
          Pn8 XVI

MAIN BIBLIOGRAPHY

Carroll, Vern, ed.
    1975 Pacific Atoll Populations. ASAO Monograph No. 3.
          Honolulu: University Press of Hawaii. 528 pp.
          P XVI

Carroll, Vern and Tobias Soulik
    1973 Nukuoro Lexicon. PALI Language Texts: Polynesia.
          Honolulu: University Press of Hawaii. 833 pp.
          Pn8 XIII

Carter, Jackson
    1972 Truk: A land Problem. M.A. Thesis, Wichita State
          University, Wichita, Kansas.
          T1 II1 X

Caughey, Frances B.
    1971 Pregnancy and childbirth on Uman, Truk. M.A. Thesis,
          University of Pennsylvania, Philadelphia.
          T1 II

Caughey, John Lyon IV
    1970 Cultural values in a Micronesian Society [Uman, Truk]. Ph.D.
          Dissertation, University of Pennsylvania, Philadelphia.
          Available from University Microfilms, Ann Arbor: No. 71-7788.
          T1 II2

Cayford, Marilyn L.
    1971 Transport strategy in Micronesia. M.A. Thesis, University
          of Washington, Seattle.
          M X

Chakravarti, Diptiman and Edward E. Held
    1963 Chemical and radiochemical composition of the Rongelapese
          Diet. Journal of Food Science, 28(2):221-228.
          Ms15 XIV

Chambers, Anne
    1971 A study of the relocation of two Marshallese atoll Communi-
          ties. Kroeber Anthropological Society Papers, 44:30-47.
          Ms11 Ms13 II7

Chambers, Keith S.
    1972 Tale traditions of Eastern Micronesia: A comparative study
          of Marshallese, Gilbertese and Nauruan folk Narrative.
          M.A. Thesis, University of California, Berkeley.
          Ms VIII

Chan, George L.
    1967 Health problems of coral atoll Populations. South
          Pacific Bulletin, 17(3):24-26.
          P XIV

MAIN BIBLIOGRAPHY

Chapman, Peter Sherwood
    1964 Micronesian archaeology: An annotated Bibliography.
          M.A. Thesis, Stanford University, Stanford, California.
          M III

Chapman, Peter Sherwood
    1967 Micronesia: 1960-1964. Asian Perspectives, 10:99-114.
          M III

Chapman, Peter Sherwood
    1968 Japanese contributions to Micronesian archaeology and
          material Culture. IN Prehistoric Culture in Oceania,
          I. Yawata and Y. H. Sinoto, eds. Honolulu: Bishcp
          Museum Press. pp. 67-82.
          M III

Chapman, Peter Sherwood
    1974 Micronesia 1965-1974: A Bibliography. Asian Perspectives,
          17(2):160-189.
          M IX

Chapman, Wilbert McLeod
    1946 Tuna in the Mandated Islands. Far Eastern Survey, 15(20):
          317-319.
          M VI

Chave, Margaret E.
    1948 The changing position of mixed-bloods in the Marshall
          Islands. M.A. Thesis, University of Chicago, Chicago.
          Published 1950. CIMA Report, No. 7. Washington, D.C.:
          Pacific Science Board. Mimeographed. 97 pp.
          Ms II7

Cheatham, Norden H.
    1968 Forestry and conservation in the Trust Territory of the
          Pacific Islands. South Pacific Bulletin, 18(4):41, 47.
          M I

Chung, Roy
    1975 Fertility and the social structure of Guam. IN The Impact
          of Urban Centers in the Pacific, Roland W. Force and Brenda
          Bishop, eds. Honolulu: Pacific Science Association, Bishop
          Museum. p. 255. [abstract].
          Mr1 XVI

Chutaro, Chuji
    1971 Caught in the Squeeze. Micronesian Reporter, 19(1):27-30.
          M II7

Clark, Eugenie
    1951 Lady with a Spear. New York: Harper and Row. 243 pp.
          M IX

Clark, Eugenie
    1953 Siakong--spear fisherman pre-eminent: Exploring the sea
          bottom in the Palau Islands with a diver whose feats are
          a legend of the South Seas. Natural History, 62(5):227-234.
          PL1 IX XIX

Clark, LCdr. T. O.
    1946 The administration of the former Japanese Mandated Islands.
          U.S. Naval Institute Proceedings, 72(4):511-515.
          M IX XV

Clark, Peggy, Jane H. Underwood, and Patricia Jones
    1975 Serum proteins in people of the Yap Islands. Micronesica,
          11(1):71-76.
          Y1 XVI

Clark, Roger
    1973 The Trust Territory of the Pacific Islands: Some
          Perspectives. Proceedings of the American Society
          of International Law, 67(5):17-21.
          M XVII

Cleveland, Harlan
    1963 Reflections on the Pacific Community. U.S. Department of
          State Bulletin, 48(1243):613-616.
          P XVII

Clifton, James A.
    1964 The acceptance of external political controls on Truk and
          Ponape. International Journal of Comparative Sociology
          [Leiden], 5(1):91-103.
          T1 Pn1 XII XVII

Cloud, Preston E., Jr.; Robert G. Schmidt; Harold W. Burke; Allen N.
          Nichol; Dan A. Davis; Ray E. Zarza; Ralph J. McCracken
    1955 Military Geology of Saipan, Mariana Islands. Volume 1 -
          Introduction and Engineering Aspects. Prepared under the
          direction of the Chief of Engineers, U.S. Army, by the
          Intelligence Division, Office of the Engineer, Headquar-
          ters, U.S. Army Forces Far East and 8th U.S. Army, with
          personnel of the U.S. Geological Survey. Washington, D.C.:
          U.S. Army. Mimeographed. 67 pp.
          Mr2 XI

Clune, Francis J.
    1974 Archeological survey of Truk, Micronesia. Micronesica,
          10(2):205-206.
          T1 III

MAIN BIBLIOGRAPHY

Coale, George L.
1951 A study of chieftainship, missionary contact and culture
      change on Ponape, 1852-1900. M.A. Thesis, University of
      Southern California, Los Angeles.
      Pn1 II7 XII

Cockrum, Emmett Erston
1970 The emergence of modern Micronesia. Ph.D. Dissertation,
      University of Colorado, Boulder. Available from University
      Microfilms, Ann Arbor: No. 71-5878.
      M XII XVII

Coenen, Jan
1961 Agricultural development in Micronesia. South Pacific
      Bulletin, 11(3):30-32, 69.
      M I

Coenen, Jan and Jacques Barrau
1961 The breadfruit tree in Micronesia. South Pacific Bulletin,
      11(4):37.
      M I

Cohen, Herbert
1952 Class and land in Micronesia. M.A. Thesis,
      University of Chicago, Chicago.
      M II1

Colletta, Nat Joseph
1972 American schools for the natives of Ponape: A case
      study of the role of education in the development of
      cultural character among the Ponapeans of Micronesia.
      Ph.D. Dissertation, Michigan State University, East
      Lansing. Available from University Microfilms, Ann
      Arbor: No. 73-05350.
      Pn1 VII

Collier, John
1946 Micronesia and trusteeship: Test for America and crucial
      need for the World. Newsletter of the Institute of
      Ethnic Affairs, 4:1-11.
      M XVII

Collister, Cdr. Louis J.
1964 Trust Territory of the Pacific Islands--problem cr
      Opportunity? Student Thesis, U.S. Army War College,
      AWC Log 64-3-38U.
      M XVII

Conard, Robert A.; Charles E. Huggins; Bradford Cannon; Austen Lowry; and John B. Richards
    1957 Medical survey of Marshallese two years after exposure to fallout Radiation. Journal of the American Medical Association, 164(11):1192-1197.
    Ms XIV

Conard, Robert A.; H. Eugene MacDonald; Austin Lowrey; Leo M. Meyer; Stanton Cohn; Wataru W. Sutow; Baruch S. Blumberg; James W. Hollingsworth; Harvey W. Lyon; William H. Lewis, Jr.; A. A. Jaffe; Maynard Eicher; David Potter; Isaac Lanwi; Ezra Riklon; John Iaman; and Jack Helkena
    1960 Medical Survey of Rongelap People Five and Six Years After Exposure to Fallout, (with addendum on Vegetation). Upton, New York: Brookhaven National Laboratory, U.S. Atomic Energy Commission. BNL 609 (T-179). 86 pp.
    Ms15 XIV

Converse, Elizabeth
    1949 The United States as Trustee--I. Far Eastern Survey, 18(22):260-263. Reprinted 1950. South Pacific, 4(3):33-38.
    M XVII

Converse, Elizabeth
    1949 The United States as Trustee--II. Far Eastern Survey, 18(24):277-283. Reprinted 1950. South Pacific, 4(6):99-106.
    M XVII

Coolidge, Harold J.
    1948 The Pacific Science Board. Far Eastern Survey, 17(11):193-194.
    P IX

Coolidge, Harold J., ed.
    1948 Conservation in Micronesia. Washington, D.C.: Pacific Science Board, National Research Council. 70 pp.
    M I

Coolidge, Harold J.
    1951 Science lends a hand. The far-flung islands of the Trust Territory received aid under the Navy's administration of the vast Area. Paradise of the Pacific [now called Honolulu Magazine], 63(5):30-31.
    M XVII

Coolidge, Harold J., ed.
    1966 Scientific Investigations in Micronesia: Final Report. Washington, D.C.: Pacific Science Board, National Research Council. 19 pp.
    M IX

MAIN BIBLIOGRAPHY

Cormack, Maribelle
 1956 The Lady was a Skipper: The Story of Eleanor Wilson,
       Missionary Extraordinary to the Marshall and Carcline
       Islands. New York: Hill and Wang. 224 pp.
       M II2

Corwin, Gilbert; Lawrence D. Bonham; Maurice J. Terman; George W. Viele
 1957 Military Geology of Pagan, Mariana Islands. Prepared under
       the direction of the Chief of Engineers, U.S. Army, by the
       Intelligence Division, Office of the Engineer, Headquarters,
       U.S. Army Japan, with personnel of the U.S. Geological
       Survey. Washington, D.C.: U.S. Army. Mimeographed. 259 pp.
       Mr5 XI

Costenoble, H.
 1974 The family tree of Chamorro. Guam Recorder, n.s., 4(2):
       25-26.
       Mr II1

Coulter, John Wesley
 1948 The United States Trust Territory of the Pacific.
       Journal of Geography, 47(7):253-267.
       M X

Coulter, John Wesley
 1957 The Pacific Dependencies of the United States. New York:
       Macmillan. 388 pp. Reviewed: 1958 by Joseph Weckler,
       American Anthropologist, 60(3):605-606.
       M XVII

Cox, Samuel Allen
 1970 An analysis of geographical influences on Micronesian
       Culture. M.A. Thesis, West Chester State College,
       West Chester, Pennsylvania.
       M X

Crane, H. R. and James B. Griffin
 1958 University of Michigan radiocarbon dates II. Science,
       127(3306):1098-1105. [dates for Yap series collected by
       E.W. Gifford and D.S. Giffcrd reported on p. 1105].
       Y1 III

Crane, H. R. and James B. Griffin
 1959 University of Michigan radiocarbon dates IV. Radiocarbon,
       1:173-198. [published by the American Journal of Science,
       Yale University; dates fcr Yap series collected by E.W.
       Gifford and D.S. Gifford reported on pp. 194-195].
       Y1 III

Crawford, David and Leona Crawford
    1967 Missionary Adventures in the South Pacific. Tokyo: Charles E.
          Tuttle Co. 280 pp. Reviewed: 1969 by H.E. Maude, Journal of
          Pacific History, 4:230-231.
          M II2 XII

Crawford, H. E., G. C. Hamman, and Isaac Lanwi
    1954 Ophthalmological survey of the Trust Territory of the
          Pacific Islands. South Pacific Commission Technical
          Paper, No. 67. Noumea: South Pacific Commission. 16 pp.
          M XIV

Crocombe, Ron
    1968 The Peace Corps in Micronesia. Papua and New Guinea
          Volunteer [Port Moresby], 17:3-4.
          M II7

Crofts, George D. and Emilie G. Johnston
    1975 Governor Gregorio Santa Maria saves and enlarges the Col-
          lege of San Juan de Letran. Guam Recorder, n.s., 5(1):
          24-28.
          Mr1 XII

Cronkite, E. P., V. P. Bond, and C. L. Dunham, eds.
    1956 Some Effects of Ionizing Radiation on Human Beings: A Report
          on the Marshallese and Americans Accidentally Exposed to Ra-
          diation from Fallout and a Discussion of Radiation Injury in
          the Human Being. U.S. Atomic Energy Commission, TID-5358.
          Washington, D.C.: U.S. Government Printing Office. 106 pp.
          Ms XIV

Crowl, Philip A.
    1960 Campaign in the Marianas. The War in the Pacific, United
          States Army in World War II, Vol. 2, Part 14. Washington,
          D.C.: Office of the Chief of Military History, Department
          of the Army. 505 pp.
          Mr XV

Crowl, Philip A. and Edmund G. Love
    1955 Seizure of the Gilberts and the Marshalls. The War in the
          Pacific, United States Army in World War II, Vol. 2, Part 6.
          Washington, D.C.: Office of the Chief of Military History,
          Department of the Army. 414 pp.
          Ms XV

Cruetz, E. and R. Beken
    1971 Air-Medec Micronesia. Proceedings [Abstracts of Papers] of
          the 12th Pacific Science Congress, 18 August-3 September,
          1971, Canberra, 1:292-293.
          M XIV

Cruz, F. "Val" (compiler)
    1967 Chamorro-English; English-Chamorro Dictionary. Hong Kong:
          The Green Pagoda Press. 255 pp.
          Mr XIII

Daeufer, Alice S. (compiler)
    1969 Pathways to Micronesia. An annotated bibliography of selected
          works. Saipan: Department of Education, Trust Territory
          of the Pacific Islands. 47 pp.
          M IX

Dahlquist, Paul A.
    1971 One pig, one yam, one sakau, and money: The changing eco-
          nomics of feasting on Ponape. Paper read at the 70th Annual
          Meeting of the American Anthropological Association, 18-21
          November, New York City.
          Pn1 II10

Dahlquist, Paul A.
    1972 The place of money in a contemporary Micronesian Society.
          Paper read at the 51st Annual Meeting of the Central States
          Anthropological Society, 27-30 April, Cleveland, Ohio.
          Pn1 II10

Dahlquist, Paul A.
    1972 Kohdo mwenge: The food complex in a changing Ponapean
          Community. Ph.D. Dissertation, Ohio State University,
          Columbus. Available from University Microfilms, Ann Arbor:
          No. 73-11479.
          Pn1 II7 II10

Dahlquist, Paul A.
    1974 Changes in Ponapean social identity: Food and social organ-
          ization in the American Period. Paper read at the 3rd Annual
          Meeting of the Association for Social Anthropology in Oceania,
          13-17 March, Asilomar, Pacific Grove, California.
          Pn1 II7

Dahlquist, Paul A.
    1974 Political development at the municipal level: Kiti,
          Ponape. IN Political Development in Micronesia, Daniel
          T. Hughes and Sherwood G. Lingenfelter, eds. Columbus:
          Ohio State University Press. pp. 178-191.
          Pn1 II3

Damm, H.
    1955 Micronesische Kultboote, Schwebealtäre und weihegaben-
          hänger. [Micronesian ritual canoes, suspended altars, and
          oblative Pendants]. Jahrbuch des Museum für Völkerkunde zu
          Leipzig [für 1954], 13:45-72.
          M II2

MAIN BIBLIOGRAPHY

Darrell, Richard W.; Sam Pieper, Jr.; Leonard T. Kurland; and Leon
    Jacobs
    1964 Chorioretinopathy and Toxoplasmosis. An epidemiologic
          study on a South Pacific Island [Truk]. Archives of
          Ophthalmology, 71(1):63-68.
          T1 XIV

Davenport, William H.
    1952 Fourteen Marshallese Riddles. Journal of American Folklore,
          65(257):265-266.
          Ms VIII

Davenport, William H.
    1953 Marshallese folklore Types. Journal of American Folklore,
          66(261):219-237.
          Ms VIII

Davenport, William H.
    1960 Marshall Island navigation Charts. Imago Mundi [The Hague],
          15:19-26. Reprinted in Bobbs-Merrill Social Science Reprint
          Series, Reprint A-48.
          Ms X

Davenport, William H.
    1962 Review of Jacques Barrau, Subsistence Agriculture in Poly-
          nesia and Micronesia. American Anthropologist, 64(2):406.
          M I

Davenport, William H.
    1964 Marshall Islands Cartography. Expedition, 6(4):10-13.
          Ms X

Davidson, James W.
    1952 The changing political role of Pacific Islands Peoples.
          South Pacific, 6(4):380-385.
          P XVII

Davidson, James W.
    1971 The decolonization of Oceania. Journal of Pacific History,
          6:133-150.
          P XVII

Davidson, Janet M.
    1966 Nukuoro--archeology on a Polynesian outlier in Micronesia.
          Proceedings [Abstracts of Papers] of the 11th Pacific Science
          Congress, 22 August-10 September, 1966, Tokyo, Vol. 9,
          Symposium No. 9, p. 6.
          Pn8 III

Davidson, Janet M.
  1967 An archeological assemblage of simple fish-hooks from Nukuoro
        Atoll. Journal of the Polynesian Society, 76(2):177-196.
        Pn8 III

Davidson, Janet M.
  1967 Archeology on coral Atolls. IN Polynesian Culture History,
        Essays in Honor of Kenneth P. Emory, Genevieve A. Highland,
        et al., eds. Honolulu: Bishop Museum Press. pp. 363-375.
        Pn8 III

Davidson, Janet M.
  1967 Preliminary archeological investigations on Ponape and other
        Eastern Caroline Islands. Micronesica, 3(2):81-95.
        Pn K III

Davidson, Janet M.
  1967 Review of Douglas Osborne, The Archaeology of the Palau
        Islands: An Intensive Survey. Journal of the Polynesian
        Society, 76(4):526-528.
        PL1 III

Davidson, Janet M.
  1968 A wooden image from Nukuoro in the Auckland Museum.
        Journal of the Polynesian Society, 77(1):77-79.
        Pn8 II4

Davidson, Janet M.
  1968 Nukuoro: Archeology cn a Polynesian outlier in Micronesia.
        IN Prehistoric Culture in Oceania, I. Yawata and Y. H.
        Sinoto, eds. Honolulu: Bishop Museum Press. pp. 51-66.
        Pn8 III

Davidson, Janet M.
  1970 Polynesian outliers and the problem of culture replacement
        in small Populations. IN Studies in Oceanic Culture History,
        Vol. 1, Roger C. Green and Marion Kelly, eds. Pacific Anthro-
        pological Records, No. 11. Honolulu: Bishop Museum,
        Department of Anthropolcgy. pp. 61-72.
        P III

Davidson, Janet M.
  1971 Archeology on Nukuoro Atoll. A Polynesian Outlier in the
        Eastern Caroline Islands. Bulletin of the Auckland Insti-
        tute and Museum, No. 9. Auckland, New Zealand. 108 pp.
        Reviewed: 1972 by Jose Garanger, Journal de la Scciete des
        Oceanistes, 28(36):311; 1973 by Erwin R. Ray, Man, n.s.,
        8(3):486-487; 1973 by John Terrell, American Anthropologist,
        75(4):1119-1121; 1974 by Jose Garanger, Journal cf the Poly-
        nesian Society, 83(2):238-239.
        Pn8 III

Davis, C. J.
    1964 Stick charts of Micronesia. Navigation, 11(1):32-37.
          Ms X

Davis, Dan
    1958 Military Geology of Saipan, Mariana Islands. Vol. II -
          Water Resources; Soils Map of Saipan, Mariana Islands;
          Geologic Map of Saipan, Mariana Islands. Prepared under
          the direction of the Chief of Engineers, U.S. Army, by the
          Intelligence Division, Office of the Engineer, Headquarters,
          U.S. Army Pacific, with personnel of the U.S. Geological
          Survey. Washington, D.C.: U.S. Army. Mimeographed. 96 pp.
          Mr2 XI

Day, A. Grove
    1971 Pacific Islands Literature: One Hundred Basic Books: A Bib-
          liography. Honolulu: University Press of Hawaii. 176 pp.
          P IX

de Beauclair, Inez [see Beauclair, Inez de]

de Brum, Oscar [see Brum, Oscar de]

de Laubenfels, M. W. [see Laubenfels, M. W. de]

de Smith, Stanley A. [see Smith, Stanley A. de]

de Young, John E. [see Young, John E. de]

Dean, Arthur
    1947 Issues in Micronesia. New York: American Institute of
          Pacific Relations. 41 pp.
          M XVII

Defngin, Francis
    1958 Yapese Names. IN The Use of Names in Micronesia, John E.
          de Young, ed. Anthropological Working Papers, No. 3. Guam:
          Office of the Staff Anthropologist, Trust Territory of the
          Pacific Islands. pp. 1-15.
          Y1 II

Defngin, Francis
    1959 Yam cultivation practices and beliefs in Yap. IN Yam Cul-
          tivation in the Trust Territory, John E. de Young, ed.
          Anthropological Working Papers, No. 4. Guam: Office of the
          Staff Anthropologist, Trust Territory of the Pacific Islands.
          pp. 38-65.
          Y1 I

Demory, Barbara
    1974 The commercialization of sakau (Ponapean Kava). Paper
          read at the 3rd Annual Meeting of the Association for
          Social Anthropology in Oceania, 13-17 March, Asilomar,
          Pacific Grove, California.
          Pn1 II7

Demory, Barbara
    1975 A look at malnutrition on Ponape. Paper read at the 4th
          Annual Meeting of the Association for Social Anthropology
          in Oceania, 26-30 March, Stuart, Florida.
          Pn1 XIV

Dennett, Raymond
    1945 U.S. Navy and dependent Areas. Far Eastern Survey, 14(8):
          93-95.
          M XVII

Devita, Philip R.
    1975 Review of David Lewis, We, the Navigators. American Anthro-
          pologist, 77(2):408-409.
          P X

Dilatush, Donald
    1945 Non-recent Chamorrcan stone and pottery implements on a
          Mariana Island. Archaeological Society of New Jersey
          Newsletter, 13:8-11.
          Mr III

Dilatush, Donald
    1946 A further note on non-recent Chamorroan stone and pottery
          implements on a Mariana Island. Archaeological Society of
          New Jersey Newsletter, 15:9-12.
          Mr III

Dilatush, Donald
    1950 Archaeological survey of Saipan Island, Marianas Group.
          Part I-Nafutan Site. Archaeological Society of New Jersey
          Bulletin, 3:2-6.
          Mr2 III

Divine, David [Arthur Durham Divine]
    1950 The King of Fassarai. New York: Macmillan. 296 pp.
          Y3 IX

Doan, David B.; Harold W. Burke; Harold G. May; and Carl H. Stensland
    1960 Military Geology of Tinian, Mariana Islands. Prepared under
          the direction of the Chief of Engineers, U.S. Army, by the
          Intelligence Division, Office of the Engineer, Headquarters,
          U.S. Army Pacific, with personnel of the U.S. Geological
          Survey. Washington, D.C.: U.S. Army. Mimeographed. 149 pp.
          Mr4 XI

MAIN BIBLIOGRAPHY

Dobbs, James C.
      1972   A macrostudy of Micronesia: The ending of a Trusteeship.
             New York Law Forum, 18(1):139-215.
             M XVII

Dodge, Ernest S.
      1963   Review of Edwin G. Burrows, Flower in My Ear, Arts and
             Ethos of Ifaluk Atoll.   Ethnohistory, 10(3):306-307.
             Y11 VIII

Dodge, Ernest S.
      1968   The American sources for Pacific ethnohistory Research.
             Ethnohistory, 15(1):1-10.
             P II9

Dodge, Ernest S.
      1974   Review of Saul H. Riesenberg, ed., A Residence of Eleven
             Years in New Holland and the Caroline Islands, by James
             F. O'Connell.   American Anthropologist, 76(4):925-926.
             Pn1 II9

Domnick, Charles and Michael Seelye
      1967   Subsistence patterns among selected Marshallese Villagers.
             IN The Laura Report, Leonard Mason, ed.   Honolulu: Depart-
             ment of Anthropology, University of Hawaii.   67 pp.
             Ms8 II10

Doran, Edwin, Jr., ed.
      1961   Land tenure in the Pacific.   A symposium of the 10th
             Pacific Science Congress.   Atoll Research Bulletin, No. 85.
             60 pp.
             P II1

Doran, Edwin, Jr.
      1972   Wa, vinta, and Trimaran.   Journal of the Polynesian
             Society, 81(2):144-159.
             T4 II4

Doty, Richard G.
      1972   Guam's role in the whaling Industry.   Guam Recorder, n.s.,
             2(4):20-27.
             Mr1 XII

Drucker, Philip
      1951   Anthropology in Trust Territory Administration.   The
             Scientific Monthly, 72(5):306-312.
             M II8

Duane, J. M.
      1969   English-Marshallese Cookbook.   Honolulu: Mid-Pacific Press.
             276 pp.
             Ms IX

Duckstad, Eric E.
      1956   Guam; Its Economy and Selected Development Opportunities.
             Prepared for the Guam Finance and Development Administra-
             tion, Territorial Government of Guam.   Menlo Park, Calif-
             ornia: Stanford Research Institute.   210 pp.
             Mr1 VI

Dugan, Paul Fleming
      1956   The early history of Guam 1521-1698.   M.A. Thesis, San
             Diego State College, San Diego.
             Mr1 XII

Duke, Cdr. Marvin L.
      1969   Micronesia: Western line of Defense.   Marine Corps
             Gazette, 53(10):39-42.
             M XV

Duncan, David D.
      1946   Yap meets the Yanks.   National Geographic, 89(3):364-372.
             Y1 XII

Duncan, Leith
      1972   Review of Kjell Akerblom, Astronomy and Navigaticn in Poly-
             nesia and Micronesia: A Survey.   Journal of the Polynesian
             Society, 81(2):272-273.
             M X

Duncan, Leith
      1972   Review of Thomas Gladwin, East Is a Big Bird: Navigation
             and Logic on Puluwat Atoll.   Journal of the Polynesian
             Society, 81(2):273-274.
             T4 II7 X   6

Dunstan, J. L.
      1947   Mission work in Micronesia.   Far Eastern Survey,
             16(21):247-250.
             M II2

Dybdal, Victor A., in association with Llcyd R. Vasey
      1973   Micronesia (United States Trust Territcry of the Pacific
             Islands); Political and Economic Outlook.   Los Angeles:
             Center for International Business.   27 pp.
             M XVII

Dyen, Isidore
      1949   On the history of Trukese Vowels.   Language, 25(4):420-436.
             T XIII

MAIN BIBLIOGRAPHY

Dyen, Isidore
    1949 A Sketch of Trukese Grammar. CIMA Report, No. 10.
          Washington, D.C.: Pacific Science Board. Reprinted 1965.
          American Oriental Essay Series No. 4, American Oriental
          Society. New Haven: American Oriental Society. 60 pp.
          T XIII

Dyen, Isidore
    1965 A Lexicostatistical Classification of the Austronesian
          Languages. International Journal of American Linguistics
          Supplement, Vol. 31, No. 1. Indiana University Publications
          in Anthropology and Linguistics, Memoir 19. Baltimore:
          Waverly Press. 64 pp.
          P XIII

Dyen, Isidore
    1971 Review of Klaus Pätzcld, Die Palau-Sprache und ihre Stellung
          zu anderen indonesischen Sprachen. [The Palau Language and
          Its Position Among Other Indonesian Languages]. Journal of
          the Polynesian Society, 80(2):247-258.
          PL1 XIII

Egami, Tomoko and Fumiko Saito
    1973 Archaeological excavation on Pagan in the Mariana Islands.
          Jinruigaku Zassi [Tokyc], 81(3):203-226.
          Mr5 III

Ehrlich, Paul
    1974 Preliminary cbservations on the German times on Fonape.
          Paper read at the 3rd Annual Meeting of the Association
          for Social Anthropolcgy in Oceania, 13-17 March, Asilomar,
          Pacific Grove, California.
          Pn1 XII

Elameto, Jesus M.
    1975 Carolinian names of common fishes in Saipan, Mariana
          Islands. Micronesica, 11(1):1-5.
          C Mr2 XIX

Elbert, Samuel H.
    1946 Kapingamarangi and Nukuoro Word List, With Notes on Ling-
          uistic Position, Pronunciation, and Grammar. Pearl Harbor:
          U.S. Naval Military Government. Mimeographed. 82 pp.
          Pn8 Pn9 XIII

Elbert, Samuel H.
    1946 Yap-English and English-Yap Word Lists, With Notes cn
          Pronunciation and Grammar. Pearl Harbor: U.S. Naval
          Military Government. Mimeographed. 129 pp.
          Y1 XIII

Elbert, Samuel H.
    1947 Trukese-English and English-Trukese Dictionary, With
          Notes on Pronunciation, Grammar, Vocabularies, Phrases.
          Pearl Harbor: U.S. Naval Military Government. 337 pp.
          T XIII

Elbert, Samuel H.
    1947 Ulithi-English and English-Ulithi Word Lists With Notes on
          Linguistic Position, Pronunciation and Grammar. Pearl Har-
          bor: U.S. Naval Military Government. Mimeographed. 90 pp.
          Y3 XIII

Elbert, Samuel H.
    1948 Grammar and Comparative Study of the Language of
          Kapingamarangi, Texts and Word lists. CIMA Report, No. 3.
          Washington, D.C.: Pacific Science Board. 289 pp.
          Pn9 XIII

Elbert, Samuel H.
    1949 Utu-Matua and other tales of Kapingamarangi. Journal of
          American Folklore, 62(245):240-246.
          Pn9 VIII

Elbert, Samuel H.
    1952 Marshallese phonemes and Orthography. A tentative Proposal.
          IN Anthropology-Geography Study of Arno Atoll, Marshall
          Islands, Leonard E. Mason, ed. Atoll Research Bulletin,
          No. 10. 1 p.
          Ms XIII

Elbert, Samuel H.
    1964 Review of Edwin Grant Burrows, Flower in My Ear, Arts and
          Ethos of Ifaluk Atoll. Journal of the Polynesian Society,
          73(1):90-92.
          Y11 VIII

Elbert, Samuel H.
    1965 Phonological expansions in outlier Polynesia. Lingua, 14:
          431-442. Indo-Pacific Linguistic Studies, Part 1, Histor-
          ical Linguistics, G.B. Milner and Eugenie J.A. Henderson,
          eds. Amsterdam: North-Holland Publishing Co.
          P XIII

Elbert, Samuel H.
    1970 Loan words in Puluwat. IN Pacific Linguistic Studies
          in Honour of Arthur Capell, S.A. Wurm and D.C. Laycock,
          eds. Pacific Linguistics, Series C, No. 13. Canberra:
          Linguistic Circle of Canberra. pp. 235-254.
          T4 XIII

MAIN BIBLIOGRAPHY

Elbert, Samuel H.
    1971 Three Legends of Puluwat and a Bit of Talk. Pacific
          Linguistics, Series D, No. 7. Canberra: Linguistic
          Circle of Canberra. 85 pp.
          T4 VIII

Elbert, Samuel H.
    1972 Puluwat Dictionary. Pacific Linguistics, Series C, No. 24.
          Canberra: Linguistic Circle of Canberra. 400 pp.
          T4 XIII

Elbert, Samuel H.
    1974 Puluwat Grammar. Pacific Linguistics, Series B, No. 29.
          Canberra: Linguistic Circle of Canberra. 137 pp.
          T4 XIII

Eldridge, Roswell; Elizabeth Ryan; Juan Rosario; and Jacob A. Brody
    1969 Amyotrophic lateral sclerosis and Parkinsonism dementia in a
          migrant population from Guam. Neurology, 19(11):1029-1037.
          Mr1 XIV

Elizan, Teresita S.; Kwang-Ming Chen; K. V. Mathai; David Dunn; and
          Leonard T. Kurland
    1966 Amyotrophic lateral sclerosis and Parkinsonism-dementia
          complex: A study in non-Chamorros of the Mariana and
          Caroline Islands. Archives of Neurology, 14(4):347-355.
          Mr C XIV XVI

Elizan, Teresita S.; Asao Hirano; Bernard M. Abrams; Richard L. Need;
          Cornelis Van Nuis; and Leonard T. Kurland
    1966 Amyotrophic lateral sclerosis Parkinsonism-dementia complex
          of Guam: Neurological Reevaluation. Archives of Neurology,
          14(4):356-368.
          Mr1 XIV

Embree, John F.
    1946 Anthropology and the War. American Association of University
          Professors Bulletin, 32(3):485-495.
          P II8

Embree, John F.
    1946 Micronesia. The Navy and Democracy. Far Eastern Survey,
          15(11):161-164.
          M XVII

Embree, John F.
    1946 Military government on Saipan and Tinian. Applied
          Anthropology [now called Human Organization], 5(1):1-39.
          Mr2 Mr4 XVII

MAIN BIBLIOGRAPHY

Embree, John F.
    1946   University of Hawaii research in Micronesia.
           American Anthropologist, 48(3):476-477.
           M II V X XIX

Embree, John F.
    1948   Kickball and some other parallels between Siam and
           Micronesia. Journal of the Siam Society, 37:33-38.
           M IV

Embree, John F.
    1949   American military Government. IN Social Structure, Essays
           Presented to A.R. Radcliffe-Brown, Meyer Fortes, ed. London:
           Oxford University Press. pp. 207-225.
           M XVII

Embree, John F.
    1950   Letter to the Editor: A note on ethnocentrism in Anthro-
           pology. American Anthropologist, 52(3):430-432. [see
           Fischer 1951].
           M II8

Embree, John F.
    1950   Review of Alexander Spoehr, Majuro: A Village in the
           Marshall Islands. American Anthropologist, 52(4):533-535.
           Ms8 II

Emerick, Richard G.
    1958   Land tenure in the Marianas. IN Land Tenure Patterns in the
           Trust Territory of the Pacific Islands, John E. de Young, ed.
           Guam: Office of the Staff Anthropologist, Trust Territory of
           the Pacific Islands. pp. 217-250.
           Mr II1

Emerick, Richard G.
    1960   Homesteading on Ponape: A study and analysis of a resettle-
           ment program of the U.S. Trust Territory Government in Micro-
           nesia. Ph.D. Dissertation, University of Pennsylvania,
           Philadelphia. Available from University Microfilms, Ann
           Arbor: No. 60-03647.
           Pn1 II

Emerick, Richard G.
    1967   Review of Willard R. Bascom, Ponape: A Pacific Economy
           in Transition. American Anthropologist, 69(2):250.
           Pn1 II10

Emerson, Rupert; Lawrence S. Finkelstein; E. L. Bartlett; George H.
      McLane; Roy E. James
   1949 America's Pacific Dependencies. A Survey of American
         Colonial Policies and of Administration and Progress
         Toward Self-Rule in Alaska, Hawaii, Guam, Samoa and
         the Trust Territory. New York: American Institute of
         Pacific Relations. 134 pp.
         M XVII

Emery, Kenneth O., Joshua I. Tracey, Jr., and H. S. Ladd
   1954 Geology of Bikini and nearby Atolls. Part 1 of U.S. Geo-
         logical Survey Professional Paper, 260-A. Washington, D.C.:
         U.S. Government Printing Office. 265 pp.
         Ms13 XI

Emory, Kenneth P.
   1947 South Seas diary; Report from the South Pacific; Life on
         Kapingamarangi; Kapingamarangi Farewell. The Honolulu
         Advertiser, Sunday Polynesian, August 31; September 7;
         October 19; and November 30.
         Pn9 IX

Emory, Kenneth P.
   1949 Anthropological Study of Kapingamarangi. CIMA Report,
         No. 8. Washington, D.C.: Pacific Science Board. 276 pp.
         Pn9 II

Emory, Kenneth P.
   1949 Myths and tales from Kapingamarangi, a Polynesian
         inhabited island in Micronesia. Journal of American
         Folklore, 62(245):230-239.
         Pn9 VIII

Emory, Kenneth P.
   1965 Kapingamarangi: Social and Religious Life of a Polynesian
         Atoll. B.P. Bishop Museum Bulletin, No. 228. Honolulu:
         Bishop Museum Press. 358 pp. Reviewed: 1966 by Raymond
         Firth, American Anthropologist, 68(2), Part 1:537-539;
         1968 by Michael D. Lieber, Journal of Pacific History, 3:229;
         1968 by Katharine Lucmala, Journal of American Folklore,
         81(319):86-87.
         Pn9 II

Emory, Kenneth P. and Yosihiko H. Sinoto
   1959 Radiocarbon dates significant for Pacific Anthropology.
         Supplement to the Pacific Science Association Bulletin,
         11(3):1-15.
         P III

MAIN BIBLIOGRAPHY

Erdland, August
    1955 Grammatik und Wörterbuch der Marshall-Sprache in Mikronesien.
          [Grammar and Dictionary of the Marshallese language in Micro-
          nesia]. 2nd edition. Micro-Bibliotheca Anthropcs, Vol.
          22. Freiburg, Suisse: Anthropos Institut. 491 pp.
          Ms XIII

Fages, Jean and Thomas B. McGrath
    1975 Tourism development in Guam and Tahiti: A Comparison. IN
          The Impact of Urban Centers in the Pacific, Roland W. Force
          and Brenda Bishop, eds. Honolulu: Pacific Science Associa-
          tion, Bishop Museum. pp. 27-32.
          Mr1 VI

Faivre, J. P.
    1972 Review of Dorothy Shineberg, ed., The Trading Voyages of
          Andrew Cheyne, 1841-1844. Journal de la Societe des
          Oceanistes, 28(36):311-312.
          M XII

Falanruw, M. V. C.
    1971 Conservation in Micronesia. Atoll Research Bulletin, No.
          148:18-20.
          M X

Feeney, T. J.
    1952 Letters from Likiep. New York: Pandick Press. 259 pp.
          Ms4 II2

Feldkamp, Frederick
    1945 Civil affairs on Saipan. Asia, 45(1):33-37.
          Mr2 XV XVII

Fifield, Russel H.
    1946 Disposal of the Carolines, Marshalls, and Marianas
          at the Paris Peace Conference. American Historical
          Review, 51(3):472-479.
          M XVII

Fink, T. Ross
    1948 United States Naval policies on education in dependent Areas.
          Ph.D. Dissertation, University of North Carolina, Chapel Hill.
          M VII

Finney, Ben R.
    1970 Review of Kjell Akerblom, Astronomy and Navigaticn in Poly-
          nesia and Micronesia: A Survey. American Anthropologist,
          72(1):134-135.
          M X

-81-

Firth, Raymond
1966 Review of Kenneth P. Emory, Kapingamarangi: Social
      and Religious Life of a Polynesian Atoll. American
      Anthropologist, 68(2), Part 1:537-539.
      Pn9 II

Fischer, Ann M.
1950 The role of the Trukese mother and its effect on child
      Training. SIM Report, No. 8. Washington, D.C.: Pacific
      Science Board. 148 pp.
      T1 VII

Fischer, Ann M.
1950 Trukese privacy Patterns. Research Reviews [Office of
      Naval Research], July, pp. 9-15.
      T1 II1

Fischer, Ann M.
1957 The role of the Trukese mother and its effect on child
      Training. Ph.D. Dissertation, Radcliffe College, Cambridge.
      T1 VII

Fischer, Ann M.
1963 Reproduction in Truk. Ethnology, 2(4):526-540.
      T1 II1 XIV

Fischer, Ann M.
1970 Field work in five Cultures. IN Women in the Field: Anthro-
      pological Experiences, Peggy Golde, ed. Chicago: Aldine.
      pp. 267-289.
      T1 Pn1 II

Fischer, John L.
1951 Letter to the Editor: Applied anthropology and the Admin-
      istration. American Anthropologist, 53(1):133-134. [see
      Embree 1950].
      M II8

Fischer, John L.
1955 Avunculocal residence on Losap. American Anthropologist,
      57(5):1025-1032.
      T8 II1

Fischer, John L.
1955 Language and folktale in Truk and Ponape: A study in cultural
      Integration. Ph.D. Dissertation, Harvard University,
      Cambridge.
      T1 Pn1 VIII XIII

MAIN BIBLIOGRAPHY

Fischer, John L.
    1956 The position of men and women in Truk and Ponape: A
          comparative analysis of kinship terminology and Folktales.
          Journal of American Folklore, 69(271):55-62.
          T1 Pn1 II1 VIII

Fischer, John L.
    1957 Totemism on Truk and Ponape. American Anthropologist, 59(2):
          250-265. Reprinted 1968. IN Introduction to Cultural Anthro-
          pology, Essays in the Scope and Methods of the Science of Man,
          James A. Clifton, ed. New York: Houghton and Mifflin.
          pp. 388-401.
          T1 Pn1 II2

Fischer, John L.
    1958 The classification of residence in Censuses. American
          Anthropologist, 60(3):508-517. Reprinted in Bobbs-Merrill
          Reprint Series, Reprint A-67. [see also Fischer 1959;
          Goodenough 1956; Raulet 1959].
          T1 II1

Fischer, John L.
    1958 Contemporary Ponape Island land Tenure, IN Land Tenure Pat-
          terns in the Trust Territory of the Pacific Islands, John
          E. de Young, ed. Guam: Office of the Staff Anthropologist,
          Trust Territory of the Pacific Islands. pp. 77-160.
          Pn1 II1

Fischer, John L.
    1958 Folktales, social structure, and environment in two Polynesian
          Outliers. Journal of the Polynesian Society, 67(1):11-36.
          Pn8 Pn9 II1 VIII

Fischer, John L.
    1958 Native land tenure in the Truk District. IN Land Tenure
          Patterns in the Trust Territory of the Pacific Islands,
          John E. de Young, ed. Guam: Office of the Staff Anthro-
          pologist, Trust Territory of the Pacific Islands.
          pp. 161-215.
          T II1

Fischer, John L.
    1959 A note on terminology for primary Kin. Southwestern Journal
          of Anthropology [now called Journal of Anthropological
          Research], 15(4):348-354.
          Pn1 II1

Fischer, John L.
    1959 Meter in Eastern Carolinian oral Literature. Journal
          of American Folklore, 72(283):47-52.
          Pn T VIII

Fischer, John L.
   1959   Reply to Raulet.   American Anthropologist, 61(4):679-681.
          [see Fischer 1958; Gcodenough 1956; Raulet 1959].
          T1 II1

Fischer, John L.
   1960   Sequence and structure in Folktales.   IN Men and Cultures,
          A.F.C. Wallace, ed.   Selected Papers of the 5th International
          Congress of Anthropological and Ethnological Sciences, 1956.
          Philadelphia: University of Pennsylvania Press.   pp. 442-446.
          T1 Pn1 VIII

Fischer, John L.
   1961   The retention rate of Chamorro basic Vocabulary.   Lingua,
          10(3):255-266.
          Mr XIII

Fischer, John L.
   1961   The Japanese schools fcr the natives of Truk, Caroline
          Islands.   Human Organization, 20(2):83-88.   Reprinted 1963.
          IN Education and Culture, George Spindler, ed.   New York:
          Holt, Rinehart and Winston.   pp. 512-529.
          T VII

Fischer, Jchn L.
   1963   Review of William Lessa, Tales from Ulithi Atoll.   American
          Anthropologist, 65(3), Part 1:746-747.
          Y3 VIII

Fischer, John L.
   1964   The abandonment of Nan Matol, ancient capital of Ponape.
          Micronesica, 1(182):49-54.
          Pn1 III

Fischer, John L.
   1964   Review of Edwin Grant Burrows, Flower in My Ear, Arts
          and Ethos of Ifaluk Atoll.   American Anthropologist, 66(2):
          460-461.
          Y11 VIII

Fischer, John L.
   1964   Semi-castration cn Pcnape.   Paper read at the 7th Interna-
          tional Congress of Anthropological and Ethnological
          Sciences, August, Moscow.   Section 16: Religious Beliefs
          and Mythology.   8:89-97.
          Pn1 II2 II6

MAIN BIBLIOGRAPHY

Fischer, John L.
    1965 The stylistic significance of consonantal _sandhi_ in Truke
          and Ponapean. American Anthropologist, 67(6), Part 1:
          1495-1502. Reprinted 1972 with additions. IN Directions in
          Sociolinguistics: The Ethnography of Communication, J.J.
          Gumperz and Dell Hymes, eds. New York: Holt, Rinehart and
          Winston. pp. 498-511.
          T Pn XIII

Fischer, John L.
    1965 Levi-Strauss versus Freud on totemism: Data from Ponape.
          Paper read at the Annual Meeting of the American Association
          for the Advancement of Science, Section H, Anthropology,
          30 December, Berkeley, California.
          Pn1 II1

Fischer, John L.
    1966 Interrogatives in Ponapean: Some semantic and grammatical
          Aspects. IN Report of the 17th Annual Round Table Meeting
          on Linguistics and Language Studies. Georgetown University
          Monograph Series on Languages and Linguistics, Nc. 19,
          Francis P. Dineen, ed. Washington, D.C.: Georgetown Uni-
          versity Press. pp. 1-17.
          Pn1 XIII

Fischer, John L.
    1966 A Ponapean Oedipus tale, a structural and sociopsychological
          Analysis. Journal of American Folklore, 79(311):109-129.
          Reprinted 1966. IN The Anthropologist Looks at Myth, Mel-
          ville Jacobs, compiler, and John Greenway, ed. Austin:
          University of Texas Press. pp. 109-129.
          Pn1 VIII

Fischer, John L.
    1966 Syntax and social structure: Truk and Ponape. IN
          Sociolinguistics, William Bright, ed. Proceedings of
          the U.C.L.A. Sociolinguistics Conference, 1964. The
          Hague: Mouton and Co. pp. 168-187.
          T1 Pn1 II1 XIII

Fischer, John L.
    1968 Folktale in the Eastern Carolines. IN Peoples and
          Cultures of the Pacific, A.P. Vayda, ed. New York:
          Natural History Press. pp. 380-382. [Excerpted from
          Fischer and Fischer 1957, The Eastern Carolines].
          T Pn VIII

MAIN BIBLIOGRAPHY

Fischer, John L.
    1968 Microethnology: Small-Scale comparative studies (with
          appendix consisting of Totemism in Truk and Ponape, 1957).
          IN Introduction to Cultural Anthropology, Essays in the
          Scope and Methods of the Science of Man, James A. Clifton,
          ed. New York: Houghton and Mifflin. pp. 374-401.
          T1 Pn1 II1 II2

Fischer, John L.
    1969 Honorific speech and social structure: A comparison
          of Japanese and Ponapean. Journal of the Polynesian
          Society, 78(3):417-422.
          Pn1 II1

Fischer, John L.
    1969 Letter: "Starfish infestation: Hypothesis." Science,
          165(3894):645.
          M XIX

Fischer, John L.
    1970 Adoption on Ponape. IN Adoption in Eastern Oceania, Vern
          Carroll, ed. ASAO Monograph No. 1. Honolulu: University
          of Hawaii Press. pp. 292-313.
          Pn1 II1

Fischer, John L.
    1971 Review of Byron W. Bender, Spoken Marshallese. Language,
          47(3):734-736.
          Ms XIII

Fischer, John L.
    1974 The role of the traditional chiefs on Ponape in the American
          Period. IN Political Development in Micronesia, Daniel T.
          Hughes and Sherwood G. Lingenfelter, eds. Columbus: Ohio
          State University Press. pp. 166-177.
          Pn1 II3

Fischer, John L.
    1974 Micronesian Cultures. Encyclopaedia Britannica, 15th ed.,
          12:122-127. Chicago: Encyclopaedia Britannica, Inc.
          M II

Fischer, John L.
    1974 Review of Roland W. Force and Maryanne Force, Just One
          House: A Description and Analysis of Kinship in the Palau
          Islands. American Anthropologist, 76(3):625-626.
          PL1 II1

MAIN BIBLIOGRAPHY

Fischer, John L.
    1974   Some characteristics of kava drinkers cn Ponape.   Paper read
           at the 3rd Annual Meeting of the Association for Social
           Anthropology in Oceania, 13-17 March, Asilomar, Pacific
           Grove, California.
           Pn1 II

Fischer, John L., with the assistance of Ann M. Fischer
    1957   The Eastern Carolines.   HRAF Behavior Science Monograph.
           New Haven: HRAF Press.   Reprinted with minor additions 1966
           and 1970.   New Haven: HRAF Press.   276 pp.
           C II

Fischer, John L., Ann M. Fischer, and Frank J. Mahony
    1959   Totemism and Allergy.   International Journal of Social
           Psychiatry, 5(1):33-40.
           Pn1 II6

Fischer, John L., Saul H. Riesenberg, and M. G. Whiting (translators
           and editors)
    n.d.   The Book of Luelen: A Ponapean Manuscript History.   Canberra:
           Australian National University Press, forthcoming.
           Pn1 II9

Fischer, John L. and Marc J. Swartz
    1960   Socio-psychological aspects of some Trukese and Ponapean love
           Songs.   Journal of American Folklore, 73(289):218-224.
           T Pn1 II6

Fischer, John L., Roger Ward, and Martha Ward
    n.d.   Ponapean conceptions of Incest.   IN Incest Prohibitions
           in Polynesia and Micronesia, Vern Caroll, ed.   ASAO
           Monograph Series.   Honolulu: University Press of Hawaii,
           forthcoming.
           Pn1 II1

Fite, Jerry
    1970   Colonizing Paradise.   Washington Monthly, 2(10):50-58.
           M XVII

Fletcher, Jack E.
    1971   Notes on herb medicine in Guam.   Economic Botany, 25(1):
           60-62.
           Mr1 V XIV

Flora, Marie Jo-Ann
    1969   Analysis of the segmental phonemes of Palauan.   Languages
           and Linguistics, 4(1):1-30.
           PL1 XIII

MAIN BIBLIOGRAPHY

Flora, Marie Jo-Ann
    1974 Palauan phonology and Morphology. Ph.D. Dissertation,
          University of California, San Diego. Available from
          University Microfilms, Ann Arbor: No. 74-23965.
          PL1 XIII

Force, Roland W.
    1957 Palau exhibit traces change in a Pacific Culture. Chicago
          Natural History Museum Bulletin [now called Field Museum
          of Natural History Bulletin], 28(3):3-4, 7.
          PL1 II7

Force, Roland W.
    1958 Leadership and cultural change in Palau. Ph.D. Disser-
          tation, Stanford University, Stanford, California.
          Published 1960. Fieldiana: Anthropology, Vol. 50. Chicago:
          Chicago Natural History Museum. 211 pp. Reviewed: 1960 by
          Homer G. Barnett, American Anthropologist, 62(6):1099-1101;
          1960 by Paula Brown, Journal of the Polynesian Society,
          69(3):297-298; 1961 by Jeremy Beckett, Oceania, 32(2):155-156.
          PL1 II3 II7

Force, Roland W.
    1960 Review of E. W. Gifford and D. S. Gifford, Archaeological
          Excavations in Yap. American Anthropologist, 62(6):1106.
          Y1 III

Force, Roland W.
    1961 Palauan paradox: Some comments on kinship Terminology.
          Paper read at the 42nd Annual Meeting of the Central
          States Anthropological Society, 4-6 May, Columbus, Ohio.
          PL1 II1

Force, Roland W.
    1961 Political change in Palau. Abstracts of Symposium Papers,
          10th Pacific Science Congress, 21 August-6 September, 1961,
          Honolulu. pp. 88-89.
          PL1 II3

Force, Roland W.
    1961 Review of E.W. Gifford and D.S. Gifford, Archaeological
          Excavations in Yap. Archaeology, 14(3):221.
          Y1 III

Force, Roland W.
    1964 Micronesian Peoples. Encyclopedia International 1963-1964,
          1st ed., 12:51. New York: Grolier. Condensed and reprinted
          1965. IN Grolier Universal Encyclopedia. New York: Grolier.
          M II

-88-

Force, Roland W., ed.
    1965 Induced Political Change in the Pacific: A Symposium.
          Honolulu: Bishop Museum Press. 103 pp. Reviewed: 1966 by
          Homer G. Barnett, American Anthropologist, 68(2), Part 1:
          540-542.
          P II3

Force, Roland W.
    1966 Micronesians. The World Book Encyclopedia, 16:62-65.
          Chicago: Field Enterprises, Educational Corporation.
          M II

Force, Roland W.
    1973 The Guam experiment: Beginning of a new Day? Guam Recorder,
          n.s., 3(2):3-4.
          Mr1 XVII

Force, Roland W. and Maryanne Force
    1959 Palauan money: Some preliminary comments on material and
          Origins. Journal of the Polynesian Society, 68(1):40-44.
          Also published 1963. Proceedings of the 9th Pacific Science
          Congress, 18 November-9 December, 1957, Bangkok, 3:52-54.
          PL1 II4

Force, Roland W. and Maryanne Force
    1961 Keys to cultural Understanding. Science, 133(3460):1202-1206.
          PL1 XIII

Force, Roland W. and Maryanne Force
    1965 Political change in Micronesia. IN Induced Political Change
          in the Pacific: A Symposium, Roland W. Force, ed. Honolulu:
          Bishop Museum Press. pp. 7-16.
          M II3

Force, Roland W. and Maryanne Force
    1972 Just One House: A Description and Analysis of Kinship in the
          Palau Islands. B.P. Bishop Museum Bulletin, No. 235. Hono-
          lulu: Bishop Museum Press. 143 pp. Reviewed: 1974 by John
          L. Fischer, American Anthropologist, 76(3):625-626; 1974 by
          William H. Alkire, Journal of the Polynesian Society, 83(3):
          379-381; 1974 by Peter B. Huber, Man, n.s., 9(4):650-651.
          PL1 II1

Force, Roland W. and Maryanne Force
    1975 Kith, kin, and fellow Urbanites. IN The Impact of Urban
          Centers in the Pacific, Roland W. Force and Brenda Bishop,
          eds. Honolulu: Pacific Science Association, Bishop Museum.
          pp. 193-223.
          P II7

MAIN BIBLIOGRAPHY

Ford, C. Christopher
    1974 Adult education in Micronesia: Problems and Prospects.
          Paper read at the 8th Waigani Seminar, 5-10 May, Port
          Moresby, Papua-New Guinea.
          M VII

Fosberg, F. Raymond
    1946 Botanical Report on Micronesia. IN U.S. Commercial Company's
          Economic Survey of Micronesia, Report No. 13, Part 1 [Part 2
          by Edward Hosaka]. Honolulu: U.S. Commercial Company.
          Mimeographed. 350 pp.
          M V

Fosberg, F. Raymond
    1947 Micronesian mangroves. A journey by motorized sampan to a
          peak development of land-building swamps in the Carolines.
          Journal of the New York Botanical Garden, 48(570):128-138.
          C V

Fosberg, F. Raymond
    1948 Salinity and atoll Vegetation. Proceedings of the Hawaiian
          Academy of Science, 23rd Annual Meeting, p. 8. [abstract].
          M V

Fosberg, F. Raymond
    1949 Atoll vegetation and Salinity. Pacific Science, 3(1):89-92.
          M V

Fosberg, F. Raymond
    1951 Coral atoll symposium: Basic information on the present
          status of scientific knowledge pertaining to atoll Ecology.
          Washington, D.C.: Pacific Science Board, National Research
          Council.
          P X

Fosberg, F. Raymond
    1953 A conservation program for Micronesia. Proceedings of
          the 7th Pacific Science Congress, 2 February-4 March,
          1949, Auckland, New Zealand, 4:670-673.
          M I X

Fosberg, F. Raymond
    1953 Vegetation of central Pacific atolls, a brief Summary.
          Atoll Research Bulletin, No. 23. 26 pp.
          Ms C V

Fosberg, F. Raymond
    1954 Soils of the Northern Marshall atolls, with special
          reference to the Jemc Series. Soil Science, 78(2):99-107.
          Ms XI

MAIN BIBLIOGRAPHY

Fosberg, F. Raymond
    1955 The Northern Marshall Islands Expedition: 1951-1952. Part 1.
          Atoll Research Bulletin, No. 38. 37 pp. Part 2. Atoll
          Research Bulletin, No. 39:1-22.
          Ms IX

Fosberg, F. Raymond
    1957 Lonely Pokak [Taongi]. The Living Wilderness, 12(62):1-4.
          Ms27 X

Fosberg, F. Raymond
    1957 Soils, vegetation, and agriculture on coral Atolls. Pro-
          ceedings of the 8th Pacific Science Congress, 16-18 Nov-
          ember, 1953, Quezon City, Philippines, 3A:1037-1047.
          Ms I V XI

Fosberg, F. Raymond
    1958 Vascular flora of Pagan Island, Northern Marianas. Pacific
          Science, 12(1):17-20.
          Mr5 V

Fosberg, F. Raymond
    1959 The Vegetation of Micronesia. SIM Report, No. 25, Part 1.
          Washington, D.C.: Pacific Science Board. 158 pp.
          M V

Fosberg, F. Raymond
    1960 The Vegetation of Micronesia I. General Descriptions, the
          Vegetation of the Marianas Islands, and Detailed Consid-
          eration of the Vegetation of Guam. American Museum of
          Natural History Bulletin, 119:1-75. Reviewed: 1962 by
          William A. Niering, Ecology, 43(2):353-354.
          M Mr Mr1 V

Fosberg, F. Raymond
    1963 Dynamics of atoll Vegetation. Proceedings of the 9th
          Pacific Science Congress, 18 November-9 December, 1957,
          Bangkok, 4:114-117.
          P V

Fosberg, F. Raymond, ed.
    1963 Man's Place in the Island Ecosystem. Honolulu: Bishop Museum
          Press. 264 pp. Reviewed: 1964 by Alexander Spoehr, American
          Anthropologist, 66(3), Part 1:685-686.
          P X

Fosberg, F. Raymond
    1966 Northern Marshall Islands land biota: Birds. Atoll
          Research Bulletin, No. 114. 35 pp.
          Ms XIX

MAIN BIBLIOGRAPHY

Fosberg, F. Raymond
    1966 Review of William H. Alkire, Lamotrek Atoll and Inter-Island
          Socioeconomic Ties. Atoll Research Bulletin, No. 117:7-8.
          Y9 II1

Fosberg, F. Raymond
    1969 Observations on the green turtle in the Marshall Islands.
          Atoll Research Bulletin, No. 135:9-12.
          Ms XIX

Fosberg, F. Raymond
    1969 Plants of Satawal Island, Caroline Islands. Atoll
          Research Bulletin, No. 132. 13 pp.
          Y10 V

Fosberg, F. Raymond
    1975 Review of David Lewis, We, the Navigators. Atoll Research
          Bulletin, No. 185:32.
          P X

Fosberg, F. Raymond and Dorothy Carroll
    1965 Terrestrial sediments and soils of the Northern Marshall
          Islands. Atoll Research Bulletin, No. 113. 156 pp.
          Ms XI

Fosberg, F. Raymond and Gilbert Corwin
    1958 A fossil flora from Pagan, Mariana Islands. Pacific Science,
          12(1):3-16.
          Mr5 V

Fosberg, F. Raymond and Michael Evans
    1969 A collection of plants from Fais, Caroline Islands.
          Atoll Research Bulletin, No. 133. 15 pp.
          Y4 V

Fosberg, F. Raymond and Marie-Helene Sachet, eds.
    1953 Handbook for atoll Research (second preliminary edition).
          Atoll Research Bulletin, No. 17. 129 pp.
          P IX

Foster, Stephen William
    1972 Review of Vern Carroll, ed., Adoption in Eastern Oceania.
          Journal of the Polynesian Society, 81(2):268-270.
          P II1

Foundation for the Peoples of the South Pacific
    1971 A Socio-Economic Survey of Micronesia Made by the Founda-
          tion for the Peoples of the South Pacific, February-October
          1971. New York: Foundation for the Peoples of the South
          Pacific (FSP Survey No. 7). 328 pp.
          M VI

MAIN BIBLIOGRAPHY

Fox, Morris G.
    1971 Strengthening the Contribution of Social Services to the
          Development of the Trust Territory of the Pacific Islands.
          Noumea: South Pacific Commission. 114 pp.
          M VI

Frake, Charles O.
    1956 Malayo-Polynesian land Tenure. American Anthropclogist,
          58(1):170-173. [see Gocdenough 1955].
          P II1

Freeman, Lila L.
    1972 Island Legends. Guam Recorder, n.s., 2(4):9-11.
          Mr VIII

Freeman, Otis W., ed.
    1951 Geography of the Pacific. New York: John Wiley and Sons.
          573 pp.
          P X

Friends of Micronesia
    1971 to present. Friends cf Micronesia Quarterly Newsletter.
          2325 McKinley, Berkeley, California, 94703.
          M II

Friis, Herman R.
    1967 The Pacific Basin. American Geography Society Special
          Publication, No. 38. 457 pp.
          P X

Gale, Roger
    1973 Anthropological colonialism in Micronesia. Association for
          Anthropology in Micronesia Newsletter, 2(1):2-19. [see
          Mason 1973].
          M II

Gale, Roger
    1973 No one warned the Micrcnesians. The Nation, 216(6):166-169.
          M XV XVII

Gale, Roger
    1974 Letter from Guam. Far Eastern Economic Review, 86(37):74.
          [20 September 1974].
          Mr1 VI

Gale, Roger
    1974 Return to Bikini? The Progressive, 38:12-13. [Cctober].
          Ms13 XII

Gale, Roger
    1974   Tinian: New base in Asia.   International Bulletin, [26 July
           1974].
           Mr4 XVII

Gallahue, Edward E.
    1946   The Economy of the Mariana Islands.   IN U.S. Commercial
           Company's Economic Survey of Micronesia, Report No. 5.
           Honolulu: U.S. Commercial Company.   Mimeographed.
           Mr VI

Gallahue, Edward E.
    1953   Changing agricultural economy of Micronesia.   Proceedings of
           the 7th Pacific Science Congress, 2 February-4 March, 1949,
           Auckland, New Zealand, 7:155-158.
           M I

Garanger, Jose
    1972   Review of Janet Davidson, Archaeology on Nukuoro Atoll,
           A Polynesian Outlier in the Eastern Caroline Islands.
           Journal de la Societe des Oceanistes, 28(36):311.
           Pn8 III

Garanger, Jose
    1974   Review of Janet Davidson, Archaeology on Nukuoro Atoll,
           A Polynesian Outlier in the Eastern Caroline Islands.
           Journal of the Polynesian Society, 83(2):238-239.
           Pn8 III

Garland, J.
    1961   Chamorro text, Guam.   Working Papers of the Summer Institute
           of Linguistics [Grand Forks, North Dakota], 5:95-97.
           Mr1 XIII

Garvin, Paul L.
    1949   Linguistic Study of Ponape.   CIMA Report, No. 2.   Washing-
           ton, D.C.: Pacific Science Board.   278 pp.
           Pn1 XIII

Garvin, Paul L.
    1954   Delimitation of syntactic units.   Language, 30(3):345-348.
           Pn1 XIII

Garvin, Paul L.
    1954   Literacy as a problem in language and Culture.   IN Report of
           the 5th Annual Round Table Meeting on Linguistics and
           Language Teaching.   Georgetown University Monograph Series
           on Languages and Linguistics, Monograph No. 7, Hugo J.
           Mueller, ed.   Washington, D.C.: Georgetown University
           Press.   pp. 117-129.
           Pn1 XIII

Garvin, Paul L.
    1958 Syntactic units and Operations. Proceedings of the 8th
          International Congress of Linguists, pp. 626-632. Oslo:
          Oslo University Press.
          Pn1 XIII

Garvin, Paul L.
    1959 The standard language problem: Concepts and Methods.
          Anthropological Linguistics, 1(3):28-31.
          Pn1 XIII

Garvin, Paul L.
    1962 A study of inductive method in Syntax. Word, 18(1&2):
          107-120.
          Pn1 XIII

Garvin, Paul L.
    1962 Ponapean Morphophonemics. Phonetica, 8(2):115-127.
          Pn1 XIII

Garvin, Paul L.
    1971 The sound pattern of Ponapean. Travaux du Cercle Linguis-
          tiques de Prague, 4(1):47-61.
          Pn1 XIII

Garvin, Paul L. and Saul H. Riesenberg
    1952 Respect behavior on Ponape: An ethnolinguistic Study.
          American Anthropologist, 54(2), Part 1:201-220.
          Pn1 II3 XIII

Gathercole, Peter W.
    1967 Review of Douglas Osborne, The Archaeology of the Palau
          Islands: An Intensive Survey. Man, n.s., 2(4):637.
          PL1 III

Gavan, James A.
    1952 Growth of Guamanian children--some methodological Questions.
          American Journal of Physical Anthropology, 10(1):132-135.
          Mr1 XVI

Georgia Center for Continuing Education
    1974 The Bikinians. 16 mm. documentary film, written and
          directed by Hill Bermont, cinematography by John Packwood,
          Art Blum and David Horwatt, eds. Color. 28.5 minutes.
          Distributed by: WNET/13 Media Services, 356 West 58th
          Street, New York, New York 10019. [see Kiste 1974].
          Ms13 Ms24 II II7

Georgia Center for Continuing Education
  1974 That Uncertain Paradise. 16 mm. documentary film, writ-
        ten and directed by Hill Bermont, cinematography by
        John Packwood, Art Blum and David Horwatt, eds. Color.
        57 minutes. Distributed by: WNET/13 Media Services,
        356 West 58th Street, New York, New York 10019.
        M II7

Gerry, Roger G., Stanley T. Smith, and M. Lyle Calton
  1952 The oral characteristics of Guamanians, including the
        effects of betel-chewing on the oral Tissues. Oral
        Surgery, Oral Medicine, and Oral Pathology, 5(7):762-781;
        5(8):884-894; 5(9):1004-1011.
        Mr1 XIV

Gibbs, C. J., Jr. and D. C. Gajdusek
  1972 Amyotrophic lateral sclerosis, Parkinson's disease,
        and the amyotrophic lateral sclerosis-Parkinsonism-
        dementia complex on Guam, a review and summary of
        attempts to demonstrate infection as the Aetiolcgy.
        Journal of Clinical Pathology, 25, Supplement 6:132-140.
        Mr1 XIV

Gibson, Robert E.
  1959 Education in the Trust Territory of the Pacific
        Islands. IN Community Education. National Society for
        Study of Education, 58th Yearbook, Nelson B. Henry, ed.
        Chicago: University of Chicago Press. pp. 117-136.
        M VII

Gifford, Edward W.
  1958 Review of Alexander Spoehr, Marianas Prehistory.
        American Anthropologist, 60(1), Part 1:206-207.
        Mr III

Gifford, Edward W. and Delila S. Gifford
  1959 Archeological Excavations in Yap. Anthropological Records,
        18(2):149-224. Berkeley and Los Angeles: University of
        California Press. Reviewed: 1960 by Roland W. Force,
        American Anthropologist, 62(6):1106; 1960 by Wilhelm G.
        Solheim II, Asian Perspectives, 4(1&2):99-100; 1960 by
        Alexander Spoehr, Journal of the Polynesian Society, 69(2):
        175; 1961 by Roland W. Force, Archaeology, 14(3):221.
        Y1 III

Gilchrist, Huntington
  1944 The Japanese Islands: Annexation or Trusteeship?
        Foreign Affairs, 22(4):635-642.
        M XVII

Gilchrist, Huntington
1946 Trusteeship and the colonial system. Proceedings
      of the Academy of Political Science, 22(2):203-217.
      M XVII

Gilliam, John D.
1975 Guam: Can the port be free when the economy is Not? IN
      The Impact of Urban Centers in the Pacific, Roland W.
      Force and Brenda Bishop, eds. Honolulu: Pacific Science
      Association, Bishop Museum. pp. 123-129.
      Mr1 VI

Gillmar, Jack and Russell Weigel
1968 The Impact of an In-Country Peace Corps Training Program on
      the Host Country: An Investigation of an In-Country Peace
      Corps Training Program Conducted in Micronesia During the
      Summer of 1968. Cambridge, Massachusetts: Human Develop-
      ment Foundation. 163 pp.
      Pn1 II7

Gladwin, Thomas
1950 Civil administration on Truk, a Rejoinder. Human Organ-
      ization, 9(4):15-24. [see Hall 1950].
      T1 II8

Gladwin, Thomas
1952 Personality and development on Truk. Ph.D. Dissertation,
      Yale University, New Haven.
      T1 II6

Gladwin, Thomas
1953 The role of man and woman on Truk: A problem in
      personality and Culture. Transactions of the New
      York Academy of Sciences, Series II, 15(8):305-309.
      T1 II6

Gladwin, Thomas
1956 Anthropology and administration in the Trust Territory of
      the Pacific Islands. IN Some Uses of Anthropology: Theore-
      tical and Applied. Washington, D.C.: The Anthropological
      Society of Washington. pp. 58-65.
      M II8

Gladwin, Thomas
1958 Canoe travel in the Truk area: Technology and its psycholo-
      gical Correlates. American Anthropologist, 60(5):893-899.
      Reprinted in Bobbs-Merrill Social Science Reprint Series,
      Reprint A-80.
      T II6

MAIN BIBLIOGRAPHY

Gladwin, Thomas
    1959 Culture and individual personality integration on Truk.
        IN Culture and Mental Health, Morris Opler, ed. New
        York: Macmillan. pp. 173-210.
        T1 II6

Gladwin, Thomas
    1960 The need: Better ways of teaching children to Think.
        IN Freeing Capacity to Learn, Alexander Frazier, ed. Wash-
        ington Association for Supervision and Curriculum Devel-
        opment. Washington, D.C.: National Education Association.
        pp. 23-29.
        P VII

Gladwin, Thomas
    1961 Oceania. IN Psychological Anthropology: Approaches to
        Culture and Personality, Francis L. K. Hsu, ed.
        Homewood, Illinois: Dorsey Press. pp. 135-171.
        P II6

Gladwin, Thomas
    1964 Culture and logical Process. IN Explorations in Cultural
        Anthropology: Essays in Honor of G.P. Murdock, Ward H.
        Goodenough, ed. New York: McGraw-Hill. pp. 167-177.
        Reprinted 1974. IN Culture and Cognition: Readings in
        Cross-Cultural Psychology, J.W. Berry and P.R. Dasen,
        eds. London: Methuen. pp. 27-37.
        T1 II6

Gladwin, Thomas
    1964 Petrus Mailo, Chief of Moen (Truk). IN In the Company
        of Man, Joseph B. Casagrande, ed. New York: Harper
        and Row. pp. 41-62.
        T1 II

Gladwin, Thomas
    1967 Review of William A. Lessa, Ulithi: A Micronesian Design
        for Living. American Anthropologist, 69(5):526.
        Y3 II

Gladwin, Thomas
    1970 East is a big bird: Part I. Natural History, 79(4):24-35;
        Part II. Natural History, 79(5):58-69.
        T4 II7 X

Gladwin, Thomas
    1970   East is a Big Bird: Navigation and Logic on Puluwat Atoll.
           Cambridge: Harvard University Press. 241 pp. Abridged
           version from Chapters 1-4 reprinted 1973. IN Man's
           Many Ways, Richard A. Gould, ed. New York: Harper and Row.
           pp. 130-146. Reviewed: 1971 by Ward H. Goodenough, American
           Anthropologist, 73(6):1336-1337; 1972 by Leith Duncan, Journal
           of the Polynesian Society, 81(2):273-274.
           T4 II7 X

Gladwin, Thomas and Seymour B. Sarason
    1953   Truk: Man in Paradise. Viking Fund Publications in Anthro-
           pology, No. 20. New York: Wenner-Gren Foundation for Anthro-
           pological Research. 663 pp. Reprinted n.d. New York:
           Johnson Reprint Corporation. Reviewed: 1955 by David M.
           Schneider, American Anthropologist, 57(5):1098-1101.
           T1 II6

Glassman, Sidney F.
    1950   Ponape's national Beverage. Research Reviews [Office of
           Naval Research], July, pp. 16-18.
           Pn1 II

Glassman, Sidney F.
    1951   The flora of Ponape. Ph.D. Dissertation, University of
           Oklahoma, Norman. Published 1952. B. P. Bishop Museum
           Bulletin, No. 209. Honolulu: Bishop Museum Press. 152 pp.
           [see Stone 1960].
           Pn1 V

Glassman, Sidney F.
    1953   New plant records from Eastern Caroline Islands, with a
           comparative study of the native plant Names. Pacific
           Science, 7(3):291-311.
           C V

Glassman, Sidney F.
    1957   The flora of Ponape and its phytogeographical Affiliation.
           Proceedings of the 8th Pacific Science Congress, 16-18
           November, Quezon City, Philippines, 4:201-216.
           Pn1 V

Glenn, Thelma H.
    1975   The Guam Museum. South Pacific Bulletin, 25(1):28-30.
           Mr1 II4

Glosser, J. W. and E. P. Yarnell
    1970   Rabies control on Guam. Public Health Reports [now called
           Health Service Reports], 85(12):1113-1120.
           Mr1 XIV

MAIN BIBLIOGRAPHY

Goding, M. W. and T. Remengsau
1964 The Trust Territory of the Pacific Islands. Statements made
in the United Nations Trusteeship Council. U.S. Department of State Bulletin, 50(1305):1007-1020.
* M XVII

Goding, M. W. and V. N. Santos
1963 The Trust Territory of the Pacific Islands. Statements made
in the United Nations Trusteeship Council. U.S. Department of State Bulletin, 49(1258):207-229.
M XVII

Goo, Fannie and Albert H. Banner
1963 A preliminary compilation of animal and plant names
of the Mariana Islands. Kaneohe: Hawaii Marine Laboratory,
University of Hawaii. 40 pp.
Mr XIII

Goo, Fannie and Albert H. Banner
1963 A preliminary compilation of animal and plant names
of the Caroline Islands. Kaneohe: Hawaii Marine
Laboratory, University of Hawaii. 47 pp.
C XIII

Goo, Fannie and Albert H. Banner
1963 A preliminary compilation of Marshallese animal and plant
Names. Kaneohe: Hawaii Marine Laboratory, University
of Hawaii. 39 pp.
Ms XIII

Goodenough, Ruth Gallagher
1970 Adoption on Romonum, Truk. IN Adoption in Eastern
Oceania, Vern Carroll, ed. ASAO Monograph No. 1.
Honolulu: University of Hawaii Press. pp. 314-340.
T1 II1

Goodenough, Ward H.
1949 A grammar of social Interaction. Ph.D. Dissertation,
Yale University, New Haven.
T1 II1

Goodenough, Ward H.
1949 Premarital freedom on Truk: Theory and Practice. American
Anthropologist, 51(4):615-620.
T1 II1

Goodenough, Ward H.
   1951 Property, Kin, and Ccmmunity on Truk.   Yale University
         Publications in Anthropology, No. 46.   New Haven: Yale
         University Press.   192 pp.   Reprinted 1966.   Hamden,
         Connecticut: Archon Bocks.   Reviewed: 1952 by William A.
         Lessa, American Anthropologist, 54(4):540-541.
         T1 II1

Goodenough, Ward H.
   1951 Native astronomy in Micronesia, a rudimentary Science.   The
         Scientific Monthly, 73(2):105-110.
         C X

Goodenough, Ward H.
   1953 Native Astronomy in the Central Carolines.   University
         of Pennsylvania Museum Monographs, Philadelphia.   46 pp.
         C X

Goodenough, Ward H.
   1955 A problem in Malayo-Polynesian social Organizaticn.   Amer-
         ican Anthropologist, 57(1):71-83.   Reprinted in Bobbs-Merrill
         Social Science Reprint Series, Reprint A-90.   Reprinted
         1968.   IN Kinship and Social Organization, Paul Bohannon
         and John Middleton, eds.   Garden City, New York: Natural
         History Press.   pp. 195-211.   Also reprinted 1968.   IN
         Peoples and Cultures of the Pacific, Andrew P. Vayda, ed.
         Garden City, New York: Natural History Press.   pp. 133-156.
         [see Frake 1956].
         M II1   6

Goodenough, Ward H.
   1955 Survival of the soul cn Truk.   Paper read at the 54th Annual
         Meeting of the American Anthropological Association, 17-19
         November, Boston.
         T1 II2

Goodenough, Ward H.
   1956 A Christmas on Truk.   The School in Rose Valley Farents
         Bulletin, No. 176.   December, pp. 1-2.
         T1 II

Goodenough, Ward H.
   1956 Componential analysis and the study of Meaning.   Language,
         32(1):195-216.   Reprinted in Bobbs-Merrill Social Science
         Reprint Series, Reprint A-91.   Reprinted 1968.   IN Kinship
         and Social Organization, Paul Bohannon and Jchn Middleton,
         eds.   Garden City, New York: Natural History Press.   pp.
         93-124.
         T1 II1

Goodenough, Ward H.
1956 Residence Rules. Southwestern Journal of Anthropology [now
called Journal of Anthropological Research], 12(1):22-37.
Reprinted in Bobbs-Merrill Social Science Reprint Series,
Reprint A-92. Reprinted 1968. IN Marriage, Family and
Residence, Paul Bohannen and John Middleton, eds. Garden
City, New York: Natural History Press. pp. 296-316. [see
Fischer 1958, 1959; Raulet 1959].
T1 II1

Goodenough, Ward H.
1957 Oceania and the problem of controls in the study of
cultural and human Evolution. Journal of the Polynesian
Society, 66(2):146-155.
P II7

Goodenough, Ward H.
1963 The long or double consonants of Trukese. Proceedings
of the 9th Pacific Science Congress, 18 November-9 December,
1957, Bangkok, 3:77-80.
T1 XIII

Goodenough, Ward H.
1963 Some applications of Guttman scale analysis to ethnography
and culture Theory. Southwestern Journal of Anthropology
[now called Journal of Anthropological Research], 19(3):
235-250.
T1 II

Goodenough, Ward H.
1964 Property and language on Truk: Some methodological Considerations. IN Language in Culture and Society: A Reader
in Linguistics and Anthropology, Dell Hymes, ed. New York:
Harper and Row. pp. 185-188. [reprinted with slight
revisions by the author from Property, Kin, and Community
on Truk, 1951].
T1 II1 XIII

Goodenough, Ward H.
1965 Personal names and modes of address in two Oceanic Societies.
IN Context and Meaning in Cultural Anthropology, Melford E.
Spiro, ed. New York: Free Press. pp. 265-276.
T1 II1 II6

Goodenough, Ward H.
1965 Rethinking 'status' and 'role': Toward a general model
of the cultural organization of social Relationships. IN
The Relevance of Models for Social Anthropology, Michael
Banton, ed. ASA Monograph No. 1. London: Tavistock
Publications. pp. 1-24.
T1 II1

MAIN BIBLIOGRAPHY

Goodenough, Ward H.
    1966 The tale of Pupily-Eyeballs-Thing, A Truk ghost Story,
           as told by Boutau K. Efot. Expedition, 8(2):23-29. Re-
           printed 1966. Micronesian Reporter, 14(3):7-11.
           T1 VIII

Goodenough, Ward H.
    1966 Human purpose in Life. Zygon, Journal of Religion and
           Science, 1(3):217-229.
           T1 II2 II6

Goodenough, Ward H.
    1966 Notes on Truk's place Names. Micronesica, 2(2):95-129.
           T1 X

Goodenough, Ward H.
    1968 Arts and crafts in Truk. Expedition, 11(1):13-15.
           T1 II4

Goodenough, Ward H.
    1970 Micronesia's People. IN The Story of Micronesia: With an
           Introductory Guide to Sources of Information. Washington,
           D.C.: Peace Corps School Partnership Program. pp. 6-9.
           M II

Goodenough, Ward H.
    1971 A similarity in cultural and linguistic Change. Paper
           read at the 70th Annual Meeting of the American Anthropo-
           logical Association, 18-21 November, New York City.
           T1 II7 XIII

Goodenough, Ward H.
    1971 Corporations: Reply to Cochrane. American Anthropologist,
           73(5):1150-1152.
           T1 II1

Goodenough, Ward H.
    1971 Review of Thomas Gladwin, East is a Big Bird: Navigation
           and Logic on Puluwat Atoll. American Anthropologist,
           73(6):1336-1337.
           T4 II7 X

Goodenough, Ward H.
    1972 Social implications of population Control. Expedition,
           14(3):11-14.
           Y1 XVI

MAIN BIBLIOGRAPHY

Goodenough, Ward H.
    1974 Changing social organization on Romonum, Truk, 1947-1965.
          IN Social Organization and the Applications of Anthropology:
          Essays in Honor of Lauriston Sharp, R.J. Smith, ed. Ithaca:
          Cornell University Press. pp. 62-93.
          T1 II1

Goodenough, Ward H.
    1974 Toward an anthropologically useful definition of Religion.
          IN Changing Perspectives in the Scientific Study of Reli-
          gion, Alan W. Eister, ed. New York: John Wiley and Sons.
          pp. 165-184.
          T1 II2

Goodenough, Ward H.
    1975 A terminal illness in Truk. Paper read at the 4th Annual
          Meeting of the Association for Social Anthropology in
          Oceania, 26-30 March, Stuart, Florida.
          T1 XIV

Goodenough, Ward H. and Hiroshi Sugita
    n.d. Trukese-English Dictionary. PALI Language Texts: Micronesia.
          Honolulu: University Press of Hawaii, forthcoming.
          T XIII

Gooding, Niles Russell
    1962 The administration of the Trust Territory of the Pacific
          Islands, 1945-1962. M.A. Thesis, American University,
          Washington, D.C.
          M XVII

Gould, K. L., K. L. Herrmann, and J. J. Witte
    1971 The epidemiology of measles in the United States Trust
          Territory of the Pacific Islands. American Journal of
          Public Health, 61(8):1602-1614.
          M XIV

Grace, George W.
    1959 The position of the Polynesian language within the Austro-
          nesian (Malayo-Polynesian) Language Family. International
          Journal of American Linguistics Supplement, Vol. 25, No. 3.
          Indiana University Publications in Anthropology and Linguis-
          tics, Memoir 16. Baltimore: Waverly Press. 77 pp.
          P XIII

Grace, George W.
    1970 Languages in Oceania. Working Papers in Linguistics, 2(3):
          1-24. Honolulu: Department of Linguistics, University of
          Hawaii.
          P XIII

MAIN BIBLIOGRAPHY

Graham, Robert
    1974 Tinian, the history cf an Island. Guam Recorder, n.s.,
          4(3):13-18.
          Mr4 XII

Grahlfs, Francis L., Jr.
    1955 The effects of Japanese cccupation in Micronesia.
          M.A. Thesis, Columbia University, New York.
          M XVII

Grattan, C. Hartley
    1944 Those Japanese Mandates. Harper's Magazine, 188(1124):145-
          153.
          M XVII

Greaves, F. C.
    1948 The health services prcgram in the Trust Territory of the
          Pacific Islands. U.S. Naval Medical Bulletin, 48(6):925-940.
          M XIV

Green, Roger C. and Marion Kelly, eds.
    1970 Pacific Islands, COWA [Council for Old World Archeology]
          Surveys and Bibliographies, Area 21, No. IV. Boston:
          Boston University Press. 15 pp.
          P III IX

Greenberg, Stephen, Larry Hall, and Taddese Beyene
    1969 The Palauan Verb. Languages and Linguistics, 4(1):68-90.
          PL1 XIII

Gressitt, J. L.
    1952 Description of Kayangel Atoll, Palau Islands. Atoll
          Research Bulletin, Nc. 14. 6 pp.
          PL1 X

Gressitt, J. L.
    1953 Notes on Ngaruangle and Kayangel Atolls, Palau Islands,
          Atoll Research Bulletin, No. 21. 5 pp.
          PL1 X

Greulich, William Walter
    1951 The growth and development status of Guamanian schcol
          children in 1947. American Journal of Physical Anthro-
          pology, 9(1):55-70.
          Mr1 XVI

Grey, Eve
    1951 Legends of Micronesia. Book I, 119 pp. Book II, 134 pp.
          Honolulu: Office of the High Commissioner.
          M VIII

Griffing, Robert P., Jr.
    1951 An exhibition of Micronesian art and Life. Paradise of
          the Pacific [now called Honolulu Magazine], 63(5):13, 16.
          M IV

Griswold, Lawrence
    1972 Confusion in the confetti Islands. Sea Power, 15(10):12-17.
          M XVII

Guam Business and Professional Women
    1959 Learn Chamorro Quickly. Agana, Guam: Guam Business and
          Professional Women. 82 pp.
          Mr XIII

Guam Recorder
    1972 to present. New Series. Published by the Micronesian Area
          Research Center, University of Guam, Agana, Guam, 96910.
          M IX

Gutmann, James
    1973 Micronesia: Politics and Education. The Virginia
          Quarterly Review, 49(1):29-37.
          M VII

Haddock, Robert L.
    1972 Guam declared rabies Free. South Pacific Bulletin,
          22(3):24-25.
          Mr1 XIV

Haddock, Robert L.
    1974 A hole full of History. Guam Recorder, n.s., 4(1):20-22.
          Mr XII

Hagaman, Roberta M.
    1974 Divorce, remarriage, and fertility in a Micronesian
          Population. Micronesica, 10(2):237-242.
          Y1 XVI

Hagiwara, George and Max Mori
    1965 Coir fiber-industry in Micronesia. South Pacific Bulletin,
          15(4):43-46.
          M II4

Haigwood, Col. Paul B.
    1972 Japan and the Mandates. IN National Security and Inter-
          national Trusteeship in the Pacific, W. Louis, ed. Anna-
          polis: Naval Institute Press. pp. 97-109.
          M XV XVII

Hainline, Lydia Jane [see Underwood, Jane Hainline]

MAIN BIBLIOGRAPHY

Halferty, Nancy
    1974 Bilingual education in Truk. Micronesian Reporter, 22(3):
          17-19.
          T1 VII

Hall, Edward T., Jr.
    1950 Military government cn Truk. Human Organization,
          9(2):25-30. [see Gladwin 1950].
          T1 XV

Hall, Edward T., Jr. and Karl J. Pelzer
    1946 The Economy of the Truk Islands, an Anthropological and
          Economic Survey. IN U.S. Commercial Company's Economic
          Survey of Micronesia, Report No. 17. Honolulu: U.S.
          Commercial Company. Mimeographed. 114 pp.
          T VI

Hall, Robert Anderscn, Jr.
    1945 English loan words in Micronesian Languages.
          Language, 21(3):214-219.
          M XIII

Halpern, Katherine Spencer
    1973 Obituary of Ann Fisher. American Anthropologist, 75(1):
          292-294.
          M IX

Hammon, W. McD.
    1953 Japanese encephalitis and other related infections on Guam.
          Proceedings of the 7th Pacific Science Congress, 2 February-
          4 March, 1949, Auckland, New Zealand, 7:341-347.
          Mr1 XIV

Hammon, W. McD. and Gladys Sather
    1953 Neutralization test survey with three types of
          poliomyelitis and viruses in children of San Francisco,
          Mexico City and Guam. American Journal of Hygiene [now
          called American Journal cf Epidemiology], 57(2):185-193.
          Mr1 XIV

Hankin, Jean H. and L. E. Dickenson
    1972 Urbanization, diet and potential health effects in Palau.
          American Journal of Clinical Nutrition, 25(3):348-353.
          PL1 II7 XIV

Hankin, Jean H.; Dwayne M. Reed; Darwin Labarthe; Milton Nichaman; and
          Reuel Stallones
    1970 Dietary and disease patterns among Micronesians.
          American Journal of Clinical Nutrition, 23(3):346-357.
          M XIV

MAIN BIBLIOGRAPHY

Hanson, Lenore C.
    1966   Archeological methods and problems in the Western Pacific
            with special reference to Micronesia and its Relationships.
            M.A. Thesis, University of Pittsburgh, Pittsburgh.
            M III

Harris, Sarah Ellen
    1953   Attempts to determine the blood group of aboriginal
            inhabitants of the Marianas and Hawaiian Islands by
            serological study of their Bones. M.Sc. Thesis,
            University of Hawaii, Honolulu.
            Mr XVI

Harrison, Sheldon P.
    n.d.   A Reference Grammar of Mokilese. PALI Language Texts: Micro-
            nesia. Honolulu: University Press of Hawaii, forthcoming.
            Pn6 XIII

Harrison, Sheldon P.
    1973   Reduplication in Micronesian Languages. Working Papers
            in Linguistics, 5(8):57-92. Honolulu: Department cf
            Linguistics, University cf Hawaii.
            M XIII

Hart, Thomas C.
    1948   The United States and the Pacific Islands. Annals of the
            American Academy of Political and Social Science, 255:115-
            123.
            M XVII

Hartmann, Floyd W.
    1947   Prevalence of dental caries in two groups of children in
            Micronesia. Journal of the American Dental Association,
            35(10):753-754.
            M XIV

Hasebe, K.
    1944   The Pingelap Islanders. South Sea Sciences, 16:13-18.
            Pn7 II

Haser, Sachuo and Kibby White
    1969   The problem of teenage boys on Moen, Truk: A test of a popu-
            lar Diagnosis. IN The Truk Report, Stephen Boggs, ed. Hon-
            olulu: Department of Anthropology, University of Hawaii. 32 p
            T1 II7

Hatanaka, Sachiko
    1967   The process of cultural change in Micronesia under the
            Japanese Mandate. IN Bunka Jinruigaku, M. Gamo, T. Okayashi,
            and S. Muratake, eds. Tokyo: Kadokawa Shoten. pp. 65-124.
            M II7 XII

MAIN BIBLIOGRAPHY

Hatheway, William H.
    1953 The land vegetation of Arno Atoll, Marshall Islands.
          Atoll Research Bulletin, No. 16. 29 pp.
          Ms9 V

Hatheway, William H.
    1957 Agricultural notes on the Southern Marshall Islands.
          Atoll Research Bulletin, No. 55. 9 pp.
          Ms I

Haudricourt, A. G.
    1969 Review of Arthur Capell, Grammar and Vocabulary of the Lang-
          uage of Sonsorol-Tobi. Journal de la Societe des Oceanistes,
          25:404.
          PL3 PL4 XIII

Hawaii Architects & Engineers, Inc.
    1967 Goals and Policies, Trust Territory of the Pacific Islands
          Physical Planning Program. Honolulu: Hawaii Architects
          and Engineers. Mimeographed. 33 pp.
          M XVII

Hawaii Architects & Engineers, Inc.
    1968 Cultural Considerations for Planning in Micronesia.
          Pre-Final Submission, Trust Territory Physical Planning
          Program. Honolulu: Hawaii Architects and Engineers.
          Mimeographed. 114 pp.
          M II

Hawaii Architects & Engineers, Inc.
    1968 Ebeye and Carlson Islands, Marshall Islands District. Final
          Report, Trust Territory Physical Planning Program. Honolulu:
          Hawaii Architects and Engineers. Mimeographed. 68 pp.
          Ms19 XVII

Hawaii Architects & Engineers, Inc.
    1968 Koror, Palau District. Final Report, Trust Territory Physical
          Planning Program. Honolulu: Hawaii Architects and Engineers.
          Mimeographed. 88 pp.
          PL1 XVII

Hawaii Architects & Engineers, Inc.
    1968 Majuro, Marshall Islands District. Final Report, Trust Terri-
          tory Physical Planning Program. Honolulu: Hawaii Architects
          and Engineers. Mimeographed. 77 pp.
          Ms8 XVII

Hawaii Architects & Engineers, Inc.
    1968 Moen Island, Truk District. Final Report, Trust Territory
          Physical Planning Program. Honolulu: Hawaii Architects
          and Engineers. Mimeographed. 74 pp.
          T1 XVII

Hawaii Architects & Engineers, Inc.
    1968   Notes on Anthropological Considerations for Planning in
         Micronesia: Micronesian Structures and Living Patterns;
         Homes for Micronesians. Trust Territory Planning Program.
         Second Consideration. Honolulu: Hawaii Architects and
         Engineers. Mimeographed. 29 pp.
         M II

Hawaii Architects & Engineers, Inc.
    1968   Ponape Island, Ponape District. Final Report, Trust Territory
         Physical Planning Program. Honolulu: Hawaii Architects and
         Engineers. Mimeographed. 70 pp.
         Pn1 XVII

Hawaii Architects & Engineers, Inc.
    1968   Progress Report on Planning Legislation Needs. Pre-Final
         Submission, Trust Territory Physical Planning Program.
         Honolulu: Hawaii Architects and Engineers. Mimeographed.
         27 pp.
         M XVII

Hawaii Architects & Engineers, Inc.
    1968   Saipan, Mariana Islands District. Final Report, Trust Terri-
         tory Physical Planning Program. Honolulu: Hawaii Architects
         and Engineers. Mimeographed. 79 pp.
         Mr2 XVII

Hawaii Architects & Engineers, Inc.
    1968   Yap, Yap District. Final Report, Trust Territory Physical
         Planning Program. Honolulu: Hawaii Architects and Engineers.
         66 pp.
         Y1 XVII

Hawaii Architects & Engineers, Inc.
    1972   Rota, Mariana Islands. Final Report, Trust Territory Physical
         Planning Program. Honolulu: Hawaii Architects and Engineers.
         Mimeographed.
         Mr3 XVII

Hawaii Architects & Engineers, Inc.
    1972   Tol, Truk District. Final Report, Trust Territory Physical
         Planning Program. Honolulu: Hawaii Architects and Engineers.
         Mimeographed.
         T1 XVII

Hawaii Architects & Engineers, Inc.
    1972   Wotje, Marshall Islands. Final Report, Trust Territory
         Physical Planning Program. Honolulu: Hawaii Architects and
         Engineers. Mimeographed.
         Ms5 XVII

MAIN BIBLIOGRAPHY

Hawaii Architects & Engineers, Inc.
    1973 Babelthuap, Palau Islands. Final Report, Trust Territory
          Physical Planning Program. Honolulu: Hawaii Architects and
          Engineers. Mimeographed.
          PL1 XVII

Hawkins, James
    1969 Factors affecting Micronesian political Development.
          IN Political Modernization of Micronesia, A Sympcsium.
          Santa Cruz, California: Center for South Pacific Studies.
          19 pp. Reprinted 1972. Micronesica, 8(1&2):1-11.
          M XVII

Hawkins, James
    1969 Requirements for Micronesian political Development. IN
          Political Modernization of Micronesia, A Symposium. Santa
          Cruz, California: Center for South Pacific Studies. 5 pp.
          M XVII

Heath, Laurel
    1975 Education for confusion: A study of education in the
          Mariana Islands 1688-1941. Journal of Pacific History,
          10(1):20-37.
          Mr VII XII

Heine, Carl
    1965 A historical study of political development and the
          prospect for self-government in the United States
          Pacific Trust Territory. B.A. Thesis, Pacific University,
          Forest Grove, Oregon.
          M XII XVII

Heine, Carl
    1969 Micronesia's Future Political Status Commission: Its rendez-
          vous with Destiny. Journal of Pacific History, 4:127-132.
          M XVII

Heine, Carl
    1970 Micronesia is confused about what it Wants. Pacific
          Islands Monthly, 41(9):18-19.
          M XVII

Heine, Carl
    1970 Micronesia: Unification and the coming of Self-Gcvernment.
          IN The Pclitics of Melanesia, Marian W. Ward, ed. Canberra:
          Australian National University Press. pp. 193-206.
          M XVII

MAIN BIBLIOGRAPHY

Heine, Carl
    1974 Micronesia at the Crossroads: A Reappraisal of the Micro-
          nesian Political Dilemma. Honolulu: University Press
          of Hawaii. 210 pp. Reviewed: 1975 by Norma N. King,
          Pacific Asian Studies, 1(1):79-80; 1975 by Peter J. Hemp-
          enstall, Journal of Pacific History, 10(2):122-123; 1975
          by Robert C. Kiste, Reviews in Anthropology, 2(3):in press.
          M XVII

Helfand, Harvey
    1974 The pirate and Palau. Micronesian Reporter, 22(3):20-22.
          PL1 XII

Helfman, Gene S. and John E. Randall
    1973 Palauan fish Names. Pacific Science, 27(2):136-153.
          PL1 XIX

Hempenstall, Peter John
    1973 Indigenous resistance to German rule in the Pacific
          colonies of Samoa, Ponape and New Guinea, 1884 to 1914.
          D.Phil. Dissertation, Oxford University, Oxford, England.
          Pn1 XII

Hempenstall, Peter John
    1975 Resistance in the German Pacific Empire: Towards a theory
          of early colonial Response. Journal of the Polynesian
          Society, 84(1):5-24.
          Pn1 XII

Hempenstall, Peter John
    1975 Review of Carl Heine, Micronesia at the Crossroads: A
          Reappraisal of the Micronesian Political Dilemma. Journal
          of Pacific History, 10(2):122-123.
          M XVII

Henning, Theodore F.
    1961 Buritis in Paradise. New York: Greenwich Book Publishers.
          252 pp.
          M IX

Henrickson, Paul R.
    1968 Two forms of primitive art in Micronesia. Micronesica,
          4(1):39-48.
          Mr1 PL1 III IV

Henry, William E.
    1954 Letter to the Editor: Trukese T.A.T.'s. American
          Anthropologist, 56:889.
          T1 II6

MAIN BIBLIOGRAPHY

Hernandes, Faustino, S. J.
    1951 Marriage problems and customs in the Carolines and Mar-
          shalls. World Mission [now called Enterprise], 2:101-102.
          C Ms II1

Hetzel, Alice M.
    1959 Health survey of the Trust Territory of the Pacific Islands.
          U.S. Armed Forces Medical Journal, 10(10):1100-1222.
          M XIV

Hewes, Gordon W.
    1955 Review of Alexander Spoehr, Saipan, The Ethnology
          of a War-Devastated Island. American Anthropologist,
          57(2), Part 1:358-359.
          Mr2 II

Hezel, Francis X.
    n.d. Foreign ship contacts with Truk Islands. Moen, Truk:
          Micronesian Seminar. Mimeographed. 8 pp.
          T XII

Hezel, Francis X.
    1970 Catholic missions in the Caroline and Marshall Islands.
          A survey of historical Materials. Journal of Pacific
          History, 5:213-227.
          C Ms XII

Hezel, Francis X.
    1971 Spanish Capuchins in the Carolines. Part 1. Micronesian
          Reporter, 19(2):32-40. Part 2. Micronesian Reporter,
          19(3):36-42.
          C II2

Hezel, Francis X.
    1972 Review of Dorothy Shineberg, ed., The Trading Voyages of
          Andrew Cheyne, 1841-1844. Journal of Pacific History, 7:
          231-232.
          M XII

Hezel, Francis X.
    1972 The westernization of Truk: A backward Glance.
          Micronesian Reporter, 20(4):24-31.
          T1 II7

Hezel, Francis X.
    1972 Sailors Beware! Foreign contact with Truk in the last
          Century. Guam Recorder, n.s., 2(4):82-84.
          T1 XII

MAIN BIBLIOGRAPHY

Hezel, Francis X.
    1973   The beginnings of foreign contact with Truk.   Journal of
           Pacific History, 8:51-73.
           T1 XII

Hezel, Francis X.
    1973   The first European visit to Truk.   Guam Recorder, n.s.,
           3(3):38-40.
           T1 XII

Hezel, Francis X.
    1973   The school Industry.   Friends of Micronesia Newsletter,
           3(2):19-22.
           M VII

Hezel, Francis X.
    1973   Reflections on Micronesia's Economy.   Micronitor [Majuro,
           Marshall Islands; now called Micronesian Independent],
           4(29):1-2.
           M VI

Hezel, Francis X.
    1973   Schools: Micronesia's biggest Industry.   Pacific
           Daily News, March 25, pp. 2A-3A.
           M VII

Hezel, Francis X.
    1974   Dumont D'Urville on Truk.   Guam Recorder, n.s.,   4(3):42-50.
           T1 XII

Hezel, Francis X.
    1974   Unholy mackerel and the almighty Buck.   Friends of
           Micronesia Newsletter, 4(1):15-19.
           M II7 VII

Hezel, Francis X.
    1975   A Yankee trader in Yap: Crayton Philo Holcomb.   Journal
           of Pacific History, 10(1):3-19.
           Y1 XII

Hezel, Francis X.
    1975   Indigenization as a missionary goal in the Caroline and
           Marshall Islands.   Paper read at the 4th Annual Meeting of
           the Association for Social Anthropology in Oceania, 26-30
           March, Stuart, Florida.
           C Ms II2

Hezel, Francis X. and Charles Reafsnyder
    1971 Micronesia: A Changing Society. 2 Volumes: Teacher's Guide
          and Student Booklet. Teacher's Guide, 198 pp. Student
          Booklet, 145 pp. Saipan: Marianas District Department of
          Education. Reviewed: 1972 by John Singleton, Association
          for Anthropology in Micronesia Newsletter, 1(1):17-20.
          M VII

Hezel, Francis X. and Charles Reafsnyder
    1972 Micronesia through the Years. 2 Volumes: Teacher's Guide
          and Student Resource Book. Teacher's Guide, 359 pp.
          Student Resource Book, 115 pp. Saipan: Department
          of Education, Trust Territory of the Pacific Islands.
          M VII

Hezel, Francis X. and Maria Teresa del Valle
    1972 Early European contact with the Western Carolines:
          1525-1750. Journal of Pacific History, 7:26-44.
          C XII

Hiatt, Robert W. (compiler)
    1969 Contributions by the University of Hawaii and the East-West
          Center to the Development of Micronesia. Honolulu: The
          Research Corporation of the University of Hawaii. 43 pp.
          M IX

Hiatt, Robert W., H. I. Fisher, and Floyd W. Hartmann
    1947 Uncle Sam's most primitive Wards. Paradise of the Pacific
          [now called Honolulu Magazine], 59:48-51.
          M IX

Hiatt, Robert W., H. I. Fisher, and Floyd W. Hartmann
    1947 Yap Re-discovered. Paradise of the Pacific [now called
          Honolulu Magazine], 59:22-26.
          Y1 IX

Hiatt, Robert W., Leonard E. Mason and D. Cox
    1951 The Arno Atoll Project. Proceedings of the Hawaii Academy
          of Science, 26th Annual Meeting, p. 5. [abstract].
          Ms9 IX

Hijikata, Hisakatsu
    1953 Dittilapal-Satewal. [Folktales of Satawal]. Tokyo:
          Sanseido Publishing Co. [in Japanese].
          Y10 VIII

MAIN BIBLIOGRAPHY

Hijikata, Hisakatsu
    1956 Report on consecrated stone images and other stone works in
         Palau, Micronesia. Minzokugaku-Kenkyu [Tokyo], 20(3&4):
         1-53. [in Japanese]. Translated into English and reprinted
         1973. Stone images of Palau. Micronesian Area Research
         Center Publication, No. 3. Agana, Guam: Garrison and
         McCarter. 93 pp.
         PL1 II4 III

Hijikata, Hisakatsu
    1960 Ceramics with decoration found in the Island Palao, Micro-
         nesia. Jinruigaku Kenkyu, 7(1&2):66-89. [in Japanese].
         Translated into English and reprinted 1973. Some ceramics
         of Palau. Micronesian Area Research Center Publication,
         No. 2. Agana, Guam: Garrison and McCarter. 26 pp.
         PL1 II4 III

Hill, Peter J. R. and Benjamin C. Stone
    1961 The vegetation of Yanagi Islet, Truk, Caroline Islands.
         Pacific Science, 15(4):261-262.
         T1 V

Hines, Neal O.
    1951 Bikini Report. The Scientific Monthly, 72(2):102-113.
         Ms13 XV XIX

Hines, Neal O.
    1952 The secret of the Marshallese Sticks. Pacific
         Discovery, 5(5):18-23.
         Ms X

Hines, Neal O.
    1962 Proving Ground: An Account of the Radiobiological Studies
         in the Pacific, 1946-1961. Seattle: University of Wash-
         ington Press. 366 pp.
         Ms XV

Hirano, Asao; Leonard T. Kurland; R. S. Krooth; and Simmons Lessell
    1961 Parkinsonism-dementia complex, an endemic disease on the
         island of Guam. I. Clinical Features. Brain, 84(4):
         642-661.
         Mr1 XIV

Hirano, Asao; Nathan Malamud; Teresita S. Elizan; and Leonard T.
         Kurland
    1966 Amyotrophic lateral sclerosis and Parkinsonism-dementia of
         Guam: Further pathologic Studies. Archives of Neurology,
         15(1):35-51.
         Mr1 XIV

Hirano, Asao, Nathan Malamud, and Leonard T. Kurland
    1961 Parkinsonism-dementia complex, an endemic disease on the
          island of Guam. II. Pathological Features. Brain,
          84(4):662-679.
          Mr1 XIV

Hiroa, Te Rangi [Peter H. Buck]
    1948 Bishop Museum Expedition to Kapingamarangi. B.P. Bishop
          Museum Bulletin, No. 194:31-40. Honolulu: Bishop Museum
          Press.
          Pn9 II IX

Hiroa, Te Rangi [Peter H. Buck]
    1949 Kapingamarangi; a Polynesian atoll in Micronesia. Pro-
          ceedings of the New Zealand Geographical Society, No. 7:13.
          Pn9 II

Hiroa, Te Rangi [Peter H. Buck]
    1950 The Material Culture of Kapingamarangi. B.P. Bishop
          Museum Bulletin, No. 200. Honolulu: Bishop Museum
          Press. 291 pp. Reviewed: 1951 by Beatrice Blackwood,
          American Anthropologist, 53(4), Part 1:549-550.
          Pn9 II4

Hiroa, Te Rangi [Peter H. Buck]
    1951 Kapingaramangi: A living Legend. Paradise of the
          Pacific [now called Honolulu Magazine], 63(5):22-27, 36-37.
          Pn9 IX

Hitch, Thomas K.
    1946 The administration of America's Pacific Islands.
          Political Science Quarterly, 61(3):384-407.
          M XVII

Hitchcock, David I., Jr.
    1974 Information and Education for Self-Government in
          Micronesia. Case study prepared for the 16th session
          of the Senior Seminar in Foreign Policy, Department
          of State. Washington, D.C.: Department of State.
          M XVII

Hobbs, William H.
    1945 The Fortress Islands of the Pacific. Ann Arbor,
          Michigan: J.W. Edwards. 186 pp.
          M XVII

Hockett, Charles F.
    1961 Recommendations on language policy in the Trust
          Territory of the Pacific Islands and the Territory
          of Guam. Agana, Guam: Department of Education,
          Government of Guam. Mimeographed. 9 pp.
          M Mr1 XIII

Hogbin, Ian
    1971   Review of Vern Carroll, ed., Adoption in Eastern Oceania.
           Mankind, 8(1):76-77.
           P II1

Hohnschopp, Henning
    1971   Untersuchung zum Para-Mikronesien-Problem unter besonderer
           Berücksichtigung der Wuvulu- und Aua-Kultur. [Examination
           of the Para-Micronesian problem with special regard to
           Wuvulu and Aua Culture]. Ph.D. Dissertation, University of
           München, München. Published 1973. München: Klaus Renner.
           215 pp.
           M III

Holbrook, Francis X.
    1969   United States Naval defense and Trans-Pacific commercial
           air routes 1933-1941. Ph.D. Dissertation, Fordham
           University, New York. Available from University Micro-
           films, Ann Arbor: No. 70-11435.
           M XV

Hollyman, K. J. (compiler)
    1960   A Checklist of Oceanic Languages (Melanesia, Micronesia,
           New Guinea, Polynesia). Te Reo Monographs. Auckland:
           Linguistic Society of New Zealand. 32 pp.
           M XIII

Holmes and Narver, Inc.
    n.d.   Report of Repatriation of the Rongelap People for the
           United States Atomic Energy Commission, Albuquerque
           Operations Office. Albuquerque, New Mexico: Holmes
           and Narver, Inc.
           Ms15 XV

Hopkins, J. W.
    1964   Toward self-government in the Trust Territory. Philippine
           Journal of Public Administration [Manila], 8(2):132-135.
           M XVII

Hops, A.
    1956   Ueber die Einmaligkeit der Marshall-Stabkarten im Stillen
           Ozean. [Concerning the uniqueness of the Marshallese
           stick charts in the Pacific Ocean]. Zeitschrift für Eth-
           nologie, 81(1):104-110.
           Ms X

Horay, Patrick J.
    1972   Education and acculturation in Marshall Island Schools.
           M.A. Thesis, University of Kansas, Lawrence.
           Ms VII

MAIN BIBLIOGRAPHY

Hosaka, Edward Y.
    1946 Botanical report on Micronesia. IN U.S. Commercial
          Company's Economic Survey of Micronesia, Report No. 13,
          Part 2. [Part 1 by F. Raymond Fosberg]. Honolulu:
          U.S. Ccmmercial Company. Mimeographed. 68 pp.; 83 plates.
          M V

Hough, Frank O.
    1947 The Island War: The United States Marine Corps in
          the Pacific. Philadelphia: Lippincott Co. 413 pp.
          P XV

Houston, Neil T.
    1954 Commercial Problems in the Trust Territory Follcwing Termin-
          ation of the Island Trading Company. SRI Project 894. Stan-
          ford, California: Stanford Research Institute. 81 pp.
          M VI

Howells, William W.
    1970 Anthropometric grouping analysis of Pacific Peoples. Arche-
          ology and Physical Anthrcpology in Oceania, 5(3):192-217.
          P XVI

Howells, William W.
    1973 The Pacific Islanders. New York: Scribner's. 299 pp.
          P XVI

Hsu, Robert W.
    1960 Palauan Phonology. M.S. Thesis, Georgetown University,
          Washington, D.C.
          PL1 XIII

Hsu, Robert W.
    1969 Phonology and morphophonemics of Yapese. Ph.D. Dissertation,
          University of California, Berkeley. Available from Uni-
          versity Microfilms, Ann Arbor: No. 69-18934.
          Y1 XIII

Hsu, Robert W.
    1969 Apocope and umlaut in Yapese. Working Papers in Linguistics,
          1(5):93-106. Honolulu: Department of Linguistics, University
          of Hawaii.
          Y1 XIII

Huber, Peter B.
    1974 Review of Roland Force and Maryanne Force, Just Cne House:
          A Description and Analysis of Kinship in the Palau Islands.
          Man, n.s., 9(4):650-651.
          PL1 II1

MAIN BIBLIOGRAPHY

Hughes, Daniel T.
    1968 Democracy in a traditional society: A role analysis
          of the political system of Ponape. Ph.D. Dissertation,
          Catholic University, Washington, D.C. Available from
          University Microfilms, Ann Arbor: No. 68-8009.
          Pn1 II3

Hughes, Daniel T.
    1969 Conflict and harmony: Roles of councilman and section
          chief cn Ponape. Oceania, 40(1):32-41.
          Pn1 II3

Hughes, Daniel T.
    1969 Democracy in a traditional society: Two hypotheses
          on Role. American Anthropologist, 71(1):36-45.
          Pn1 II3

Hughes, Daniel T.
    1969 Reciprocal influence of traditional and democratic
          leadership rcles cn Ponape. Ethnology, 8(3):278-291.
          Pn1 II3

Hughes, Daniel T.
    1970 Political Conflict and Harmony on Ponape. New Haven:
          HRAFlex Books. 256 pp.
          Pn1 II3

Hughes, Daniel T.
    1971 A Bibliographic Resource for Demographic, Economic, and
          Social Trends in the Western Pacific. Washington, D.C.:
          National Research Council, National Academy of Sciences.
          63 pp.
          P IX

Hughes, Daniel T.
    1972 Integration of the rcle of territorial congressman
          into Ponapean Society. Oceania, 43(2):140-152.
          Pn1 II3

Hughes, Daniel T.
    1972 Traditional versus modern sources of legitimacy for modern
          political leadership positions in Micronesia. Paper read
          at the 1st Annual Meeting of the Association for Sccial
          Anthropology in Oceania, 29 March-1 April, Orcas Island,
          Washington.
          M II3

Hughes, Daniel T.
    1973 Democracy in the Philippines and on Ponape: A ccmparison
          of two political systems structured on the U.S. Model.
          Micronesica, 9(1):1-10.
          Pn1 II3

Hughes, Daniel T.
    1974 Changes in the value system associated with traditional
          Ponapean leadership Positions. Paper read at the 3rd Annual
          Meeting of the Association for Social Anthropolcgy in
          Oceania, 13-17 March, Asilomar, Pacific Grove, California.
          Pn1 II3

Hughes, Daniel T.
    1974 Obstacles to the integration of the district legislature
          into Ponapean Society. IN Political Development in
          Micronesia, Daniel T. Hughes and Sherwood G. Lingenfelter,
          eds. Columbus: Ohio State University Press. pp. 93-109.
          Pn1 II3

Hughes, Daniel T. and Sherwood G. Lingenfelter, eds.
    1974 Political Development in Micronesia. Columbus: Chio
          State University Press. 333 pp. Reviewed: 1975 by
          Robert C. Kiste, Reviews in Anthropology, 2(3):in press.
          M II3

Hughes, Daniel T. and Douglas Mapou
    1973 Structural variation of rank in traditional Micrcnesian
          Society. Paper read at the 72nd Annual Meeting of the
          American Anthropological Association, 28 November-2
          December, New Orleans.
          M II1 II3

Hughes, Daniel T. and James McLeod
    1973 Typology of colonial administrative Approaches. Paper read
          at the 2nd Annual Meeting of the Association for Social
          Anthropology in Oceania, 21-25 March, Orcas Island, Wash-
          ington.
          M II3

Hunt, Edward E., Jr.
    1950 A view cf somatology and serology in Micronesia.
          American Journal of Physical Anthropology, 8(2):157-184.
          M XVI

Hunt, Edward E., Jr.
    1951 Physique, social class and crime among the Yap Islanders.
          American Journal of Physical Anthropology, 9(2):241-242.
          Y1 XVI

Hunt, Edward E., Jr.
    1951 Studies of physical anthropology in Micronesia.
          Ph.D. Dissertation, Harvard University, Cambridge.
          M XVI

Hunt, Edward E., Jr.
    1965 Polymorphisms of the ABO blood groups and sex ratios of
          live births in seven human Populations. Human Biology,
          37(2):156-161.
          Y1 XVI

Hunt, Edward E., Jr.
    1966 Metrical variability and population size in Micronesians.
          Annals of the New York Academy of Sciences, 134:632-638.
          M XVI

Hunt, Edward E., Jr., Nathaniel R. Kidder, and David M. Schneider
    1954 The depopulation of Yap. Human Biology, 26(1):21-51.
          Y1 XVI

Hunt, Edward E., Jr.; Nathaniel R. Kidder; David M. Schneider;
    and William D. Stevens
    1949 The Micronesians of Yap and Their Depopulation. Report of
          the Peabody Museum Expedition tc Yap Island, Micronesia,
          1947-1948. Cambridge: Peabody Museum, Harvard University.
          223 pp. Also published 1949. CIMA Report, No. 24. Wash-
          ington, D.C.: Pacific Science Board. 223 pp.
          Y1 XVI

Hunt, Edward E., Jr., William A. Lessa, and Arobati Hicking
    1965 The sex ratio of live births in three Pacific Island
          populations (Yap, Samoa and New Guinea). Human Biology,
          37(2):148-155.
          Y1 XVI

Hunt, Edward E., Jr. and Jamshed Mavalwala
    1964 Finger ridge counts in the Micronesians of Yap. Micro-
          nesica, 1(1&2):55-58.
          Y1 XVI

Hunter, Col. Clyde W.
    1972 The Marshall Islands. IN Naticnal Security and Inter-
          national Trusteeship in the Pacific, W.R. Louis, ed.
          Annapolis: Naval Institute Press. pp. 133-140.
          Ms XV XVII

Hussels, I. E. and Newton E. Morton
    1972 Pingelap and Mokil Atolls: Achromatopsia. American
          Journal of Human Genetics, 24(3):304-309.
          Pn6 Pn7 XVI

Hynd, George W.
    1974 Religion and magic among the ancient Chamorro.
          Guam Recorder, n.s., 4(1):23-24.
          Mr II2

MAIN BIBLIOGRAPHY

Imaizumi, Y. and Newton E. Morton
    1970   Isolation by distance in New Guinea and Micronesia.
           Archaeology and Physical Anthropology in Oceania,
           5(3):218-235.
           M XVI

Inman, N.
    1967   Notes on some poisonous plants of Guam. Micronesica, 3(1):
           55-66.
           Mr1 V

Isely, Jeter A. and Philip A. Crowl
    1951   The U.S. Marines and Amphibious War; Its Theory and Its
           Practice in the Pacific. Princeton: Princeton University
           Press. 636 pp.
           P XV

Ittel, W. H.
    1949   Sailing canoes of the Marshall Islands. U.S. Naval
           Institute Proceedings, 75(5):589.
           Ms II4

Izui, Hisanosuke
    1949   A propos d'une table de correspondances de phonemes Balau.
           [Remarks on a table of correspondences of Palauan phonemes].
           Gengo Kenkyu, 14:40-48.
           PL1 XIII

Izui, Hisanosuke
    1965   The languages of Micronesia: Their unity and Diversity.
           Lingua, 14:349-359. Indo-Pacific Linguistic Studies, Part
           1, Historical Linguistics, G.B. Milner and Eugenie J.A.
           Henderson, eds. Amsterdam: North-Holland Publishing Co.
           M XIII

Jackman, Harry H.
    1964   Co-operative housing at Metalanim, Ponape, Trust Territory of
           the Pacific Islands. South Pacific Bulletin, 14(4):24-26.
           Pn1 XVII

Jackman, Harry H.
    1967   America in the West Pacific: Integrating 90,000
           Micronesians. New Guinea, 1(8):48-53.
           M XVII

Jackman, Harry H.
    1969   Review of Willard R. Bascom, Ponape: A Pacific Economy
           in Transition. Oceania, 39(4):312-315.
           Pn1 VI

MAIN BIBLIOGRAPHY

Jacobs, Robert M.
    1971 The effects of acculturation on the traditional narratives of
         Palau. Journal of American Folklore, 84(331-334):428-435.
         PL1 II7 VIII

Jacobson, Harold K.
    1960 Our "colonial" problem in the Pacific. Foreign Affairs,
         39(1):56-66.
         M XVII

Jaffee, A. A.
    1959 Dental Services in the United States Trust Territory. South
         Pacific Bulletin, 9(2):45-46, 56-57.
         M XIV

James, Roy E.
    1946 Military government: Guam. Far Eastern Survey, 15(18):273-
         277.
         Mr1 XV

James, Roy E.
    1949 The Trust Territory of the Pacific Islands. IN America's
         Pacific Dependencies, Rupert Emerson, et al., eds. New York:
         American Institute of Pacific Relations. pp. 109-126.
         M XII XVII

Janssen, Roswitha
    1971 Spiele in Mikronesien. [Games in Micronesia]. Ph.D. Dis-
         sertation, University of Bonn, Bonn.
         M IV

Jardin, C.
    1967 Food and dietary habits in Micronesia. South Pacific
         Commission Field Report. Noumea: South Pacific Com-
         mission. Mimeographed. 5 pp.
         M XIV

Jenkins, W. S.
    1946 Wartime canoe building in the Marshall Islands. American
         Neptune, 6(1):71-72.
         Ms II4

Jensen, John T.
    n.d. Yapese Reference Grammar. PALI Language Texts: Micronesia.
         Honolulu: University Press of Hawaii, forthcoming.
         Y1 XIII

Jensen, John T.
    n.d. Yapese-English Dictionary. PALI Language Texts: Micronesia.
         Honolulu: University Press of Hawaii, forthcoming.
         Y1 XIII

MAIN BIBLIOGRAPHY

Jensen, John T.
    1966 Lessons in Yapese. Honolulu: University of Hawaii Peace
          Corps Training Center. Mimeographed. Vol. 1, 236 pp.;
          Vol. 2, 387 pp.
          Y1 XIII

Jernigan, Earl Wesley
    1973 Lochukle: A Palauan art Tradition. Ph.D. Dissertation,
          University of Arizona, Tucson.
          PL1 IV

Johnson, Charles G., Richard J. Alvis, and Robert L. Hetzler
    1960 Military Geology of Yap Islands, Caroline Islands. Parts
          I and II. Prepared under the direction of the Chief of
          Engineers, U.S. Army, by the Intelligence Division, Office
          of the Engineer, Headquarters, U.S. Army Pacific, with
          personnel of the U.S. Geological Survey. Washington, D.C.:
          U.S. Army. Mimeographed. 164 pp.
          Y1 XI

Johnson, Donald D.
    1970 The Trust Territory of the Pacific Islands.
          Current History, 58(344):233-239.
          M XVII

Johnson, Donald D.
    1974 Pacific Islands, Trust Territory of the. Encyclopaedia
          Britannica, 15th ed., 13:831-836. Chicago: Encyclopaedia
          Britannica, Inc.
          M II

Johnson, James B.
    1969 Land Ownership in the Northern Mariana Islands: An
          Outline History. Saipan, Mariana Islands: Trust
          Territory of the Pacific Islands, Division of Land
          Management, Mariana Islands District. 67 pp.
          Mr II1

Johnson, Robert G.
    1959 Recommendations for the administration of the schools
          of Guam in light of the island Culture. Ph.D. Disser-
          tation, Florida State University, Tallahassee. Available
          from University Microfilms, Ann Arbor: No. 59-01758.
          Mr1 VII

Johnston, Agueda I.
    1965 Christmas on Guam. Pacific Profile, 3(10):6-7.
          Mr1 II

MAIN BIBLIOGRAPHY

Johnston, Emilie G.
    1971 Micronesian nutrition Bibliography. Micronesica,
          8(1&2):197-210.
          M IX XIV

Johnston, Emilie G.
    1972 Chamorro tools, implements and Utensils. Guam
          Recorder, n.s., 1(2&3):58-59.
          Mr II4

Johnston, Emilie G.
    1972 References to the latte of the Mariana Islands. Guam
          Recorder, n.s., 2(1):8-11.
          Mr III

Johnston, Emilie G.
    1973 Bibliography of Micronesian native Medicine. Guam: Micro-
          nesian Area Research Center, University of Guam. 10 pp.
          M IX XIV

Johnston, Emilie G.
    1974 Spanish dikes in the Agana Swamp. Guam Recorder, n.s.,
          4(3):11-12.
          Mr1 III XII

Johnston, William J.
    1970 The United States as a Pacific Power. Current History,
          58(344):193-195.
          M XVII

Jones, Garth Nelson
    1954 Administration of the Trust Territory of the Pacific
          Islands. Ph.D. Dissertation, University of Utah, Salt
          Lake City.
          M XVII

Jordheim, G. D. and Inger A. Olsen
    1963 The use of a non-verbal test of intelligence in the Trust
          Territory of the Pacific Islands. American Anthropologist,
          65(5):1122-1125. [see Kearney 1964; King 1964].
          M II6

Joseph, Alice and Veronica F. Murray
    1951 Chamorros and Carolinians of Saipan: Personality Studies.
          CIMA Report, No. 12. Washington, D.C.: Pacific Science
          Board. 381 pp. Reprinted 1951. Cambridge: Harvard
          University Press. 381 pp. Reprinted 1971. Westport,
          Connecticut: Greenwocd Press. Reviewed: 1952 by Ernest
          Beaglehcle, American Anthropolcgist, 54(4):547-548.
          Mr2 C II6

MAIN BIBLIOGRAPHY

Joseph, Alice and Veronica F. Murray
    1957 Rorschachs of 100 Chamorro and 99 Carolinian Children.
          Microcard Publications of Primary Records in Culture and
          Personality, Volume 2. Madison, Wisconsin: The Microcard
          Foundation.
          Mr2 C II6

Josephs, Lewis S.
    n.d. Palauan Reference Grammar. PALI Language Texts: Micronesia.
          Honolulu: University Press of Hawaii, forthcoming.
          PL1 XIII

Kabua, Phillip and Nancy Pollock
    1967 The ecological bases of political power in Laura Community.
          IN The Laura Report, Leonard E. Mason, ed. Honolulu:
          Department of Anthropology, University of Hawaii. 88 pp.
          Ms8 II3

Kaeppler, Adrienne
    1967 Micronesia--Linguistics. Man in the Pacific, 7:4. Honolulu:
          Pacific Scientific Information Center, Bishop Museum.
          M XIII

Kahlo, G.
    1960 Die Mikronesische Frage. [The Micronesian Question].
          Wissenschaftliche Zeitschrift der Universität Leipzig,
          9(1):119-124.
          M II

Kahn, E. J., Jr.
    1966 The small islands: America and its Responsibility.
          Saturday Review, 49(41):45-46.
          M XVII

Kahn, E. J., Jr.
    1966 A Reporter in Micronesia. New York: W.W. Norton and Co.
          313 pp.
          M IX

Kahn, E. J., Jr.
    1971 A reporter at large: Micronesia Revisited. New
          Yorker Magazine, 47(44):98-115.
          M IX

Kaneshiro, Shigeru
    1958 Land tenure in the Palau Islands. IN Land Tenure Patterns
          in the Trust Territory of the Pacific Islands, John E. de
          Young, ed. Guam: Office of the Staff Anthropologist,
          Trust Territory of the Pacific Islands. pp. 289-336.
          PL1 II1

Kanost, R. F.
    1970 Localization in the Trust Territory of the Pacific Islands.
          IN The Politics of Melanesia, Marian W. Ward, ed. Canberra:
          Australian National University Press. pp. 321-364.
          M XVII

Karig, Walter
    1948 The Fortunate Islands, A Pacific Interlude; An Account of
          the Pleasant Lands and People in the United States Trust
          Territory of the Pacific. New York: Rinehart and Co.   226 pp
          M IX

Karolle, Bruce G.
    1973 A geography of Guam Island. Guam Recorder, n.s., 3(3):16-25.
          Mr1 X

Kay, Alan
    1974 Population growth in Micronesia. Micronesian Reporter,
          22(2):13-22.
          M XVI

Kearney, G. E.
    1964 Comment on 'The use of a non-verbal test of intelligence in
          the Trust Territory of the Pacific Islands' by Jordheim and
          Olsen. American Anthropologist, 66(6), Part 1:1395-1396.
          [see Jordheim and Olsen 1963; King 1964].
          M II6

Keesing, Felix M.
    1945 The former Japanese Mandated Islands. Far Eastern Survey,
          14(19):269-271.
          M XVII

Keesing, Felix M.
    1945 People of the Mandates. Far Eastern Survey, 14(20):288-291.
          M II

Keesing, Felix M.
    1947 Administration in Pacific Islands. Far Eastern Survey,
          16(6):61-65.
          M XVII

Keesing, Felix M.
    1949 Experiments in training overseas Administrators.
          Human Organization, 8(4):20-22.
          M II8

Keesing, Felix M.
    1959 Field Guide to Oceania. Field Guide Series No. 1,
          Publication 701. Washington, D.C.: National Academy
          of Science. 51 pp.
          P IX

MAIN BIBLIOGRAPHY

Kehoe, Monika
    1973 English on Guam. Guam Recorder, n.s., 3(1):41-44.
          Mr1 XIII

Kenady, Reid M., Jr.
    1962 The soils of Rongelap Atoll, Marshall Islands. M.S. Thesis,
          University of Washingtcn, Seattle.
          Ms15 XI

Kennally, Most Rev. Vincent I., S.J.
    1961 Oceania: A missionary Commentary. World Mission [now
          called Enterprise], 12:103-108.
          P II1 II2

Kennedy, T. F.
    1966 A Descriptive Atlas of the Pacific Islands. New Zealand,
          Australia, Polynesia, Melanesia, Micronesia, Philippines.
          Wellington: A. and H. and A.W. Reed. 65 pp.
          P X

Kesolei, Katherine, ed.
    1971 Cheldecheduck er Belau: Palauan Legends, No. 1.
          Koror: Palau Community Action Agency. 28 pp.
          [text in Palauan and English].
          PL1 VIII

Kidson, Cheviot S.
    1967 Genetics of human populations; Studies in Melanesia,
          Micronesia and Australia. M.D. Thesis, University
          of Sydney, Sydney.
          M XVI

Kidson, Cheviot S. and D. C. Gajdusek
    1962 Glucose-6-phosphate dehydrogenase deficiency in Micronesian
          Peoples. The Australian Journal of Science [now called
          Search], 25(2):61-62.
          M XVI

Kim, Dai You and Francis Defngin
    1960 Taro cultivation in Yap. IN Taro Cultivation, Practices and
          Beliefs, Part I (The Western Carolines), John E. de Young, ed.
          Anthropological Working Papers, No. 6. Guam: Office of the
          Staff Anthropologist, Trust Territory of the Pacific Islands.
          pp. 48-68.
          Y1 I

-129-

King, A. R.
    1964 Comments on Jordheim and Olsen's use of a non-verbal test of
         intelligence in the Pacific Islands Trust Territory. Amer-
         ican Anthropologist, 66(3), Part 1:640-644. [see Jordheim
         and Olsen 1963; Kearney 1964].
         M II6

King, Norma N.
    1975 Review of Carl Heine, Micronesia at the Crossroads. Pacific
         Asian Studies [University of Guam], 1(1):79-80.
         M XVII

Kirkpatrick, John
    1973 Personal names on Yap. M.A. Thesis, University of
         Chicago, Chicago.
         Y1 II

Kirkpatrick, John T. and Charles R. Broder
    n.d. Adoption and parenthood on Yap. IN Transactions in Kinship:
         Adoption and Fosterage in Oceania, Ivan Brady, ed. ASAO
         Monograph No. 4. Honolulu: University Press of Hawaii, in
         press.
         Y1 II1

Kirtley, Bacil F.
    1955 A motif-index of Polynesian, Melanesian, and Micronesian
         Narratives. Ph.D. Dissertation, Indiana University,
         Bloomington. Available from University Microfilms, Ann
         Arbor: No. 00-14660.
         M VIII

Kiste, Robert C.
    n.d. The people of Enewetak Atoll vs. the U.S. Department of
         Defense. IN Ethical Dilemmas: Anthropologists at Work,
         Michael A. Rynkiewich and James P. Spradley, eds. New York:
         John Wiley and Sons, forthcoming.
         Ms11 XV XVII

Kiste, Robert C.
    n.d. The relocation of the Bikinians. IN Exiles and Migrants in
         Oceania, Michael D. Lieber, ed. ASAO Monograph Series.
         Honolulu: University Press of Hawaii, forthcoming.
         Ms13 Ms24 II7

Kiste, Robert C.
    1967 Changing patterns of land tenure and social organization
         among the Ex-Bikini Marshallese. Ph.D. Dissertation,
         University of Oregon, Eugene. Available from University
         Microfilms, Ann Arbor: No. 68-3995.
         Ms13 Ms24 II7

Kiste, Robert C.
1968 Kili Island: A Study of the Relocation of the Ex-Bikini
      Marshallese. Eugene: Department of Anthropology, Univer-
      sity of Oregon. 393 pp.
      Ms13 Ms24 II7

Kiste, Robert C.
1968 Variations in Marshallese cross-cousin terminology
      and Behavior. Paper read at the 67th Annual Meeting
      of the American Anthropological Association, 21-24
      November, Seattle.
      Ms II1

Kiste, Robert C.
1971 Review of Byron W. Bender, Spoken Marshallese: An Intensive
      Language Course with Grammatical Notes and Glossary, and
      Donald W. Topping, Spoken Chamorro: An Intensive Language
      Course with Grammatical Notes and Glossary. American
      Anthropologist, 73(2):407-408.
      Ms Mr XIII

Kiste, Robert C.
1972 Relocation and technological change in Micronesia. IN
      Technology and Social Change, H. Russell Bernard and
      Pertti Pelto, eds. New York: Macmillan. pp. 72-107.
      Ms13 Ms24 II4 II7

Kiste, Robert C.
1974 The Bikinians: A Study in Forced Migration. The Kiste and
      Ogan Social Change Series in Anthropology. Menlo Park,
      California: Cummings Publishing Co. 212 pp. Reviewed:
      1975 by Mac Marshall, American Anthropologist, 77:in press.
      [see Georgia Center for Continuing Education 1974].
      Ms13 Ms24 II7

Kiste, Robert C.
1975 Eniwetok resettlement project: Opinions concerning the
      Eniwetok people's reactions to AEC's conclusion that
      northern islands of Eniwetok Atoll may not be Resettled.
      IN Environmental Impact Statement: Cleanup, Rehabilitation,
      Resettlement of Enewetak Atoll--Marshall Islands. Volume
      IIA of IV. Washington, D.C.: Defense Nuclear Agency.
      Ms11 XV XVII

Kiste, Robert C.
1975 Micronesia: The politics of the Colonized. Review of Carl
      Heine, Micronesia at the Crossroads; and Daniel T. Hughes
      and Sherwood G. Lingenfelter, eds., Political Development
      in Micronesia. Reviews in Anthropology, 2(3):in press.
      M XVII

MAIN BIBLIOGRAPHY

Kiste, Robert C. and Michael A. Rynkiewich
    n.d.   Incest and exogamy: A comparative study of two Marshall
           Island Populations. IN Incest Prohibitions in Polynesia
           and Micronesia, Vern Carroll, ed. ASAO Monograph Series.
           Honolulu: University Press of Hawaii, forthcoming.
           Ms9 Ms13 II1

Kiste, Robert C. and Paul D. Schaefer
    1974   Review of Conrad Bentzen in collaboration with Mel Sloan,
           "Mokil," a documentary film. American Anthropologist,
           76(3):715-717.
           Pn6 II

Klarwill, P. E.
    1955   Review of Erhard Schlesier, Die Erscheinungsformen des
           Männerhauses und das Klubwesen in Mikronesien. [The char-
           acteristic forms taken by men's houses and the nature of
           club life in Micronesia]. Journal of the Polynesian
           Society, 64(2):244.
           M II1 II4

Klingman, Lawrence and Gerald Green
    1950   His Majesty O'Keefe. New York: Charles Scribner's Sons.
           356 pp.
           Y1 IX

Kluge, P. F.
    1947   Operation Crossroads. National Geographic, 91(4):519-530.
           Ms13 XV

Kluge, P. F.
    1968   Official Visitor's Guidebook to the Trust Territory
           of the Pacific Islands. Saipan: Public Information
           Office (in cooperation with the Office of Tourism and
           Economic Development and Air Micronesia). 49 pp.
           M IX

Kluge, P. F.
    1971   Micronesia: America's troubled Pacific Ward. Reader's
           Digest, 99(596):161-164.
           M IX

Knudson, Kenneth E.
    1970   Resource fluctuation, productivity, and social organization
           on Micronesian coral Islands. Ph.D. Dissertation, Univer-
           sity of Oregon, Eugene. Available from University Micro-
           films, Ann Arbor: No. 71-1328.
           M II5

MAIN BIBLIOGRAPHY

Ko, Young Kuk
    1962 The segmental phonemes of Marshallese, including
          spectrographic study of the Vowels. M.S. Thesis,
          Georgetown University, Washington, D.C.
          Ms XIII

Koch, Gerd
    1966 The Polynesian-Micronesian 'Culture Boundary'. Prcceedings
          [Abstracts of Papers] of the 11th Pacific Science Congress,
          22 August-10 September, 1966, Tokyo, 9:2.
          M II

Koerner, D. R.
    1952 Amyotrophic lateral sclerosis on Guam: A clinical study
          and review of the Literature. Annals of Internal Medicine,
          37(6):1204-1220.
          Mr1 XIV

Kohl, Manfred Waldemar
    1971 Lagoon in the Pacific. The Stcry of Truk. Schooley's
          Mountain, New Jersey: Liebenzell Mission. 62 pp.
          T1 II2

Koskinen, Aarne A.
    1964 Review of Byron Bender, A Linguistic Analysis of the
          Place-Names of the Marshall Islands. Journal of the
          Polynesian Society, 73(1):92-94.
          Ms XIII

Kostelnik, Mary B.
    1971 Democracy in Micronesia: An examination of its fcrm and
          Meaning. M.A. Thesis, Ohio State University, Columbus.
          M XVII

Kurland, Leonard T.
    1957 Epidemiologic investigations of amyotrophic lateral scle-
          rosis. III. A genetic interpretation of incidence and
          geographic Distribution. Proceedings of the Staff Meet-
          ings, Mayo Clinic, 32(17):449-462.
          Mr XIV XVI

Kurland, Leonard T.
    1963 High incidence of neurological disease in an island popu-
          lation. IN The Genetics of Migrant and Isolate Populations,
          Elizabeth Goldschmidt, ed. Baltimore: Published for the
          Association for the Aid of Crippled Children by the Williams
          and Wilkins Co. pp. 195-214.
          Mr1 XIV XVI

Kurland, Leonard T.; Asao Hirano; Nathan Malamud; and Simmons Lessell
    1961 Parkinsonism-dementia complex, an endemic disease on the
          island of Guam: Clinical, pathological, genetic and epi-
          demiological Features. Transactions of the American
          Neurological Association for 1961, 86:115-120.
          Mr1 XIV XVI

Kurland, Leonard T. and Donald W. Mulder
    1954 Epidemiologic investigations of amyotrophic lateral scle-
          rosis. 1. Preliminary report on geographic distribution,
          with special reference to the Mariana Islands, including
          clinical and pathologic Observations. Neurology, 4(5):
          355-378; 4(6):438-448.
          Mr XIV XVI

Kurland, Leonard T. and Donald W. Mulder
    1955 Epidemiologic investigations of amyotrophic lateral scle-
          rosis. 2. Familial aggregations indicative of dominant
          Inheritance. Neurolcgy, 5(3):182-196; 5(4):249-268.
          Mr XIV XVI

Labarthe, Darwin; Dwayne Reed; Jacob A. Brody; and Reuel Stallones
    1972 Health effects of modernization in Palau. American Journal
          of Epidemiology, 98(3):161-174.
          PL1 II7 XIV

Labby, David
    n.d. Incest as cannibalism: The Yapese Analysis. IN Incest
          Prohibitions in Polynesia and Micronesia, Vern Carroll,
          ed. ASAO Monograph Series. Honolulu: University Press
          of Hawaii, forthcoming.
          Y1 II1

Labby, David
    1972 The anthropology of others: An analysis of the traditional
          ideology of Yap, Western Caroline Islands. Ph.D. Disserta-
          tion, University of Chicago, Chicago.
          Y1 II1

Labby, David
    1973 Old Glory and the new Yap. Natural History, 82(6):26-37.
          Y1 II7

Lane, Capt. Dwight A.
    1972 Micronesia and Self-Determination. IN National Security
          and International Trusteeship in the Pacific, W.R. Louis, ed.
          Annapolis: Naval Institute Press. pp. 67-79.
          M XV XVII

Lang, Werner
    1951   Steinbauten in Mikronesien. [Stone buildings in Micronesia].
           Ph.D. Dissertation, Georg-August Universität, Göttingen.
           M II4 III

Latta, F. Christian
    1972   On stress and vowel harmony in Chamorro. Oceanic Ling-
           uistics, 11(2):140-151.
           Mr XIII

Lattimore, Eleanor
    1945   Pacific Ocean or American Lake? Far Eastern Survey,
           14(22):313-316.
           P XV XVII

Laubenfels, M. W. de
    1950   Native Navigators. Research Reviews [Office of Naval
           Research], June, pp. 7-12.
           M X

Lawrence, Pensile and John E. de Young
    1958   The use of names in Ponapean Society. IN The Use of Names
           in Micronesia, John E. de Young, ed. Anthropological Work-
           ing Papers, No. 3. Guam: Office of the Staff Anthropolo-
           gist, Trust Territory of the Pacific Islands. pp. 55-79.
           Pn1 II

Lee, Kee-dong
    n.d.   A Kusaien-English Dictionary. PALI Language Texts: Micro-
           nesia. Honolulu: University Press of Hawaii, forthcoming.
           K XIII

Lee, Kee-dong
    n.d.   A Reference Grammar of Kusaiean. PALI Language Texts: Micro-
           nesia. Honolulu: University Press of Hawaii, forthcoming.
           K XIII

Lee, Kee-dong
    1972   Some derivational rules of Kusaiean. Working Papers in
           Linguistics, 4(1):45-69. Honolulu: Department of
           Linguistics, University of Hawaii.
           K XIII

Lee, Kee-dong
    1973   Verbal aspect in Kusaiean and Ponapean. Working Papers
           in Linguistics, 5(9):23-66. Honolulu: Department of
           Linguistics, University of Hawaii.
           K Pn1 XIII

MAIN BIBLIOGRAPHY

Leon Guerrero, Wilfred P. and Robert Ota
    1974 Implications of the Land-Grant status of the University of
          Guam to the development of the Territory of Guam. Guam
          Recorder, n.s., 4(2):44-48.
          Mr1 VII

Lessa, William A.
    n.d. The apotheosis of Marespa. IN Directions in Pacific Tradi-
          tional Literature: Essays in Honor of Katharine Luomala,
          Adrienne L. Kaeppler and H. Arlo Nimmo, eds. B.P. Bishop
          Museum Special Publication, No. 61. Honolulu: Bishop
          Museum Press, in press.
          Y3 II2 VIII

Lessa, William A.
    1950 The place of Ulithi in the Yap Empire. Human Organization,
          9(1):16-18.
          Y3 II3

Lessa, William A.
    1950 The Ethnography of Ulithi Atoll. CIMA Report, No. 28.
          Washington, D.C.: Pacific Science Board. 269 pp.
          Y3 II

Lessa, William A.
    1950 Ulithi and the outer native World. American Anthropologist,
          52(1):27-52.
          Y3 II

Lessa, William A.
    1952 Review of Ward H. Goodenough, Property, Kin, and Community
          on Truk. American Anthropologist, 54(4):540-541.
          T1 II1

Lessa, William A.
    1953 Neueste Amerikanische ethnologische Forschung in Ozeania.
          [The most recent American ethnographic research in
          Oceania]. Zeitschrift für Ethnologie, 78(2):224-230.
          P II

Lessa, William A.
    1955 Depopulation on Ulithi. Human Biology, 27(3):161-183.
          Y3 XVI

Lessa, William A.
    1955 Review of Edwin G. Burrows and Melford E. Spiro, An Atoll
          Culture, Ethnography of Ifaluk in the Central Carolines.
          American Anthropologist, 57(5):1090.
          Y11 II

Lessa, William A.
    1955 Review of Edwin G. Burrows and Melford E. Spiro, An Atoll
          Culture, Ethnography of Ifaluk in the Central Carolines.
          Journal of the Polynesian Society, 64(1):171.
          Y11 II

Lessa, William A.
    1956 Myth and blackmail in the Western Carolines. Journal of
          the Polynesian Society, 65(1):66-74.
          W VIII

Lessa, William A.
    1956 Oedipus-type tales in Oceania. Journal of American
          Folklore, 69(271):63-73. Reprinted 1965. On the symbolism
          of Oedipus. IN The Study of Folklore, Alan Dundes, ed.
          Englewood Cliffs, New Jersey: Prentice-Hall. pp. 114-125.
          Y3 VIII

Lessa, William A.
    1957 Modified Thematic Apperception Tests of 99 Ulithian Males
          and Females. Microcard Publications of Primary Records in
          Culture and Personality, Vol. 2, No. 26. Madison, Wisconsin:
          The Microcard Foundation. 483 pp.
          Y3 II6

Lessa, William A.
    1959 Divining from knots in the Carolines. Journal of the
          Polynesian Society, 68(3):188-204.
          C II2

Lessa, William A.
    1961 Sorcery on Ifaluk. American Anthropologist, 63(4):817-820.
          [see Beauclair 1963; Spiro 1961].
          Y11 II2

Lessa, William A.
    1961 Tales from Ulithi Atoll: A Comparative Study in Oceanic
          Folklore. University of California Publications, Folklore
          Studies, No. 13. Berkeley and Los Angeles: University of
          California Press. 493 pp. Reviewed: 1963 by John L.
          Fischer, American Anthropologist, 65(3), Part 1:746-747.
          Y3 VIII

Lessa, William A.
    1962 The decreasing power of myth on Ulithi. Journal of
          American Folklore, 75(296):153-159. Reprinted 1965. IN
          Reader in Comparative Religion: An Anthropological
          Approach, 2nd edition, William A. Lessa and Evon
          Z. Vogt, eds. New York: Harper and Row. pp. 180-185.
          Y3 VIII

MAIN BIBLIOGRAPHY

Lessa, William A.
  1962 An evaluation of early descriptions of Carolinian Culture.
        Ethnohistory, 9(4):313-403.
        C II9

Lessa, William A.
  1964 The social effects of Typhoon Ophelia (1960) on Ulithi.
        Micronesica, 1(1&2):1-47. Reprinted 1968. IN Peoples
        and Cultures of the Pacific, Andrew P. Vayda, ed. Garden
        City, New York: Natural History Press. pp. 330-379.
        Y3 II7

Lessa, William A.
  1964 Review of John E. de Young, ed., The Use of Names by Micro-
        nesians. Journal of the Polynesian Society, 73(1):95-96.
        M II

Lessa, William A.
  1964 Review of Robert K. McKnight, Mnemonics in Pre-literate
        Palau. Journal of the Polynesian Society, 73(1):94-95.
        PL1 II

Lessa, William A.
  1966 Discoverer-of-the-Sun, mythology as a reflection of Culture.
        Journal of American Folklore, 79(311):3-51. Reprinted 1966.
        IN The Anthropologist Looks at Myth, Melville Jacobs, com-
        piler, and John Greenway, ed. Austin: University of Texas
        Press. pp. 3-51. Reprinted in abridged form 1972. IN
        Mythology, Pierre Maranda, ed. Penguin Modern Sociology
        Readings. Harmondsworth: Penguin Books. pp. 71-110.
        Y3 VIII

Lessa, William A.
  1966 Review of William H. Alkire, Lamotrek Atoll and Inter-Island
        Socioeconomic Ties. American Anthropologist, 68(5):1274-1275.
        Y9 II1

Lessa, William A.
  1966 Ulithi: A Micronesian Design for Living. New York: Holt,
        Rinehart and Winston. 118 pp. Reviewed: 1967 by K.O.L.
        Burridge, Man, n.s., 2(1):155; 1967 by Thomas Gladwin, Amer-
        ican Anthropologist, 69(5):526.
        Y3 II

Lessa, William A.
  1969 The Chinese trigrams in Micronesia. Journal of American
        Folklore, 82(326):353-362.
        M VIII

-138-

Lessa, William A.
    1973 Review of Saul H. Riesenberg, ed., A Residence of Eleven
          Years in New Holland and the Caroline Islands, by James F.
          O'Connell. Journal of Pacific History, 8:222.
          C II9

Lessa, William A.
    1974 Drake in the Marianas? Micronesica, 10(1):7-11.
          Mr XII

Lessa, William A.
    1974 Francis Drake in Mindanao? Journal of Pacific History,
          9:55-64.
          PL1 XII

Lessa, William A.
    1975 Drake's Island of Thieves: Ethnological Sleuthing. Hono-
          lulu: University Press of Hawaii. 289 pp.
          PL1 XII

Lessa, William A.
    1975 The Portuguese discovery of the Iles of Sequeira. Micro-
          nesica, 11(1):35-70.
          Y PL XII

Lessa, William A. and Tracy Lay
    1953 The somatology of Ulithi Atoll. American Journal of
          Physical Anthropology, 11(3):405-412.
          Y3 XVI

Lessa, William A. and George C. Meyers
    1962 Population dynamics of an atoll Community. Population
          Studies, 15(3):244-257.
          Y3 XVI

Lessa, William A. and Marvin Spiegelman
    1954 Ulithian Personality as Seen Through Ethnological Materials
          and Thematic Test Analysis. University of California
          Publications in Culture and Society, 2(5):243-301. Berkeley
          and Los Angeles: University of California Press. Reviewed:
          1955 by Anthony F.C. Wallace, American Anthropologist, 57(2),
          Part 1:392-393.
          Y3 II6

Lessell, Simmons; Asao Hirano; Jose M. Torres; and Leonard T. Kurland
    1962 Parkinson-dementia complex. Epidemiological considerations
          in the Chamorros of the Mariana Islands and California.
          Archives of Neurology, 7(5):377-385.
          Mr XIV

MAIN BIBLIOGRAPHY

Lessell, Simmons, Jose M. Torres, and Leonard T. Kurland
    1962 Seizure disorders in a Guamanian Village. Archives of
          Neurology, 7(1):37-44.
          Mr1 XIV

Lester, Mark
    1966 Lessons in Ponapean. Honolulu: University of Hawaii Peace
          Corps Training Center. Mimeographed.
          Pn1 XIII

Levi, Warner
    1948 American attitudes toward Pacific Islands, 1914-1919.
          Pacific Historical Review, 17(1):55-64.
          P XVII

Levy, Robert I.
    1969 Personality Studies in Polynesia and Micronesia, Stability
          and Change. Social Science Research Institute Working
          Papers, No. 8. Honolulu: Social Science Research Insti-
          tute, University of Hawaii. 55 pp.
          M II6

Lewis, David
    1969 Navigational techniques of the early Polynesians and
          Micronesians. Journal of the Australian Institute of
          Navigation, 3(2):1-16.
          M X

Lewis, David
    1970 A return voyage between Puluwat and Saipan using Micronesian
          navigational Techniques. Journal of the Polynesian Society,
          80(4):437-448.
          T4 X

Lewis, David
    1970 Polynesian and Micronesian navigational Techniques.
          Journal of the Institute of Navigation, 23(4):432-447.
          M X

Lewis, David
    1971 'Expanding' the target in indigenous Navigation.
          Journal of Pacific History, 6:83-95.
          T4 X

Lewis, David
    1972 The Gospel according to St. Andrew. Journal of Pacific
          History, 7:223-225. [see Sharp 1972].
          P X

MAIN BIBLIOGRAPHY

Lewis, David
    1972 We, the Navigators. The Ancient Art of Landfinding
          in the Pacific. Honolulu: University Press of Hawaii.
          345 pp. Reviewed: 1973 by Gordon R. Lewthwaite, Journal of
          Pacific History, 8:224-225; 1973 by Amani Racule, Pacific
          Perspective, 2(1):57-58; 1974 by M.W. Richey, The Geograph-
          ical Journal, 140(1):114-117; 1975 by F. Raymond Fosberg,
          Atoll Research Bulletin, No. 185:32; 1975 by Philip R.
          Devita, American Anthropologist, 77(2):408-409.
          P X

Lewis, David
    1974 Wind, wave, star and Bird. National Geographic,
          146(6):746-755, 770-781.
          T4 X

Lewis, J. L.
    n.d. Kusaien Acculturation. CIMA Report, No. 17. Washington,
  [1948] D.C.: Pacific Science Board. 139 pp. Reprinted 1967.
          Kusaien Acculturation 1824-1948. Saipan: Division of
          Land Management, Resources and Development, Trust Ter-
          ritory of the Pacific Islands. 99 pp.
          K II7

Lewthwaite, Gordon R.
    1973 Review of David Lewis, We, the Navigators. Journal
          of Pacific History, 8:224-225.
          P X

Leysne, Humphrey W.
    1952 Food for Kili. Micronesian Monthly [now called Micro-
          nesian Reporter], 1(5):4, 9, 18.
          Ms24 II7

LeBar, Frank M.
    1951 Trukese material culture, a study in analytical Method.
          Ph.D. Dissertation, Yale University, New Haven. Pub-
          lished 1952. CIMA Report, No. 13. Washington, D.C.:
          Pacific Science Board. Reprinted 1964. The Material
          Culture of Truk. Yale University Publications in Anthro-
          pology, No. 68. New Haven: Yale University Press.
          185 pp. Reviewed: 1967 by D.R. Moore, Archaeology and
          Physical Anthropology in Oceania, 2(2):168.
          T1 II4

LeBar, Frank M.
    1963 Some aspects of canoe and house construction on Truk.
          Ethnology, 2(1):55-69.
          T1 II4

MAIN BIBLIOGRAPHY

LeBar, Frank M.
    1964 A household survey of economic goods on Romonum Island,
          Truk. IN Explorations in Cultural Anthropology, Essays
          in Honor of G.P. Murdock, Ward H. Goodenough, ed. New
          York: McGraw-Hill. pp. 335-349.
          T1 II4 II10

Libby, W. F.
    1952 Chicago radiocarbon dates, III. Science, 116:673-681.
          [dates for Saipan and Tinian series collected by Alexander
          Spoehr reported on pp. 680-681].
          Mr4 III

Lieber, Michael D.
    n.d. The process of change: A relocated Kapingamarangi community
          on Ponape. IN Exiles and Migrants in Oceania, Michael D.
          Lieber, ed. ASAO Monograph Series. Honolulu: University
          Press of Hawaii, forthcoming.
          Pn1 Pn9 II7

Lieber, Michael D.
    n.d. Incest and responsibility on Kapingamarangi. IN Incest
          Prohibitions in Polynesia and Micronesia, Vern Carroll,
          ed. ASAO Monograph Series. Honolulu: University Press
          of Hawaii, forthcoming.
          Pn9 II1

Lieber, Michael D., ed.
    n.d. Exiles and Migrants in Oceania. ASAO Monograph Series.
          Honolulu: University Press of Hawaii, forthcoming.
          P II7

Lieber, Michael D.
    1968 The nature of the relationship between kinship and land
          tenure on Kapingamarangi Atoll. Ph.D. Dissertation, Univer-
          sity of Pittsburgh, Pittsburgh. Available from University
          Microfilms, Ann Arbor: No. 69-12710.
          Pn9 II1

Lieber, Michael D.
    1968 Kapingamarangi: Kinship Terminology. Paper read at
          the 67th Annual Meeting of the American Anthropological
          Association, 21-24 November, Seattle.
          Pn9 II1

Lieber, Michael D.
    1968 Porakiet: A Kapingamarangi Colony on Ponape. Eugene:
          Department of Anthropology, University of Oregon. 228 pp.
          Reviewed: 1969 by H.E. Maude, Journal of Pacific History,
          4:230-231.
          Pn1 Pn9 II7

Lieber, Michael D.
    1968   Review of Kenneth P. Emory, Kapingamarangi: Social and
           Religious Life of a Polynesian Atoll. Journal of Pacific
           History, 3:229.
           Pn9 II

Lieber, Michael D.
    1970   Adoption on Kapingamarangi. IN Adoption in Eastern
           Oceania, Vern Carroll, ed. ASAO Monograph No. 1.
           Honolulu: University of Hawaii Press. pp. 158-205.
           Pn9 II1

Lieber, Michael D.
    1970   Review of Saul H. Riesenberg, The Native Polity cf Ponape.
           American Anthropologist, 72(4):899-900.
           Pn1 II3

Lieber, Michael D.
    1973   To be 'only a woman' on Kapingamarangi: The penultimate
           Insult? Paper read at the 2nd Annual Meeting of the
           Association for Social Anthropology in Oceania, 21-25 March,
           Orcas Island, Washington.
           Pn9 II1

Lieber, Michael D.
    1974   Land tenure on Kapingamarangi. IN Land Tenure in Oceania,
           Henry Lundsgaarde, ed. ASAO Monograph No. 2. Honolulu:
           University Press of Hawaii. pp. 70-99.
           Pn9 II1

Lieber, Michael D. and Kalio H. Dikepa
    1974   Kapingamarangi Lexicon. PALI Language Texts: Polynesia.
           Honolulu: University Press of Hawaii. 382 pp.
           Pn9 XIII

Lincoln, Cdr. John R.
    1972   The Mariana Islands. IN National Security and
           International Trusteeship in the Pacific, W.R. Louis
           ed. Annapolis: Naval Institute Press. pp. 119-132.
           Mr XV XVII

Lingenfelter, Richard E.
    1967   Presses of the Pacific Islands, 1817-1867. A History
           of the First Half Century of Printing in the Pacific
           Islands. Los Angeles: The Plantin Press. 132 pp.
           P XII

MAIN BIBLIOGRAPHY

Lingenfelter, Sherwood G.
    1971 The process of elite formation in a changing Micronesian
          Society. Paper read at the 70th Annual Meeting of the
          American Anthropological Association, 18-21 November, New
          York City.
          Y1 II3 II7

Lingenfelter, Sherwood G.
    1971 Social structure and political change in Yap. Ph.D. Disser-
          tation, University of Pittsburgh, Pittsburgh. Available
          from University Microfilms, Ann Arbor: No. 72-7562.
          Y1 II1 II3

Lingenfelter, Sherwood G.
    1973 Action group formation and cultural differentiation
          of land and sea activities in Yap, Western Caroline
          Islands. Paper read at the 72nd Annual Meeting of the
          American Anthropological Association, 28 November-
          2 December, New Orleans.
          Y1 II1

Lingenfelter, Sherwood G.
    1974 Administrative officials, Peace Corps lawyers, and directed
          change on Yap. IN Political Development in Micronesia, Dan-
          iel T. Hughes and Sherwood G. Lingenfelter, eds. Columbus:
          Ohio State University Press. pp. 54-71.
          Y1 II3 II7

Lingenfelter, Sherwood G.
    1975 Yap: Political Leadership and Culture Change in an Island
          Society. Honolulu: University Press of Hawaii. 271 pp.
          Y1 II3 II7

Lisco, Herman and Robert Conard
    1967 Chromosome studies on Marshall Islanders exposed to
          fallout Radiation. Science, 157(3787):445-447.
          Ms15 XVI

Loeb, E. M.
    1947 Social organization and the long house in Southeast
          Asia and Micronesia. Far Eastern Quarterly [now called
          Journal of Asian Studies], 6(2):168-172.
          M II1

Logan-Smith, Nat
    1962 A descriptive analysis of the personnel program for
          the Micronesian employees of the government of the
          Trust Territory of the Pacific Islands. M.A. Thesis,
          University of Hawaii, Honolulu.
          M XVII

MAIN BIBLIOGRAPHY

Long, Austin
    1965   Smithsonian Institution radiocarbon measurements II.
           Radiocarbon, 7:245-256. [published by the American
           Journal of Science, Yale University; dates for Ponape series
           collected by Clifford Evans, Betty Meggers, and Saul H.
           Riesenberg reported cn pp. 253-254].
           Pn1 III

Loomis, Albertine
    1970   To All People. A History of the Hawaii Conference of the
           United Church of Christ. Honolulu: United Church of Christ,
           and Kingsport, Tennessee: Kingsport Press. 417 pp.
           M II2 XII

Lopinot, Callistus, O.F.M. Cap.
    1964   Die Karolinenmission der Spanischen und deutschen Kapuziner,
           1886-1919. [The Caroline Mission of the Spanish and Ger-
           man Capuchins, 1886-1919]. Rome. 29 pp. Translated from
           the German by the Micronesian Seminar and reprinted 1966.
           Moen, Truk: Micronesian Seminar. 56 pp.
           C II2

Lord, Anthony S.
    1971   Landholding groups: A new solution to an old problem,
           Mokil Atcll, Micronesia. Paper read at the 70th Annual
           Meeting of the American Anthropological Association,
           18-21 November, New York City.
           Pn6 II1

Lord, Anthony S.
    1974   Acculturation and cultural identity: The Mokilese Case.
           Paper read at the 3rd Annual Meeting of the Association for
           Social Anthropology in Oceania, 13-17 March, Asilomar,
           Pacific Grove, California.
           Pn6 II7

Lorrach, P. von
    1953   Grammatik der Yap-Sprache in Mikronesien. [Grammar of the
           Yapese language in Micronesia]. Anthropos, Micrc-Bibliotheca,
           Vol. 6. Freiburg, Suisse: Anthropos Institut. 431 pp.
           Y1 XIII

Louis, William Roger, ed.
    1972   National Security and International Trusteeship in the
           Pacific. Annapolis: Naval Institute Press. 182 pp.
           Reviewed: 1975 by T.B. Millar, Journal of Pacific History,
           10(2):125-126.
           M XV XVII

MAIN BIBLIOGRAPHY

Lundsgaarde, Henry P., ed.
    1974 Land Tenure in Oceania. ASAO Monograph No. 2. Honolulu:
          University Press of Hawaii. 288 pp.
          P II1

Luomala, Katharine
    1949 Micronesian Mythology. IN Standard Dictionary of Folklore,
          Myth and Legend, Maria Leach, ed. Volume 2. New York:
          Funk and Wagnalls. pp. 717-722.
          M VIII

Luomala, Katharine
    1951 Micronesian informants as Collectors. Journal
          of American Folklore, 64(252):221.
          M VIII

Luomala, Katharine
    1958 Review of Alfred Tetens, Among the Savages of the
          South Seas, translated by Florence M. Spoehr.
          American Anthropologist, 60(6), Part 1:1232-1233.
          M XII

Luomala, Katharine
    1963 Review of Edwin G. Burrows, Flower in My Ear, Arts
          and Ethos of Ifaluk Atoll. Pacific Historical Review,
          32(4):419-420.
          Y11 VIII

Luomala, Katharine
    1966 Numskull clans and tales: Their structure and function in
          asymmetrical joking Relationships. Journal of American Folk-
          lore, 79(311):157-194. Reprinted 1966. IN The Anthropolo-
          gist Looks at Myth, Melville Jacobs, compiler, and John
          Greenway, ed. Austin: University of Texas Press. pp. 157-194
          M VIII

Luomala, Katharine
    1968 Review of Kenneth P. Emory, Kapingamarangi, Social and
          Religious Life of a Polynesian Atoll. Journal of
          American Folklore, 81(319):86-87.
          Pn9 II

Lyman, Richard, Jr.
    1946 Report on the Marshalls, Carolines and Marianas. IN U.S.
          Commercial Company's Economic Survey of Micronesia, Report
          No. 16. Honolulu: U.S. Commercial Company. Mimeographed.
          32 pp.
          M VI

MAIN BIBLIOGRAPHY

Mackenzie, J. Boyd
    1960 Breadfruit cultivation practices and beliefs in the
          Marshall Islands. Anthropological Working Papers, No. 8.
          Guam: Office of the Staff Anthropologist, Trust Territory
          of the Pacific Islands. 17 pp.
          Ms I

Mackenzie, J. Boyd
    1961 Population and economy of Jaluit. Atoll Research Bulletin,
          No. 75:81-87.
          Ms23 II7 X

MacMeekin, Daniel H.
    1975 Land law and change cn Truk. IN The Impact of Urban Centers
          in the Pacific, Roland W. Force and Brenda Bishop, eds.
          Honolulu: Pacific Science Association, Bishop Museum.
          pp. 145-162.
          T1 II1 II7

MacMillan, Howard G.
    1946 Report on agricultural conditions in Micronesia. IN U.S.
          Commercial Company's Economic Survey of Micronesia, Report
          No. 11. Honolulu: U.S. Commercial Company. Mimeographed.
          52 pp.
          M I

MacQuarrie, Alan M.
    1969 The effects of political modernization in Micronesia: The
          job of Nation-Building. IN Political Modernization of
          Micronesia, A Symposium. Santa Cruz, California: Center
          for South Pacific Studies. 12 pp.
          M II3

Mahone, Rene C.
    1974 Biography of Guam's last Spaniard. Guam Recorder, n.s.,
          4(1):16-19.
          Mr1 XII

Mahoney, Francis B.
    1950 Projective psychological findings in Palau Personality.
          M.A. Thesis, University of Chicago, Chicago. Also CIMA
          Report, No. 22. Washington, D.C.: Pacific Science Board.
          PL1 II6

Mahoney, Francis B.
    1957 Rorschachs and Modified TATs of 120 Palau Men and Women.
          Microcard Publications of Primary Records in Culture and
          Personality, Volume 2. Madison, Wisconsin: The Microcard
          Foundation.
          PL1 II6

Mahoney, Francis B.
1958 Land tenure patterns on Yap Island. IN Land Tenure Pat-
terns in the Trust Territory of the Pacific Islands, John
E. de Young, ed. Guam: Office of the Staff Anthropologist,
Trust Territory of the Pacific Islands. pp. 251-287.
Y1 II1

Mahoney, Francis B.
1961 Micronesia. Encyclopaedia Britannica, 15:430. Chicago:
Encyclopaedia Britannica, Inc.
M II

Mahoney, Francis B.
1974 Social and Cultural Factors Relating to the Cause and
Control of Alcohol Abuse Among Micronesian Youth.
Prepared for the Government of the Trust Territory
of the Pacific Islands under Contract: TT 174-8 with
James R. Leonard Associates, Inc., Washington, D.C. 78 pp.
M II7

Mahony, Frank J.
1957 The innovation of a savings institution on Moen Island,
Truk: A preliminary Report. Anthropological Working Papers,
No. 2. Guam: Office of the Staff Anthropologist, Trust
Territory of the Pacific Islands. 51 pp. Revised and
reprinted 1960. American Anthropologist, 62(3):465-482.
T1 II8 II10

Mahony, Frank J.
1958 Trukese Names. IN The Use of Names in Micronesia, John E.
de Young, ed. Anthropological Working Papers, No. 3. Guam:
Office of the Staff Anthropologist, Trust Territory of the
Pacific Islands. pp. 80-98.
T1 II

Mahony, Frank J.
1959 Anthropology and public Health. South Pacific Bulletin,
9(4):54-59.
M II8

Mahony, Frank J.
1960 Taro cultivation in Ponape. IN Taro Cultivation Practices
and Beliefs, Part II (The Eastern Carolines and the Marshall
Islands), John E. de Young, ed. Anthropological Working
Papers, No. 6. Guam: Office of the Staff Anthropologist,
Trust Territory of the Pacific Islands. pp. 99-132.
Pn1 I

Mahony, Frank J.
     1960   Taro cultivation in Truk. IN Taro Cultivation Practices
            and Beliefs, Part II (The Eastern Carolines and the Mar-
            shall Islands), John E. de Young, ed. Anthropolcgical
            Working Papers, No. 6. Guam: Office of the Staff Anthropo-
            logist, Trust Territcry of the Pacific Islands. pp. 69-98.
            T I

Mahony, Frank J.
     1970   A Trukese theory of Medicine. Ph.D. Dissertation,
            Stanford University, Stanford, California. Available
            from University Microfilms, Ann Arbor: No. 70-18439.
            T1 XIV

Mahony, Frank J. and Pensile Lawrence
     1959   Ponapean yam Cultivation. IN Yam Cultivation in the
            Trust Territory, John E. de Young, ed. Anthropological
            Working Papers, No. 4. Guam: Office of the Staff Anthropo-
            logist, Trust Territory of the Pacific Islands. pp. 1-13.
            Pn1 I

Maki, John M.
     1947   US strategic area or UN Trusteeship? Far Eastern Survey,
            16(15):175-178.
            M XVII

Malamud, Nathan, Asao Hirano, and Leonard T. Kurland
     1961   Pathoanatomic changes in amyotrophic lateral sclerosis on
            Guam with special reference to the occurrence of neurofi-
            brillary Changes. Archives of Neurology, 5(4):401-415.
            Mr1 XIV

Malcolm, Sheila
     1955   Diet and Nutrition in the Trust Territory of the Pacific
            Islands: A Survey. South Pacific Commission Technical
            Paper, No. 83. Noumea: South Pacific Commission. 41 pp.
            M XIV

Malcolm, Sheila
     1958   The Diet of Mothers and Children on the Island of
            Guam. South Pacific Ccmmission Technical Paper,
            No. 113. Noumea: South Pacific Commission. 35 pp.
            Mr1 XIV

Manchester, Curtis A.
     1951   The Caroline Islands. IN Geography of the Pacific, Otis W.
            Freeman, ed. New York: John Wiley and Sons. pp. 236-269.
            C X

MAIN BIBLIOGRAPHY

Mancill, Grace S. and Frances S. Woods
    1969 Morphology and syntax of Palauan Nominals. Languages
          and Linguistics, 4(1):31-67.
          PL1 XIII

Mander-Jones, Phyllis
    1967 A guide to manuscripts in the British Isles relating
          to Australia, New Zealand, and the Pacific Islands.
          Journal of Pacific History, 2:189-190.
          P XII

Mander, Linden A.
    1956 The U.N. Mission's 1956 survey of the Pacific Trust
          Territory. Pacific Affairs, 29(2):367-374.
          M XVII

Maramba, Manuela G.
    1960 The economics of food and nutrition in the United States
          Trust Territory of the Pacific Islands, April 25-June 2,
          1959. South Pacific Commission Technical Informaticn
          Circular, No. 39. Noumea: South Pacific Commission. 35 pp.
          M XIV

Marck, Jeffrey C.
    1974 A lexico-statistical model for nuclear Micronesian origins,
          settlement, and post colonization cultural Interaction.
          Paper read at the 53rd Annual Meeting of the Central States
          Anthropological Society, 27-30 March, Chicago. [Central
          States Student Prize Paper for 1974].
          M III XIII

Marck, Jeffrey C.
    1975 The origin and dispersal of the Proto Nuclear Micronesians.
          M.A. Thesis, University of Iowa, Iowa City.
          M III XIII

Markwith, Carl
    1946 Farewell to Bikini. National Geographic, 90(1):97-116.
          Ms13 IX

Marshall, Colin
    1951 Report on forestry in the Trust Territory of the Pacific
          Islands. SIM Report, No. 14. Washington, D.C.: Pacific
          Science Board. 94 pp.
          M I

Marshall, J. T., Jr.
    1951 Vertebrate ecology of Arno Atoll, Marshall Islands. Atoll
          Research Bulletin, No. 3:1-38.
          Ms9 XIX

MAIN BIBLIOGRAPHY

Marshall, Mac
    n.d.   Incest and endogamy on Namoluk Atoll. IN Incest Prohibi-
           tions in Polynesia and Micronesia, Vern Carroll, ed. ASAO
           Monograph Series. Honolulu: University Press of Hawaii,
           forthcoming.
           T10 II1

Marshall, Mac
    n.d.   Solidarity or sterility? Adoption and fosterage on Namoluk
           Atoll. IN Transactions in Kinship: Adoption and Fosterage
           in Oceania, Ivan Brady, ed. ASAO Monograph No. 4. Hono-
           lulu: University Press of Hawaii, in press.
           T10 II1

Marshall, Mac
    1971   Notes on birds from Namoluk Atoll. Micronesica, 7(1&2):
           234-236.
           T10 XIX

Marshall, Mac
    1972   Of cats and rats and Toxoplasma gondii at Namoluk. Micro-
           nesian Reporter, 20(2):30-31.
           T10 XIV

Marshall, Mac [Keith]
    1972   The structure of solidarity and alliance on Namoluk Atoll.
           Ph.D. Dissertation, University of Washington, Seattle.
           Available from University Microfilms, Ann Arbor: No. 72-28629.
           T10 II1

Marshall, Mac
    1974   Research bibliography of alcohol and kava studies in
           Oceania. Micronesica, 10(2):299-306.
           P IX

Marshall, Mac
    1974   Review of Robert Wenkam and Byron Baker, Micronesia:
           The Breadfruit Revolution. American Anthropologist,
           76(3):598-599.
           M IX

Marshall, Mac
    1975   The natural history of Namoluk Atoll, Eastern Caroline
           Islands. Atoll Research Bulletin, No. 189. 53 pp.
           T10 V XIX

Marshall, Mac
    1975   The politics of prohibition on Namoluk Atoll. Journal of
           Studies on Alcohol [formerly called Quarterly Journal of
           Studies on Alcohol], 36(5):597-610.
           T10 II3

MAIN BIBLIOGRAPHY

Marshall, Mac
    1975 Changing patterns of marriage and migration on Namoluk
         Atoll. IN Pacific Atoll Populations, Vern Carroll, ed.
         ASAO Monograph No. 3. Honolulu: University Press of
         Hawaii. pp. 160-211.
         T10 II1 XVI

Marshall, Mac
    1975 Review of Robert C. Kiste, The Bikinians: A Study in Forced
         Migration. American Anthropologist, 77:in press.
         Ms13 Ms24 II

Marshall, Mac and Mark Borthwick
    1974 Consensus, dissensus, and Guttman scales: The Namoluk Case.
         Journal of Anthropolcgical Research [formerly called
         Southwestern Journal of Anthropology], 30(4):in press.
         T10 II3

Marshall, Mac and Leslie B. Marshall
    1975 Holy and unholy spirits: The effects of missionization on
         alcohol use in Eastern Micronesia. Paper read at the 4th
         Annual Meeting of the Association for Social Anthropology
         in Oceania, 26-30 March, Stuart, Florida.
         M II2 XII

Marshall, Mac and Leslie B. Marshall
    1975 Opening Pandora's bottle: Reconstructing Micronesians'
         early contacts with alcoholic Beverages. Paper read at
         the 4th Annual Meeting of the Association for Social
         Anthropology in Oceania, 26-30 March, Stuart, Florida.
         M II7 XII

Marston, Geoffrey
    1969 Termination of Trusteeship. International and Comparative
         Law Quarterly, 18(1):1-40.
         M XVII

Maruyama, Michiro
    1954 Anatahan. Translated from the Japanese by Younghill Kang.
         New York: Hermitage House. 206 pp.
         Mr6 IX

Masland, Richard L., Seymour B. Sarason, and Thomas Gladwin
    1958 Mental Subnormality: Biological, Psychological, and Cul-
         tural Factors. New York: Basic Books. 422 pp.
         T1 II6 XVIII

Mason, Arnold C.; Gilbert Corwin; Cleaves L. Rodgers; Paul C. Elmquist;
    Anton J. Vessel; and Ralph J. McCracken
    1956 Military Geology of Palau Islands, Caroline Islands. Pre-
          pared under the direction of the Chief of Engineers, U.S.
          Army, by the Intelligence Division, Office of the Engineer,
          Headquarters, U.S. Army Forces Far East and 8th U.S. Army
          (Rear), with personnel of the U.S. Geological Survey. Wash-
          ington, D.C.: Department of the Army. Mimeographed. 285 pp.
          PL1 XI

Mason, Leonard E.
    1946 The economic organization of the Marshall Islanders. IN
          U.S. Commercial Company's Economic Survey of Micronesia,
          Report No. 9. Honolulu: U.S. Commercial Company. Mimeo-
          graphed. 150 pp. + 29 photographs.
          Ms VI

Mason, Leonard E.
    1948 Micronesia: Isolation or Assimilation? Hawaii Institute
          of Pacific Relations Nctes, 3:1-7.
          M II3

Mason, Leonard E.
    1948 Review of Laura Thompson, Guam and Its People (rev. 3rd ed.).
          Pacific Affairs, 21(1):95.
          Mr1 II

Mason, Leonard E.
    1948 Trusteeship in Micronesia. Far Eastern Survey, 17(9):
          105-108.
          M XVII

Mason, Leonard E.
    1949 The Marshallese look to Uncle Sam. Think, 15(2):5, 32.
          Ms XVII

Mason, Leonard E.
    1950 The Bikinians: A transplanted Population. Human Organ-
          ization, 9(1):5-15.
          Ms13 Ms24 II7

Mason, Leonard E.
    1950 Cultural adaptation of the Bikini Islanders to a new
          Environment. Proceedings of the 25th Annual Meeting of
          the Hawaiian Academy of Science, 1949-1950, p. 5. [abstract].
          Ms13 Ms24 II7

Mason, Leonard E.
    1951 A changing world--Micronesia. Paradise of the Pacific
          [now called Honolulu Magazine], 63(5):14-16.
          M II

MAIN BIBLIOGRAPHY

Mason, Leonard E.
    1951 An interpretation of "native custom" in a changing
         Oceanic Society. IN U.S. Trust Territory of the Pacific
         Islands Basic Information, July, pp. 112-115. Honolulu:
         Office of the High Commissioner. Reprinted 1953. IN Pro-
         ceedings of the 7th Pacific Science Congress, 2 February-
         4 March, 1949, Auckland, New Zealand, 7:95-102.
         M II7 II8

Mason, Leonard E.
    1951 Man in the culture-environment Relationship. Atoll
         Research Bulletin, No. 2:12-13.
         P II5

Mason, Leonard E.
    1951 Marshalls, Gilberts, Ocean Island, and Nauru.
         IN Geography of the Pacific, Otis W. Freeman, ed.
         New York: John Wiley and Sons. pp. 270-297.
         Ms X

Mason, Leonard E.
    1953 Anthropology in American Micronesia: A progress Report.
         Clearinghouse Bulletin of Research in Human Organization,
         2(3):1-5.
         M II

Mason, Leonard E.
    1953 Re-establishment of a copra industry in the Marshall
         Islands. Proceedings of the 7th Pacific Science Congress,
         2 February-4 March, 1949, Auckland, New Zealand, 7:159-162.
         Ms II10

Mason, Leonard E.
    1953 Suggestions for investigating the culture of atoll People.
         IN Handbook for Atoll Research, 2nd preliminary ed., F.
         Raymond Fosberg and Marie-Helene Sachet, eds. Atoll
         Research Bulletin, No. 17:111-115.
         M II

Mason, Leonard E.
    1954 Relocation of the Bikini Marshallese: A study in group
         Migration. Ph.D. Dissertation, Yale University, New
         Haven. Available from University Microfilms, Ann Arbor:
         No. 70-12452.
         Ms13 Ms24 II7

MAIN BIBLIOGRAPHY

Mason, Leonard E.
    1957 Ecologic change and culture pattern in the resettlement of
          Bikini Marshallese. IN Cultural Stability and Cultural
          Change, Verne F. Ray, ed. Proceedings of the 1957 Annual
          Spring Meeting of the American Ethnological Society.
          Seattle: University cf Washington Press. pp. 1-6.
          Ms13 Ms24 II7 II8

Mason, Leonard E.
    1958 Habitat and social change on Kili Island. Proceedings of the
          Hawaiian Academy of Science, 1957-1958, pp. 21-22. [abstract].
          Ms24 II7

Mason, Leonard E.
    1958 Kili community in Transition. South Pacific Bulletin,
          8(2):32-35, 46.
          Ms24 II7

Mason, Leonard E.
    1959 Space, the scarce commodity in atoll Living. Prcceedings of
          the Hawaiian Academy of Science, 1958-1959, p. 24. [abstract].
          Ms9 II1 II5

Mason, Leonard E.
    1959 Suprafamilial authority and economic process in Micronesian
          Atolls. Humanities,-Cahiers de l'Institut de Science Eco-
          nomique Appliquee, No. 96, November 1959, serie v, No. 1,
          Paris, I.S.E.A. pp. 87-118. Reprinted 1968. IN Peoples
          and Cultures of the Pacific, Andrew P. Vayda, ed. Garden
          City, New York: Natural History Press. pp. 299-329.
          Ms C II1

Mason, Lecnard E.
    1960 Art forms and culture history in Micronesia. Paper read at
          the 59th Annual Meeting of the American Anthropological
          Association, 17-20 November, Minneapolis.
          M III IV

Mason, Leonard E.
    1961 Changing family crganization among Ex-Bikini Marshallese.
          Abstracts of the 10th Pacific Science Congress, 21 August-
          6 September, 1961, Honolulu. Honolulu: Bishop Museum Press.
          pp. 116-117.
          Ms13 Ms24 II7

Mason, Leonard E.
    1962 Habitat, man and Culture. Pacific Viewpcint, 3(2):3-7.
          P II5 X

MAIN BIBLIOGRAPHY

Mason, Leonard E.
    1962 Micronesia. Encyclopaedia Britannica, 15:429-430. Chicago:
          Encyclopaedia Britannica, Inc.
          M II

Mason, Leonard E.
    1963 Changes in decision-making in a displaced Micronesian
          Community. Paper read at the 62nd Annual Meeting of the
          American Anthropological Association, 21-24 November,
          San Francisco, California.
          Ms13 Ms24 II3

Mason, Leonard E.
    1963 Micronesia. IN Enciclopedia Universale dell Arte, Rome,
          11:306-309. [in Italian; also in English edition, Ency-
          clopaedia of World Art, 9:918-930. New York: McGraw-Hill].
          M II

Mason, Leonard E.
    1966 Anthropological and other social science research in the
          Trust Territory of the Pacific Islands. Micronesian Pro-
          gram Bulletin, No. 1. Honolulu: Department of Anthropology,
          University of Hawaii. 7 pp.
          M II

Mason, Leonard E.
    1966 Early Micronesian voyaging: A Comment. Oceania, 37(2):155.
          [see Riesenberg 1965; Sharp 1966].
          M III

Mason, Leonard E.
    1967 The mapping of Majuro Island (Laura). IN The Laura Report,
          Leonard Mason, ed. Honolulu: Department of Anthropology,
          University of Hawaii. 30 pp.
          Ms8 II

Mason, Leonard E.
    1967 Research problems and ethics in Micronesia. A survey
          undertaken for the Committee on Research Problems and
          Ethics, American Anthropological Association, Ralph L.
          Beals, Chairman. Micronesian Program Bulletin (Special
          Issue). Honolulu: Department of Anthropology, Univer-
          sity of Hawaii. 21 pp.
          M II8

Mason, Leonard E., ed.
    1967 The Laura Report. A Field Report of Training and Research
          in Majuro Atoll, Marshall Islands. Honolulu: Department of
          Anthropology, University of Hawaii. 288 pp.
          Ms8 II

MAIN BIBLIOGRAPHY

Mason, Leonard E.
   1968   The ethnology of Micronesia. IN Peoples and Cultures of
          the Pacific, Andrew P. Vayda, ed. Garden City, New York:
          Natural History Press. pp. 275-298.
          M II

Mason, Leonard E.
   1969   Anthropological research in Micronesia, 1954-1968.
          Anthropologica, n.s., 11(1):85-115.
          M II IX

Mason, Leonard E.
   1969   Popular participation in the development of Trust
          Territory Self-Government. IN Political Modernization of
          Micronesia, A Symposium. Santa Cruz, California: Center
          for South Pacific Studies. 6 pp.
          M II3

Mason, Leonard E.
   1972   Comments on political future of Micronesia. Micronesica,
          8(1&2):37-40.
          M II3

Mason, Leonard E.
   1972   La Micronesie. IN Encyclopaedia de la Pleiade: Ethnologie
          Regionale, I[Afrique-Oceanie]:1196-1235. Paris: Gallimard.
          [in French].
          M II

Mason, Leonard E.
   1973   The anthropological presence in Micronesia. Association
          for Anthropology in Micronesia Newsletter, 2(1):19-31.
          [see Gale 1973].
          M II II8

Mason, Leonard E.
   1974   Unity and disunity in Micronesia: Internal problems and
          future Status. IN Political Development in Micronesia,
          Daniel T. Hughes and Sherwood G. Lingenfelter, eds.
          Columbus: Ohio State University Press. pp. 203-262.
          M II3

Mason, Leonard E.
   1975   The many faces of Micronesia: District Center and Outer
          Island Culture. Pacific Asian Studies [University of Guam],
          1(1):5-37.
          M II

Mason, Leonard E., Jack Tobin, and O. Wade
    1950 Anthropology-Geography study of Arno Atoll, Marshall
          Islands. SIM Report, No. 7. Reprinted 1952. Atoll
          Research Bulletin, No. 10. 21 pp.
          Ms9 X

Mason, Leonard E. and Harry Uyehara
    1953 A quantitative study of certain aspects of the man-land
          relationship in Marshallese economy at Arno Island. IN
          Handbook for Atoll Research, (2nd preliminary edition),
          F. Raymond Fosberg and Marie-Helene Sachet, eds. Atoll
          Research Bulletin, No. 17:116-121.
          Ms9 II5 II10

Mathai, K. V.
    1970 Amyotrophic lateral sclerosis and Parkinsonism dementia
          in the Marianas. American Journal of Tropical Medicine
          and Hygiene, 19(1):151-154.
          Mr XIV

Mathiot, Madeline
    1955 Chamorro phonemics with morphophonemic Notes.
          M.S. Thesis, Georgetown University, Washington, D.C.
          Mr XIII

Matsumuro, Kazuaki
    1969 Pepper culture in the Eastern Caroline Islands.
          South Pacific Bulletin, 19(4):39-42.
          Pn1 I

Matthews, William K.
    1950 Characteristics of Micronesian. Lingua, 2(4):419-437.
          M XIII

Maude, H. E.
    1966 Review of Paul Carano and Pedro C. Sanchez, A Complete
          History of Guam. Journal of Pacific History, 1:243-245.
          Mr1 XII

Maude, H. E.
    1969 Review of David Crawford and Leona Crawford, Missionary
          Adventures in the South Pacific. Journal of Pacific
          History, 4:230-231.
          M II2 XII

Maude, H. E.
    1969 Review of Michael D. Lieber, Porakiet: A Kapingamarangi
          Colony on Ponape. Journal of Pacific History, 4:230-231.
          Pn1 Pn9 II7

MAIN BIBLIOGRAPHY

Maude, H. E.
    1969 Review of Saul H. Riesenberg, The Native Polity cf
          Ponape. Journal of Pacific History, 4:230-231.
          Pn1 II3

Mavalwala, Jamshed and Edward E. Hunt, Jr.
    1964 Finger and palm prints of the Micronesians of Yap. Zeit-
          schrift für Morphologie und Anthropologie, 55(1):11-23.
          Y1 XVI

May, Walther
    1957 Die Erziehung in Micronesien. [Education in Micronesia].
          Ph.D. Dissertation, University of Bonn, Bonn.
          M VII

Mayr, Ernst
    1945 The land and fresh-water birds of Micronesia. IN Birds of
          the Southwest Pacific, by Ernst Mayr. New York: Macmillan.
          pp. 283-302.
          M XIX

McCall, Louis Edmund
    1973 A study comparing scholastic achievement, social adjustment
          and moral values of parcchial and public school students at
          the ninth grade level on Guam. Ed.D. Dissertaticn, Southern
          Baptist Theological Seminary, Louisville, Kentucky. Avail-
          able from University Microfilms, Ann Arbor: No. 74-2183.
          Mr1 II2 VII

McCarthy, F. D.
    1958 Review of Alexander Spoehr, Marianas Prehistory.
          Oceania, 28(3):240-241.
          Mr III

McCauley, David P.
    1967 Lessons in Ponapean. Honolulu: University of Hawaii Peace
          Corps Training Center. Mimeographed.
          Pn1 XIII

McCauley, David P. and H. E. S. George
    1966 Lessons in Kusaiean. Honolulu: University of Hawaii Peace
          Corps Training Center. Mimeographed.
          K XIII

McClain, E. G. and R. W. Clopton
    1949 Guamanian Songs. Journal of American Folklore, 62(245):
          217-229.
          Mr1 IV

McClam, Virginia G.
    1971 United States public policy and its implementation in the
          Trust Territory of the Pacific Islands, 1947-1967. Ph.D.
          Dissertation, Harvard University, Cambridge.
          M XVII

McClam, Virginia G.
    1972 The Micronesian Islands: Economic self-sufficiency versus
          political Self-Determination. IN Micronesian Realities:
          Political and Economic, Frances McReynolds Smith, ed.
          Santa Cruz, California: Center for South Pacific Studies.
          pp. 175-193.
          M VI

McCoy, Michael A.
    1973 A renaissance in Carolinian-Marianas Voyaging. Journal of
          the Polynesian Society, 82(4):355-365.
          Mr C X

McCoy, Michael A.
    1973 Fish--something Old. Micronesian Reporter, 21(2):11-14.
          W II5

McCoy, Michael A.
    1974 Man and turtle in the Central Carolines. Micronesica,
          10(2):207-222.
          W II5

McCracken, Ralph J.
    1951 Soil geography of Palau and Saipan. M.A. Thesis, Cornell
          University, Ithaca.
          PL1 Mr2 XI

McCracken, Ralph J.
    1953 A preliminary report on the soils of Saipan, Mariana Is-
          lands. Pacific Science, 7(3):267-277.
          Mr2 XI

McDonald, Hugh
    1949 Trusteeship in the Pacific. Sydney: Angus and Robertson.
          M XVII

McGrath, Thomas B.
    1964 The Micronesian Seminar. The Jesuit, Winter, pp. 9-11.
          M II2

McGrath, Thomas B.
    1968 Anxiety and conformity in traditional Micronesian Life.
          M.A. Thesis, Catholic University, Washington, D.C.
          M II6

MAIN BIBLIOGRAPHY

McGrath, Thomas B.
    1972   The proas of the Marianas.   Guam Recorder, n.s., 1(2&3):
           48-52.
           Mr II4

McGrath, Thomas B.
    1972   Conservation of indigenous cultural heritage in Guam and
           Micronesia: A partial Survey.   Anthropological Forum,
           3(2):189-196.
           M Mr1 II

McGrath, Thomas B.
    1973   Abortion: Some observations about Guam.   Journal
           de la Societe des Oceanistes, 29(39):218-222.
           Mr1 II2 XIV XVI

McGrath, Thomas B.
    1973   The Joachim deBrum Papers.   Journal of Pacific History,
           8:181-185.
           M Ms XII

McGrath, Thomas B.
    1973   Sakau in tomw.   Sarawi in Tomw.   Oceania, 44(1):64-67.
           Reprinted 1973.   Guam Recorder, n.s., 3(3):47-50.
           Pn1 II2

McGrath, William A.
    1971   Resolving the land Dilemma.   Micronesian Repcrter,
           19(1):9-16.
           M II1 XII

McGrath, William A.
    1972   The effects of urban drift in the Palau district of
           Micronesia.   IN Change and Development in Rural Melanesia,
           Marion Ward, ed.   Papers delivered at the 5th Waigani
           Seminar, Port Moresby, Papua-New Guinea.   Canberra:
           Allans Printers.   pp. 130-150.
           PL II7

McGrath, William A. and K. Aaron Mitchell (compilers)
    1971   Trust Territory of the Pacific Islands: 5th Lands and
           Surveys Conference, October 1971, held at District Head-
           quarters, Koror, Palau District.   Vol. 1: Backgrcund
           Papers.   Saipan: Department of Resources and Development,
           Division of Lands and Surveys.   275 pp.
           M X

McGrath, William A. and Walter Scott Wilson
    1971   The Marshall, Caroline and Marianas Islands: Too many for-
           eign Precedents.   IN Land Tenure in the Pacific, Ron Cro-
           combe, ed.   London: Oxford University Press.   pp. 172-191.
           M II1

McIntire, Elliot G. (compiler)
    1960 A Library Brochure: Kapingamarangi Atoll, Caroline Islands,
          William L. Thomas, Jr., ed. Prepared for the Pacific Missile
          Range, Point Mugu, California. Riverside, California: Univ-
          ersity of California at Riverside. 57 pp.
          Pn9 X

McIntire, Elliot G. (compiler)
    1960 Taongi Atoll, Marshall Islands: A Library Summary, William
          L. Thomas, Jr., ed. Prepared for the Pacific Missile Range,
          Point Mugu, California. Riverside, California: University
          of California at Riverside. 17 pp.
          Ms27 X

McKee, Edwin D.
    1956 Geology of Kapingamarangi Atoll, Caroline Islands.
          SIM Report, No. 23. Washington, D.C.: Pacific Science
          Board. 38 pp. Reprinted 1956. Atoll Research Bulletin,
          No. 50. 38 pp. Reprinted 1958. Bulletin of the Geolo-
          gical Society of America, 69(3):241-278.
          Pn9 XI

McKinley, Robert
    1973 Review of Vern Carroll, ed., Adoption in Eastern Oceania.
          Journal of Asian Studies, 32(4):734-737.
          P II1

McKinney, Robert Quentin
    1947 Micronesia under German Rule 1885-1914. M.A. Thesis,
          Stanford University, Stanford, California.
          M XII

McKnight, Robert K.
    n.d. Commas in microcosm: The movement of Southwestern Islanders
          to Palau, Micronesia. IN Exiles and Migrants in Oceania,
          Michael D. Lieber, ed. ASAO Monograph Series. Honolulu:
          University Press of Hawaii, forthcoming.
          PL II7

McKnight, Robert K.
    1958 Palauan Names. IN The Use of Names in Micronesia, John E.
          de Young, ed. Anthropological Working Papers, No. 3. Guam:
          Office of the Staff Anthropologist, Trust Territory of the
          Pacific Islands. pp. 16-54.
          PL1 II

MAIN BIBLIOGRAPHY

McKnight, Robert K.
   1959   The Oyabun-Kobun in Palau, a master-apprentice System.
          Anthropological Working Papers, No. 5. Guam: Office
          of the Staff Anthropologist, Trust Territory of the Pacific
          Islands. 17 pp. Reviewed: 1961 by Allan H. Smith, American
          Anthropologist, 63(2), Part 1:426-428.
          PL1 II7 VII

McKnight, Robert K.
   1960   Breadfruit cultivation practices and beliefs in Palau.
          Anthropological Working Papers, No. 7. Guam: Office
          of the Staff Anthropolcgist, Trust Territory of the
          Pacific Islands. 25 pp. Reviewed: 1961 by Allan H.
          Smith, American Anthropologist, 63(2), Part 1:426-428.
          PL1 I

McKnight, Robert K.
   1960   Competition in Palau. Ph.D. Dissertation, Ohio State
          University, Columbus. Available from University
          Microfilms, Ann Arbor: No. 61-926.
          PL1 II1

McKnight, Robert K.
   1961   The mouth that explains: Mesaod Ngerel, an allegcry in
          Palauan political Lore. Palau Museum Publication, No. 2.
          Koror, Palau Islands. 8 pp.
          PL1 II3 VIII

McKnight, Robert K.
   1961   Mnemonics in preliterate Palau. Anthropological Wcrking
          Papers, No. 9. Guam: Office of the Staff Anthropologist,
          Trust Territory of the Pacific Islands. 36 pp. Reviewed:
          1964 by William A. Lessa, Journal of the Polynesian Society,
          73(1):94-95.
          PL1 II VIII

McKnight, Robert K. [authorship unacknowledged]
   1963   The changing face cf Palauan Custom. Micronesian Reporter,
          11(1):28-32.
          PL1 II7

McKnight, Robert K.
   1964   Handicrafts of the Trust Territory of the Pacific Islands.
          South Pacific Bulletin, 14(2):37-40.
          M II4 IV

McKnight, Robert K.
   1964   Orachl's drawings: Palauan rock Paintings. Micronesian
          Research Working Papers, No. 1. Saipan: Literature Produc-
          tion Center, Trust Territory of the Pacific Islands. 28 pp.
          PL1 IV

McKnight, Robert K.
    1964 Shell inlay: Art of Palau. Micronesian Reporter, 12(2):10-14.
          PL1 II4 IV

McKnight, Robert K.
    1967 Palauan story Boards. Lore, 17(3):82-88.
          PL1 II4 IV

McKnight, Robert K.
    1968 Palauan culture heroes as agents of Change. Paper read
          at the Annual Meeting of the Southwestern Anthropological
          Association, 10-12 April, San Diego, California.
          PL1 II7

McKnight, Robert K.
    1968 Proverbs of Palau. Journal of American Folklore, 81(319):
          3-33.
          PL1 VIII

McKnight, Robert K.
    1969 Political leadership in Micronesia. Paper read at the
          Symposium on Political Modernization of Micronesia, 27-29
          March, Santa Cruz, California.
          M II3

McKnight, Robert K.
    1969 Rigid models and ridiculous boundaries: Political develop-
          ment and practice in Palau--circa 1945-64. IN Political
          Modernization of Micronesia, A Symposium. Santa Cruz,
          California: Center for South Pacific Studies. Reprinted
          1972. Micronesica, 8(1&2):23-35.
          PL1 II3

McKnight, Robert K.
    1971 Past and future culture change: A quest for variant
          Explanations. IN Human Futuristics, M. Maruyama and J.A.
          Dator, eds. Honolulu: Social Science Research Institute,
          University of Hawaii. pp. 193-204.
          P II7

McKnight, Robert K.
    1971 Two models of assimilation and change in Micronesia. Paper
          read at the Annual Meeting of the Southwestern Anthropolo-
          gical Association, 29 April-1 May, Tucson, Arizona.
          M II7

MAIN BIBLIOGRAPHY

McKnight, Robert K.
  1974 Rigid models and ridiculous boundaries: Political devel-
        opment and practice in Palau, circa 1955-1964. IN Poli-
        tical Development in Micronesia, Daniel T. Hughes and
        Sherwood G. Lingenfelter, eds. Columbus: Ohio State
        University Press. pp. 37-53.
        PL1 II3

McKnight, Robert K.
  1975 Competition and status in Palau, a short analysis of verti-
        cal and horizontal Divisions. Paper read at the 4th Annual
        Meeting of the Association for Social Anthropology in
        Oceania, 26-30 March, Stuart, Florida.
        PL1 II1

McKnight, Robert K. and Lester Hazell
  1972 Folklore and culture change: Part I, eliciting non-western
        Ideologies (McKnight). Part II, Andaman, Trobriand, Ulithi
        and Hopi (Hazell). Paper read at the Annual Meeting of the
        American Folklore Society, 16-19 November, Austin, Texas.
        Y3 VIII

McKnight, Robert K. and Adalbert Obak
  1959 Yam cultivation in the Palau District. IN Yam Cultivation
        in the Trust Territory, John E. de Young, ed. Anthropolo-
        gical Working Papers, No. 4. Guam: Office of the Staff
        Anthropologist, Trust Territory of the Pacific Islands.
        pp. 14-37.
        PL1 I

McKnight, Robert K. and Adalbert Obak
  1960 Taro cultivation in Palau. IN Taro Cultivation Practices and
        Beliefs, Part I (The Western Carolines), John E. de Young, ed.
        Anthropological Working Papers, No. 6. Guam: Office of the
        Staff Anthropologist, Trust Territory of the Pacific Islands.
        pp. 1-47.
        PL1 I

McLean, Mervyn
  1972 Review of Mary A. Browning, Micronesian Heritage. Journal
        of the Polynesian Society, 81(2):279-282.
        M IV

McLeod, James R.
  1973 An analysis of Westernization: The new elites of developing
        Nations. Paper read at the 72nd Annual Meeting of the
        American Anthropological Association, 28 November-2 December,
        New Orleans.
        M II7

-165-

McManus, Edward
    n.d. Palauan-English Dictionary, Lewis S. Josephs and Masa-aki
          Emesiochl, eds. PALI Language Texts: Micronesia. Hono-
          lulu: University Press of Hawaii, forthcoming.
          PL1 XIII

McNair, Philip K.; Robert R. Garison; John H. Gilpin; Byron M. Briggs;
          Lucien G. Estes; George H. LaMaze; Roland J. Hurst; George G.
          Appel; Robert V. Davis; David DeLaPena; Walter P. Claypool;
          and Carl N. Hayes
    1949 Report of a medical survey of the Yap District of the
          Western Caroline Islands of the Trust Territory of the
          Pacific Islands. The Hospital Corps Quarterly [Supplement
          to the U.S. Naval Medical Bulletin], 22(4):5-19.
          Y XIV

McPhetres, Sam
    1975 Review of James C. Webb, Jr., Micronesia and the United
          States' Pacific Strategy: A Blueprint for the 1980s.
          Marianas Variety News and Views [Saipan], 4(19):6.
          M XV XVII

McVey, Jim
    1973 Fish--something New. Micronesian Reporter, 21(2):15-18.
          PL1 VI

Meggitt, Mervyn J.
    1960 Review of Homer Barnett, Being a Palauan. Oceania,
          31(1):83.
          PL1 II

Meller, Norman
    1958 Validity of records in the South Seas. Political
          Research: Organization and Design, 2(2):8-9.
          P XVII

Meller, Norman
    1959 Bilingualism in island legislatures of the Pacific
          as an index of acculturation: A Hypothesis. Sociology
          and Social Research, 43(6):408-414.
          P II7 XVII

Meller, Norman
    1960 Political changes in American Pacific Dependencies.
          Far Eastern Survey, 29(7):97-101.
          Mr1 Ms II3 XVII

Meller, Norman
    1965 Political change in the Pacific. Asian Survey, 5(5):245-254.
          P II3 XVII

MAIN BIBLIOGRAPHY

Meller, Norman
    1965   Three American legislative bodies in the Pacific.   IN
           Induced Political Change in the Pacific, Roland W. Force,
           ed.   Honolulu: Bishop Museum Press.   pp. 41-53.
           P II3 XVII

Meller, Norman
    1966   The identification and classification of Legislatures.
           Philippine Journal of Public Administration [Manila], 10(4):
           308-319.
           M XVII

Meller, Norman
    1967   Districting a new legislature in Micronesia.
           Asian Survey, 7(7):457-468.
           M XVII

Meller, Norman
    1967   Representational role types: A research Note.
           American Political Science Review, 61(2):474-477.
           M XVII

Meller, Norman
    1968   American Pacific outposts: Guam, Samoa, and the Trust
           Territory.   State Government, 41(3):204-211.
           M Mr1 XVII

Meller, Norman
    1969   American legislatures in the Pacific.   State Government,
           42(3):186-189.
           P XVII

Meller, Norman
    1969   The Congress of Micronesia--A unifying and modernizing
           Force.   In Political Modernization of Micronesia, A Sympo-
           sium.   Santa Cruz, California: Center for South Pacific
           Studies.   18 pp.   Reprinted 1972.   Micronesica, 8(1&2):13-22.
           M XVII

Meller, Norman
    1970   Indigenous leadership in the Trust Territory of the Pacific
           Islands.   IN Development Administration in Asia, Edward
           Weidner, ed.   Durham: Duke University Press.   pp. 309-335.
           M XVII

Meller, Norman
    1973   Legislative staff in Oceania as a focus for Research.   IN
           Legislatures in Comparative Perspective, Allan Kornberg,
           ed.   New York: McKay.   pp. 314-334.
           P XVII

MAIN BIBLIOGRAPHY

Meller, Norman
    1973 The Pacific legislature--spearhead for political Change.
          Paper read at the 2nd Annual Meeting of the Association for
          Social Anthropology in Oceania, 21-25 March, Orcas Island,
          Washington.
          P XVII

Meller, Norman
    1974 Micronesian political change in Perspective. IN Political
          Development in Micronesia, Daniel T. Hughes and Sherwood G.
          Lingenfelter, eds. Columbus: Ohio State University Press.
          pp. 263-277.
          M XVII

Meller, Norman, with the assistance of Terza Meller
    1969 The Congress of Micronesia. Development of the Legislative
          Process in the Trust Territory of the Pacific Islands.
          Honolulu: University of Hawaii Press. 480 pp. Reviewed:
          1971 by Vern Carroll, American Anthropologist, 73(4):884-885.
          M XVII

Meredith, J. C.
    1958 The Tatooed Man. New York: Duell, Sloan and Pearce. 90 pp.
          [Horace Holden].
          PL XII

Metelski, John B.
    1974 Micronesia and free association: Can federalism save Them?
          California Western International Law Journal, 5(1):162-183.
          Reprinted 1975. Micronesian Independent [Majuro, Mar-
          shall Islands], 6(17):2, 5-7, 10-14. [May 9, 1975].
          M XVII

Metge, Joan
    1971 Review of Vern Carroll, ed., Adoption in Eastern Oceania.
          Man, n.s., 6(3):518.
          P II1

Micronesian Program Bulletin
    1966 to 1969. Bulletins Nos. 1-6, published by the Department
          of Anthropology, University of Hawaii. [no longer published].
          M II

Micronesian Reporter
    1951 to present. Quarterly publication of the Public Infor-
          mation Office, Trust Territory of the Pacific Islands,
          Saipan, Mariana Islands, 96950. [formerly called
          Micronesian Monthly].
          M IX

Micronesian Seminar
    1967 Bibliography of library materials: Micronesian Seminar
          Research Library. Compiled at Woodstock College, Woodstock,
          Maryland. 65 pp. [library now located at Xavier High
          School, Moen, Truk, Eastern Caroline Islands, 96942].
          M IX

Micronesian Seminar
    1973 Proceedings of a Seminar on Moral Issues Related to Political
          Status, 3-9 June, Kolonia, Ponape. Moen, Truk: Micronesian
          Seminar. Mimeographed. 101 pp.
          M II3 XVII

Micronesian Seminar
    1974 Education for what? Proceedings of a Conference on Micro-
          nesian Education, 7-11 January, Kolonia, Ponape. Moen, Truk:
          Micronesian Seminar. Mimeographed. 26 pp. + appendices.
          M VII

Micronesian Seminar
    1975 Developing Micronesia's People. Proceedings of a Conference
          on Human Development Sponsored by the Micronesian Seminar,
          4-8 March, Kolonia, Ponape. Moen, Truk: Micronesian
          Seminar. Mimeographed. 18 pp.
          M II7

Micronesian Seminar (translations)
    n.d. Translation from the French of the account of his visit to
          Truk from Voyage au Pole sud et l'Oceanie...1837-1840, by
          Jules Dumont d'Urville. Paris 1841-1846, Vol. 5, pp. 120-167.
          T1 XII

Micronesian Seminar (translations)
    n.d. Translation from the Spanish of the account of the first Euro-
          pean visit to Truk in 1565 by Arellano, from Coleccion de do-
          cumentos ineditos III Madrid 1887, pp. 11-25.
          T1 XII

Micronesian Seminar (translations)
    n.d. Translation of "Some Remarks about the Religious views of
          our Islanders," by an anonymous missionary. Unpublished
          MSS, Truk, 1915, 17 pp.
          T1 II2

Micronesian Seminar (translations)
    1965 Translation from the Spanish of "Missions in the
          Caroline and Marshall Islands," by Faustino Hernandez,
          S.J., 1955. Originally published as Mision de las Islas
          Carolinas y Marshalls. Madrid. 52 pp. Duplicated 28 pp.
          C Ms II2

MAIN BIBLIOGRAPHY

Micronesian Seminar (translations)
1965 Translation from the Spanish of "The Discovery and
      description cf the Garbanzos Islands," by John Anthony
      Cantova, S. J. Letter quoted in Carrasco 1881,
      "Descubrimiento y descripcion de las Islas Garbanzos."
      Boletin de la Sociedad Geografica de Madrid, 10:263-279.
      Duplicated, 23 pp.
      Y3 XII

Micronesian Seminar (translations)
1966 Translation from the French of "Letter of Fr. Cantova
      to Fr. William D'Aubenton." Lettres edifiantes,
      Aime-Martin, ed. 18(Paris 1728):188-246.
      Mr1 II2

Micronesian Seminar (translations)
1967 Translation from the German of "Letter from the Caroline,
      Philippine and Mariana Islands, May 10, 1731." by Victor
      Walter, S.J. Die Katholischen Missionen, No. 1 (1886).
      Duplicated, 3 pp.
      C Mr II2

Micronesian Seminar (translations)
1967 Translation from the German of "The occupation of the
      Marianas and the Carolines by the Japanese." Die
      Katholischen Missionen, No. 3 (1915), pp. 64-66.
      Mr C XII

Micronesian Seminar (translations)
1967 Translation from the German of "The Carolines and their Inhab-
      itants." Die Katholischen Missionen, No. 1 (1886), pp. 1-6.
      C II

Micronesian Seminar (translations)
1967 Translation from the German of "The First missionary
      attempts in the Carolines," Die Katholischen Missionen,
      No. 8 (1886), pp. 167-171; No. 11 (1886), pp. 225-228.
      C II2

Micronesian Seminar (translations)
1967 Translation from the German of, "The Capuchin Mission in
      the Carolines (late nineteenth century). Duplicated. 1 p.
      C II2

Micronesian Seminar (translations)
1969 Translaticn from the German of "Die religion der Palauer."
      by J.S. Kubary. In Allerlei aus Volks-und Menschen Kunde,
      A. Bastian, ed. Vol. 1, Berlin, 1888, pp. 3-66.
      PL1 II2

MAIN BIBLIOGRAPHY

Micronesian Seminar (translations)
  1969 Translation from the German of "Religious beliefs and
        practices of the inhabitants of Yap," by Augustine Walleser,
        O.F.M. Cap., 1913. Anthropos, 8:607-629, 1044-1068.
        Y1 II2

Micronesian Seminar Bulletin
  1965 to present. Published occasionally by the Micronesian
        Seminar, c/o Xavier High School, Moen, Truk, Eastern
        Caroline Islands, 96942.
        M IX

Micronesica
  1964 to present. Journal of the University of Guam, P.O. Box EK,
        Agana, Guam, Mariana Islands, 96910.
        M IX

Midkiff, Frank E.
  1953 Administering the Pacific Trust Territory. U.S.
        Department of State Bulletin, 29(736):150-157.
        M XVII

Midkiff, Frank E.
  1953 Problems in the administration of the Pacific Trust
        Territory. U.S. Department of State Bulletin, 29(732):
        22-26.
        M XVII

Midkiff, Frank E.
  1954 Problems of the Pacific Trust. U.S. Department
        of State Bulletin, 31(787):141-145.
        M XVII

Midkiff, Frank E.
  1954 United States Administration of the Trust Territory
        of the Pacific Islands. U.S. Department of State
        Bulletin, 31(786):96-109.
        M XVII

Miguar, Leo
  1964 The coconut in Micronesia. Micronesian Reporter, 12(5):4-7,
        15. Reprinted 1965. Agricultural Extension Circular, No. 3.
        Saipan: Publications Office, Trust Territory of the Pacific
        Islands. 9 pp.
        M I

MAIN BIBLIOGRAPHY

Mihaly, Eugene B.
    1970 United States strategy in the Western Pacific and the
          Micronesia Dilemma. Paper read at the Conference of the
          Pacific, 27 September-3 October, Vina del Mar, Chile
          [sponsored by the Institute of International Studies,
          University of Chile].
          M XVII

Mihaly, Eugene B.
    1973 Micronesia: A U.S. strategic pawn of 2000 South Sea Islands.
          War/Peace Report, 12(6):17-21.
          M XVII

Mihaly, Eugene B.
    1974 Neutralization of Pacific Island states: A Proposal. IN
          Political Development in Micronesia, Daniel T. Hughes and
          Sherwood G. Lingenfelter, eds. Columbus: Ohio State Univer-
          sity Press. pp. 299-309.
          P XVII

Mihaly, Eugene B.
    1974 Tremors in the Western Pacific. Micronesian freedom and
          United States Security. Foreign Affairs, 52(4):839-849.
          Reprinted 1974. Micronesian Independent, [Majuro, Marshall
          Islands], 5(29):2,3,8,11. [September 3, 1974].
          M XVII

Mikoletsky, Nikolaus
    1968 Mikronesische Eingeborenenliteratur. [Micronesian native
          Literature]. Kindlers Literatur Lexikon [Zurich], 4:2606-
          2622.
          M VIII

Mikoletsky, Nikolaus
    1972 Kulturhistorische Untersuchungen zum Hauptlingstum auf
          Ponape und Kusae (Zentralmikronesien). [A cultural his-
          torical investigation of the kingdoms of Ponape and
          Kusaie (Central Micronesia)]. Archiv für Völkerkunde,
          26(1):119-164.
          Pn1 K II9 III

Mikoletsky, Nikolaus
    1972 Kulturhistorische Untersuchungen zum Hauptlingstum von
          Ponape und Kusae (Zentralmikronesien). [A cultural his-
          torical investigation of the kingdoms of Ponape and
          Kusaie (Central Micronesia)]. Ph.D. Dissertation, Uni-
          versity of München, München.
          Pn1 K II9 III

MAIN BIBLIOGRAPHY

Milhurn, J. D.
    1959 Health and sanitation study of Arno Atoll. Atoll Research
          Bulletin, No. 62. 7 pp.
          Ms9 XIV

Millar, T. B.
    1975 Review of William R. Louis, ed., National Security and
          International Trusteeship in the Pacific. Journal of
          Pacific History, 10(2):125-126.
          M XV XVII

Miller, Carey D., Mary Murai, and Florence Pen.
    1956 The use of pandanus fruit as food in Micronesia.
          Pacific Science, 10(1):3-16.
          M I

Miller, Ralph E.
    1953 Health report at Kapingamarangi. Atoll Research Bulletin,
          No. 20. 42 pp.
          Pn9 XIV

Miller, William O.
    1969 The United Nations and Oceania: New dimensions in the
          Cold War Refrain. Naval War College Review, 21(10):45-59.
          P XVII

Milne, Carmen and Michael Steward
    1967 The inheritance of land rights in Laura. IN The Laura
          Report, Leonard E. Mason, ed. Honolulu: Department of
          Anthropology, University of Hawaii. 48 pp.
          Ms8 II1

Milne, James
    1953 Meto--Marshallese Navigation. Proceedings of the 28th
          Annual Meeting of the Hawaiian Academy of Science, 1952-
          1953. p. 6.
          Ms X

Milner, George
    1956 Political progress in Micronesia. M.A. Thesis, Princeton
          University, Princeton.
          M XVII

Mink, Patsy T.
    1971 Micronesia: Our bungled Trust. Texas International Law
          Forum [now called Texas International Law Journal],
          6(2):181-207.
          M XVII

MAIN BIBLIOGRAPHY

Mirrer, Bonnie M.
    1971 Educational change in Truk, Micronesia. M.A. Thesis,
          Ohio State University, Columbus.
          T1 VII

Mitchell, I. S.
    1972 Review of Vern Carroll, ed., Adoption in Eastern Oceania.
          Practical Anthropology [now called Missiology], 19(6):
          237-238.
          P II1

Mitchell, Roger E.
    1967 A study of the cultural, historical and acculturative
          factors influencing the repertoires of two Trukese
          Informants. Ph.D. Dissertation, Indiana University,
          Bloomington. Available from University Microfilms,
          Ann Arbor: No. 68-2335.
          T1 VIII XII

Mitchell, Roger E.
    1968 Genre and function in Eastern Carolinian Narratives. Asian
          Folklore Studies [Tokyo], 27(2):1-15.
          C VIII

Mitchell, Roger E.
    1968 The Oedipus myth and complex in Oceania with special refer-
          ence to Truk. Asian Folklore Studies [Tokyo], 27(1):131-145.
          T1 VIII

Mitchell, Roger E.
    1970 Oral tradition and Micronesian history: A microcosmic
          Approach. Journal of Pacific History, 5:33-41.
          M T II9

Mitchell, Roger E.
    1971 Kubary: The first Micronesian Reporter. Micronesian
          Reporter, 19(3):43-45.
          M IX

Mitchell, Roger E.
    1972 Micronesian folklore and culture Change. Journal of the
          Folklore Institute [Indiana University], 9(1):28-44.
          M II7 VIII

Mitchell, Roger E.
    1973 Micronesian Folktales. Asian Folklore Studies, Volume
          32. Nagoya: Asian Folklore Institute. 281 pp.
          C Ms VIII

Montvel-Cohen, Marvin
    1970 Canoes in Micronesia. Micronesian Working Papers, No. 2.
          Agana: University of Guam, Gallery of Art. 17 pp.
          M II4

Montvel-Cohen, Marvin
    1974 The arts of Micronesia: A selective Survey. Paper read
          at the Conference on The Art of Oceania, 21-26 August,
          Hamilton, Ontario, Canada.
          M IV

Moore, D. R.
    1967 Review of Frank LeBar, The Material Culture of Truk.
          Archaeology and Physical Anthropology in Oceania, 2(2):168.
          T1 II4

Moore, Philip H.
    1974 Familiar plants of Agana. Guam Recorder, n.s., 4(2):39-43.
          Mr1 V

Moore, W. Robert
    1945 Our new military wards, the Marshalls. National
          Geographic Magazine, 88(3):325-360.
          Ms XV

Moore, W. Robert
    1945 South from Saipan. National Geographic Magazine, 87(4):
          441-474.
          Mr2 XV

Moore, W. Robert
    1948 Pacific wards of Uncle Sam? National Geographic,
          94(1):73-104.
          M XVII

Moore, W. Robert
    1952 Grass-skirted Yap. National Geographic, 102(6):805-826.
          Y1 IX

Moos, Felix
    1972 Strategy and occupation: The U.S. and Japan in the
          Pacific (Micronesia). Paper read at the 1st Annual
          Meeting of the Association for Social Anthropology in
          Oceania, 29 March-1 April, Orcas Island, Washington.
          M XVII

Moos, Felix
    1974 The old and the new: Japan and the United States in the
          Pacific. IN Political Development in Micronesia, Daniel
          T. Hughes and Sherwood G. Lingenfelter, eds. Columbus:
          Ohio State University Press. pp. 278-298.
          P XVII

Morgan, H. Wayne
    1965 Making Peace with Spain: The Diary of Whitelaw Reid,
          September-December, 1898. Austin: University of Texas
          Press. 276 pp.
          M XVII

Morgiewicz, Cdr. Daniel J.
    1968 Micronesia: Especial Trust. U.S. Naval Institute Pro-
          ceedings, 94(10):68-79.
          M XVII

Morison, Samuel E.
    1944 Historical Notes on the Gilbert and Marshall Islands.
          American Neptune, 4(2):87-118.
          Ms XII

Morrill, Sibley S.
    1970 Ponape: Where American Colonialism Confronts Black Magic,
          Five Kingdoms, and the Mysterious Ruins cf Nan-Madol.
          San Francisco: Cadlecn Press. 253 pp. Reviewed: 1972 by
          Saul H. Riesenberg, Association for Anthropology in Micro-
          nesia Newsletter, 1(2):18-19.
          Pn1 II

Morton, Louis
    1967 The Marianas. Military Review, 47(7):71-82.
          Mr XII XV

Morton, Newton E.
    1973 Population structure of Micronesia. IN Methods and
          Theories of Anthropological Genetics, Michael H. Crawford
          and P.L. Workman, eds. Albuquerque: University cf New
          Mexico Press. pp. 333-366.
          M XVI

Morton, Newton E. and D. L. Greene
    1972 Pingelap and Mokil Atolls: Anthropometrics. American
          Journal of Human Genetics, 24(3):299-303.
          Pn6 Pn7 XVI

Morton, Newton E.; D. E. Harris; S. Yee; and R. Lew
    1971 Pingelap and Mokil Atolls: Migration. American
          Journal of Human Genetics, 23(4):339-349.
          Pn6 Pn7 XVI

Morton, Newton E., J. N. Hurd, and G. F. Little
    1973 Pingelap and Mokil Atolls: A problem in populaticn
          Structure. IN Methods and Theories of Anthropological
          Genetics, Michael H. Crawford and P.L. Wcrkman, eds.
          Albuquerque: University of New Mexico Press. pp. 315-332.
          Pn6 Pn7 XVI

MAIN BIBLIOGRAPHY

Morton, Newton E. and J. M. Lalouel
    1973 Bioassay of kinship in Micronesia. American Journal of
          Physical Anthropology, 38(3):709-719.
          M XVI

Morton, Newton E. and J. M. Lalouel
    1973 Topology of kinship in Micronesia. American Journal of
          Human Genetics, 25(4):422-432.
          M XVI

Morton, Newton E.; R. Lew; I. E. Hussels; and G. F. Little
    1972 Pingelap and Mokil Atolls: Clans and cognate Frequencies.
          American Journal of Human Genetics, 24(3):290-298.
          Pn6 Pn7 XVI

Morton, Newton E.; R. Lew; I. E. Hussels; and G. F. Little
    1972 Pingelap and Mokil Atolls: Historical Genetics.
          American Journal of Human Genetics, 24(3):277-289.
          Pn6 Pn7 XVI

Morton, Newton E.; I. Roisenberg; R. Lew; and S. Yee
    1971 Pingelap and Mokil Atolls: Genealogy. American
          Journal of Human Genetics, 23(4):350-360.
          Pn6 Pn7 XVI

Morton, Newton E. and Manabu Yamamoto
    1973 Blood groups and haptoglobins in the Eastern Carolines.
          American Journal of Physical Anthropology, 38(3):695-698.
          Pn K XVI

Mulder, Donald W. and Leonard T. Kurland
    1954 Amyotrophic lateral sclerosis in Micronesia. Proceedings
          of the Staff Meetings, Mayo Clinic, 29(26):666-670.
          M XIV

Mulder, Donald W., Leonard T. Kurland, and Lorenzo L. G. Iriarte
    1954 Neurologic diseases on the island of Guam. U.S. Armed
          Forces Medical Journal, 5(12):1724-1739.
          Mr1 XIV

Munoz, Ben G.
    1975 Law enforcement in Guam. IN The Impact of Urban Centers in
          the Pacific, Roland W. Force and Brenda Bishop, eds. Hono-
          lulu: Pacific Science Association, Bishop Museum. pp. 257-
          264.
          Mr1 XVII

Murai, Mary
    1954 Food patterns in the Caroline and Marshall Islands.
          Journal of the American Dietetic Association, 30(2):154-158.
          C Ms XIV

Murai, Mary
    1954 Nutrition study in Micronesia. Atoll Research Bulletin,
          No. 27. 239 pp.
          M XIV

Murai, Mary, Florence Pen, and Carey D. Miller
    1958 Some Tropical South Pacific Island Foods: Description,
          History, Use, Composition, and Nutritive Value. Honolulu:
          University of Hawaii Press. 159 pp. Reprinted 1970.
          Honolulu: University of Hawaii Press.
          C Ms XIV

Murai, Mary, Florence Pen, and Carey D. Miller
    1963 Nutritive value of coconut Sap. Proceedings of the 9th
          Pacific Science Congress, 18 November-9 December, 1957,
          Bangkok, 15:142-144.
          P XIV

Murdock, George P.
    1948 Anthropology in Micronesia. Transactions of the New York
          Academy of Sciences, 11(1):9-16. Reprinted 1965. IN Cul-
          ture and Society, Twenty-Four Essays by George P. Murdock.
          Pittsburgh: University of Pittsburgh Press. pp. 237-248.
          M II

Murdock, George P.
    1948 New light on the peoples of Micronesia. Science,
          108(2808):423-425.
          M II

Murdock, George P.
    1948 Waging baseball in Truk. Newsweek, 32(9):69-70.
          Reprinted 1965. IN Culture and Society, Twenty-four
          Essays by George P. Murdock. Pittsburgh: University
          of Pittsburgh Press. pp. 291-293.
          T1 IV XV

Murdock, George P.
    1949 Social organization and government in Micronesia. CIMA
          Report, No. 19. Washington, D.C.: Pacific Science Board.
          10 pp.
          M II1

Murdock, George P.
    1953 Administrative needs and objectives in Micronesia. Proceed-
          ings of the 7th Pacific Science Congress, 2 February-4 March,
          1949, Auckland, New Zealand, 7:62. [abstract].
          M XVII

MAIN BIBLIOGRAPHY

Murdock, George P.
    1953 Cultural sub-areas in Micronesia. Proceedings of the 7th
          Pacific Science Congress, 2 February-4 March, 1949, Auck-
          land, New Zealand, 7:215-216. [abstract].
          M II

Murdock, George P.
    1954 Review of Bernhard Stillfried, Die Soziale Organisation
          in Mikronesien. [Social Organization of Micronesia].
          American Anthropologist, 56(6), Part 1:1122-1123.
          M II1

Murdock, George P.
    1963 Human influences on the ecosystems of high islands of the
          tropical Pacific. IN Man's Place in the Island Ecosystem,
          F. Raymond Fosberg, ed. Honolulu: Bishop Museum Press.
          pp. 145-154.
          P II5

Murdock, George P.
    1964 Genetic classification of the Austronesian languages:
          A key to Oceanic culture History. Ethnology, 3(2):117-126.
          P XIII

Murdock, George P. and Ward H. Goodenough
    1947 Social organization cf Truk. Southwestern Journal of
          Anthropology [now called Journal of Anthropological
          Research], 3(4):331-343. Reprinted 1965. IN Culture and
          Society, Twenty-four Essays by George P. Murdock. Pitts-
          burgh: University of Pittsburgh Press. pp. 218-235.
          T1 II1

Murphy, Joseph
    1975 Life-Style on Guam: Communication and Community. IN The
          Impact of Urban Centers in the Pacific, Roland W. Force
          and Brenda Bishop, eds. Honolulu: Pacific Science Asso-
          ciation, Bishop Museum. pp. 115-119.
          Mr1 II7

Murphy, Raymond E.
    1948 Landownership on a Micronesian Atoll. The Geographical
          Review, 38(4):598-614.
          Pn6 II1

Murphy, Raymond E.
    1949 'High' and 'Low' islands in the Eastern Carolines. The
          Geographical Review, 39(3):425-439.
          Pn K X

Murphy, Raymond E.
    1950 The economic geography of a Micronesian Atoll. Annals
          of the Association of American Geographers, 40 (1):58-83.
          Pn6 II10

Murphy, Raymond E.
    1950 Geographic studies in the Easternmost Carolines. CIMA
          Report, No. 5. Washington, D.C.: Pacific Science Board.
          Pn K X

Murphy, Raymond E.
    1950 Review of Alexander Spoehr, Majuro: A Village in the
          Marshall Islands. The Geographical Review, 40 (3):504-505.
          Ms8 II

Murphy, Raymond E.
    1953 Changing patterns of agriculture in the Easternmost Caro-
          lines. Proceedings of the 7th Pacific Science Congress,
          2 February-4 March, 1949, Auckland, New Zealand, 7:163-170.
          Pn I

Murphy, Robert T.
    1974 A Postal History Cancellation Study of the U.S. Pacific
          (Including the Trust Territories). Houston: L.B. Johnson
          Space Center Stamp Club.
          M IX XII

Murrill, Rupert I.
    1948 Ponape: A Micronesian culture of the Caroline Islands.
          Transactions of the New York Academy of Science, Series II,
          10 (4):154-158.
          Pn1 II

Murrill, Rupert I.
    1949 A blood pressure study of the natives of Ponape Island,
          Eastern Carolines. Human Biology, 21(1):47-57.
          Pn1 XIV

Murrill, Rupert I.
    1950 Population, Physical Characteristics and Constitutional
          Typology of the Ponape Islanders, Eastern Carolines. CIMA
          Report, No. 9. Washington, D.C.: Pacific Science Board.
          Pn1 XVI

Murrill, Rupert I.
    1950 Vital statistics of Ponape Island, Eastern Carolines.
          American Journal of Physical Anthropology, 8 (2):185-194.
          Pn1 XVI

MAIN BIBLIOGRAPHY

Myrianthopoulos, Ntinos C. and Samuel J. L. Pieper, Jr.
    1959 The ABO and Rh blood groups among the Chamorros of Guam
          with reference to anthropologic and genetic problems in
          the Area. American Journal of Physical Anthropology,
          17(2):105-108.
          Mr1 XVI

Nagao, Clarence M. and Masao Nakayama
    1969 A study of school-community relations in Truk. IN The Truk
          Report, Stephen Boggs, ed. Honolulu: Department of Anthro-
          pology, University of Hawaii. 37 pp.
          T1 VII

Narr, Karl J.
    1970 Review of Douglas Osborne, The Archaeology of the Palau
          Islands. Anthropos, 65:1074-1075.
          PL1 III

Nason, Anita Kay
    1970 An analysis of communicated social change on Etal Island.
          Master of Communications Thesis, University of Washington,
          Seattle.
          T11a II7

Nason, James D.
    n.d. The effects of social change on marine technology in a
          Pacific atoll Community. IN Approaches to Maritime
          Anthropology: Examples from the Pacific Shores, Richard
          Casteel and George Quimby, eds. World Anthropology Series.
          The Hague: Mouton, forthcoming.
          T11a II4 II7

Nason, James D.
    1967 Ecological aspects of cultural stability and culture
          change in Micronesia. M.A. Thesis, University of
          Washington, Seattle.
          M II5

Nason, James D.
    1970 Clan and copra: Modernization on Etal Island, Eastern
          Caroline Islands. Ph.D. Dissertation, University of
          Washington, Seattle. Available from University Micro-
          films, Ann Arbor: No. 71-1008.
          T11a II7

Nason, James D.
    1972 Political change: An outer island Perspective. IN
          Political Development in Micronesia, Daniel T. Hughes and
          Sherwood G. Lingenfelter, eds. Columbus: Ohio State Uni-
          versity Press. pp. 119-142.
          T11a II3

Nason, James D.
    1975 The strength of the land--community perception of popula-
          tion on Etal Island. IN Pacific Atoll Populations, Vern
          Carroll, ed. ASAO Mcnograph No. 3. Honolulu: University
          Press of Hawaii. pp. 117-159.
          T11a II5 XVI

Nason, James D.
    1975 Civilizing the heathen: Missionaries and social change in
          the Mortlock Islands. Paper read at the 4th Annual Meeting
          of the Association for Social Anthropology in Oceania, 26-
          30 March, Stuart, Flcrida.
          T11a II2 II7

Nason, James D.
    1975 Reconnaisance and plat mapping of coral atolls: A simpli-
          fied rangefinder Method. Atoll Research Bulletin, No. 185:
          13-20.
          T11a X

Nason, James D.
    1975 Sardines and other fried fish: The consumption of
          alcoholic beverages on a Micronesian Island. Journal
          of Studies on Alcohol [formerly called Quarterly Journal
          of Studies on Alcohol], 36(5):611-625.
          T11a II7

Nathan Associates, Inc., Robert R.
    1967 Economic Development Plan for Micronesia: Summary and Index.
          Prepared for the High Commissioner of the Trust Territory
          of the Pacific Islands. Washington, D.C.: Nathan Associates.
          Mimeographed. 73 pp.
          M VI

Neas, Maynard
    1961 Land ownership patterns in the Marshall Islands. IN Land
          Tenure in the Pacific: A Symposium of the 10th Pacific
          Science Congress. Atoll Research Bulletin, No. 85:17-23.
          Ms II1

Newlon, Robert Edward
    1949 Evolution of the United States' position in Micrcnesia.
          M.A. Thesis, University of Chicago, Chicago.
          M XVII

Niering, William A.
    1956 Bioecology of Kapingamarangi Atoll, Caroline Islands: Ter-
          restrial Aspects. SIM Report, No. 22. Washingtcn, D.C.:
          Pacific Science Board. 32 pp. Reprinted 1956. Atoll
          Research Bulletin, Nc. 49. 32 pp.
          Pn9 X

MAIN BIBLIOGRAPHY

Niering, William A.
    1961   Observations on Puluwat and Gaferut, Caroline Islands.
            Atoll Research Bulletin, No. 76. 10 pp.
            T4 Y13 V X

Niering, William A.
    1962   Review of F. Raymond Fosberg, The Vegetation of Micronesia.
            Ecology, 43(2):353-354.
            M V

Niering, William A.
    1963   Terrestrial ecology of Kapingamarangi Atoll, Caroline
            Islands. Ecological Monographs, 33(2):131-160.
            Pn9 X

Nishi, Midori
    1968   An evaluation of Japanese agricultural and fishery
            developments in Micronesia during the Japanese
            Mandate, 1914-1941. Micronesica, 4(1):1-18.
            M I VI

Nørlund, Mogens Christian
    1966   Den forsvundne verden. Mikronesien. [The Vanished World.
            Micronesia]. København: Carit Andersen. 200 pp.
            M IX

Nozikov, Nikolai N.
    1946   Russian Voyages Round the World, M.A. Sergeyev, ed.
            Translated from the Russian by Ernst and Mira Lesser.
            London: Hutchinson and Co. 165 pp.
            P XII

Nugent, L. E., Jr.
    1946   Coral reefs in the Gilbert, Marshall, and Caroline Islands.
            Bulletin of the Geological Society of America, 57(2):
            735-780.
            C Ms XI

Nystrom, Cdr. Frederic L.
    1972   The Caroline Islands. IN National Security and Inter-
            national Trusteeship in the Pacific, W.R. Louis, ed.
            Annapolis: Naval Institute Press. pp. 110-118.
            C XV XVII

O'Brien, Ilma E.
    1971   Missionaries on Ponape: Induced social and political
            Change. The Australian National University Historical
            Journal, 8(20):53-64.
            Pn1 II2 II7

O'Connor, LCdr. Edward C.
   1969   Micronesia--America's Western frontier in the East.   M.S.
          Thesis, George Washington University, Washington, D.C.
          Published 1970.   Micronesia: America's frontier in the Far
          East.   The National War College Forum [Fort Lesley J.
          McNair, Washington, D.C.], 9th issue, pp. 57-80.
          M XVII

Oakley, Richard G.
   1946   Entomological Observations in the Marshall, Caroline and
          Mariana Islands.   IN U.S. Commercial Company's Economic
          Survey of Micronesia, Report No. 14, Part 2 [Part 1 by
          Henry Townes].   Honolulu: U.S. Commercial Company.
          Mimeographed.   82 pp.
          M XIX

Obak, Adalbert and Robert K. McKnight
   1964   Mesubed Dingal: Patron deity of Kites.   Micronesian Reporter,
          12(7):15-16.
          PL1 II2 II4

Obak, Adalbert and Robert K. McKnight
   1966   Palauan Proverbs.   Micronesian Research Working Papers,
          No. 2.   Saipan: Publications Office, Trust Territory of
          the Pacific Islands.   23 pp.
          PL1 VIII

Obak, Adalbert and Robert K. McKnight
   1969   Kadam, the Palauan Kite.   Lore, 19(2):49-57.
          PL1 II4

Oberdorfer, Don
   1964   America's neglected colonial Paradise.   The Saturday
          Evening Post, 237(8):24-35.   [February 29, 1964].
          M XVII

Oberem, Udo
   1951   Die frühe Herrenkultur der Mikronesischen Staaten (Ein Beitrag
          zum Wesen der Herrenkultur).   [The ruling class of the early
          civilization of the Micronesian states (a contribution to the
          nature of upper-class Civilization)].   Ph.D. Dissertation,
          University of Bonn, Bonn.
          M II3

Oberem, Udo
   1953   Staatsaufbau in Mikronesien.   [The formation of states in
          Micronesia].   Zeitschrift für vergleichende Rechtswissen-
          schaft, 56:104-150.
          M II3

Ogata, S. Bert
    1960   Traditional coconut culture on Yap.   South Pacific Bulletin,
            19(4):50-54.
            Y1 I

Okumiya, Lt. Gen. Masatake
    1968   For sugar boats or Submarines?   U.S. Naval Institute Pro-
            ceedings, 94(8):66-73. [see Peeke 1968].
            M XV

Oliver, Douglas L., ed.
    1951   Planning Micronesia's Future, A Summary of the United
            States Commercial Company's Economic Survey of Micronesia,
            1946. Cambridge, Massachusetts: Harvard University Press.
            Reprinted 1971. Honolulu: University of Hawaii Press.
            94 pp. Reviewed: 1971 by Maria Teresa del Valle, Micro-
            nesica, 7(1&2):246-247.
            M II7 VI

Osborne, Carolyn and Douglas Osborne
    1969   Construction of the Bai. IN Bai Rangerechel ur Charchur
            [Palau Museum Bai on Koror]. Koror, Palau Islands: Palau
            Museum. pp. 16-20.
            PL1 II4

Osborne, Douglas
    1947   Archeology of Guam: A progress Report.   American Anthro-
            pologist, 49(3):518-524.
            Mr1 III

Osborne, Douglas
    1958   The Palau Islands: Stepping stones into the Pacific.
            Archaeology, 11(3):162-171.
            PL1 III

Osborne, Douglas
    1959   Review of Alfred Tetens, Among the Savages of the South
            Seas, translated by Florence M. Spoehr. Journal of the
            Polynesian Society, 68(1):50-51.
            M XII

Osborne, Douglas
    1960   Review of Alfred Tetens, Among the Savages of the South Seas,
            translated by Florence M. Spoehr. Archaeology, 13(4):299-300.
            M XII

Osborne, Douglas
    1961   Archeology in Micronesia: Background, Palau studies and sug-
            gestions for the Future. Asian Perspectives, 5(2):156-163.
            PL1 III

Osborne, Douglas
      1966   The Archaeology of the Palau Islands, an Intensive Survey.
             B.P. Bishop Museum Bulletin, No. 230.   Honolulu: Bishop
             Museum Press.   497 pp.   Reviewed: 1967 by Janet M. Davidson,
             Journal of the Polynesian Society, 76(4):526-528; 1967 by
             Peter W. Gathercole, Man, n.s., 2(4):637; 1967 by Fred M.
             Reinman, Asian Perspectives, 10:174-176; 1968 by Leon Sin-
             der, American Anthropologist, 70(4):815-816; 1970 by Karl
             J. Narr, Anthropos, 65:1074-1075.
             PL1 III

Otobed, Demei O.
      1975   Conservation priorities in Micronesia.   IN The Impact of
             Urban Centers in the Pacific, Roland W. Force and Brenda
             Bishop, eds.   Honolulu: Pacific Science Association, Bishop
             Museum.   pp. 73-79.
             M I X

Owen, Hera W.
      1973   Bat Soup, and Other Recipes From the South Seas.   Seattle:
             Graphic Press.   48 pp.
             M IX

Owen, Hera W., ed.
      1973   Charles Gibbons: Visions of old Palau.   Micronesian Working
             Papers, No. 4.   Agana: University of Guam, Gallery of Art.
             35 pp.
             PL1 XII

Owen, Hera W.
      1974   A museum in Micronesia.   South Pacific Bulletin, 24(1):19-22.
             PL1 II4 II9

Owen, Robert P.
      1969   The status of conservation in the Trust Territory of the
             Pacific Islands.   Micronesica, 5(2):303-306.
             M I X

Pätzold, Klaus
      1968   Die Palau-Sprache und ihre Stellung zu anderen indonesischen
             Sprachen.   [The Palau Language and Its Position Among Other
             Indonesian Languages].   Veröffentlichugen des Seminars für
             Indonesische und Südseesprachen der Universität Hamburg,
             Band 6.   Berlin: Dietrich Reimer.   186 pp.   Reviewed: 1971
             by Isidore Dyen, Journal of the Polynesian Society, 80(2):
             247-258.
             PL1 XIII

Paler, Abraham D.
      1975   Draw-a-man: The IQ test for Guam Children.   Pacific Asian
             Studies [University of Guam], 1(1):50-54.
             Mr1 XVIII

Paszkowski, Lech
    1971 John Stanislaw Kubary-naturalist and ethnographer of the
          Pacific Islands. Australian Zoologist, 16(2):43-70.
          M II XIX

Pawley, Andrew
    1967 The relationships of Polynesian outlier Languages. Journal
          of the Polynesian Society, 76(3):259-296.
          P Pn8 Pn9 XIII

Pawley, Andrew
    1972 On the internal relationships of Eastern Oceanic Lang-
          uages. IN Studies in Oceanic Culture History, Volume 3,
          Roger C. Green and Marion Kelly, eds. Pacific Anthropo-
          logical Records, No. 13. Honolulu: Department of Anthro-
          pology, B.P. Bishop Museum. pp. 1-142.
          P XIII

Pawley, Andrew and Roger C. Green
    1973 Dating the dispersal of the Oceanic Languages. Working
          Papers in Linguistics, 5(7):1-48. Honolulu: Department
          of Linguistics, University of Hawaii.
          P XIII

Peace Corps
    1969 Peace Corps Health Program for the Trust Territory of the
          Pacific Islands. Honolulu: University of Hawaii. 121 pp.
          M XIV

Peace Corps
    1969 The Story of Micronesia: With an Introductory Guide to
          Sources of Information. Washington, D.C.: Peace Corps.
          M IX

Peacock, Dan
    1961 The new Pacific Islands Central School. South Pacific
          Bulletin, 11(1):57.
          Pn1 M VII

Peacock, Dan
    1963 The Pacific Islands Central School Library. South Pacific
          Bulletin, 13(4):53-54.
          Pn1 M VII

Peacock, Dan
    1965 Training island Librarians. South Pacific Bulletin, 15(1):
          41-43.
          M VII

Pearse, Richard and Keith A. Bezanson
    1970 Education and Modernization in Micronesia: A Case Study in
          Development and Development Planning. Stanford, Califor-
          nia: Stanford International Development Educaticn Center,
          School of Education, Stanford University. 96 pp.
          M II7 VII

Peeke, C. E. B.
    1968 For sugar boats or Submarines? U.S. Naval Institute
          Proceedings, 94(11):108. [see Okumiya 1968].
          M XV

Pelep, Stew
    1960 Ponape fishermen set up successful Cooperative. South
          Pacific Bulletin, 10(4):48.
          Pn1 VI

Pellett, Marcian, O.F.M., Cap. and Alexander Spoehr
    1961 Marianas archeology: Report on an excavation on Tirian.
          Journal of the Polynesian Society, 70(3):321-325.
          Mr4 III

Pelzer, Karl J.
    1947 Agriculture in the Truk Islands. Foreign Agriculture,
          11(6):74-81.
          T1 I

Pelzer, Karl J.
    1950 Micronesia--a changing Frontier. World Politics, 2(2):
          251-266.
          M XVII

Perez, Gerald S. A.
    1975 Guam conservation Priorities. IN The Impact of Urban Cen-
          ters in the Pacific, Roland W. Force and Brenda Bishop, eds.
          Honolulu: Pacific Science Association, Bishop Museum.
          pp. 89-96.
          Mr1 I X

Perkins, Whitney T.
    1962 Denial of Empire: The United States and Its Dependencies.
          Leyden: A.W. Sythoff. 381 pp.
          P XVII

Peter, Jim
    1973 Odyssey on Anatahan. Micronesian Reporter, 21(1):40-46.
          Mr6 XV

Peterson, Carl R.; James A. Bryan, II; Jerome Kern; Kenneth L. Hermann;
and Ronald R. Robertc
   1965 Poliomyelitis in an isolated population: Report of a type
         1 epidemic in the Marshall Islands, 1963. American Journal
         of Epidemiolcgy, 82(3):273-296.
         Ms XIV

Pettay, Louanna
   1959 Racial affinity of prehistoric Guam. Proceedings of the
         Indiana Academy of Science for 1958, 68:58. [abstract].
         Mr1 III

Phillip, Alex
   1971 Role of the U.S. Military in Micronesia. IN Micronesian
         Realities; Political and Economic, Frances McReynolds Smith,
         ed. Santa Cruz, California: Center for South Pacific
         Studies. pp. 237-244.
         M XV

Pickerill, Cicely P.
   1954 Pacific Islands Central School. South Pacific Bulletin,
         4(2):23.
         T1 M VII

Piddington, Ralph
   1958 Review of Homer Barnett, Anthropology in Administration.
         Journal of the Polynesian Society, 67(4):427-429.
         M II8

Pierard, Richard V.
   1964 The German colonial society, 1882-1914. Ph.D. Dissertation,
         State University of Iowa, Iowa City. Available from Univer-
         sity Microfilms, Ann Arbor: No. 65-499.
         P VI XVII

Pieris, W. V. D.
   1955 The manufacture of copra in the Pacific Islands.
         South Pacific Commission Technical Paper, No. 82.
         Noumea: South Pacific Commission. 37 pp.
         P VI

Piper, Arthur M.
   1946 Water Resources of Guam and the Ex-Japanese Mandated
         Islands of the Western Pacific. IN U.S. Commercial Com-
         pany's Economic Survey of Micronesia, Report No. 4. Hono-
         lulu: U.S. Commercial Company. Mimeographed. 117 pp.
         M XI

Pla Carceles, Jose
   1951 Espana en la Micronesia. [Spain in Micronesia]. Revista
         de Indias, 11(43&44):29-59.
         M XII

Plato, Chris C., Paul Brown, and D. C. Gajdusek
    1972 Dermatoglyphics of the Micronesians from the Outer Islands
          of Yap. Zeitschrift für Morphologie und Anthropologie,
          64(1):29-44.
          W XVI

Plato, Chris C. and Manuel T. Cruz
    1966 Blood group and haptoglobin frequencies of the Trukese of
          Micronesia. Acta Genetica et Statistica Medica [now called
          Human Heredity], 16(1):74-83.
          T1 XVI

Plato, Chris C. and Manuel T. Cruz
    1967 Blood group and haptoglobin frequencies of the Chamorros of
          Guam. American Journal of Human Genetics, 19(6):722-731.
          Mr1 XVI

Plato, Chris C., Manuel T. Cruz, and Leonard T. Kurland
    1964 Frequency of glucose-6-phosphate dehydrogenase deficiency,
          red-green colour blindness and Xga blood-group among
          Chamorros. Nature, 202(4933):728.
          Mr XIV XVI

Plato, Chris C., Manuel T. Cruz, and Leonard T. Kurland
    1969 Amyotrophic lateral sclerosis/Parkinsonism dementia complex of
          Guam: Further genetic Investigations. American Journal of
          Human Genetics, 21(3):133-141.
          Mr1 XIV XVI

Plato, Chris C. and Jerry D. Niswander
    1967 Dermatoglyphics of the Trukese of Micronesia. Human
          Biology, 39(2):176-181.
          T1 XVI

Plato, Chris C.; Dwayne M. Reed; Teresita S. Elizan; and Leonard T.
          Kurland
    1967 Amyotrophic lateral sclerosis/Parkinsonism-dementia complex
          of Guam. IV. Familial and genetic Investigations. American
          Journal of Human Genetics, 19(5):617-632.
          Mr1 XIV XVI

Plato, Chris C., D. L. Rucknagel, and Leonard T. Kurland
    1966 Blood group investigations on the Carolinians and
          Chamorros of Saipan. American Journal of Physical
          Anthropology, 24(2):147-154.
          Mr2 C XVI

Plato, Chris C. and Jane Hainline Underwood
    1969 Dermatoglyphics of the Micronesians of Yap. Human
          Biology, 41(2):271-274.
          Y1 XVI

Platt, William J. and Philip H. Sorensen
    1967 Planning for Education and Manpower in Micronesia. Summary
          report prepared for the Trust Territory of the Pacific
          Islands. Menlo Park, California: Stanford Research Institute.
          26 pp.
          M VII

Playdon, Capt. George W., U.S.C.G. (Ret.)
    1967 The significance of Marshallese stick Charts. Journal of
          the Institute of Navigation, 20(2):155-166.
          Ms X

Plaza, Felicia
    1971 Origin of the word Chamorro. Guam Recorder, n.s., 1(1):4-5.
          Mr XIII

Plaza, Felicia
    1973 Lattes of the Marianas. Guam Recorder, n.s., 3(1):6-9.
          Mr III

Poignant, Roslyn
    1967 Oceanic Mythology. The Myths of Polynesia, Micronesia,
          Melanesia, Australia. London: Paul Hamlyn. 141 pp.
          P VIII

Pollock, Nancy J.
    n.d. The origin of clans on Namu, Marshall Islands. IN Directions
          in Pacific Traditional Literature: Essays in Honor of Kath-
          arine Luomala, Adrienne L. Kaeppler and H. Arlo Nimmo, eds.
          B.P. Bishop Museum Special Publication, No. 61. Honolulu:
          Bishop Museum Press, in press.
          Ms21 VIII

Pollock, Nancy J.
    n.d. The risks of dietary change, a Pacific atoll Example.
          IN Gastronomy, The Anthropology of Food and Food Habits,
          M. Arnott, ed. World Anthropology Series. The Hague:
          Mouton, forthcoming.
          Ms21 XIV

Pollock, Nancy J.
    1970 Breadfruit and breadwinning on Namu Atoll, Marshall
          Islands. Ph.D. Dissertation, University of Hawaii,
          Honolulu. Available from University Microfilms, Ann
          Arbor: No. 71-12211.
          Ms21 II10

Pollock, Nancy J.
1972 Namu--an atoll population on the Move. Paper read at the
Conference on Atoll Populations, East-West Center Population
Institute, 27-30 December, Honolulu, Hawaii.
Ms21 XVI

Pollock, Nancy J.
1973 Breadfruit or rice: Dietary choice on a Micronesian
Atoll. Journal of Ecology of Food and Nutrition, 2:1-9.
Ms21 XIV

Pollock, Nancy J.
1974 Household economic strategies on Namu Atoll, Marshall
Islands. Paper read at the 3rd Annual Meeting of the
Association for Social Anthropology in Oceania, 13-17
March, Asilomar, Pacific Grove, California.
Ms21 II10

Pollock, Nancy J.
1974 Land tenure and land usage on Namu Atoll. IN Land Tenure
in Oceania, Henry Lundsgaarde, ed. ASAO Monograph No. 2.
Honolulu: University Press of Hawaii. pp. 100-129.
Ms21 II1

Pollock, Nancy J., J. M. Lalouel, and Newton E. Morton
1972 Kinship and inbreeding on Namu Atoll (Marshall Islands).
Human Biology, 44(3):459-474.
Ms21 XVI

Pomeroy, Earl Spencer
1948 American policy respecting the Marshalls, Carolines
and Marianas, 1898-1941. Pacific Historical Review,
17(1):43-53.
M XVII

Pomeroy, Earl Spencer
1951 Pacific Outpost. American Strategy in Guam and Micronesia.
Stanford, California: Stanford University Press. 198 pp.
Mr1 M XVII

Porter, Catherine
1944 Guam. Far Eastern Survey, 13(6):54-55.
Mr1 II XVII

Porter, Catherine
1944 The Japanese Mandates. Far Eastern Survey, 13(5):46-48.
M II XVII

Powells, Guy
1970 Political alternatives in Micronesia. Pacific Affairs,
43(1):84-90.
M XVII

Pramuanradhakarn Thiravetya
    1969 Current influence of traditional leaders and their atti-
          tudes and expectations toward modern leaders on Truk. IN
          The Truk Report, Stephen Boggs, ed. Honolulu: Department
          of Anthropology, University of Hawaii. 18 pp.
          T1 II3

Price, Monroe E.
    1972 Land tenure and the constitution: Protecting Micronesian
          cultural Integrity. IN Micronesian Realities: Political
          and Economic, Frances McReynolds Smith, ed. Santa Cruz,
          California: Center for South Pacific Studies. pp. 59-71.
          M II1

Price, Willard
    1944 Japan's Islands of Mystery. New York: John Day. 264 pp.
          M IX

Price, Willard
    1944 Ponape: A nut to Crack. Asia and the Americas, 44(3):105-109.
          Pn1 IX

Price, Willard
    1966 America's Paradise Lost. New York: John Day Co. 240 pp.
          M IX

Purcell, David Campell, Jr.
    1967 Japanese expansion in the South Pacific, 1890-1935. Ph.D.
          Dissertation, University of Pennsylvania, Philadelphia.
          Available from University Microfilms, Ann Arbor: No. 68-4607.
          P XII XVII

Purcell, David Campbell, Jr.
    1971 Japanese entrepreneurs in the Mariana, Marshall, and Caro-
          line Islands. IN East Across the Pacific. Historical
          and Sociological Studies of Japanese Immigration and
          Assimilation, Hilary Conroy and T. Scott Miyakawa, eds.
          Santa Barbara, California: American Bibliographical
          Center, Clio Press. pp. 56-70.
          M XII

Quackenbush, Edward M.
    1966 Lessons in Ulithian. Honolulu: University of Hawaii Peace
          Corps Training Center. Mimeographed. 123 pp.
          Y3 XIII

Quackenbush, Edward M.
    1968 From Sonsorol to Truk: A dialect Chain. Ph.D. Disser-
          tation, University of Michigan, Ann Arbor. Available
          from University Microfilms, Ann Arbor: No. 69-02375.
          C XIII

MAIN BIBLIOGRAPHY

Quackenbush, Hiroko C.
     1966   Lessons in Pulapese. Honolulu: University of Hawaii Peace
            Corps Training Center. Mimeographed. 76 pp.
            T5 XIII

Quackenbush, Hiroko C.
     1970   Studies in the phonology of some Trukic Dialects. Ph.D.
            Dissertation, University of Michigan, Ann Arbor. Avail-
            able from University Microfilms, Ann Arbor: No. 71-23851.
            C XIII

Quigg, Philip W.
     1969   Coming of age in Micronesia. Foreign Affairs, 47(3):493-508.
            Reprinted 1969. Micronesian Reporter, 17(4):24-31.
            M XVII

Quinn, P. E.
     1945   Diplomatic struggle for the Carolines, 1898. Pacific
            Historical Review, 14(3):290-302.
            C XII

Racule, Amani
     1973   Review of David Lewis, We, The Navigators. Pacific
            Perspective, 2(1):57-58.
            P X

Radford, Admiral Arthur
     1951   The Navy in Micronesia. Paradise of the Pacific [now
            called Honolulu Magazine], 63(5):18-20.
            M XV

Rainey, Mary C. and George L. Boughton
     1975   The socialization of children on Guam: An annotated biblio-
            graphy and Review. Pacific Asian Studies [University of
            Guam], 1(1):72-78.
            Mr1 IX XVIII

Raken, Yokitaro and Robert Edmondson
     1969   Representative democracy in Truk District, the development
            and operation of a new political Form. IN The Truk Report,
            Stephen Boggs, ed. Honolulu: Department of Anthropology,
            University of Hawaii. 34 pp.
            T II3

Ramarui, David
     1975   Education in Micronesia: Practicalities and Impracticalities.
            IN The Impact of Urban Centers in the Pacific, Roland W.
            Force and Brenda Bishop, eds. Honolulu: Pacific Science
            Association, Bishop Museum. pp. 307-316.
            M VII

MAIN BIBLIOGRAPHY

Rappaport, Michael D.
    1972 The constitution of Micronesia: Problems and questions to
          be Considered. IN Micronesian Realities: Political and
          Economic, Frances McReynolds Smith, ed. Santa Cruz, Cal-
          ifornia: Center for South Pacific Studies. pp. 47-57.
          M XVII

Rattan, Sumitra
    1972 The Yap controversy and its Significance. Journal of
          Pacific History, 7:124-136.
          Y1 XII

Raulet, Harry M.
    1959 A note on Fischer's residence Typology. American Anthro-
          pologist, 61(1):108-112. [see Fischer 1958, 1959; Goode-
          nough 1956].
          T1 II1

Ray, Erwin R.
    1973 Review of Janet Davidson, Archaeology on Nukuoro Atoll.
          Man, n.s., 8(3):486-487.
          Pn8 III

Read, Kenneth R. H.
    1971 Palauan tuna Fishing. Oceans, 4(4):30-35.
          PL1 II10

Read, Kenneth R. H.
    1972 Kayangel Atoll. Oceans, 5(6):10-17.
          PL1 IX

Read, Kenneth R. H.
    1974 The rock islands of Palau. Oceans, 7(6):10-17.
          PL1 IX

Reed, Dwayne M.
    1974 Modernization and health in Micronesia. Oceans, 7(6):18-23.
          M II7 XIV

Reed, Dwayne M.
    1975 Health effects of modernization in Micronesia. IN The
          Impact of Urban Centers in the Pacific, Roland W. Force
          and Brenda Bishop, eds. Honolulu: Pacific Science Asso-
          ciation, Bishop Museum. pp. 267-280.
          M II7 XIV

Reed, Dwayne M. and Jacob A. Brody
    1975 Amyotrophic lateral sclerosis and Parkinsonism-dementia
          on Guam, 1945-1972. I. Descriptive Epidemiology. Amer-
          ican Journal of Epidemiology, 101(4):287-301.
          Mr1 XIV XVI

MAIN BIBLIOGRAPHY

Reed, Dwayne M., Darwin Labarthe, and Reuel Stallones
  1970 Health effects of Westernization and migration among
    Chamorros. American Journal of Epidemiology, 92(2):94-112.
    Mr1 Mr3 II7 XIV

Reed, Dwayne M., Darwin Labarthe, and Reuel Stallones
  1972 Epidemiologic studies of serum uric acid levels among
    Micronesians. Arthritis and Rheumatism, 15(4):381-390.
    M XIV

Reed, Dwayne M.; Chris C. Plato; Teresita S. Elizan; and Leonard T.
    Kurland
  1966 The amyotrophic lateral sclerosis/Parkinsonism dementia
    complex: A ten-year follow-up on Guam. I. Epidemiologic
    Studies. American Journal of Epidemiology, 83(1):54-73.
    Mr1 XIV

Reed, Dwayne M., Jose M. Torres, and Jacob A. Brody
  1975 Amyotrophic lateral sclerosis and Parkinsonism-dementia on
    Guam, 1945-1972. II. Familial and genetic Studies. Amer-
    ican Journal of Epidemiology, 101(4):302-310.
    Mr1 XIV XVI

Reed, Erik K.
  1952 Archeology and History of Guam. Washington, D.C: National
    Park Service, Department of the Interior. 133 pp.
    Reviewed: 1955 by G.H.S. Bushnell, Antiquity, 29(113):56-57.
    Mr1 III

Reed, Erik K.
  1954 Archeology in Guam, 1952: A status Report. American
    Anthropologist, 56(5), Part 1:877-879.
    Mr1 III

Rehg, Kenneth L.
  n.d. Ponapean Reference Grammar. PALI Language Texts: Micro-
    nesia. Honolulu: University Press of Hawaii, forthcoming.
    Pn1 XIII

Rehg, Kenneth L.
  1973 On the history of Ponapean Phonology. Working Papers in
    Linguistics, 5(8):17-55. Honolulu: Department of
    Linguistics, University of Hawaii.
    Pn1 XIII

Rehg, Kenneth L. and Damien Sohl
  n.d. Ponapean-English Dictionary. PALI Language Texts: Micro-
    nesia. Honolulu: University Press of Hawaii, forthcoming.
    Pn1 XIII

Reinman, Fred M.
   1965   Maritime adaptation: An aspect of Oceanic Economy.   Ph.D.
          Dissertation, University of California, Los Angeles.
          Available from University Microfilms, Ann Arbor: No. 65-
          04700.
          P II10 III

Reinman, Fred M.
   1967   Fishing: An Aspect of Oceanic Economy, An Archeological
          Approach.   Fieldiana Anthropology, Vol. 54(2).   Chicago:
          Field Museum of Natural History.   208 pp.
          P III

Reinman, Fred M.
   1967   Notes on an archeological survey of Guam, Marianas
          Islands, 1965-66.   Preliminary report to National
          Science Foundation.   Chicago: Field Museum of
          Natural History.   Duplicated.   50 pp.
          Mr1 III

Reinman, Fred M.
   1967   Review of Douglas Osborne, The Archaeology of the Palau
          Islands: An Intensive Survey.   Asian Perspectives, 10:
          174-176.
          PL1 III

Reinman, Fred M.
   1968   Guam prehistory: A preliminary field Report.   IN Prehis-
          toric Culture in Oceania, I. Yawata and Y.H. Sinoto, eds.
          Honolulu: Bishop Museum Press.   pp. 41-50.   Reprinted
          1973.   Guam Recorder, n.s., 3(1):10-14.
          Mr1 III

Reinman, Fred M.
   1968   Radiocarbon dates from Guam, Mariana Islands.   Journal
          of the Polynesian Society, 77(1):80-82.
          Mr1 III

Reinman, Fred M.
   1972   An Archaeological Survey and Preliminary Test Excavations on
          the Island of Guam, Marianas Islands, 1965-66.   Los Angeles:
          California State University at Los Angeles.   Duplicated.
          155 pp., 2 appendices and 45 plates.
          Mr1 III

MAIN BIBLIOGRAPHY

Richard, LCdr. Dorothy
    1957 U.S. Naval Administration of the Trust Territory of the
          Pacific Islands. Washington, D.C.: Office of the Chief of
          Naval Operations. 3 vols. Vol. 1: The Wartime Military
          Government Period 1942-1945. 767 pp. Vol. 2: The Post-War
          Military Government Era 1945-1947. 573 pp. Vol. 3: The
          Trusteeship Period 1947-1951. 1340 pp.
          M XV

Richardson, Frank
    1960 Preliminary report on the birds of Rongelap and Eniwetok,
          especially in relaticn to soil and plant Development. M.S.
          Thesis, University of Washington, Seattle.
          Ms11 Ms15 XIX

Richardson, Paul D.
    1971 A Study of the Socio-Cultural Factors of Guam, A Portion
          of the First Phase of the General Master Plan for the
          Territory of Guam. Agana: Greenleaf/Telesca-Ahn. [Type-
          script located in Micronesian Area Research Center,
          University of Guam]. 132 pp.
          Mr1 II

Richey, M. W.
    1974 Review of David Lewis, We, The Navigators. The Gecgraphical
          Journal, 140(1):114-117.
          P X

Riesenberg, Saul H.
    1948 Archeological remains in Ponape. IN Conservation in
          Micronesia, Harold J. Coolidge, ed. Washington, D.C.:
          Pacific Science Bcard. p. 26.
          Pn1 III

Riesenberg, Saul H.
    1948 Magic and medicine in Ponape. Southwestern Journal of
          Anthropology [now called Journal of Anthropological
          Research], 4(4):406-429.
          Pn1 II2 XIV

Riesenberg, Saul H.
    1948 Ponapean Political and Social Organizaticn. CIMA Report,
          No. 15. Washington, D.C.: Pacific Science Bcard. 255 pp.
          Pn1 II3

Riesenberg, Saul H.
    1950 The cultural position cf Ponape in Oceania. Ph.D. Disser-
          tation, University of California, Berkeley.
          Pn1 II

Riesenberg, Saul H.
    1951 People in Micronesia. Paradise of the Pacific [now
        called Honolulu Magazine], 63(5):25-27, 37.
        M IX

Riesenberg, Saul H.
    1951 Ponapean Omens. Journal of American Folklore, 65(258):
        351-352.
        Pn1 VIII

Riesenberg, Saul H.
    1953 Land tenure problems in the Trust Territory. Abstracts of
        the 8th Pacific Science Congress, 16-18 November, 1953,
        Quezon City, Philippines, p. 399.
        M II1

Riesenberg, Saul H.
    1954 Community development project at Kili. Micronesian
        Monthly [now called Micronesian Reporter], 3(8):19-20.
        Ms24 II7 XVII

Riesenberg, Saul H.
    1954 Modern atomic Exiles. Micronesian Monthly [now called
        Micronesian Reporter], 3(3):21-23. Also published in
        the Honolulu Advertiser, 15-17 July, 1954.
        Ms13 II7

Riesenberg, Saul H.
    1955 Review of Erhard Schlesier, Die Erscheinungsformen des
        Männerhauses und das Klubwesen in Mikronesien. [The
        Characteristic Forms Taken by Men's Houses and the Nature
        of Club Life in Micronesia]. American Anthropologist,
        57(5):1081-1083.
        M II1 II4

Riesenberg, Saul H.
    1959 A New Guinea canoe prow found in the Marshall Islands.
        Journal of the Polynesian Society, 68(1):45-46. [see
        Sinoto 1959].
        Ms II4

Riesenberg, Saul H.
    1959 A Pacific voyager's Hoax. Ethnohistory, 6(3):238-264.
        Pn1 XII

Riesenberg, Saul H.
    1959 Review of John de Young, ed., The Use of Names by
        Micronesians. American Anthropologist, 61(6):1136-1137.
        M II1

Riesenberg, Saul H.
    1965 Table of voyages affecting Micronesian Islands. Oceania,
          36(2):155-168. [see Mason 1966; Sharp 1966].
          M X XII

Riesenberg, Saul H.
    1966 The Ngatik Massacre. Micronesian Reporter, 14(5):
          9-12, 29-30.
          Pn5 II9

Riesenberg, Saul H.
    1968 The tatooed Irishman. The Smithsonian Journal of History,
          3:1-18. [James O'Connell].
          Pn1 XII

Riesenberg, Saul H.
    1968 The Native Polity of Ponape. Smithsonian Contritutions
          to Anthropology, Vol. 10. Washington, D.C.: Smithsonian
          Institution Press. 115 pp. Reviewed: 1968/1969 by Wil-
          liam H. Alkire, Anthropos, 63/64:1039-1040; 1969 by H.E.
          Maude, Journal of Pacific History, 4:230-231; 1969 by J.
          Soustelle, Journal de la Societe des Oceanistes, 25:401;
          1970 by Michael D. Lieber, American Anthropologist,
          72(4):899-900.
          Pn1 II3

Riesenberg, Saul H., ed.
    1972 A Residence of Eleven Years in New Holland and the Caroline
          Islands, by James F. O'Connell. Pacific History Series, No.
          4. Canberra: Australian National University Press. 232 pp.
          Reviewed: 1973 by William A. Lessa, Journal of Pacific
          History, 8:222; 1974 by Ernest S. Dodge, American Anthro-
          pologist, 76(4):925-926.
          Pn1 XII

Riesenberg, Saul H.
    1972 The organisation of navigational knowledge on Puluwat.
          Journal of the Polynesian Society, 81(1):19-56.
          T4 X

Riesenberg, Saul H.
    1972 Review of Sibley S. Morrill, Ponape: Where American
          Colonialism Confronts Black Magic, Five Kingdoms and the
          Mysterious Ruins of Nan-Madol. Association for Anthro-
          pology in Micronesia Newsletter, 1(2):18-19.
          Pn1 II9

Riesenberg, Saul H.
    1975 The ghost islands of the Carolines. Micronesica,
          11(1):7-33.
          C XII

Riesenberg, Saul H., O. A. Bushnell, and S. E. N. Harris
    1953 Blood groups of aboriginal Chamorros and Hawaiians as
          determined by serological analysis of skeletal Remains.
          Abstracts of the 8th Pacific Science Congress, 16-18 Novem-
          ber, 1953, Quezon City, Philippines, pp. 525-526.
          Mr XVI

Riesenberg, Saul H. and Samuel H. Elbert
    1971 The poi of the Meeting. Journal of the Polynesian
          Society, 80(2):217-227.
          T4 II

Riesenberg, Saul H. and John L. Fischer
    1955 Some Ponapean Proverbs. Journal of American Folklore,
          68(267):9-18.
          Pn1 VIII

Riesenberg, Saul H. and A. H. Gayton
    1952 Caroline Island belt Weaving. Southwestern Journal of
          Anthropology [now called Journal of Anthropological Re-
          search], 8(3):342-375.
          C II4

Riesenberg, Saul H. and Shigeru Kaneshiro
    1960 A Caroline Islands Script. Bureau of American Ethnology
          Bulletin, No. 173. Anthropological Papers, No. 60:269-333.
          Washington, D.C.: Smithsonian Institution. Reviewed: 1961
          by Bruce Biggs, Journal of the Polynesian Society, 70(2):
          254-255.
          W T1 XIII

Riesenfeld, Alphonse
    1951 Some observations on the pottery of the Palau Islands.
          Far Eastern Quarterly [now called Journal of Asian Studies],
          10(2):178-180.
          PL1 III

Riley, Frank
    1969 Storm over Micronesia. Saturday Review, 52(37):56-60, 90-93.
          M IX

Riley, Frank
    1970 Micronesia...hotel on Truk kicks off a new travel Era.
          Pacific Travel News, September, pp. 55-59.
          T1 IX

Ripperton, John C.
    1946 Report on Some Agricultural Aspects of Micronesia. IN
          U.S. Commercial Company's Economic Survey of Micronesia,
          Report No. 17. Honolulu: U.S. Commercial Company. Mimeo-
          graphed. 31 pp.
          M I

Risco, A. and Msgr. O. L. Calvo, eds.
    1970 The Apostle of the Marianas: The Life, Labors and Martyrdom
          of Ven. Diego Luis de San Vitores 1627-1672, translated by
          J.M.H. Ledesma. Guam: Diocese of Guam. 234 pp. [trans-
          lation of the 1935 Spanish edition].
          Mr II2

Ritzenthaler, Robert E.
    1949 Native Money of Palau. CIMA Report, No. 27. Washington,
          D.C.: Pacific Science Board. 44 pp. Reprinted 1954.
          Milwaukee Public Museum Publications in Anthropology, No.
          1. 44 pp. Reviewed: 1955 by David M. Schneider, Amer-
          ican Anthropologist, 57(2), Part 1:357; 1957 by Allan H.
          Smith, Asian Perspectives, 1(1&2):117.
          PL1 II4

Rively, William E., S.J.
    1953 The Story of the "Romance". New York: Rinehart and Co.
          241 pp.
          T II2 IX

Robbins, Robert R.
    1947 United States Trusteeship for the Territory of the Pacific
          Islands. U.S. Department of State Bulletin, 16(401):416-423.
          M XVII

Robbins, Robert R.
    1968 Law Note. Michigan Law Review, 66(6):1227-1292.
          M XVII

Robbins, Robert R.
    1969 Political future of Micronesia and the timing of Self-
          Determination. IN Political Modernization of Micronesia,
          A Symposium. Santa Cruz, California: Center for South
          Pacific Studies. 21 pp.
          M XVII

Robbins, Robert R.
    1973 United States territcries in Mid-Century. IN The American
          Territorial System, John P. Bloom, ed. Athens, Chio: Ohio
          University Press. pp. 200-226.
          P XVII

Rogers, Oliver C.
    1946 Report on Soils of Micronesia. IN U.S. Commercial
          Company's Economic Survey cf Micronesia, Report No. 12.
          Honolulu: U.S. Commercial Company. Mimeographed. 21 pp.
          M XI

MAIN BIBLIOGRAPHY

Rosen, Leon; Guy Loison; Jacques Laigret; and Gordon D. Wallace
1967   Studies in eosinophilic meningitis 3. Epidemiolcgic and
clinical observations on Pacific Islands and the possible
etiologic role of Angiostrongylus Cantonensis. American
Journal of Epidemiology, 85(1):17-44.
P XIV

Roucek, Joseph S.
1965   The Pacific in Geopolitics. Contemporary Review,
206(1189):63-76.
P XVII

Rowley, Charles D.
1972   Transition to independence: Some New Guinea background
for some current Micronesian Problems. IN Micronesian
Realities: Pclitical and Economic, Frances McReynolds
Smith, ed. Santa Cruz, California: Center fcr Scuth
Pacific Studies. pp. 255-285.
M XVII

Royce, Joseph and Ted Murray
1971   Work and play in Kapingamarangi, past and Present.
Micronesica, 7(1&2):1-17.
Pn9 IV

Rynkiewich, Michael A.
n.d.   The underdevelopment of anthropological Ethics. IN Ethical
Dilemmas: Anthropologists at Work, Michael A. Rynkiewich
and James P. Spradley, eds. New York: John Wiley and Sons,
forthcoming.
Ms9 II8

Rynkiewich, Michael A.
n.d.   Adoption and land tenure among Arno Marshallese. IN
Transactions in Kinship: Adoption and Fosterage in Oceania,
Ivan Brady, ed. ASAO Mcnograph No. 4. Honolulu: Univer-
sity Press of Hawaii, in press.
Ms9 II1

Rynkiewich, Michael A.
1972   Demography and social structure on Arno Atoll. Paper
read at the Conference cn Pacific Atoll Populations,
East-West Center Population Institute, 27-30 December,
Honolulu, Hawaii.
Ms9 II1 XVI

Rynkiewich, Michael A.
1972   Land tenure among Arnc Marshallese. Ph.D. Dissertation,
University of Minnesota, Minneapolis. Available from
University Microfilms, Ann Arbor: No. 72-32314.
Ms9 II1

Rynkiewich, Michael A.
    1974   The ossification of local politics: The impact of colonialism
           on a Marshall Islands Atoll.   IN Political Development in
           Micronesia, Daniel T. Hughes and Sherwood G. Lingenfelter,
           eds.   Columbus: Ohio State University Press.   pp. 143-165.
           Ms9 II3

Rynkiewich, Michael A.
    1974   Coming home to Bokelab.   IN Conformity and Conflict:
           Readings in Cultural Anthropology, James P. Spradley and
           David W. McCurdy, eds.   2nd edition.   Boston: Little, Brown
           and Co.   pp. 130-142.
           Ms II1

Sachet, Marie-Helene
    1966   Coral islands as ecological Laboratories.   Micronesica,
           3(1):45-50.
           M X

Sachet, Marie-Helene and F. Raymond Fosberg
    1955   Island Bibliographies: Micronesian Botany, Land Environ-
           ment and Ecology of Coral Atolls, Vegetation of Tropical
           Pacific Islands.   Washington, D.C.: National Academy of
           Sciences.   577 pp.   Reprinted n.d.   Springfield, Virginia:
           National Technical Information Service.   Document No.
           AD-738 566.
           M V X XIX

Sachet, Marie-Helene and F. Raymond Fosberg
    1971   Island Bibliographies Supplement: Micronesian Botany, Land
           Environment and Ecology of Coral Atolls, Vegetation of Tro-
           pical Pacific Islands.   Washington, D.C.: National Academy
           of Sciences.   427 pp.
           M V X XIX

Sady, Emil J.
    1950   The Department of the Interior and Pacific Islands Adminis-
           tration.   Public Administration Review, 10(1):13-19.
           P XVII

Sady, Emil J.
    1956   The United Nations and Dependent Peoples.   Washington, D.C.:
           The Brookings Institute.   205 pp.
           P XVII

Sahara, Tamotsu
    1967   Land Classification Program Proposal for the Trust Territory
           of the Pacific Islands.   Honolulu: Land Study Bureau, Univ-
           ersity of Hawaii.   30 pp.
           M X

Sahir, Abul Hasan
    1966   United States' Trust Territory in the Pacific Islands: A
            potential Sea-State. M.A. Thesis, University of Hawaii,
            Honolulu.
            M XVII

Salcedo, Carl
    1970   The search for medicinal plants in Micronesia.   Micronesian
            Reporter, 18(3):10-17.
            M V XIV

Salii, Lazarus E.
    1972   Liberation and conquest in Micronesia.   Pacific Islands
            Monthly, 43(6):37-40, 123.
            M XVII

San Agustin, Joe T.
    1965   United States guaranteed municipal obligations for the
            Territory of Guam. M.A. Thesis, George Washington Uni-
            versity, Washington, D.C.
            Mr1 XVII

Sanchez, Gregorio C.
    1975   Planning and its aftermath on Guam.   IN The Impact of Urban
            Centers in the Pacific, Roland W. Force and Brenda Bishop,
            eds.   Honolulu: Pacific Science Association, Bishop Museum.
            pp. 97-105.
            Mr1 VI

Sanchez, Pedro C.
    1975   The new Guam: A challenge to human Values.   IN The Impact of
            Urban Centers in the Pacific, Roland W. Force and Brenda
            Bishop, eds.   Honolulu: Pacific Science Association, Bishop
            Museum.   pp. 83-88.
            Mr1 II2

Sanvitores, Diego Luis de
    1954   Lingua Mariana. [The Marianas Language]. Anthropos, Micro-
            Bibliotheca, Vol. 14.   Freiburg, Suisse: Anthropos Institut.
            45 pp.
            Mr XIII

Sasuke, N.
    1953   Breadfruit, yams and taros of Ponape Island.   Proceedings
            of the 7th Pacific Science Congress, 2 February-4 March,
            1949, Auckland, 6:159-170.
            Pn1 I V

Saunders, Marin Grace
    1960   Cross-Cultural study of coalitions in the Triad.   M.A.
            Thesis, University of Hawaii, Honolulu.
            M II1

Sayre, Francis B.
    1948   American trusteeship in the Pacific. Proceedings of the
           Academy of Political Science, 22(4):406-416.
           M XVII

Sayre, Francis B.
    1950   The Pacific islands we Hold.   Atlantic Monthly, 185(1):70-75.
           P XVII

Sayre, Francis B.
    1951   Trust Territories' progress toward Self-Government.   U.S.
           Department of State Bulletin, 25(652):1024-1027.
           M XVII

Schaefer, Paul D.
    1975   From "king" to pastor: The acquisition of Christianity on
           Kusaie.   Paper read at the 4th Annual Meeting of the Asso-
           ciation for Social Anthropology in Oceania, 26-30 March,
           Stuart, Florida.
           K II2

Schlesier, Erhard
    1951   Die Erscheinungsformen des Männerhauses und das Klubwesen
           in Mikronesien.   Eine ethno-sociologische Untersuchung.
           [The Characteristic Forms Taken by Men's Houses and the
           Nature of Club Life in Micronesia.   An Ethnosociological
           Study].   Ph.D. Dissertation, Georg-August University of
           Göttingen, Göttingen.   Published 1953.   The Hague: Mouton.
           208 pp.   Reviewed: 1954 by Arthur Capell, Oceania, 25(1&2):
           133-135; 1955 by P.E. Klarwill, Journal of the Polynesian
           Society, 64(2):244; 1955 by Saul H. Riesenberg, American
           Anthropologist, 57(5): 1081-1083.
           M II1 II4

Schlesier, Erhard
    1952   Zum problem "Männerhaus".   [Concerning the problem of
           "men's houses."].   Zeitschrift für Ethnologie, 77(1):133-136.
           M II1

Schlesier, Erhard
    1954   Eine alte Quelle über Lemarafat, Zentralkarolinen.   [An old
           source concerning Lemarafat, Central Carolines].   Ethnos
           [Stockholm], 19(1-4):127-138.
           T2 XII

Schmidt, P. W.
    1953   Die Mythologien und Religionen der Mikronesier.   [Mythology
           and religion of the Micronesians].   Archiv für Völkerkunde,
           8(1):172-227.
           M II2

Schneider, David M.
    1949 The kinship system and village organization of Yap, West
          Caroline Islands, Micronesia: A structural and functional
          Account. Ph.D. Dissertation, Harvard University, Cambridge.
          Y1 II1

Schneider, David M.
    1953 Yap kinship terminology and kin Groups. American Anthro-
          pologist, 55(2):215-236.
          Y1 II1

Schneider, David M.
    1955 Abortion and depopulation on a Pacific Island. IN Health,
          Culture and Community: Case Studies of Public Reactions to
          Health Programs, Benjamin D. Paul and Walter B. Miller, eds.
          New York: Russell Sage Foundation. pp. 211-235. Reprinted
          1968. IN Peoples and Cultures of the Pacific, Andrew P.
          Vayda, ed. Garden City, New York: Natural History Press.
          pp. 383-406. Reprinted 1975. IN The Human Way: Read-
          ings in Anthropology, H. Russell Bernard, ed. New York:
          Macmillan. pp. 365-376. [see Underwood 1973].
          Y1 XVI

Schneider, David M.
    1955 Review of Robert E. Ritzenthaler, Native Money of Palau.
          American Anthropologist, 57(2), Part 1:357.
          PL1 II4

Schneider, David M.
    1955 Review of Thomas Gladwin and Seymour Sarason, Truk: Man in
          Paradise. American Anthropologist, 57(5):1098-1101.
          T1 II6

Schneider, David M.
    1957 Political organization, supernatural sanctions, and the pun-
          ishment for incest on Yap. American Anthropologist, 59(5):
          791-800. Reprinted in Bobbs-Merrill Social Science Reprint
          Series, Reprint A-201. Reprinted 1970. IN Cultures of the
          Pacific: Selected Readings, Thomas G. Harding and Ben J.
          Wallace, eds. New York: Free Press. pp. 232-241.
          Y1 II3

Schneider, David M.
    1957 Truk. IN Matrilineal Kinship, David M. Schneider and
          Kathleen Gough, eds. Berkeley and Los Angeles:
          University of California Press. pp. 202-233.
          T1 II1

Schneider, David M.
    1957 Typhoons on Yap. Human Organization, 16(2):10-15.
          Y1 II7

MAIN BIBLIOGRAPHY

Schneider, David M.
    1962   Double descent on Yap. Journal of the Polynesian Society,
            71(1):1-24. Reprinted in Bobbs-Merrill Social Science
            Reprint Series, Reprint A-341.
            Y1 II1

Schneider, David M.
    1966   Review of C.R.H. Taylor, A Pacific Bibliography: Printed
            Matter Relating to the Native Peoples of Polynesia, Melanesia
            and Micronesia. American Anthropologist, 68(5):1276-1277.
            P IX

Schneider, David M.
    1968   Virgin Birth. Man, n.s., 3(1):126-129.
            Y1 II1

Schneider, David M.
    1969   A re-analysis of the kinship system of Yap in the light of
            Dumont's Statement. Paper read at the Wenner-Gren Symposium
            on Kinship and Locality [Symposium No. 46], 23 August-1 Sep-
            tember, Burg Wartenstein, Austria.
            Y1 II1

Schneider, David M.
    1974   Depopulation and the Yap Tabinau. IN Social Organizati
            the Applications of Anthropology, Essays in Honor of Lauriston
            Sharp, Robert J. Smith, ed. Ithaca: Cornell University
            Press. pp. 94-113.
            Y1 II1

Schultz, Leonard P.; Earl S. Herald; Ernest A. Lachner; Arthur D.
            Welander; and Loren P. Woods
    1953   Fishes of the Marshall and Marianas Islands. Volume 1.
            Families Asymmetrontidae through Siganidae. U.S. National
            Museum Bulletin, No. 202. Washington, D.C.: Smithsonian
            Institution. 685 pp.
            Ms Mr XIX

Schultz, Leonard P.; Wilbert M. Chapman; Ernest A. Lachner; and Loren
            P. Woods
    1960   Fishes of the Marshall and Marianas Islands. Volume 2.
            Families Mullidae through Stromateidae. U.S. National
            Museum Bulletin, No. 202. Washington, D.C.: Smithsonian
            Institution. 438 pp.
            Ms Mr XIX

Schultz, Leonard P., Loren P. Woods, and Ernest A. Lachner
    1966   Fishes of the Marshall and Marianas Islands. Volume 3.
            Families Kraemeriidae through Antennariidae. U.S. Nat-
            ional Museum Bulletin, No. 202. Washington, D.C.:
            Smithsonian Institution. 176 pp.
            Ms Mr XIX

MAIN BIBLIOGRAPHY

Searles, P. J.
    1974 Spanish Galleons. [Part 1]. Guam Recorder, n.s., 4(3):51-60.
          Mr XII

Searles, P. J.
    1975 Spanish Galleons. [Part 2]. Guam Recorder, n.s., 5(1):56-61.
          Mr XII

Sedwick, Ensign Benjamin Frank
    1946 Puken Aueuen Fosun Ingnes (Ngeni Chon Sukunun Chuk). [Spoken
          English Primer (for Trukese Students)]. Pearl Harbor: U.S.
          Naval Military Government, 14th Naval District Publications
          and Printing Office. 110 pp.
          T1 XIII

Segalen, Martine
    1971 Review of Vern Caroll, ed., Adoption in Eastern Cceania.
          L'anthropologie, 15(5&6):515-516.
          P II1

Seiden, William
    1960 Chamorro Phonemes. Anthropological Linguistics, 2(4):6-35.
          Mr XIII

Severance, Craig J.
    1974 Sanction and sakau: The accessibility and social ccntrol of
          alcohol on Pis-Losap. Paper read at the 3rd Annual Meeting
          of the Association for Social Anthropology in Oceania, 13-17
          March, Asilomar, Pacific Grove, California.
          T8 Pn1 II1

Severance, Craig J.
    1975 Becoming Ponapean: The accomodation of the Pis-Lcsap Home-
          steaders. Paper read at the 4th Annual Meeting of the Asso-
          ciation for Social Anthropology in Oceania, 26-30 March,
          Stuart, Florida.
          T8 Pn1 II7

Shahan, James Buhl
    1951 American colonial administration in the Western Pacific:
          A study in civil-military Relations. Ph.D. Dissertation,
          Ohio State University, Columbus.
          M XVII

Shapiro, Harry L.
    1953 Physical anthropology cf Micronesia: Discussion. Proceed-
          ings of the 7th Pacific Science Congress, 2 February-4 March,
          1949, Auckland, New Zealand, 7:216-217.
          M XVI

MAIN BIBLIOGRAPHY

Sharp, Andrew
    1960 Discovery of the Pacific Islands.   London: Oxford
          University Press.   259 pp.
          P XII

Sharp, Andrew
    1966 Early Micronesian Voyaging.   Oceania, 37(1):64-65.   [see
          Mason 1966; Riesenberg 1965].
          M X

Sharp, Andrew
    1972 David Lewis on indigenous Pacific Navigation.   Journal of
          Pacific History, 7:222-223.   [see Lewis 1972].
          P X

Sheridan, Francis P.
    1954 Why strategic areas? A study of the trusteeship agreement
          for the former Japanese Mandated Islands administered by
          the United States of America. M.A. Thesis, Columbia Uni-
          versity, New York.
          M XVII

Shineberg, Dorothy, ed.
    1971 The Trading Voyages of Andrew Cheyne 1841-1844.   Pacific
          History Series, No. 3.   Honolulu: University of Hawaii Press.
          Reviewed: 1972 by J.P. Faivre, Journal de la Societe des
          Oceanistes, 28(36):311-312; 1972 by Francis X. Hezel, Jour-
          nal of Pacific History, 7:231-232; 1973 by Ernest S. Dodge,
          Man, n.s., 8(1):136.
          M XII

Shinozaki, Nobuo
    1953 Summary of the investigation on mixed-blood families of
          Micronesian with European or other Races. Proceedings of
          the 7th Pacific Science Congress, 2 February-4 March,
          1949, Auckland, New Zealand, 7:12.   [abstract].
          M XVI

Shurcliff, W. A.
    1947 Bombs at Bikini: The Official Report of Operation Cross-
          roads.   New York: William H. Wise and Co.   212 pp.
          Ms13 XV

Shutler, Richard, Jr.
    1958 Review of Alexander Spoehr, Marianas Prehistory.   Asian
          Perspectives, 2(1):84-85.
          Mr III

Shutler, Richard, Jr.
    1961 Peopling of the Pacific in the light of radiocarbon Dating.
          Asian Perspectives, 5(2):207-212.
          P III

Sicard, Charles
    1974 Micronesian children with a foreign Parent. Micronesian
          Reporter, 22(4):20-24.
          M II1

Sigler, Jay A.
    1960 American administration of the Pacific Islands Trust Terri-
          tory. Journal of East Asiatic Studies [University of Manila],
          9(2&3):52-63.
          M XVII

Silk, Ekpap
    1969 Creation of the Future Political Status Commissicn of the
          Congress of Micronesia. IN Political Modernization of
          Micronesia, A Symposium. Santa Cruz, California: Center
          for South Pacific Studies. 6 pp.
          M XVII

Simmons, D. R.
    1970 Palau cave paintings on Aulong Island. Records of the Auck-
          land Institute and Museum, 7:171-173.
          PL1 II4 IV

Simmons, J. S.; T. F. Whayne; G. W. Anderson; H. M. Horack; and
          collaborators
    1944 Global Epidemiology: A Geography of Disease and Sani-
          tation. Philadelphia: Lippincott. 504 pp.
          M XIV

Simmons, R. T.
    1956 A report on blood group genetical surveys in Eastern Asia,
          Indonesia, Melanesia, Micronesia, Polynesia, and Australia
          in the study of Man. Anthropos, 51:500-512.
          M XVI

Simmons, R. T.; J. J. Graydon; D. C. Gajdusek; and Paul Brown
    1965 Blood group genetic variations in natives of the Caroline
          Islands and in other parts of Micronesia. Oceania, 36(2):
          132-170.
          M XVI

Simmons, R. T., J. J. Graydon, and N. M. Semple
    1953 A blood group genetical survey in Micronesia: Palauans,
          Trukese, and Kapingas. Medical Journal of Australia
          [40th year], 2(16):589-596.
          C XVI

Simmons, R. T.; J. J. Graydon; N. M. Semple; Joseph P. Birdsell;
      John D. Milbourne; and J. R. Lee
   1952 A collaborative genetical survey in Marshall Islanders.
      American Journal of Physical Anthropology, 10(1):31-54.
      Ms XVI

Sinder, Leon
   1968 Review of Douglas Osborne, The Archaeology of the Palau
      Islands: An Intensive Survey. American Anthropologist,
      70(4):815-816.
      PL1 III

Singleton, John
   1972 Review of Francis X. Hezel and Charles B. Reafsnyder,
      Micronesia: A Changing Society. Association for Anthro-
      pology in Micronesia Newsletter, 1(1):17-20.
      M VII

Singleton, John
   1974 Education, planning and political development in Micronesia.
      IN Political Development in Micronesia, Daniel T. Hughes
      and Sherwood G. Lingenfelter, eds. Columbus: Ohio State
      University Press. pp. 72-92.
      M II3 VII

Singleton, John
   1974 The U.S. Trust Territory in the Pacific. Vital Issues,
      23(7):1-6.
      M XVII

Sinha, D. P.
   1969 Review of William H. Alkire, Lamotrek Atoll and Inter-Island
      Socioeconomic Ties. Oceania, 40(1):82.
      Y9 II1

Sinoto, Yosihiko H.
   1959 Drifting canoe prows. Journal of the Polynesian Society,
      68(4):354-355. [see Riesenberg 1959].
      Ms II4

Skinner, Carlton
   1972 The economic base and role of the private investor in
      Micronesia. IN Micronesian Realities: Political and
      Economic, Frances McReynolds Smith, ed. Santa Cruz, Cal-
      ifornia: Center for South Pacific Studies. pp. 195-207.
      M VI

Sloan, N. R.; R. M. Worth; B. Jano; P. Pasal; and C. C. Shepard
   1972 Acedapsone in leprosy chemoprophylaxis: Field trial in
      three high-prevalence villages in Micronesia. International
      Journal of Leprosy, 40(1):40-47.
      Pn1 Pn7 XIV

Sloan, N. R.; R. M. Worth; B. Jano; P. Fasal; and C. C. Shepard
    1972 Acedapsone in leprosy treatment: Trial in 68 active cases in
          Micronesia. International Journal of Leprosy, 4C(1):48-52.
          M Pn7 XIV

Smith, Alfred G.
    1951 Gamwoelhaelhi Ishilh Weleeya. [Guide to Woleai Spelling].
          Honolulu: Office of the High Commissioner. Mimeographed.
          51 pp.
          Y6 XIII

Smith, Alfred G.
    1951 Ki Luwn Specl Kosray. [Guide to Kusaien Spelling]. Hono-
          lulu: Office of the High Commissioner. Mimeographed.
          26 pp.
          K XIII

Smith, Alfred G.
    1951 Wahween Jibehhleh Kajin Marshall. [Guide to Marshallese
          Spelling]. Honolulu: Office of the High Commissioner.
          Mimeographed. 26 pp.
          Ms XIII

Smith, Alfred G.
    1956 Literacy promotion in an underdeveloped Area. Ph.D.
          Dissertation, University of Wisconsin, Madison. Available
          from University Microfilms, Ann Arbor: No. 56-3168.
          M VII

Smith, Alfred G. and John P. Kennedy
    1960 The extension of incest taboos in the Woleai, Micronesia.
          American Anthropologist, 62(4):643-647.
          W II1

Smith, Allan H.
    1956 Attitudes and relationships (American-Micronesian).
          Micronesian Monthly [now called Micronesian Reporter],
          4(1):26-31.
          M XVII

Smith, Allan H.
    1957 Report on research in Micronesian ethnology and
          Archaeology. Asian Perspectives, 1(1):112-119.
          M II III

Smith, Allan H.
    1957 Review of Robert E. Ritzenthaler, Native Money of Palau.
          Asian Perspectives, 1(1&2):117.
          PL1 II4

Smith, Allan H.
1958 Report on research in Micronesian ethnology and
      Archaeology. Asian Perspectives, 2(1):68-85.
      M II III

Smith, Allan H.
1959 Micronesia. Asian Perspectives, 3(1):53-55.
      M III

Smith, Allan H.
1960 Micronesia. Asian Perspectives, 4(1&2):95-100.
      M III

Smith, Allan H.
1961 Micronesia. Asian Perspectives, 5(1):79-87.
      M III

Smith, Allan H.
1961 Review of John de Young, ed., Taro Cultivation Practices
      and Beliefs: Part I. The Western Carolines. Part II.
      The Eastern Carolines and the Marshall Islands; John E. de
      Young, ed., Yam Cultivation in the Trust Territory; Robert K.
      McKnight, The Oyabun-Kobun in Palau; and Robert K. McKnight,
      Breadfruit Cultivation Practices and Beliefs in Palau,
      American Anthropologist, 63(2), Part 1:426-428.
      M PL1 I II7 VII

Smith, Daniel C.
1972 Issues in the economic development of Micronesia: Tourism
      as an Example. IN Micronesian Realities: Political and
      Economic, Frances McReynolds Smith, ed. Santa Cruz, Cal-
      ifornia: Center for South Pacific Studies. pp. 217-234.
      M VI

Smith, Donald F.
1968 Education of the Micronesian with emphasis on the
      historical Development. Ed.D. Dissertation, American
      University, Washington, D.C. Available from University
      Microfilms, Ann Arbor: No. 68-14968.
      M VII

Smith, Donald F.
1969 American education in the Trust Territory of the Pacific
      Islands. Educational Leadership, 27(1):71-77.
      M VII

Smith, Donald F.
1970 The Micronesian Occupational Center (at Koror, Palau).
      South Pacific Bulletin, 20(1):25-26.
      PL1 VII

MAIN BIBLIOGRAPHY

Smith, Donald F.
   1971   A glimpse of German education in Micronesia, 1899-1914.
         Papua-New Guinea Journal of Education, 7(2):50-51.
         M VII

Smith, Donald F.
   1971   The political evolution of Micronesia toward Self-Deter-
         mination. Asian Studies, 9(1):79-86.
         M XVII

Smith, Donald F.
   1973   Diversity in Micronesia. Current History, 65(387):
         221-223, 225.
         M XVII

Smith, Frances McReynolds
   1972   From Trust Territory to nationhood: Political progress
         in Micronesia. IN Micronesian Realities: Political
         and Economic, Frances McReynolds Smith, ed. Santa Cruz,
         California: Center for South Pacific Studies. pp. 93-114.
         M XVII

Smith, Frances McReynolds, ed.
   1972   Micronesian Realities: Political and Economic. Seminar
         Series, No. 2. Santa Cruz, California: Center for South
         Pacific Studies. 288 pp.
         M VI XVII

Smith, Howard F.
   1971   The forced-pace modernisation of Micronesia. Pacific
         Viewpoint, 12(2):163-170.
         M II7

Smith, James Jerome
   n.d.   Rotanese fosterage: Counterexample of an Oceanic Pattern.
         IN Transactions in Kinship: Adoption and Fosterage in
         Oceania, Ivan Brady, ed. ASAO Monograph No. 4. Honolulu:
         University Press of Hawaii, in press.
         Mr3 II1

Smith, James Jerome
   1971   Intergenerational land transactions on Rota, Mariana
         Islands. Paper read at the 70th Annual Meeting of the
         American Anthropological Association, 18-21 November, New
         York City.
         Mr3 II1

MAIN BIBLIOGRAPHY

Smith, James Jerome
1972   Intergenerational land transactions on Rota, Mariana
        Islands: A study of ethnographic Theory. Ph.D. Disser-
        tation, University of Arizona, Tucson. Available from
        University Microfilms, Ann Arbor: No. 72-31842.
        Mr3 II1

Smith, James Jerome
1973   The population of Rota, May 1971. IN Rota: Master Plan.
        Honolulu: Hawaii Architects and Engineers, Incorporated.
        Appendix G.
        Mr3 XVI

Smith, James Jerome
1973   Land tenure on Rota: Yesterday, today and Tomorrow.
        Association for Anthropology in Micronesia Newsletter,
        2(2):9-12.
        Mr3 II1

Smith, James Jerome
1973   Types and general location of private land tenure on Rota
        exclusive of Songsong Village. IN Rota: Master Plan.
        Honolulu: Hawaii Architects and Engineers, Incorporated.
        Appendix H.
        Mr3 II1

Smith, James Jerome
1974   Household economic strategies on Rota, Mariana Islands.
        Paper read at the 3rd Annual Meeting of the Association
        for Social Anthropology in Oceania, 13-17 March, Asilomar,
        Pacific Grove, California.
        Mr3 II10

Smith, James Jerome
1974   Land tenure on Rota, Mariana Islands. Micronesica,
        10(2):223-236.
        Mr3 II1

Smith, James Jerome
1975   Review of Donald M. Topping with the assistance of Bernadita
        C. Dungca, Chamorro Reference Grammar. American Anthropolo-
        gist, 77(1):127.
        Mr XIII

Smith, Robert Clark
1970   Some problems of modernization in a Pacific Island Setting.
        M.A. Thesis, University of Kansas, Lawrence.
        Pn1 II7

MAIN BIBLIOGRAPHY

Smith, Robert O.
    1946 Survey of the Fisheries of the Former Japanese Mandated
          Islands. IN U.S. Commercial Company's Economic Survey of
          Micronesia, Report No. 10. Honolulu: U.S. Commercial
          Company. Mimeographed. 98 pp.
          M VI

Smith, Stanley A. de
    1969 Options for Micronesia: A potential crisis for America's
          Pacific Trust Territory. New York University Center for
          International Studies Policy Papers, 3(1):1-29.
          M XVII

Smith, Stanley A. de
    1970 Microstates and Micronesia: Problems of America's Pacific
          Islands and Other Minute Territories. New York: New York
          University Press. 193 pp.
          M XVII

Sohn, Ho-min
    1969 An outline of Ulithian Grammar. Ph.D. Dissertation, Uni-
          versity of Hawaii, Honolulu. Available from University
          Microfilms, Ann Arbor: No. 70-4318.
          Y3 XIII

Sohn, Ho-min
    1971 a-raising in Woleaian. Working Papers in Linguistics,
          3(8):15-36. Honolulu: Department of Linguistics,
          University of Hawaii.
          W XIII

Sohn, Ho-min
    1973 Relative clause formation in Micronesian Languages.
          Working Papers in Linguistics, 5(8):93-124. Honclulu:
          Department of Linguistics, University of Hawaii.
          M XIII

Sohn, Ho-min
    1975 A Reference Grammar of Woleaian. PALI Language Texts:
          Micronesia. Honolulu: University Press of Hawaii. 308 pp.
          W XIII

Sohn, Ho-min and Byron W. Bender
    1973 A Ulithian Grammar. Pacific Linguistics, Series C, No. 27.
          Canberra: Linguistic Circle of Canberra. 398 pp.
          Y3 XIII

Solenberger, Robert R.
    1953 The social and cultural position of Micronesian minorities
          on Guam. South Pacific Commission Technical Paper, No. 49.
          Noumea: South Pacific Commission. 11 pp.
          Mr1 II

Solenberger, Robert R.
    1953- Recent changes in Chamorro direction Terminology.
    1954 Oceania, 24(2):132-141.
          Mr XIII

Solenberger, Robert R.
    1960 Contrasting patterns of Carolinian population distribution
          in the Marianas. IN Men and Cultures, A.F.C. Wallace, ed.
          Selected Papers of the 5th International Congress of Anthro-
          pological and Ethnological Sciences, 1956. Philadelphia:
          University of Pennsylvania Press. pp. 513-518.
          Mr C XVI

Solenberger, Robert R.
    1962 The social meaning of language choice in the Marianas.
          Anthropological Linguistics, 4(1):59-64.
          Mr XIII

Solenberger, Robert R.
    1964 Continuity of local political institutions in the Marianas.
          Human Organization, 23(1):53-60.
          Mr II3

Solenberger, Robert R.
    1967 The changing role of rice in the Marianas Islands.
          Micronesica, 3(2):97-103.
          Mr I

Solenberger, Robert R.
    1968 Cultural conflict and language learning in Micronesia.
          Proceedings of the 8th International Congress of Anthro-
          pological and Ethnological Sciences, Vol. 2, Section B-8.
          Tokyo: Science Council of Japan. pp. 364-367.
          M II7 XIII

Solheim, Wilhelm G., II
    1952 Oceanic pottery Manufacture. Journal of East Asiatic Studies
          [University of Manila], 1(2):1-39.
          M II4

Solheim, Wilhelm G., II
    1960 Review of E.W. Gifford and D.S. Gifford, Archaeological
          Excavations in Yap. Asian Perspectives, 4:99-100.
          Y1 III

Someki, Atsushi
    1945 Micronesia no Fudo to Mingu. [Peoples and Customs in
          Micronesia]. Tokyo: Shoko Shoin. 488 pp.
          M II

Soucie, Edward
    1963 Jesuit Brothers in the Caroline-Marshall Islands Mission.
          The Jesuit, Autumn, pp. 3-7.
          C Ms II2

Soucie, Edward
    1964 Fr. Hugh Costigan, S.J. and Ponape, Caroline Islands.
          The Jesuit, Winter, pp. 3-5.
          Pn1 II2

Souder, Paul B.
    1963 Poisonous plants on Guam. IN Venemous and Poisonous Animals
          and Noxious Plants of the Pacific Region, H.L. Keegan and
          and W.V. MacFarlane, eds. Oxford: Pergamon Press. pp. 15-29.
          Mr1 V

Souder, Paul B.
    1971 Guam: Land tenure in a Fortress. IN Land Tenure in the
          Pacific, Ron Crocombe, ed.   London: Oxford University Press.
          pp. 192-205.
          Mr1 II1

Soustelle, J.
    1969 Review of Saul H. Riesenberg, The Native Polity cf Ponape.
          Journal de la Societe des Oceanistes, 25:401.
          Pn1 II3

Spiro, Melford E.
    1950 The problem of aggression in a South Sea Culture. Ph.D.
          Dissertation, Northwestern University, Evanston.
          Y11 II6

Spiro, Melford E.
    1950 A psychotic personality in the South Seas. Psychiatry,
          13(2):189-204.
          Y11 II6

Spiro, Melford E.
    1951 Some Ifaluk myths and folk Tales. Journal of American
          Folklore, 64(253):289-302.
          Y11 VIII

Spiro, Melford E.
    1952 Ghosts, Ifaluk, and teleological Functionalism. American
          Anthropologist, 54(4):497-503. Reprinted in Bobbs-Merrill
          Social Science Reprint Series, Reprint A-351. Reprinted
          1965. IN A Reader in Comparative Religion: An Anthropo-
          logical Approach, 2nd edition, William A. Lessa and Evon Z.
          Vogt, eds. New York: Harper and Row. pp. 432-436.
          Y11 II2

Spiro, Melford E.
    1953 A typology of functional Analysis. Explorations, 1(1):84-94.
          Y11 II

Spiro, Melford E.
    1953 Ghosts: An anthropological inquiry into learning and
          Perception. Journal of Abnormal and Social Psychology
          [now called Journal cf Abnormal Psychology], 43(3):376-
          382. Reprinted 1967. IN Personalities and Cultures,
          Readings in Psychological Anthropology, Robert Hunt, ed.
          Garden City, New York: Natural History Press. pp. 238-250.
          Y11 II6

Spiro, Melford E.
    1957 156 Rorschachs, 126 Modified TATs, 83 Stewart ERTs, 82
          Bavela MITs, and 54 Dreams of Ifaluk Men, Women, and
          Children. Microcard Publicaticns of Primary Records in
          Culture and Personality, Volume 2. Madison, Wisconsin:
          The Microcard Foundaticn.
          Y11 II6

Spiro, Melford E.
    1959 Cultural heritage, personal tensions, and mental illness
          in a South Sea Culture. IN Culture and Mental Health,
          Marvin K. Opler, ed. New York: Macmillan. pp. 141-171.
          Y11 II6

Spiro, Melford E.
    1961 Sorcery, evil spirits and functional analysis: A Rejoinder.
          American Anthropologist, 63(4):820-824. [see Beauclair
          1963; Lessa 1961].
          Y11 II2

Spoehr, Alexander
    1946 The Marshall Islands and Trans-Pacific Aviation. The
          Geographical Review, 36(3):447-451.
          Ms X

Spoehr, Alexander
    1947 Micronesian Expediticn completes Work (Majurc). Chicago
          Natural History Museum Bulletin [now called Field Museum
          of Natural History Bulletin], 18(9):1-2, 8.
          Ms8 IX

Spoehr, Alexander
    1949 The generation type kinship system in the Marshall and
          Gilbert Islands. Southwestern Journal of Anthrcpology [now
          called Journal of Anthropological Research], 5(2):107-116.
          Ms II1

Spoehr, Alexander
    1949 Life in the Marshall Islands. Research Reviews [Office
        of Naval Research], April, pp. 1-6.
        Ms II IX

Spoehr, Alexander
    1949 Majuro, A Village in the Marshall Islands. Fieldiana:
        Anthropology, Vol. 39. Chicago: Natural History Museum.
        266 pp. Also published 1949. CIMA Report, No. 1. Washing-
        ton, D.C.: Pacific Science Board. 266 pp. Reprinted
        1966. New York: Kraus Reprint Corporation. Reviewed:
        1950 by John F. Embree, American Anthropologist, 52(4):
        533-535; 1950 by Raymond E. Murphy, The Geographical
        Review, 40(3):504-505.
        Ms8 II

Spoehr, Alexander
    1950 Digging in Micronesia. Chicago Natural History Museum
        Bulletin [now called Field Museum of Natural History Bulle-
        tin], 21(8):6-7.
        M III

Spoehr, Alexander
    1950 Expedition to Marianas completes work. Chicago Natural
        History Museum Bulletin [now called Field Museum of Natural
        History Bulletin], 21(12):8.
        Mr II

Spoehr, Alexander
    1950 Exploring man's past in isles of the South Pacific.
        Chicago Natural History Museum Bulletin [now called Field
        Museum of Natural History Bulletin], 21(5):3, 8.
        Mr III

Spoehr, Alexander
    1950 Notice on Marianas Archaeology. Chicago Natural History
        Museum Bulletin [now called Field Museum of Natural His-
        tory Bulletin], 21(1):3-5.
        Mr III

Spoehr, Alexander
    1950 Report from Micronesia. Chicago Natural History Museum
        Bulletin [now called Field Museum of Natural History
        Bulletin], 21(4):7.
        M IX

Spoehr, Alexander
    1951 The peoples living in U.S. Trust Territory and Guam. Chicago
        Natural History Museum Bulletin [now called Field Museum of
        Natural History Bulletin], 22(2):3.
        M Mr1 II

MAIN BIBLIOGRAPHY

Spoehr, Alexander
  1951 Anthropology and the Trust Territory: A summary of recent
        Researches. Clearinghouse Bulletin of Research in Human
        Organization, 1(2):1-3.
        M II

Spoehr, Alexander
  1951 Marianas expedition excavates ancient "ghost" Homes.
        Chicago Natural History Museum Bulletin [now called
        Field Museum of Natural History Bulletin], 22(1):3-5.
        Mr III

Spoehr, Alexander
  1951 The Tinian Chamorros. Human Organization, 10(4):16-20.
        Mr4 II7

Spoehr, Alexander
  1952 Time perspective in Micronesia and Polynesia. Southwestern
        Journal of Anthropology [now called Journal of Anthropolo-
        gical Research], 8(4):457-465.
        M II6

Spoehr, Alexander
  1953 Anthropology and coral atoll field Research. Atoll
        Research Bulletin, No. 17:109-110.
        P II

Spoehr, Alexander
  1954 Saipan, the Ethnology of a War-Devastated Island. Field-
        iana: Anthropology, Vol. 41. Chicago: Natural History
        Museum. 383 pp. Reviewed: 1955 by Gordon W. Hewes, American
        Anthropologist, 57(2), Part 1:358-359.
        Mr2 II

Spoehr, Alexander
  1955 Human background of Pacific Science. The Scientific
        Monthly, 81(1):3-9.
        P IX

Spoehr, Alexander
  1957 Relation of humans to the atoll Environment. Proceedings
        of the 8th Pacific Science Congress, 16-18 November, 1953,
        Quezon City, Philippines, 3A:1049-1052.
        P X

MAIN BIBLIOGRAPHY

Spoehr, Alexander
  1957 Marianas Prehistory: Archeological Survey and Excavations
        on Saipan, Tinian, and Rota. Fieldiana: Anthropology,
        Vol. 48. Chicago: Natural History Museum. 187 pp.
        Reviewed: 1958 by Edward W. Gifford, American Anthropo-
        logist, 60(1), Part 1:206-207; 1958 by F.D. McCarthy,
        Oceania, 28(3):240-241; 1958 by Richard Shutler, Jr.,
        Asian Perspectives, 2(1):84-85.
        Mr III

Spoehr, Alexander
  1960 Port town and hinterland in the Pacific Islands. American
        Anthropologist, 62(4):586-592. Reprinted 1970. IN Cultures
        of the Pacific: Selected Readings, Thomas G. Harding and
        Ben J. Wallace, eds. New York: Free Press. pp. 412-418.
        P II7

Spoehr, Alexander
  1960 Review of E.W. Gifford and D.S. Gifford, Archaeological
        Investigations in Yap. Journal of the Polynesian Society,
        69(2):175.
        Y1 III

Spoehr, Alexander
  1964 Review of F. Raymond Fosberg, ed., Man's Place in the Island
        Ecosystem: A Symposium. American Anthropologist, 66(3),
        Part 1:685-686.
        P X

Spoehr, Alexander (compiler)
  1966 Bibliography of the Tri-Institutional Pacific Program, 1953-
        1964 (TRIPP). Honolulu: Pacific Scientific Information
        Center, Bishop Museum. Mimeographed. 11 pp.
        P IX

Spoehr, Alexander
  1966 The part and the whole: Reflections on the study of a
        Region. American Anthropologist, 68(3):629-640.
        P II

Spoehr, Alexander
  1973 Life of the Chamorros in the Marianas. Guam Recorder, n.s.,
        3(2):13-14.
        Mr II

Spoehr, Alexander (Chairman); Kenneth P. Emory; Edward W. Gifford;
        Gordon MacGregor; and Douglas Osborne
  1951 A program for Micronesian Archaeology. Recommendations of
        the Sub-Committee on Pacific Archaeology, National Research
        Council. American Anthropologist, 53(4), Part 1:594-597.
        M III

Spoehr, Florence Mann
1963   White Falcon. The House of Godeffroy and Its Commercial and
        Scientific Role in the Pacific. Palo Alto, California:
        Pacific Books. 120 pp.
        P XII

St. John, Harold
1948   Plant records from the Caroline Islands, Micronesia.
        Pacific Plant Studies, No. 8. Pacific Science, 2(4):272-273.
        C V

St. John, Harold
1948   Report on the flora of Pingelap Atoll, Caroline Islands,
        Micronesia, and observations on the vocabulary of the
        native Inhabitants. Pacific Plant Studies, No. 7. Pacific
        Science, 2(2):96-113.
        Pn7 V

St. John, Harold
1951   Plant records from Aur Atoll and Majuro Atoll, Marshall
        Islands, Micronesia. Pacific Plant Studies, No. 9.
        Pacific Science, 5(3):279-286.
        Ms7 Ms8 V

St. John, Harold
1957   Adventive plants in the Marshalls before 1941. Proceedings
        of the 8th Pacific Science Congress, 16-18 November, 1953,
        Quezon City, Philippines, 4:227. [abstract].
        Ms V

St. John, Harold
1960   Flora of Eniwetok Atoll. Pacific Science, 14(4):313-336.
        Ms11 V

St. John, Harold and Leonard Mason
1953   Vernacular names of the plants of Bikini, Marshall Islands.
        Pacific Plant Studies, No. 12. Pacific Science, 7(2):165-168.
        Ms13 V

Stanford University, School of Naval Administration
1948   Handbook on the Trust Territory of the Pacific Islands; A
        Handbook for Use in Training and Administration Prepared at
        the School of Naval Administration, Hoover Institute, Stan-
        ford University. Washington, D.C.: Office of the Chief of
        Naval Operations. 311 pp.
        M XV XVII

Stanhope, John M.; Jacob A. Brody; Edward Brink; and Charles F. Morris
1972   Convulsions among the Chamorro people of Guam, Mariana
        Islands--I. Seizure Disorders. American Journal of
        Epidemiology, 95(3):292-298.
        Mr1 XIV

Stanhope, John M.; Jacob A. Brody; Edward Brink; and Charles E. Morris
    1972 Convulsions among the Chamorro people of Guam, Mariana
          Islands--II. Febrile Convulsions. American Journal of
          Epidemiology, 95(3):299-304.
          Mr1 XIV

Stanhope, John M., Jacob A. Brody, and Charles E. Morris
    1972 Epidemiologic features of amyotrophic lateral sclerosis
          and Parkinsonism-dementia, Guam, Mariana Islands.
          International Journal of Epidemiology, 1(3):199-210.
          Mr1 XIV XVI

Stark, John T. and Richard L. Hay
    1963 Geology and petrology of volcanic rocks of the Truk Islands,
          East Caroline Islands. U.S. Geological Survey Professional
          Paper, No. 409. Washington, D.C.: U.S. Geological Survey.
          41 pp.
          T1 XI

Stark, John T.; James E. Paseur; Richard L. Hay; Harold G. May; and
          Elmer D. Patterson
    1958 Military Geology of Truk, Caroline Islands. Prepared under
          the direction of the Chief of Engineers, U.S. Army, by the
          Intelligence Division, Office of the Engineer, Headquarters,
          U.S. Army Pacific, with personnel of the U.S. Geological
          Survey. Washington, D.C.: Department of the Army. Mimeo-
          graphed. 205 pp.
          T1 XI

Steager, Peter William
    1972 Food in its social context on Puluwat, Eastern Caroline
          Islands. Ph.D. Dissertation, University of California,
          Berkeley.
          T4 II10

Steager, Peter William
    1974 Where does art begin on Puluwat? Paper read at the
          Conference on The Art of Oceania, 21-26 August,
          Hamilton, Ontario, Canada.
          T4 IV

Steinberg, A. G. and Newton E. Morton
    1973 Immunoglobulins in the Eastern Carolines. American
          Journal of Physical Anthropology, 38(3):699-702.
          Pn K XVI

Stensland, Carl H.
    1957 The soils of Guam. Proceedings of the 8th Pacific Science
          Congress, 16-18 November, 1953, Quezon City, Philippines,
          2:270-271. [abstract].
          Mr1 XI

Stephenson, 1st Lt. F. A.
    1971 Talofofo cave Writing. Guam Recorder, n.s., 1(1):10-11.
          Mr1 III

Stevens, Russell L.
    1953 Guam, U.S.A.: Birth of a Territory. Honolulu: Tcngg
          Publishing Co. 151 pp.
          Mr1 IX XVII

Stevens, William D.
    1949 A study of depopulation on Yap Island. Ph.D. Dissertation,
          Harvard University, Cambridge.
          Y1 XVI

Stewart, J. L.
    1971 Rubella-Deafened children in Guam. South Pacific Bulletin,
          21(3):15-17.
          Mr1 XIV

Stewart, T. D. and Alexander Spoehr
    1952 Evidence on the paleopathology of Yaws. Bulletin of the
          History of Medicine, 26(6):538-553.
          Mr4 III XIV

Stillfried, Bernhard
    1953 Die Soziale Organisaticn in Mikronesien. [Social Organi-
          zation in Micronesia]. Acta Ethnologica et Linguistica.
          Nr. 4, Institut für Völkerkunde der Universität Wien,
          Verlag Herold Wien. 132 pp. Reviewed: 1954 by George P.
          Murdock, American Anthropologist, 56(6), Part 1:1122-1123.
          M II1

Stillfried, Bernhard
    1956 Mutterrechtliche Verwandtschaftszüge auf den Zentralkaro-
          linen und ihre Problematik. [Matrilineal kinship in the
          Central Carolines and its difficulties of Soluticn].
          Zeitschrift für Ethnologie, 81(1):95-103.
          M II1

Stoddart, D. R.
    1968 Catastrophic human interference with coral atoll Ecosystems.
          Geography, 53(1):25-40.
          P X

Stone, Benjamin C.
    1959 The flora of Namonuito and the Hall Islands. Pacific
          Science, 13(1):88-104.
          T2 T3 V

MAIN BIBLIOGRAPHY

Stone, Benjamin C.
  1960 Corrections and additions to the flora of the Hall Islands
        and to the flora of Ponape. Pacific Science, 14(4):408-410.
        [see Glassman 1952; Stone 1959].
        T2 Pn1 V

Stone, Benjamin C.
  1960 The wild and cultivated Pandanus of the Marshall Islands.
        Ph.D. Dissertation, University of Hawaii, Honolulu. Avail-
        able from University Microfilms, Ann Arbor: No. 60-05332.
        Ms I V

Stone, Benjamin C.
  1961 Pandanus pistillaris in the Caroline Islands: An example
        of long-range Oceanic Dispersal. Pacific Science, 15(4):
        610-614.
        C V X

Stone, Benjamin C.
  1963 The role of pandanus in the culture of the Marshall Islands.
        IN Plants and the Migrations of Pacific Peoples, Jacques
        Barrau, ed. Honolulu: Bishop Museum Press pp. 61-74.
        Ms I

Stone, Benjamin C.
  1963 Appendix: Marshallese cultivar index and distribution
        of the names by Atoll. IN Plants and the Migrations
        of Pacific Peoples, Jacques Barrau, ed. Honolulu:
        Bishop Museum Press. pp. 75-82.
        Ms V

Stone, Benjamin C.
  1966 Cultivated pandanus in Kapingamarangi Atoll. Journal
        of the Polynesian Society, 75(4):430-436.
        Pn9 I

Stone, Benjamin C.
  1966 Some vernacular names of plants from Kapingamarangi and
        Nukuoro Atolls, Caroline Islands. Micronesica, 2(2):131-132.
        Pn8 Pn9 V

Stone, Benjamin C.
  1967 The flora of Romonum Island, Truk Lagoon, Caroline Islands.
        Pacific Science, 21(1):98-114.
        T1 V

Stone, Benjamin C.
  1971 The flora of Guam. Micronesica, 6:1-659. Reviewed: 1975
        by E.H. Bryan, Jr., Atoll Research Bulletin, No. 185:27-28.
        Mr1 V

MAIN BIBLIOGRAPHY

Stone, Earl L., Jr.
    1951 The agriculture of Arno Atoll, Marshall Islands. Atoll
          Research Bulletin, No. 6. 46 pp.
          Ms9 I

Stone, Earl L., Jr.
    1951 The soils of Arno Atoll, Marshall Islands. SIM Report,
          No. 10. Washington, D.C.: Pacific Science Board. 52 pp.
          Reprinted 1951. Atoll Research Bulletin, No. 5. 56 pp.
          Ms9 XI

Stone, Earl L., Jr.
    1953 Summary of information on atoll Soils. Atoll Research
          Bulletin, No. 22. 6 pp.
          M Ms9 XI

Strance, Almi
    1972 Role of women in Micronesia: Marshall Islands as an Example.
          Parts I and II. IN Micronesian Realities: Political and
          Economic, Frances McReynolds Smith, ed. Santa Cruz, Calif-
          ornia: Center for South Pacific Studies. pp. 249-253.
          Ms II1

Street, John M. (compiler)
    1960 Eniwetok Atoll, Marshall Islands: A library Brochure,
          William L. Thomas, Jr., ed. Prepared for the Pacific
          Missile Range, Point Mugu, California. Riverside, Calif-
          ornia: University of California at Riverside. 63 pp.
          Ms11 X

Stuckenrath, Robert, Jr.
    1967 University of Pennsylvania radiocarbon dates X. Radio-
          carbon, 9:333-345. [published by the American Journal
          of Science, Yale University; dates for Nukuoro series
          collected by Janet M. Davidson on p. 341].
          Pn8 III

Stumpf, Margaret K.
    1970 Palauan value orientation and Education. Ed.D. Dissertation,
          Teachers College, Columbia University, New York. Available
          from University Microfilms, Ann Arbor: No. 71-5601.
          PL1 II2 VII

Stumpf, Margaret K.
    1972 Money of Palau. Guam Recorder, n.s., 1(2&3):70-72.
          PL1 II4

Stumpf, Margaret K.
    1972 Palau--islands of Diversity. Guam Recorder, n.s., 2(1):50-52.
          PL1 IX

MAIN BIBLIOGRAPHY

Suda, Akiyoshi
  1952 Bibliography on physical anthropology of the Micronesian.
        Jinruigaku Zassi [Tokyo], 62(3):147-153. [in Japanese].
        M IX XVI

Sugimura, Kenichi
  1953 Culture contact and culture change in Eastern Micronesia.
        Proceedings of the 7th Pacific Science Congress, 2 February-
        4 March, 1949, Auckland, New Zealand, 7:221-222. [abstract].
        Pn1 Ms II7

Sugita, Hiroshi
  n.d. Trukese Reference Grammar. PALI Language Texts: Micro-
        nesia. Honolulu: University Press of Hawaii, forthcoming.
        T XIII

Sugita, Hiroshi
  1973 Comparison of verb-object relationships in Micronesian
        Languages. Working Papers in Linguistics, 5(9):67-75.
        Honolulu: Department of Linguistics, University of Hawaii.
        M XIII

Sullivan, Julius
  1957 The Phoenix Rises: A Mission History of Guam. New York:
        Seraphic Mass Association. 231 pp.
        Mr1 II2 XII

Sussman, Leon N., Leo H. Meyer, and Robert A. Conard
  1959 Blood groupings in Marshallese. Science, 129(3349):644-645.
        Ms15 XVI

Sutow, W. W., Robert A. Conard, and K. M. Griffith
  1965 Growth status of children exposed to fallout radiation on
        Marshall Islands. Pediatrics, 36(5):721-731.
        Ms XIV

Swartz, Marc J.
  1958 The social organization of behavior: Relations among
        kinsmen cn Romonum, Truk. Ph.D. Dissertation, Harvard
        University, Cambridge.
        T1 II1

Swartz, Marc J.
  1958 Sexuality and aggression on Romonum, Truk. American
        Anthropologist, 60(3):467-486.
        T1 II6

Swartz, Marc J.
  1959 Leadership and status conflict on Romonum, Truk. South-
        western Journal of Anthropology [now called Journal of
        Anthropological Research], 15(2):213-218.
        T1 II3

Swartz, Marc J.
      1960   Situational determinants of kinship Terminology. South-
             western Journal of Anthropology [now called Journal of
             Anthropological Research], 16(4):393-397.
             T1 II1

Swartz, Marc J.
      1961   Negative Ethnocentrism. Journal of Conflict Resclution,
             5(1):75-81.
             T1 II6

Swartz, Marc J.
      1962   Recruiting labor for fissionary descent lines on Romonum,
             Truk. Southwestern Journal of Anthropolcgy [now called
             Journal of Anthropological Research], 18(4):351-364.
             T1 II1

Swartz, Marc J.
      1965   Personality and structure: Political acquiesence in Truk.
             IN Induced Political Change in the Pacific: A Symposium,
             Roland W. Force, ed. Honolulu: Bishop Museum Press.
             pp. 17-39.
             T1 II3 II6

Sykes, Egerton, ed.
      1960   The archaeology of the Caroline Islands. New World
             Antiquity, 7(2):23.
             C III

Sykes, Egerton, ed.
      1961   The archaeology of Micronesia. New World Antiquity, 8(6):
             68-70, 75-76.
             M III

Tabb, John R.
      1966   Public Finance in Micronesia. Prepared for the High
             Commissioner of the Trust Territory of the Pacific Islands
             by Robert R. Nathan Associates, Inc., Consulting Economists.
             Washington, D.C.: Nathan Associates. Mimeographed. 79 pp.
             M VI

Takayama, Jun
      1973   The second excavation of Muchon on Rota. Kokogaku
             Zassi [Tokyo], 77:16-19. [in Japanese].
             Mr3 III

MAIN BIBLIOGRAPHY

Takayama, Jun and Tomoko Egami
     1971 Archeology on Rota in the Marianas Islands: Preliminary
           Report on the First Excavation of the Latte Site (m-1).
           Reports of Pacific Archeological Survey, No. 1. Hirat-
           suka City: Tokai University. 31 pp.; 12 plates.
           Mr3 III

Takayama, Jun and Toshihiko Seki
     1973 Preliminary Archaeolcgical Investigations on the Island
           of Tol in Truk. Reports of Pacific Archaeological Survey,
           No. 2. Hiratsuka City: Tokai University. 65 pp.; 24 plates.
           T1 III

Tansill, William Raymond
     1951 Guam and Its Administration. Public Affairs Bulletin, No.
           95. Washington, D.C.: Library of Congress, Legislative
           Reference Bureau. 140 pp.
           Mr1 XVII

Tashian, Richard E., Chris C. Plato, and Thomas B. Shows, Jr.
     1963 Inherited variant of erythrocyte carbonic anhydrase in
           Micronesians from Guam and Saipan. Science, 140(3562):53-54.
           Mr1 Mr2 XVI

Tate, Merze and Doris M. Hull
     1964 Effects of nuclear explosions on Pacific Islanders.
           Pacific Historical Review, 33(4):379-393.
           Ms XIV XVII

Tauber, Irene and Chungnim C. Han
     1950 Micronesian islands under United Nations' trusteeship:
           Demographic Paradox. Population Index, 16(2):93-115.
           M XVI

Taylor, Clyde Romer Hughes
     1965 A Pacific Bibliography. Printed Matter Relating to the
           Native People of Polynesia, Melanesia and Micronesia.
           2nd edition. Oxford: Clarendon Press. 692 pp. Reviewed:
           1966 by David M. Schneider, American Anthropologist, 68(5):
           1276-1277.
           P IX

Taylor, John L.
     1949 Guam: Focus of the Western Pacific. Journal of Geography,
           48(1):27-38.
           Mr1 X

Taylor, John L.
     1951 Saipan: A study in land Utilization. Economic Geography,
           27(4):340-347.
           Mr2 X

Taylor, Theodore W.; J. A. Giddings; Henry C. Wolfgram; and Leonard E.
    Mason
    1951 Management Survey of the Government of the Trust Territory
        of the Pacific Islands: A Report of a Management Improve-
        ment Survey to the Department of the Interior, Containing
        Recommendations for the Future Civilian Administration of
        the Trust Territory. 2 vols. Washington, D.C.: Government
        Printing Office (Office of Territories, Department of the
        Interior). Vol. 1, 164 pp.; Vol. 2, 151 pp.
        M XVII

Taylor, William R.
    1950 Plants of Bikini and cther Northern Marshall Islands. Uni-
        versity of Michigan Studies, Scientific Series, Vol. 18, No.
        15. Ann Arbor: University of Michigan Press. 227 pp.
        Ms13 Ms V

Terrell, John
    1973 Review of Janet M. Davidson, Archaeology on Nukucro Atoll:
        A Polynesian Outlier in the Eastern Caroline Islands.
        American Anthropologist, 75(4):1119-1121.
        Pn8 III

Tetens, Alfred
    1958 Among the Savages of the South Seas, Memoirs of Micronesia,
        1862-1868, translated from the German by Florence M. Spoehr.
        Stanford: Stanford University Press. 107 pp. Reviewed:
        1958 by Katharine Luomala, American Anthropologist, 60(6),
        Part 1:1232-1233; 1959 by Douglas Osborne, Journal of the
        Polynesian Society, 68(1):50-51; 1960 by Douglas Osborne,
        Archaeology, 13(4):299-300.
        M XII

Thomas, Theodore Hubert
    1957 The aims and organization of the Trust Territory of the
        Pacific Islands. M.A. Thesis, Duke University, Curham,
        North Carolina.
        M XVII

Thompson, Laura
    1944 Guam: Study in military Government. Far Eastern Survey,
        13(16):149-154.
        Mr1 XV

Thompson, Laura
    1944 The women of Guam. Asia and the Americas, 44(9):412-415.
        Mr1 II

MAIN BIBLIOGRAPHY

Thompson, Laura
    1945   The Native Culture of the Marianas Islands. B.P. Bishop
            Museum Bulletin, No. 185. Honolulu: Bishop Museum Press.
            48 pp. Reviewed: 1947 by John Useem, American Anthropo-
            logist, 49(2):304-305.
            Mr II

Thompson, Laura
    1946   Crisis on Guam. Far Eastern Quarterly [now called
            Journal of Asian Studies], 7(1):5-11.
            Mr1 II7 XVII

Thompson, Laura
    1947   Guam and Its People: A Study of Cultural Change and
            Colonial Education. With a Village Journal by Jesus C.
            Parainas. 3rd revised edition. Princeton: Princeton
            University Press. 367 pp. Reprinted 1969. Westport,
            Connecticut: Greenwood Press. Reviewed: 1948 by Leonard
            E. Mason, Pacific Affairs, 21(1):95.
            Mr1 II7

Thompson, Laura
    1947   Guam's bombed-out Capital. Far Eastern Survey, 16(6):66-69.
            Mr1 XV

Thompson, Laura
    1948   A model trusteeship for Micronesia. Newsletter of the
            Institute of Ethnic Affairs, October, pp. 6-8.
            M XVII

Thompson, Laura
    1949   The basic conservaticn Problem. The Scientific Monthly,
            68(2):129-131.
            M X

Thompson, Laura
    1969   People of Guam. IN The Secret of Culture, Nine Community
            Studies, by Laura Thompson. New York: Random House. pp.
            52-69.
            Mr1 II

Tinker, Spencer
    1950   Some Marshall Islands fish Traps. Occasional Papers of
            the B.P. Bishop Museum, 20(7):89-93.
            Ms II4

MAIN BIBLIOGRAPHY

Tobin, Jack A.
    1952 Land tenure in the Marshall Islands. Atoll Research Bulle-
         tin, No. 11. 36 pp. Reprinted 1958. IN Land Tenure Pat-
         terns in the Trust Territory of the Pacific Islands, John E.
         de Young, ed. Guam: Office of the Staff Anthropclcgist,
         Trust Territcry of the Pacific Islands. pp. 1-76.
         Ms II1

Tobin, Jack A.
    1967 The resettlement of the Eniwetok people: A study of a
         displaced community in the Marshall Islands. Ph.D. Dis-
         sertation, University of California, Berkeley. Available
         from University Microfilms, Ann Arbor: No. 68-5837.
         Ms11 Ms12 II7

Tobin, Jack A.
    1970 The legend of Lijibake. Micronesian Reporter, 18(1):16-17.
         Ms8 VIII

Tobin, Jack A.
    1970 Jabwor: Former capitol of the Marshall Islands. Micronesian
         Reporter, 18(4):20-30.
         Ms23 XII

Tobin, Jack A.
    1970 Report on Bikini Atoll. Pacific Islands Monthly,
         41(5):44-46.
         Ms13 II7 XV

Tobin, Jack A.; Gustav Weilbacher; Edward Iwaniec; Frank Mahony;
         Shigeru Kaneshiro; and Richard Emerick
    1957 Notes on the present regulations and practices of harvesting
         sea turtle and sea turtle eggs in the Trust Territcry of
         the Pacific Islands. Anthropological Working Papers, No. 1.
         Guam: Office of the Staff Anthropologist, Trust Territory
         of the Pacific Islands. 26 pp.
         M II5 X

Tolerton, Burt and Jerome Rauch
      n.d. Social Organization, Land Tenure and Subsistence Economy
    [1949] of Lukunor, Nomoi Islands. CIMA Report, No. 26. Wash-
           ington, D.C.: Pacific Science Board. 209 pp.
           T11b II

Tonkinson, Robert
    1975 Review of Robert Wenkam and Byron Baker, Micronesia: The
         Breadfruit Revolution. Pacific Affairs, 48(1):146-147.
         M IX

-234-

MAIN BIBLIOGRAPHY

Toomin, Philip R. and Pauline M. Toomin
    1963 Black Robe and Grass Skirt. New York: Horizon Press.
          286 pp.
          M IX XVII

Topping, Donald M.
    1962 Loanblends: A tool for Linguists. Language Learning,
          12(2):281-287.
          Mr XIII

Topping, Donald M.
    1963 Chamorro structure and the teaching of English. Ph.D.
          Dissertation, Michigan State University, East Lansing.
          Available from University Microfilms, Ann Arbor: No.
          64-07549.
          Mr XIII

Topping, Donald M.
    1964 Contrastive analysis and sandhi Alternation. Language
          Learning, 14(3):99-107.
          T XIII

Topping, Donald M.
    1966 Lessons in Chamorro. Honolulu: University of Hawaii Peace
          Corps Training Center. Mimeographed.
          Mr XIII

Topping, Donald M.
    1968 Chamorro vowel Harmony. Oceanic Linguistics, 7(1):67-79.
          Mr XIII

Topping, Donald M.
    1973 Spoken Chamorro Tomorrow. Guam Recorder, n.s., 3(1):45-48.
          Mr XIII

Topping, Donald M., with the assistance of Bernadita C. Dungca
    1973 Chamorro Reference Grammar. PALI Language Texts: Micronesia.
          Honolulu: University Press of Hawaii. 301 pp. Reviewed:
          1975 by James Jerome Smith, American Anthropologist, 77(1):127.
          Mr XIII

Topping, Donald M., with the assistance of Pedro M. Ogo
    1969 Spoken Chamorro: An Intensive Language Course With Gramma-
          tical Notes and Glossary. PALI Language Texts: Micronesia.
          Honolulu: University of Hawaii Press. 614 pp. Reviewed:
          1971 by Arthur Capell, Oceania, 41(4):314-315; 1971 by
          Robert C. Kiste, American Anthropologist, 73(2):407-408.
          Mr XIII

MAIN BIBLIOGRAPHY

Topping, Donald M., Pedro M. Ogc, and Bernadita C. Dungca
    1975 Chamorro-English Dictionary. PALI Language Texts: Micro-
          nesia. Honolulu: University Press of Hawaii. 336 pp.
          Mr XIII

Toribiong, Johnson
    1972 Micronesia, Economic trend, land and People. IN Micronesian
          Realities: Political and Economic, Frances McReynolds Smith,
          ed. Santa Cruz, California: Center for South Pacific Studies.
          pp. 121-164.
          M VI

Torres, Jose M., Lorenzo L. G. Iriarte, and Leonard T. Kurland
    1957 Amyotrophic lateral sclerosis among Guamanians in Calif-
          ornia. California Medicine, 86(6):385-388.
          Mr1 XIV XVI

Townes, Henry K.
    1946 Results of an Entomological Inspection Tour of Micronesia.
          IN U.S. Commercial Company's Economic Survey of Micronesia,
          Report No. 14, Part 1 [Part 2 by Richard G. Oakley].
          Honolulu: U.S. Commercial Company. Mimeographed. 53 pp.
          M XIX

Tracey, Joshua I., Jr.
    1957 Geological investigations on Guam. Proceedings cf the 8th
          Pacific Science Congress, 16-18 November, 1953, Quezon
          City, Philippines, 2:270. [abstract].
          Mr1 XI

Tracey, Joshua I., Jr. et al.
    1959 Military Geology of Guam, Mariana Islands. Part 1: Des-
          cription of Terrain and Environment. Part 2: Engineering
          Aspects of Geology and Soils. Tokyo: U.S. Army, Chief of
          Engineers, Intelligence Division, Headquarters, U.S. Army
          Pacific. 282 pp.
          Mr1 XI

Tracey, Joshua I., Jr.; Seymour O. Schlanger; John T. Stark; David B.
    Doan; and Harold G. May
    1964 General Geolcgy of Guam. U.S. Geological Survey Profes-
          sional Paper, No. 403-A. Washington, D.C.: U.S. Geolo-
          gical Survey. 104 pp.
          Mr1 XI

Tracey, Joshua I., Jr., Donald P. Abbott, and Ted Arnow
    1961 Natural History of Ifaluk Atoll: Physical Environment.
          B.P. Bishop Museum Bulletin, No. 222. Honolulu: Bishop
          Museum Press. 75 pp.
          Y11 XI

MAIN BIBLIOGRAPHY

Trifonovitch, Gregory J.
 1971 Ifaluk: A brief report on some aspects of its Culture.
       Working Papers of the East-West Culture Learning Institute,
       No. 10, Honolulu: East-West Center. 103 pp.
       Y11 II

Trifonovitch, Gregory J.
 1971 Language policy, language engineering, and literacy (Trust
       Territory of the Pacific Islands). IN Current Trends in
       Linguistics, Thomas A. Sebeok, ed. Vol. 8, Part 2. The
       Hague: Mouton. pp. 1063-1087.
       M XIII

Trifonovitch, Gregory J.
 1973 Across cultures between Kuleanas. East-West Center
       Magazine, Fall, pp. 9-12.
       M II2

Trumbell, Robert
 1959 Paradise in Trust: A Report on Americans in Micronesia,
       1946-1958. New York: W. Sloane Associates. 222 pp.
       M IX

Tsuchida, Shigeru
 1965 Velarization in Marshallese. M.A. Thesis, University of
       Hawaii, Honolulu.
       Ms XIII

Turner, Gordon B.
 1950 The amphibious complex: A study of operations at Saipan.
       Ph.D. Dissertation, Princeton University, Princeton,
       New Jersey.
       Mr2 XV

Tweed, George and Blake Clark
 1945 Robinson Crusoe, USN: The Adventures of George R. Tweed,
       RM 1/C, on Jap-Held Guam. New York: McGraw Hill. 267 pp.
       Mr1 XV

Uberoi, J. S.
 1966 Review of William H. Alkire, Lamotrek Atoll and Inter-
       Island Socioeconomic Ties. Man, n.s., 1(3):426.
       Y9 II1

Udui, Kaleb
 1972 America's dilemmas in carrying out its international trus-
       teeship obligations in Micronesia. IN Micronesian Reali-
       ties: Political and Economic, Frances McReynolds Smith, ed.
       Santa Cruz, California: Center for South Pacific Studies.
       pp. 1-20.
       M XVII

Udui, Kaleb
1972 Free Association--A political status option of Self-Deter-
      mination. IN Micronesian Realities: Political and Economic,
      Frances McReynolds Smith, ed. Santa Cruz, California:
      Center for South Pacific Studies. pp. 31-46.
      M XVII

Uherbelau, Victorio
1972 Does a "domestic" Micronesia really control its Destiny?
      IN Micronesian Realities: Political and Economic, Frances
      McReynolds Smith, ed. Santa Cruz, California: Center for
      South Pacific Studies. pp. 73-91.
      M XVII

Ullman, James Ramsey
1960 A strange tale of the South Seas. Readers Digest, 77(460):
      176-181.
      T5 IX X

Ullman, James Ramsey
1963 Where the Bong Tree Grows. The Log of One Man's Journey in
      the South Pacific. New York: World Publishing Co. 316 pp.
      P IX

Uludong, Francisco T.
1969 A review of some aspects of American-Micronesian Relations.
      IN Political Modernization of Micronesia, A Symposium.
      Santa Cruz, California: Center for South Pacific Studies.
      12 pp.
      M XVII

Uludong, Francisco T.
1969 Whither Micronesia? IN Political Modernization of Micro-
      nesia, A Symposium. Santa Cruz, California: Center for
      South Pacific Studies. 4 pp.
      M XVII

Uludong, Francisco T.
1972 Comments on political future of Micronesia. Micronesica,
      8(1&2):41-42.
      M XVII

Underwood, Jane Hainline
n.d. The Afghan caper, the Yapese affair, and 'one-ups-manship'
      in Inbreeding. Festschrift in honor of Joseph P. Birdsell,
      Larry Mai, ed. Anthropology UCLA, in press.
      Y1 XVI

MAIN BIBLIOGRAPHY

Underwood, Jane Hainline
  1964 Human ecology in Micronesia: Determinants of population size, structure and Dynamics. Ph.D. Dissertation, University of California, Los Angeles. Available from University Microfilms, Ann Arbor: No. 64-07350.
  M XVI

Underwood, Jane Hainline
  1965 Blood typing data, ABO and Rh(d), collected from hospital records in Yap and Saipan: A brief Note. Human Biology, 37(2):174-177.
  Y1 Mr2 XVI

Underwood, Jane Hainline
  1965 Culture and biological Adaptation. Population and environment in Micronesia. American Anthropologist, 67(5), Part 1:1174-1197.
  M XVI

Underwood, Jane Hainline
  1966 Population and genetic (serological) variability in Micronesia. Annals of the New York Academy of Sciences, 134: 639-654.
  M XVI

Underwood, Jane Hainline
  1969 Ecological genetics of an island Population (Yap). American Journal of Physical Anthropology, 31(2):267. [abstract].
  Y1 XVI

Underwood, Jane Hainline
  1969 Preliminary investigations of demographic features and ecological variables of a Micronesian Island Population. Micronesica, 5(1):1-24.
  Y1 XVI

Underwood, Jane Hainline
  1972 Report on a preliminary examination of the skeletal remains excavated on Guam, Mariana Islands. Appendix I-A IN An Archaeological Survey and Preliminary Test Excavations on the Island of Guam, Mariana Islands, 1965-1966, by Fred M. Reinman. Los Angeles: California State University. Mimeographed.
  Mr1 XVI

Underwood, Jane Hainline
  1973 The demography of a myth: Abortion in Yap. Human Biology in Oceania, 2(2):115-127. [see Schneider 1955].
  Y1 XVI

Underwood, Jane Hainline
   1973 Population history of Guam: Context of human Micro-evolution.
         Micronesica, 9(1):11-44.
         Mr1 XVI

Underwood, Jane Hainline, Peggy Clark, and R. J. Walsh
   1969 ABO, Rh, and MNS blood typing results and other biochemical
         traits in the people of the Yap Islands. Archeology and
         Physical Anthropology in Oceania, 4(1):64-71.
         Y1 XVI

United States Department of the Army
   1971 Pacific Islands and Trust Territories: A Select Bibliography.
         Department of the Army pamphlet 550-10. Washington, D.C.:
         Department of the Army. 171 pp.
         M IX

United States Department of the Army (Forces in the Far East)
   1956 Annotated Bibliography of Geologic and Soils Literature
         of Western North Pacific Islands. Prepared under the
         direction of the Chief of Engineers, U.S. Army by the
         Intelligence Division, Office of the Engineer, Headquar-
         ters, U.S. Army Forces Far East, and 8th U.S. Army (Rear)
         with personnel of the U.S. Geological Survey. 884 pp.
         P XI

United States Department of the Army (Forces in the Far East)
   1956 Military Geography of the Northern Marshalls. Prepared
         under the direction of the Chief of Engineers, U.S. Army,
         by the Intelligence Division, Office of the Engineer,
         Headquarters, U.S. Army Forces Far East and 8th U.S.
         Army, with personnel of the U.S. Geological Survey. n.p.
         Mimeographed. 320 pp.
         Ms X

United States Department of the Navy
   1943 Military Government Handbook: Marshall Islands. OPNAV
         50E-1. Office of the Chief of Naval Operations. Wash-
         ington, D.C.: Navy Department. 113 pp.
         Ms IX XV

United States Department of the Navy
   1944 Civil Affairs Handbook: East Caroline Islands. OPNAV P22-5.
         Office of the Chief of Naval Operations. Washington D.C.:
         Navy Department. 213 pp.
         T Pn K IX XV

United States Department of the Navy
   1944 Civil Affairs Handbook: Mandated Marianas Islands.
         OPNAV P22-8. Office of the Chief of Naval Operations.
         Washington, D.C.: Navy Department. 205 pp.
         Mr IX XV

MAIN BIBLIOGRAPHY

United States Department of the Navy
    1944 Civil Affairs Handbook: West Caroline Islands. OPNAV P22-7.
          Office of the Chief of Naval Operations. Washington, D.C.:
          Navy Department. 222 pp.
          Y PL IX XV

United States Department of the Navy
    1945 Marshallese-English and English-Marshallese Dictionary.
          14th Naval District, District Intelligence Office,
          Marshall-Gilberts Area. Vol. 1, 136 pp.; Vol. 2, 121 pp.
          Ms XIII

United States Department of Health, Education and Welfare
    1973 HEW/Interior Task Force Report on Health, Sanitation,
          Education, Social Services in the Trust Territory of
          the Pacific Islands. Washington, D.C.: U.S. Department
          of Health, Education and Welfare. 208 pp.
          M VII XIV

United States Geographical Names Board
    1955 Decisions on Names in the Trust Territory of the Pacific
          Islands and Guam. Cumulative Decision List No. 5501-5503.
          Washington, D.C.: U.S. Department of the Interior. 228 pp.
          M X

United States Hydrographic Office
    1944 Caroline, Mariana, Marshall, and Gilbert Islands.
          Gazetteer, No. 6. 2nd edition. Hydrographic Office
          Publication No. 886. Washington, D.C.: U.S. Government
          Printing Office. 133 pp.
          M X

United States Trust Territory of the Pacific Islands
    1967 to present. Highlights. Saipan: Public Information
          Office, Trust Territory of the Pacific Islands. A
          bi-monthly publication.
          M IX

United States Trust Territory of the Pacific Islands
    1957 Anthropology Newsletter. Volume 1, Nos. 1-4. March-June.
          Guam: Office of the Staff Anthropologist, Trust Territory
          of the Pacific Islands. [no longer published].
          M II

United States Trust Territory of the Pacific Islands
    1973 Maps of Micronesia. Saipan: Lands and Surveys Division,
          Department of Resources and Development, Trust Territory
          of the Pacific Islands.
          M X

MAIN BIBLIOGRAPHY

United States Trust Territory of the Pacific Islands
    1975 1973 Population of the Trust Territory of the Pacific
          Islands. Saipan: Office of the High Commissioner. 292 pp.
          [results of the full-scale census of the U.S.T.T.P.I.
          conducted 18 September 1973].
          M XVI

University of Hawaii, School of Public Health
    1967 Micronesian Health Mcncgraph, No. 1. Honolulu: School of
          Public Health, University of Hawaii. 209 pp.
          M XIV

Unpingco, Norbert R.
    1975 The realities facing Guam Today. IN The Impact cf Urban
          Centers in the Pacific, Roland W. Force and Brenda Bishop,
          eds. Honolulu: Pacific Science Association, Bishop Museum.
          pp. 107-114.
          Mr1 VI

Urguhart, Alvin W. (compiler)
    1960 Majuro Atoll, Marshall Islands: A Library Brochure, William
          L. Thomas, Jr., ed. Prepared for the Pacific Missile Range,
          Point Mugu, California. Riverside, California: University
          of California at Riverside. 32 pp.
          Ms8 X

Useem, John
    1945 The changing structure cf a Micronesian Society. American
          Anthropologist, 47(4):567-588. Reprinted 1957. IN Under-
          developed Areas, Lyle Shannon, ed. New York: Harper and
          Brothers. pp. 29-37.
          PL1 II7

Useem, John
    1945 The American pattern of military government in Micronesia.
          American Journal cf Sociology, 51(2):93-102.
          M XV

Useem, John
    1945 Governing the occupied areas of the South Pacific: War time
          lessons and peace time Proposals. Applied Anthrcpology
          [now called Human Organization], 4(3):1-10.
          M II8

Useem, John
    1946 Americans as governors cf natives in the Pacific. Journal
          of Social Issues, 2(3):39-49.
          M XVII

Useem, John
    1946   Report on Yap and Palau, and the Lesser Islands of the
            Western Carolines. IN U.S. Commercial Company's Economic
            Survey of Micronesia, Report No. 6. Honolulu: U.S. Com-
            mercial Company. Mimeographed. 124 pp.
            C II

Useem, John
    1946   Social reconstruction in Micronesia. Far Eastern Survey,
            15(2):21-24.
            M XVII

Useem, John
    1947   Applied anthropology in Micronesia. Applied Anthropology
            [now called Human Organization], 6(4):1-14.
            M II8

Useem, John
    1947   Review of Laura Thompson, The Native Culture of the
            Marianas Islands. American Anthropologist, 49(2):304-305.
            Mr II

Useem, John
    1948   Human resources of Micronesia. Far Eastern Survey,
            17(1):1-4.
            M II

Useem, John
    1948   Institutions of Micronesia. Far Eastern Survey,
            17(2):22-25.
            M II

Useem, John
    1949   Report on Palau. CIMA Report, No. 21. Washington, D.C.:
            Pacific Science Board. 133 pp.
            PL1 II

Useem, John
    1950   Structure of power in Palau. Social Forces, 29(2):141-148.
            PL1 II3

Useem, John
    1952   Democracy in process: The development of democratic
            leadership in the Micronesian Islands. IN Human Problems
            in Technological Change: A Casebook, Edward H. Spicer,
            ed. New York: Russell Sage Foundation. pp. 261-280.
            PL1 II3

MAIN BIBLIOGRAPHY

Useem, John
    1952 South Sea Island strike: Labor-Management relations in the
          Caroline Islands, Micronesia [Angaur]. IN Human Problems in
          Technological Change: A Casebook, Edward H. Spicer, ed.
          New York: Russell Sage Foundation. pp. 149-164.
          PL1 II8

Useem, John
    1955 Palau. IN Culture Patterns and Technical Change, Margaret
          Mead, ed. New York: The New American Library. pp. 126-150.
          PL1 II

Ushijima, Iwao
    1967 The afterworld view and its underlying ideas among
          Micronesians. Minzokugaku-Kenkyu [Tokyo], 32(1):24-37.
          [in Japanese; resume in English].
          M II2

Ushijima, Iwao
    1969 The disorganization process of the matrilineal society
          in Micronesians. Minzokugaku-Kenkyu [Tokyo], 34(1):40-
          56. [in Japanese; resume in English].
          M II1

Utinomi, Huzio (compiler)
    1950 Bibliography of Micronesia. Honolulu, 1950. Translated
          and revised by O.A. Bushnell and others 1952. Honolulu:
          University of Hawaii Press. 157 pp.
          M IX

Valenciano, Santos and Kiyoshi J. Takasaki
    1959 Military Geology of Truk Islands, Caroline Islands. Water
          Resources Supplement. Prepared under the direction of the
          Chief of Engineers, U.S. Army, by the Intelligence Division,
          Office of the Engineer, Headquarters, U.S. Army Pacific, with
          personnel of the U.S. Geological Survey. Washington, D.C.:
          Department of the Army. Mimeographed. 81 pp.
          T1 XI

Valentine, Charles A.
    1963 Social status, political power, and native responses to
          European influence in Oceania. Anthropological Forum,
          1(1):3-55. Reprinted 1970. IN Cultures of the Pacific:
          Selected Readings, Thomas G. Harding and Ben J. Wallace,
          eds. New York: Free Press. pp. 337-384.
          M II XVII

Valle, Maria Teresa del
    1971 Review of Douglas Oliver, ed., Planning Micronesia's
          Future. Micronesica, 7(1&2):246-247.
          M II7 VI

MAIN BIBLIOGRAPHY

Valle, Maria Teresa del
    1971 The Congress of Micronesia. Guam Recorder, n.s., 1(1):52.
        M XVII

Van der Poel, Cornelius J.
    1973 Guam in Search of Its Own Identity. Agana: Social Science
        Institute, University of Guam. 2 vols. 380 pp.
        Mr1 II2

Van der Poel, Cornelius J.
    1975 Human and cultural values on Guam in a period of rapid
        Transition. IN The Impact of Urban Centers in the Pacific,
        Roland W. Force and Brenda Bishop, eds. Honolulu: Pacific
        Science Association, Bishop Museum. pp. 327-336.
        Mr1 II2 II7

Van Peenan, Mavis W.
    1971 Chamorro legends on the Island of Guam. Guam Recorder,
        n.s., 1(1):7-9.
        Mr1 VIII

Van Peenan, Mavis W.
    1972 Legends of Guam: Juan Malo and his magic Word. Creation
        cf Man. Guam Recorder, n.s., 2(1):15-16.
        Mr1 VIII

Van Steenis, C. G. G. J.
    1965 Man and plants in the tropics: An appeal to Micronesians
        for the preservation of Nature. Micronesica, 2(1):61-65.
        M I V

Vanatta, Jack
    1947 Guam, the Gem of Micronesia. Orlando, Florida: Southland
        Printing Co. 24 pp.
        Mr1 IX

Vayda, Andrew P.
    1962 Review of Marston Bates and Donald P. Abbott, Coral Island,
        Portrait of an Atoll. Journal of the Polynesian Society,
        71(1):130.
        Y11 IX

Vesper, Don
    1972 Guam as an example of U.S. Language policy. Papers of
        the 1972 Mid-America Linguistics Conference, Oklahcma State
        University, Stillwater. pp. 309-315.
        Mr1 XIII

MAIN BIBLIOGRAPHY

Vesper, Ethel R.
     1969 Grammatical and semantic classifiers as evidenced in the
           possessive construction in Kusaien. Papers of the 4th
           Annual Kansas Linguistics Conference, University of
           Kansas, Lawrence. pp. 174-183.
           K XIII

Vesper, Ethel R.
     1969 Phrase structures of Kusaien. M.A. Thesis, University of
           California, Berkeley.
           K XIII

Vesper, Ethel R.
     1970 A consideration of number in Kusaien. Anthropolcgical
           Linguistics, 12(1):20-30.
           K XIII

Vesper, Ethel R.
     1970 Kusaien possessives as relative clauses: A new Approach.
           Papers of the 5th Annual Kansas Linguistics Conference,
           University of Kansas, Lawrence. pp. 159-165.
           K XIII

Vesper, Ethel R.
     1971 A semantic characterization of Kusaien Pronouns.
           Anthropological Linguistics, 13(8):391-400.
           K XIII

Vesper, Ethel R.
     1972 Kusaien reduplication: A lexical Problem. Papers of the
           1972 Mid-America Linguistics Conference, Oklahoma State
           University, Stillwater, Oklahoma. pp. 9-15.
           K XIII

Vesper, Ethel R.
     1973 A consideration of derivation in Kusaien. Paper read at
           72nd Annual Meeting of the American Anthropological Asso-
           ciation, 28 November-2 December, New Orleans.
           K XIII

Vesper, Ethel R.
     1973 Directional affixes: More evidence for lexical Rules.
           Papers of the 1973 Mid-America Linguistics Conference,
           University of Iowa, Iowa City. pp. 342-351.
           K XIII

Vessel, A. V. and Roy W. Simonson
     1958 Soils and agriculture of the Palau Islands. Pacific
           Science, 12(4):281-298.
           PL1 I XI

MAIN BIBLIOGRAPHY

Vidich, Arthur J.
    1949 Political Factionalism in Palau, Its Rise and Development.
          CIMA Report, No. 23. Washington, D.C.: Pacific Science
          Board. 128 pp.
          PL1 II3

Vidich, Arthur J.
    1953 The political impact of colonial Administration. Ph.D.
          Dissertation, Harvard University, Cambridge.
          PL1 XVII

Vitarelli, William V.
    1968 Twenty years in Micronesia. Paper presented at the Institute
          of Advanced Projects, East-West Center, 28 October, Honolulu,
          Hawaii.
          M IX

Vitarelli, William V.
    1975 Non-Planning and social imbalance in a Marshall Island
          Community. IN The Impact of Urban Centers in the Pacific,
          Roland W. Force and Brenda Bishop, eds. Honolulu: Pacific
          Science Association, Bishop Museum. pp. 247-253.
          Ms19 II

Voegelin, Carl F. and Florence M. Voegelin
    1964 Micronesia. Anthropological Linguistics, 6(4):101-106.
          M XIII

Voegelin, Carl F. and Florence M. Voegelin
    1965 Chamorro in Micronesia. Languages of the World: Indo-
          Pacific Fascicle Four. Anthropological Linguistics,
          7(2):265-297.
          Mr XIII

Volprecht, Klaus
    1968 Nukuoro, zur Sammlung Kapitän Jeschke in Rautenstrauch-
          Joest, Museum. [Nukuoro: The collection of Captain Jeschke
          in the Rautenstrauch-Joest Museum]. Ethnologica [Köln],
          n.s., 4:532-542.
          Pn8 II4

Wainhouse, David W.
    1964 U.S. dependencies: Decolonization begins at Home. IN
          Remnants of Empire, Deryck Scarr, ed. New York: Harper
          and Row. pp. 115-130.
          P XVII

Walker, L. W.
    1945 Guam's seizure by the United States in 1898. Pacific
          Historical Review, 14(1):1-12.
          Mr1 XII

MAIN BIBLIOGRAPHY

Wallace, Anthony F. C.
      1955   Review of William A. Lessa and Marvin Spiegelman,
             Ulithian Personality as Seen Through Ethnological
             Materials and Thematic Test Analysis. American
             Anthropologist, 57(2), Part 1:392-393.
             Y3 II6

Wallace, Gordon D.
      1969   Serologic and epidemiologic observations on Toxoplasmosis
             on three Pacific Atolls. American Journal of Epidemiology,
             90(2):103-111.
             W XIV

Wallace, Gordon D.
      1969   Toxoplasmosis on Caroline Atolls. Atoll Research Bulletin,
             No. 135:9.
             W XIV

Wallace, Gordon D., Leslie B. Marshall, and Mac Marshall
      1972   Cats, rats and Toxoplasmosis on a small Pacific Island.
             American Journal of Epidemiology, 95(5):475-482.
             T10 XIV

Walter, William J.
      1951   My people of Ulithi. Jesuit Missions, October, pp. 9-10.
             Y3 II2

Walter, William J.
      1952   Micronesian medicine Man. Jesuit Missions, September, pp.
             18-20.
             M II2

Walter, William J.
      1955   Laughter on Ulithi. Jesuit Missions, October, pp. 1-2.
             Y3 IX

Walter, William J.
      1957   Ifalik...changing Paradise. Jesuit Missions,
             January-February, pp. 4-6.
             Y11 IX

Walter, William J.
      1957   Witch Doctor. Jesuit Missions, May, pp. 5-7.
             M II2

Walter, William J.
      1961   Typhoon in the Pacific. Jesuit Missions, June, pp. 8-14.
             M X

MAIN BIBLIOGRAPHY

Walzer, Peter D.; Franklin N. Judson; Kevin B. Murphy; George R.
    Healy; Donna K. English; Myron G. Schultz
    1973   Balantidiasis outbreak in Truk. American Journal of
            Tropical Medicine and Hygiene, 22(1):33-41.
            T1 XIV

Ward, Herbert T.
    1970   Flight of the Cormoran. New York: Vantage Press. 175 pp.
            M XII

Ward, Martha Coonfield
    1974   Some anthropological methods for epidemiology fieldwork:
            The Ponape blood pressure Study. Paper read at the 73rd
            Annual Meeting of the American Anthropological Association,
            19-24 November, Mexico City.
            Pn1 XIV

Ward, Roger L.
    1974   Ponapean apology rituals: Elaborations of the apology
            pattern in modern Ponape. Paper read at the 3rd Annual
            Meeting of the Association for Social Anthropology in
            Oceania, 13-17 March, Asilomar, Pacific Grove, California.
            Pn1 II2

Ward, Roger L.
    1974   Sociocultural factors in the diagnosis of illness on Ponape.
            Paper read at the 73rd Annual Meeting of the American
            Anthropological Association, 19-24 November, Mexico City.
            Pn1 XIV

Ward, Roger L.
    1975   Ponapean diagnosis: The role of symptoms in the identifica-
            tion of illness on Ponape. Paper read at the 4th Annual
            Meeting of the Association for Social Anthropology in
            Oceania, 26-30 March, Stuart, Florida.
            Pn1 XIV

Ward, William T. T.
    1955   A preliminary survey of the economic and social life of the
            Mortlock Islands people, Eastern Carolines, Trust Territory
            of Micronesia. M.A. Thesis, University of the Philippines,
            Quezon City.
            T11 II

Webb, James C., Jr.
    1974   Micronesia and the United States' Pacific Strategy: A Blue-
            print for the 1980s. New York: Praeger. 109 pp. Reviewed:
            1975 by Sam McPhetres, Marianas Variety News and Views [Sai-
            pan], 4(19):6.
            M XV XVII

MAIN BIBLIOGRAPHY

Weckler, Joseph E.
    1949 Land and Livelihood on Mokil, An Atoll in the Eastern
          Carolines. CIMA Report, No. 11, Part 1 [Part 2 by Conrad
          Bentzen]. Washington, D.C.: Pacific Science Board. 147 pp.
          Pn6 II

Weckler, Joseph E.
    1950 Review of Homer Barnett, Palauan Society. American
          Anthropologist, 52(4), Part 1:538-539.
          PL1 II

Weckler, Joseph E.
    1953 Adoption on Mokil. American Anthropologist, 55(4)555-568.
          Pn6 II1

Weckler, Joseph E.
    1958 Review of John Wesley Coulter, The Pacific Dependencies of
          the United States. American Anthropolcgist, 60(3):605-606.
          P XVII

Weckler, Joseph E.
    1959 Review of Marston Bates and Donald P. Abbott, Coral Island,
          Portrait of an Atoll. American Anthropologist, 61(4):707-708.
          Y11 IX

Wees, Marshall Paul
    1950 King-Doctor of Ulithi. The True Story of the Wartime
          Experiences of Marshall Paul Wees as Related to Francis
          Beauchesne Thcrnton. New York: Macmillan. 128 pp.
          Y3 IX

Weitzell, E. C.
    1946 The Mariana, Caroline, and Marshall Islands. The
          Scientific Monthly, 63(3):218-226.
          M I

Weitzell, E. C.
    1946 Resource development in the Pacific Mandated Islands.
          Journal of Land and Public Utility Economics, 22(3):199-212.
          M VI

Wells, Jchn W.
    1950 Geology Study cf Arno. SIM Report, No. 5. Washington,
          D.C.: Pacific Science Board. 19 pp. + 16 maps.
          Ms9 XI

Wenkam, Robert
    1971 Micronesian parks: A Proposal. Micronesian Reporter,
          19(3):9-22.
          M X

MAIN BIBLIOGRAPHY

Wenkam, Robert
    1972 Parks for the Pacific. Not Man Apart, 2(2):8-9.
          M X

Wenkam, Robert
    1974 The Great Pacific Rip-Off: Corporate Rape in the Far East.
          Chicago: Follett Publishing Co. 237 pp.
          P VI

Wenkam, Robert and Byron Baker
    1972 Micronesia: The Breadfruit Revolution. Honolulu: East-West
          Center Press. 192 pp. Reviewed: 1974 by Mac Marshall,
          American Anthropologist, 76(3):598-599; 1975 by Robert
          Tonkinson, Pacific Affairs, 48(1):146-147.
          M IX

Wenkam, Robert and Ken Brower
    1975 Micronesia: Island Wilderness. San Francisco: Friends of
          the Earth and Seabury Press. 144 pp.
          M X

Wernhardt, Karl R.
    1972 A pre-missionary manuscript record of the Chamorro,
          Micronesia. Journal of Pacific History, 7:189-194.
          Mr XII

Wiens, Herold J.
    1955 The Geography of Kapingamarangi Atoll in the Eastern Caro-
          lines. SIM Report, No. 21. Washington, D.C.: Pacific
          Science Board. 86 pp. Reprinted 1956. Atoll Research
          Bulletin, No. 48. 86 pp.
          Pn9 X

Wiens, Herold J.
    1957 Field notes on atolls visited in the Marshalls, 1956.
          Atoll Research Bulletin, No. 54. 23 pp.
          Ms X

Wiens, Herold J.
    1962 Atoll Environment and Ecology. New Haven: Yale University
          Press. 532 pp.
          P X

Wiens, Herold J.
    1962 Pacific Island Bastions of the United States. Princeton,
          New Jersey: Van Nostrand Searchlight Series. 127 pp.
          M XVII

MAIN BIBLIOGRAPHY

Wiens, Herold J.
1963 Some effects of geographic location upon land utilization in
      the coral atolls of Micronesia. Proceedings of the 9th
      Pacific Science Congress, 18 November-9 December, 1957,
      Bangkok, 3:157-162.
      M X

Wilds, Thomas
1955 How Japan fortified the Mandated Islands. U.S. Naval
      Institute Proceedings, 81(4):401-407.
      M XV

Wiliander, Hans
1972 Economic realities of Independence. IN Micronesian
      Realities: Political and Economic, Frances McReynolds Smith,
      ed. Santa Cruz, California: Center for South Pacific
      Studies. pp. 21-29.
      M VI

Wiliander, Hans
1972 Independence as a political Alternative. IN Micronesian
      Realities: Political and Economic, Frances McReynolds Smith,
      ed. Santa Cruz, California: Center for South Pacific
      Studies. pp. 21-29.
      M XVII

Williams, John Z.
1946 Administration of the natives of Saipan. Foreign Service
      Journal, 23(4):7-10.
      Mr2 XVII

Wilson, Erika
1974 Seabirds and Micronesians. Micronesian Reporter, 22(3):11-16.
      M II5 XIX

Wilson, Helen Irene
1972 The phonology and syntax of Palauan verb Affixes. Working
      Papers in Linguistics, 4(5):1-214. Honolulu: Department of
      Linguistics, University of Hawaii.
      PL1 XIII

Wilson, James
1973 The applicability of the principle of self-determination
      to the Trust Territory of the Pacific Islands. Proceedings
      of the American Society of International Law, 67(5):21-26.
      M XVII

Wilson, Peter T.
1966 Boatbuilding in the Trust Territory of the Pacific Islands.
      South Pacific Bulletin, 16(3):23-26, 33.
      M VI

MAIN BIBLIOGRAPHY

Wilson, Peter T.
    1971 Truk live-bait Survey. National Oceanic and Atmospheric
          Administration Technical Reports, National Marine Fisheries
          Service, Circular-353. Seattle: U.S. Department of Commerce,
          U.S. Government Printing Office. 10 pp.
          T1 VI XIX

Wilson, Walter Scott
    n.d. Household, land and adoption on Kusaie. IN Transactions in
          Kinship: Adoption and Fosterage in Oceania, Ivan Brady, ed.
          ASAO Monograph No. 4. Honolulu: University Press of Hawaii,
          in press.
          K II1

Wilson, Walter Scott
    1953 The copra industry in the Trust Territory of the Pacific
          Islands. South Pacific Bulletin, 3(3):33-34.
          M II10

Wilson, Walter Scott
    1968 Land, activity, and social organization of Lelu, Kusaie.
          Ph.D. Dissertation, University of Pennsylvania, Philadelphia.
          Available from University Microfilms, Ann Arbor: No. 69-5678.
          K II1

Wilson, Walter Scott
    1971 Review of Vern Carroll, ed., Adoption in Eastern Oceania.
          Micronesica, 7(1&2):244-245.
          P II1

Wilson, Walter Scott
    1974 Elements of household economic strategies on Kusaie. Paper
          Pread at the 3rd Annual Meeting of the Association for Social
          Anthropology in Oceania, 13-17 March, Asilomar, Pacific
          Grove, California.
          K II10

Wilson, Walter Scott and Singkitchy P. George
    1965 Christmas on Kusaie. Pacific Profile, 3(10):8-10, 14.
          K II

Wilson, Walter Scott and Eleanora Wilson
    n.d. Incest on Kusaie. IN Incest Prohibitions in Polynesia and
          Micronesia, Vern Carroll, ed. ASAO Monograph Series.
          Honolulu: University Press of Hawaii, forthcoming.
          K II1

Wiswell, Ella
    1974   Translation from the Russian of V.M. Golovnin's chapters
           on Hawaii and the Marianas, frcm Voyage Around the World
           on the Sloop of War Kamchatka Performed by Order of His
           Majesty the Emperor in the Years 1817, 1818, and 1819.
           Honolulu: Pacific Islands Program, University of Hawaii,
           Miscellaneous Work Papers, 1974:2.
           Mr XII

Witucki, Jeannette
    1973   Alternative analyses of Chamorro Vowels.   Anthropological
           Linguistics, 15(8):362-372.
           Mr XIII

Wolff, Robert J., R. Desanna, and J. P. Chaine
    1971   A study of knowledge, attitude and practice of ccntracep-
           tion in the Trust Territory of the Pacific Islands, 1970.
           Honolulu: International Health/Population and Family Plan-
           ning Programs, School of Public Health, University of
           Hawaii.   219 pp.
           M XIV

Womack, William W., Daniel Machir, and Justus Freimund
    1969   Adolescent psychiatry in Guam.   IN Youth: Transcultural
           Psychiatric Approach, Jules H. Masserman, ed.   New York:
           Grune and Stratton.   pp. 56-65.
           Mr1 XVIII

Wright, Rear Admiral Carleton H.
    1948   Sailing canoes of the Marshall Islands. U.S. Naval Institute
           Proceedings, 74(12):1528-1531.
           Ms II4

Wright, Rear Admiral Carleton H.
    1948   Trust Territory of the Pacific Islands.   U.S. Naval
           Institute Proceedings, 74(11):1333-1341.
           M XVII

Wright, Gordon (compiler)
    1969   A Biblicgraphy of Reports, Surveys, and Studies Prepared
           by, for, or about the Trust Territory of the Pacific Is-
           lands.   Saipan: Department of Education, Trust Territory
           of the Pacific Islands.   182 pp.
           M IX

Wypych, Konrad
    1969   W cieniu fe; sladami Jana Stanislawa Kubarego.   [In the
           Shade of the Fir Tree; Following the Footsteps of Jan
           Kubary].   Wroclaw: Polski Towarzystwo Ludoznawcze.
           181 pp.   [biography of Kubary].
           M IX

MAIN BIBLIOGRAPHY

Wypych, Konrad
    1971 Native money of the Palau Islands. Lud [Warsaw], 55:
          115-128. [in Polish; English resume].
          PL1 II4

Wyttenbach, Richard Harrington
    1971 Micronesia and strategic trusteeship: A case study in
          American politico-military Relations. Ph.D. Dissertation,
          Fletcher School of Law and Diplomacy, Tufts University,
          Medford, Massachusetts.
          M XVII

Yamada, Kozo
    1969 Land tenure in the Eastern Caroline Islands (Micronesia).
          The implications of the German land reform program in the
          Ponape District, circa 1912, in the structure of contemp-
          orary Ponapean land Holdings. Paper read at the Symposium
          on Land Tenure in Relation to Economic Development, spon-
          sored by the South Pacific Commission, 1-12 September,
          Suva, Fiji.
          Pn II1

Yamada, Kozo
    1975 A comment on land law and land ownership in Micronesia. IN
          The Impact of Urban Centers in the Pacific, Roland W. Force
          and Brenda Bishop, eds. Honolulu: Pacific Science Associ-
          ation, Bishop Museum. pp. 163-167.
          M II1

Yamaguchi, Osamu
    1966 Some observations on music-language relationships in the
          chant of Tobi and Sonsorol, Southwestern Islands of Micro-
          nesia. Proceedings [Abstracts of Papers] of the 11th
          Pacific Science Congress, 22 August-10 September, 1966,
          Tokyo, 9:10.
          PL3 PL4 IV

Yamaguchi, Osamu
    1967 The music of Palau: An ethnomusicological study of the
          classical Tradition. M.A. Thesis, University of Hawaii,
          Honolulu.
          PL1 IV

Yamaguchi, Osamu
    1968 The taxonomy of music in Palau. Journal of the Society
          for Ethnomusicology, 12(3):345-351.
          PL1 IV

Yamamoto, Manabu and Linda Fu
    1973 Red cell isozymes in the Eastern Carolines. American
          Journal of Physical Anthropology, 38(3):703-707.
          Pn K XVI

MAIN BIBLIOGRAPHY

Yamashita, Antonio C.
    1965 Attitudes and reactions toward Typhoon Karen in Guam (1962).
          Micronesica, 2(1):15-23.
          Mr1 II7

Yamashita, Antonio C. and Walter Scott Wilson
    1971 Education and culture change in Micronesia. IN Education
          in Comparative and International Perspectives, Kalil I. Gezi,
          ed. New York: Holt, Rinehart and Winston. pp. 108-118.
          M II7 VII

Yawata, Ichiro
    1944 Peculiar forms of the stone-piles on the Mariana Islands.
          Jinruigaku Zassi [Tokyo], 59(11):418-424. [in Japanese].
          Mr III

Yawata, Ichiro
    1961 A burial type among the ancient Marianas People. Kodaigaku:
          Palaeologia, 9(3):117-128. [in Japanese].
          Mr III

Yawata, Ichiro
    1961 Burial systems of ancient Mariana Islanders. Asian
          Perspectives, 5(2):164-165.
          Mr III

Yawata, Ichiro
    1963 Rice cultivation of the ancient Mariana Islanders. IN
          Plants and the Migrations of Pacific Peoples, Jacques
          Barrau, ed. Honolulu: Bishop Museum Press. pp. 91-92.
          Mr I III

Yawata, Ichiro and Yosihiko H. Sinoto, eds.
    1968 Prehistoric Culture in Oceania: A Symposium of the 11th
          Pacific Science Congress. Honolulu: Bishop Museum Press.
          179 pp. Reviewed: 1969 by Peter W. Gathercole, American
          Anthropologist, 71(4):771-774.
          P III

Yen, Douglas E.
    1962 Review of Jacques Barrau, Subsistence Agriculture in
          Polynesia and Micronesia. Journal of the Polynesian
          Society, 71(4):350-351.
          M I

Yinug, Martin
    1972 Leadership requirements in Micronesia. IN Micronesian
          Realities: Political and Economic, Frances McReynolds Smith,
          ed. Santa Cruz, California: Center for South Pacific
          Studies. pp. 245-248.
          M XVII

Yotopoulos, Pan A.
   1972   The hard realities of developing a new nation: Micronesia.
          IN Micronesian Realities: Political and Economic, Frances
          McReynolds Smith, ed.   Santa Cruz, California: Center for
          South Pacific Studies.   pp. 115-119.
          M XVII

Youd, Jean
   1961   Notes on kickball in Micronesia.   Journal of American
          Folklore, 74(291):62-64.
          M IV

Young, John E. de, ed.
   1958   The Use of Names by Micronesians.   Anthropological Working
          Papers, No. 3.   Guam: Office of the Staff Anthropologist,
          Trust Territory of the Pacific Islands.   124 pp.   Reviewed:
          1959 by Saul H. Riesenberg, American Anthropologist, 61(6):
          1136-1137; 1964 by William A. Lessa, Journal of the Poly-
          nesian Society, 73(1):95-96.
          M II

Young, John E. de, ed.
   1958   Land Tenure Patterns, Trust Territory of the Pacific Islands,
          Vol. 1.   Guam: Office of the Staff Anthropologist, Trust
          Territory of the Pacific Islands.   339 pp.
          M II1

Young, John E. de, ed.
   1959   Yam Cultivation in the Trust Territory.   Anthropological
          Working Papers, No. 4.   Guam: Office of the Staff Anthro-
          pologist, Trust Territory of the Pacific Islands.   Re-
          viewed: 1961 by Allan H. Smith, American Anthropologist,
          63(2), Part 1:426-428.
          M I

Young, John E. de, ed.
   1960   Taro Cultivation, Practices and Beliefs.   Parts I and II.
          Anthropological Working Papers, No. 6.   Guam: Office of the
          Staff Anthropologist, Trust Territory of the Pacific Islands.
          Reviewed: 1961 by Allan H. Smith, American Anthropologist,
          63(2), Part 1:426-428.
          M I

Z'graggen, J. A.
   1971   Review of Arthur Capell, Grammar and Vocabulary of the
          Language of Sonsorol-Tobi.   Anthropos, 66:292.
          PL3 PL4 XIII

MAIN BIBLIOGRAPHY

Zachary, Wyman X.
    1972 Micronesia: A viable economy, fact or Fancy? IN
         Micronesian Realities: Political and Economic, Frances
         McReynolds Smith, ed. Santa Cruz, California: Center for
         South Pacific Studies. pp. 167-171.
         M VI

Zaiger, D. and G. A. Zentmeyer
    1966 A new lethal disease of breadfruit in the Pacific Islands.
         Plant Disease Reporter [Crops Research Division, Agri-
         cultural Research Service, U.S. Department of Agriculture],
         50(12):892-896.
         M I

Zan, Yigal
    1971 A Ponapean Oedipus tale: An explanation of narrative
         Phenomenon. Anthropology UCLA, 3(1):21-25.
         Pn1 VIII

Zimbelman, Edward
    1974 A night in "Venice": Nan Madol, ancient sea city of the
         Carolines. Oceans, 7(6):32-39.
         Pn1 IX

GUIDE TO TOPICS AND AREAS

Agriculture

Micronesia (U.S.T.P.I.)
Apple, Russell A. 1972 Historic Properties Policy and Program in
Barrau, Jacques 1961 Subsistence agriculture in Polynesia and
Cheatham, Norden H. 1968 Forestry and conservation in the Trust
Coenen, Jan 1961 Agricultural development in Micronesia.
Coenen, Jan and Jacques Barrau 1961 The breadfruit tree in
Coolidge, Harold J., ed. 1948 Conservation in Micronesia.
Davenport, William H. 1962 Review of Jacques Barrau, Subsistence
Fosberg, F. Raymond 1953 A conservation program for Micronesia.
Gallahue, Edward E. 1953 Changing agricultural economy of
MacMillan, Howard G. 1946 Report on agricultural conditions in
Marshall, Colin 1951 Report on forestry in the Trust
Miguar, Leo 1964 The coconut in Micronesia.
Miller, Carey D., et al. 1956 The use of pandanus fruit as food
Nishi, Midori 1968 An evaluation of Japanese agricultural and
Otobed, Demei O. 1975 Conservation priorities in Micronesia.
Owen, Robert P. 1969 The status of conservation in the Trust
Ripperton, John C. 1946 Report on Some Agricultural Aspects of
Smith, Allan H. 1961 Review of John de Young, ed., Taro
Van Steenis, C. G. G. J. 1965 Man and plants in the tropics: An
Weitzell, E. C. 1946 The Mariana, Caroline, and Marshall Islands.
Yen, Douglas E. 1962 Review of Jacques Barrau, Subsistence
Young, John E. de, ed. 1959 Yam Cultivation in the Trust
Young, John E. de, ed. 1960 Taro Cultivation, Practices and
Zaiger, D. and G. A. Zentmeyer 1966 A new lethal disease of

Mariana Islands
Solenberger, Robert R. 1967 The changing role of rice in the
Yawata, Ichiro 1963 Rice cultivation of the ancient Mariana

Guam
Perez, Gerald S. A. 1975 Guam conservation Priorities.

Palau Islands
McKnight, Robert K. 1960 Breadfruit cultivation practices and
McKnight, Robert K. and Adalbert Obak 1959 Yam cultivation in the
McKnight, Robert K. and Adalbert Obak 1960 Taro cultivation in
Smith, Allan H. 1961 Review of John de Young, ed., Taro
Vessel, A. V. and Roy W. Simonson 1958 Soils and agriculture of

Yap Islands
Defngin, Francis 1959 Yam cultivation practices and beliefs in
Kim, Dai You and Francis Defngin 1960 Taro cultivation in Yap.
Ogata, S. Bert 1960 Traditional coconut culture on Yap.

Truk District
Mahony, Frank J. 1960 Taro cultivation in Truk.

Truk Islands - Truk Lagoon

GUIDE TO TOPICS AND AREAS

Agriculture

Pelzer, Karl J. 1947 Agriculture in the Truk Islands.

Ponape District
Murphy, Raymond E. 1953 Changing patterns of agriculture in the

Ponape
Bascom, Willard R. 1949 Subsistence farming on Ponape.
Bascom, Willard R. 1953 Ponapean subsistence Farming.
Mahony, Frank J. 1960 Taro cultivation in Ponape.
Mahony, Frank J. and Pensile Lawrence 1959 Ponapean yam
Matsumuro, Kazuaki 1969 Pepper culture in the Eastern Caroline
Sasuke, N. 1953 Breadfruit, yams and taros of Ponape Island.

Kapingamarangi
Stone, Benjamin C. 1966 Cultivated pandanus in Kapingamarangi

Marshall Islands District
Bikajle, Tion 1960 Taro culture as practised by the Marshallese.
Fosberg, F. Raymond 1957 Soils, vegetation, and agriculture on
Hatheway, William H. 1957 Agricultural notes on the Southern
Mackenzie, J. Boyd 1960 Breadfruit cultivation practices and
Stone, Benjamin C. 1960 The wild and cultivated Pandanus of the
Stone, Benjamin C. 1963 The role of pandanus in the culture of

Arno
Stone, Earl L., Jr. 1951 The agriculture of Arno Atoll, Marshall

GUIDE TO TOPICS AND AREAS

Anthropology

Pacific Islands
Association for Social Anthropology in Oceania 1967 to present.
Lessa, William A. 1953 Neueste Amerikanische ethnologische
Spoehr, Alexander 1953 Anthropology and coral atoll field
Spoehr, Alexander 1966 The part and the whole: Reflections on the

Micronesia (U.S.T.T.P.I.)
Alkire, William H. 1972 An introduction to the peoples and
Alkire, William H. 1972 Concepts of order in Southeast Asia and
Anonymous 1947 Anthropological research and related research in
Association for Anthropology in Micronesia 1972 to 1974.
Bryan, Edwin H., Jr. 1965 Life in Micronesia.
Embree, John F. 1946 University of Hawaii research in Micronesia.
Fischer, John L. 1974 Micronesian Cultures.
Force, Roland W. 1964 Micronesian Peoples.
Force, Roland W. 1966 Micronesians.
Friends of Micronesia 1971 to present.
Gale, Roger 1973 Anthropological colonialism in Micronesia.
Goodenough, Ward H. 1970 Micronesia's People.
Hawaii Architects & Engineers, Inc. 1968 Cultural Considerations
Hawaii Architects & Engineers, Inc. 1968 Notes on Anthropological
Johnson, Donald D. 1974 Pacific Islands, Trust Territory of the.
Kahlo, G. 1960 Die Mikronesische Frage.
Keesing, Felix M. 1945 People of the Mandates.
Koch, Gerd 1966 The Polynesian-Micronesian 'Culture Boundary'.
Lessa, William A. 1964 Review of John E. de Young, ed., The Use
Mahoney, Francis B. 1961 Micronesia.
Mason, Leonard E. 1951 A changing world--Micronesia.
Mason, Leonard E. 1953 Anthropology in American Micronesia: A
Mason, Leonard E. 1953 Suggestions for investigating the culture
Mason, Leonard E. 1962 Micronesia.
Mason, Leonard E. 1963 Micronesia.
Mason, Leonard E. 1966 Anthropological and other social science
Mason, Leonard E. 1968 The ethnology of Micronesia.
Mason, Leonard E. 1969 Anthropological research in Micronesia,
Mason, Leonard E. 1972 La Micronesie.
Mason, Leonard E. 1973 The anthropological presence in
Mason, Leonard E. 1975 The many faces of Micronesia: District
McGrath, Thomas B. 1972 Conservation of indigenous cultural
Micronesian Program Bulletin 1966 to 1969.
Murdock, George P. 1948 Anthropology in Micronesia.
Murdock, George P. 1948 New light on the peoples of Micronesia.
Murdock, George P. 1953 Cultural sub-areas in Micronesia.
Paszkowski, Lech 1971 John Stanislaw Kubary-naturalist and
Porter, Catherine 1944 The Japanese Mandates.
Smith, Allan H. 1957 Report on research in Micronesian ethnology
Smith, Allan H. 1958 Report on research in Micronesian ethnology
Someki, Atsushi 1945 Micronesia no Fudo to Mingu.
Spoehr, Alexander 1951 The peoples living in U.S. Trust Territory

GUIDE TO TOPICS AND AREAS

Anthropology

Spoehr, Alexander 1951 Anthropology and the Trust Territory: A
U.S.T.T.P.I. 1957 Anthropology Newsletter.
Useem, John 1948 Human resources of Micronesia.
Useem, John 1948 Institutions of Micronesia.
Valentine, Charles A. 1963 Social status, political power, and
Young, John E. de, ed. 1958 The Use of Names by Micronesians.

Mariana Islands

Ballendorf, Dirk 1973 The confidential Micronesian Reporter.
Spoehr, Alexander 1950 Expedition to Marianas completes Work.
Spoehr, Alexander 1973 Life cf the Chamorros in the Marianas.
Thompson, Laura 1945 The Native Culture of the Marianas Islands.
Useem, John 1947 Review of Laura Thompson, The Native Culture of

Guam

Johnston, Agueda I. 1965 Christmas on Guam.
Mason, Leonard E. 1948 Review of Laura Thompson, Guam and Its
McGrath, Thomas B. 1972 Conservation of indigenous cultural
Porter, Catherine 1944 Guam.
Richardson, Paul D. 1971 A Study of the Socio-Cultural Factors of
Solenberger, Robert R. 1953 The social and cultural position of
Spoehr, Alexander 1951 The peoples living in U.S. Trust Territory
Thompson, Laura 1944 The women of Guam.
Thompson, Laura 1969 People of Guam.

Saipan

Hewes, Gordon W. 1955 Review of Alexander Spoehr, Saipan, The
Spoehr, Alexander 1954 Saipan, the Ethnology of a War-Devastated

Caroline Islands

Fischer, John L. and Ann M. Fischer 1957 The Eastern Carolines.
Micronesian Seminar 1967 Translation of "The Carolines and their
Useem, John 1946 Report on Yap and Palau, and the Lesser Islands

Palau Islands

Aderkroi, David M. 1965 Palau's imported Festivity.
Barnett, Homer G. 1949 Palauan Society, A Study of Contemporary
Barnett, Homer G. 1960 Being A Palauan.
Barnett, Homer G. 1970 Palauan Journal.
Barras de Aragon, Francisco de las 1949 Las islas Palaos.
Beaglehole, Ernest 1962 Review of Homer Barnett, Being a Palauan.
Bruner, Edward M. 1961 Review of Homer G. Barnett, Being a
Lessa, William A. 1964 Review of Robert K. McKnight, Mnemonics in
McKnight, Robert K. 1958 Palauan Names.
McKnight, Robert K. 1961 Mnemonics in preliterate Palau.
Meggitt, Mervyn J. 1960 Review of Homer Barnett, Being a Palauan.
Useem, John 1949 Report on Palau.
Useem, John 1955 Palau.
Weckler, Joseph E. 1950 Review of Homer Barnett, Palauan Society.

Yap Islands

GUIDE TO TOPICS AND AREAS

Anthropology

Beauclair, Inez de 1961 Bericht aus Yap, Mikronesien.
Defngin, Francis 1958 Yapese Names.
Kirkpatrick, John 1973 Personal names on Yap.

Ulithi

Burridge, K. O. L. 1967 Review of William A. Lessa, Ulithi: A
Gladwin, Thomas 1967 Review of William A. Lessa, Ulithi: A
Lessa, William A. 1950 The Ethnography of Ulithi Atoll. CIMA
Lessa, William A. 1950 Ulithi and the outer native World.
Lessa, William A. 1966 Ulithi: A Micronesian Design for Living.

Ifaluk

Bates, Marston 1956 Ifalik, lonely paradise of the South Seas.
Burrows, Edwin Grant and Melford E. Spiro 1953 An Atoll Culture,
Lessa, William A. 1955 Review of Edwin G. Burrows and Melford E.
Lessa, William A. 1955 Review of Edwin G. Burrows and Melford E.
Spiro, Melford E. 1953 A typology of functional Analysis.
Trifonovitch, Gregory J. 1971 Ifaluk: A brief report on some

Truk Islands - Truk Lagoon

Boggs, Stephen T., ed. 1969 The Truk Report: A Report on Field
Caughey, Frances B. 1971 Pregnancy and childbirth on Uman, Truk.
Fischer, Ann M. 1970 Field work in five Cultures.
Gladwin, Thomas 1964 Petrus Mailo, Chief of Moen (Truk).
Goodenough, Ward H. 1956 A Christmas on Truk.
Goodenough, Ward H. 1963 Some applications of Guttman scale
Mahony, Frank J. 1958 Trukese Names.

Puluwat

Riesenberg, Saul H. and Samuel H. Elbert 1971 The poi of the

Mortlock Islands

Ward, William T. T. 1955 A preliminary survey of the economic and

Lukunor

Tolerton, Burt and Jerome Rauch n.d. Social Organization, Land

Ponape

Emerick, Richard G. 1960 Homesteading on Ponape: A study and
Fischer, Ann M. 1970 Field work in five Cultures.
Fischer, John L. 1974 Some characteristics of kava drinkers on
Glassman, Sidney F. 1950 Ponape's national Beverage.
Lawrence, Pensile and John E. de Young 1958 The use of names in
Morrill, Sibley S. 1970 Ponape: Where American Colonialism
Murrill, Rupert I. 1948 Ponape: A Micronesian culture of the
Riesenberg, Saul H. 1950 The cultural position of Ponape in

Mokil

Bentzen, Conrad 1949 Land and Livelihood on Mokil, an Atoll in
Bentzen, Conrad, in collaboration with Mel Sloan 1948 Mokil.
Kiste, Robert C. and Paul D. Schaefer 1974 Review of Conrad

GUIDE TO TOPICS AND AREAS

Anthropology

Weckler, Joseph E. 1949 Land and Livelihood on Mokil, An Atoll in

Pingelap
Hasebe, K. 1944 The Pingelap Islanders.

Nukuoro
Bayard, Donn T. 1966 The cultural relationships of the Polynesian

Kapingamarangi
Bayard, Donn T. 1966 The cultural relationships of the Polynesian
Emory, Kenneth P. 1949 Anthropological Study of Kapingamarangi.
Emory, Kenneth P. 1965 Kapingamarangi: Social and Religious Life
Firth, Raymond 1966 Review of Kenneth P. Emory, Kapingamarangi:
Hiroa, Te Rangi [Peter H. Buck] 1948 Bishop Museum Expedition
Hiroa, Te Rangi [Peter H. Buck] 1949 Kapingamarangi; a
Lieber, Michael D. 1968 Review of Kenneth P. Emory,
Luomala, Katharine 1968 Review of Kenneth P. Emory,

Kusaie - Kusaie District
Wilson, Walter Scott and Singkitchy P. George 1965 Christmas on

Marshall Islands District
Bikajle, Tion and John E. de Young 1958 Marshallese Names.
Bryan, Edwin H., Jr. 1972 Life in the Marshall Islands.
Spoehr, Alexander 1949 Life in the Marshall Islands.

Majuro
Embree, John F. 1950 Review of Alexander Spoehr, Majuro: A
Mason, Leonard E. 1967 The mapping of Majuro Island (Laura).
Mason, Leonard E., ed. 1967 The Laura Report.
Murphy, Raymond E. 1950 Review of Alexander Spoehr, Majuro: A
Spoehr, Alexander 1949 Majuro, A Village in the Marshall Islands.

Bikini
Georgia Center for Continuing Education 1974 The Bikinians.
Marshall, Mac 1975 Review of Robert C. Kiste, The Bikinians: A

Kwajalein
Vitarelli, William V. 1975 Non-Planning and social imbalance in a

Kili
Georgia Center for Continuing Education 1974 The Bikinians.
Marshall, Mac 1975 Review of Robert C. Kiste, The Bikinians: A

GUIDE TO TOPICS AND AREAS

Social Organization

Pacific Islands
Brady, Ivan A. 1973 Review of Vern Carroll, ed., Adoption in
Carroll, Vern, ed. n.d. Incest Prohibitions in Polynesia and
Carroll, Vern, ed. 1970 Adoption in Eastern Oceania.
Doran, Edwin, Jr., ed. 1961 Land tenure in the Pacific.
Foster, Stephen William 1972 Review of Vern Carroll, ed.,
Frake, Charles O. 1956 Malayo-Polynesian land Tenure.
Hogbin, Ian 1971 Review of Vern Carroll, ed., Adoption in Eastern
Kennally, Most Rev. Vincent I., S.J. 1961 Oceania: A missionary
Lundsgaarde, Henry P., ed. 1974 Land Tenure in Oceania.
McKinley, Robert 1973 Review of Vern Carroll, ed., Adoption in
Metge, Joan 1971 Review of Vern Carroll, ed., Adoption in Eastern
Mitchell, I. S. 1972 Review of Vern Carroll, ed., Adoption in
Segalen, Martine 1971 Review of Vern Carroll, ed., Adoption in
Wilson, Walter Scott 1971 Review of Vern Carroll, ed., Adoption

Micronesia (U.S.T.T.P.I.)
Capell, Arthur 1954 Review of Erhard Schlesier, Die
Cohen, Herbert 1952 Class and land in Micronesia.
Goodenough, Ward H. 1955 A problem in Malayo-Polynesian social
Hughes, Daniel T. and Douglas Mapou 1973 Structural variation of
Klarwill, P. E. 1955 Review of Erhard Schlesier, Die
Loeb, E. M. 1947 Social organization and the long house in
McGrath, William A. 1971 Resolving the land Dilemma.
McGrath, William A. and Walter Scott Wilson 1971 The Marshall,
Murdock, George P. 1949 Social organization and government in
Murdock, George P. 1954 Review of Bernhard Stillfried, Die
Price, Monroe E. 1972 Land tenure and the constitution:
Riesenberg, Saul H. 1953 Land tenure problems in the Trust
Riesenberg, Saul H. 1955 Review of Erhard Schlesier, Die
Riesenberg, Saul H. 1959 Review of John de Young, ed., The Use of
Saunders, Marin Grace 1960 Cross-Cultural study of coalitions in
Schlesier, Erhard 1951 Die Erscheinungsformen des Männerhauses
Schlesier, Erhard 1952 Zum problem "Männerhaus".
Sicard, Charles 1974 Micronesian children with a foreign Parent.
Stillfried, Bernhard 1953 Die Soziale Organisation in
Stillfried, Bernhard 1956 Mutterrechtliche Verwandtschaftszüge
Ushijima, Iwao 1969 The disorganization process of the
Yamada, Kozo 1975 A comment on land law and land ownership in
Young, John E. de, ed. 1958 Land Tenure Patterns, Trust Territory

Mariana Islands
Benavente, Ignacio V. 1952 Land tenure in the Northern Marianas.
Costenoble, H. 1974 The family tree of Chamorro.
Emerick, Richard G. 1958 Land tenure in the Marianas.
Johnson, James B. 1969 Land Ownership in the Northern Mariana

Guam
Souder, Paul B. 1971 Guam: Land tenure in a Fortress.

GUIDE TO TOPICS AND AREAS

Social Organization

Rota

Smith, James Jerome n.d. Rotanese fosterage: Counterexample of an
Smith, James Jerome 1971 Intergenerational land transactions on
Smith, James Jerome 1972 Intergenerational land transactions on
Smith, James Jerome 1973 Land tenure on Rota: Yesterday, today
Smith, James Jerome 1973 Types and general location of private
Smith, James Jerome 1974 Land tenure on Rota, Mariana Islands.

Caroline Islands

Hernandes, Faustino, S. J. 1951 Marriage problems and customs in
Mason, Leonard E. 1959 Suprafamilial authority and economic

Palau Islands

Alkire, William H. 1974 Review of Roland W. Force and Maryanne
Fischer, John L. 1974 Review of Roland W. Force and Maryanne
Force, Roland W. 1961 Palauan paradox: Some comments on kinship
Force, Roland W. and Maryanne Force 1972 Just One House: A
Huber, Peter B. 1974 Review of Roland Force and Maryanne Force,
Kaneshiro, Shigeru 1958 Land tenure in the Palau Islands.
McKnight, Robert K. 1960 Competition in Palau.
McKnight, Robert K. 1975 Competition and status in Palau, a short

Yap Islands

Beauclair, Inez de 1968 Social stratification in Micronesia: The
Kirkpatrick, John T. and Charles R. Broder n.d. Adoption and
Labby, David n.d. Incest as cannibalism: The Yapese Analysis.
Labby, David 1972 The anthropology of others: An analysis of the
Lingenfelter, Sherwood G. 1971 Social structure and political
Lingenfelter, Sherwood G. 1973 Action group formation and
Mahoney, Francis B. 1958 Land tenure patterns on Yap Island.
Schneider, David M. 1949 The kinship system and village
Schneider, David M. 1953 Yap kinship terminology and kin Groups.
Schneider, David M. 1962 Double descent on Yap.
Schneider, David M. 1968 Virgin Birth.
Schneider, David M. 1969 A re-analysis of the kinship system of
Schneider, David M. 1974 Depopulation and the Yap

Lamotrek

Alkire, William H. 1965 Lamotrek Atoll and Inter-Island
Fosberg, F. Raymond 1966 Review of William H. Alkire, Lamotrek
Lessa, William A. 1966 Review of William H. Alkire, Lamotrek
Sinha, D. P. 1969 Review of William H. Alkire, Lamotrek Atoll and
Uberoi, J. S. 1966 Review of William H. Alkire, Lamotrek Atoll

The Woleai

Alkire, William H. 1974 Land tenure in the Woleai.
Smith, Alfred G. and John P. Kennedy 1960 The extension of incest

Truk District

Fischer, John L. 1958 Native land tenure in the Truk District.

GUIDE TO TOPICS AND AREAS

Social Organization

Truk Islands - Truk Lagoon

Carter, Jackson 1972 Truk: A land Problem.
Fischer, Ann M. 1950 Trukese privacy Patterns.
Fischer, Ann M. 1963 Reproduction in Truk.
Fischer, John L. 1956 The position of men and women in Truk and
Fischer, John L. 1958 The classification of residence in
Fischer, John L. 1959 Reply to Raulet.
Fischer, John L. 1966 Syntax and social structure: Truk and
Fischer, John L. 1968 Microethnology: Small-Scale comparative
Goodenough, Ruth Gallagher 1970 Adoption on Romonum, Truk.
Goodenough, Ward H. 1949 A grammar of social Interaction.
Goodenough, Ward H. 1949 Premarital freedom on Truk: Theory and
Goodenough, Ward H. 1951 Property, Kin, and Community on Truk.
Goodenough, Ward H. 1956 Componential analysis and the study of
Goodenough, Ward H. 1956 Residence Rules.
Goodenough, Ward H. 1964 Property and language on Truk: Some
Goodenough, Ward H. 1965 Personal names and modes of address in
Goodenough, Ward H. 1965 Rethinking 'status' and 'role': Toward a
Goodenough, Ward H. 1971 Corporations: Reply to Cochrane.
Goodenough, Ward H. 1974 Changing social organization on Romonum,
Lessa, William A. 1952 Review of Ward H. Goodenough, Property,
MacMeekin, Daniel H. 1975 Land law and change on Truk.
Murdock and Goodenough 1947 Social organization of Truk.
Raulet, Harry M. 1959 A note on Fischer's residence Typology.
Schneider, David M. 1957 Truk.
Swartz, Marc J. 1958 The social organization of behavior:
Swartz, Marc J. 1960 Situational determinants of kinship
Swartz, Marc J. 1962 Recruiting labor for fissionary descent

Losap

Fischer, John L. 1955 Avunculocal residence on Losap.
Severance, Craig J. 1974 Sanction and sakau: The accessibility

Namoluk

Marshall, Mac n.d. Incest and endogamy on Namoluk Atoll.
Marshall, Mac n.d. Solidarity or sterility? Adoption and
Marshall, Mac [Keith] 1972 The structure of solidarity and
Marshall, Mac 1975 Changing patterns of marriage and migration on

Ponape District

Yamada, Kozo 1969 Land tenure in the Eastern Caroline Islands

Ponape

Carroll, Vern n.d. Communities and non-communities: The Nukuoro
Fischer, John L. 1956 The position of men and women in Truk and
Fischer, John L. 1958 Contemporary Ponape Island land Tenure, IN
Fischer, John L. 1959 A note on terminology for primary Kin.
Fischer, John L. 1965 Levi-Strauss versus Freud on totemism: Data
Fischer, John L. 1966 Syntax and social structure: Truk and
Fischer, John L. 1968 Microethnology: Small-Scale comparative

GUIDE TO TOPICS AND AREAS

Social Organization

Fischer, John L. 1969 Honorific speech and social structure: A
Fischer, John L. 1970 Adoption cn Ponape.
Fischer, John L., et al. n.d. Ponapean conceptions of Incest.
Severance, Craig J. 1974 Sanction and sakau: The accessibility

Mokil
Lord, Anthony S. 1971 Landholding groups: A new solution to an
Murphy, Raymond E. 1948 Landownership on a Micronesian Atoll.
Weckler, Joseph E. 1953 Adoption cn Mokil.

Nukucro
Carroll, Vern n.d. Communities and non-communities: The Nukuoro
Carroll, Vern n.d. Incest on Nukucro.
Carroll, Vern 1966 Nukuoro Kinship.
Carroll, Vern 1968 Nukuoro kinship Terms.
Carroll, Vern 1970 Adoption on Nukuoro.
Carroll, Vern 1972 The Nukuoro nction of 'Person'.
Carroll, Vern 1973 'Rape' on Nukuoro.
Fischer, John L. 1958 Folktales, social structure, and

Kapingamarangi
Fischer, John L. 1958 Folktales, social structure, and
Lieber, Michael D. n.d. Incest and responsibility on
Lieber, Michael D. 1968 The nature of the relationship between
Lieber, Michael D. 1968 Kapingamarangi: Kinship Terminology.
Lieber, Michael D. 1970 Adoption on Kapingamarangi.
Lieber, Michael D. 1973 To be 'cnly a woman' on Kapingamarangi:
Lieber, Michael D. 1974 Land tenure on Kapingamarangi.

Kusaie - Kusaie District
Wilson, Walter Scott n.d. Household, land and adoption on Kusaie.
Wilson, Walter Scott 1968 Land, activity, and social organization
Wilson, Walter Scott and Eleanora Wilson n.d. Incest on Kusaie.

Marshall Islands District
Hernandes, Faustino, S. J. 1951 Marriage problems and customs in
Kiste, Robert C. 1968 Variations in Marshallese cross-ccusin
Mason, Leonard E. 1959 Suprafamilial authority and ecconomic
Neas, Maynard 1961 Land ownership patterns in the Marshall
Rynkiewich, Michael A. 1974 Coming home to Bokelab.
Spoehr, Alexander 1949 The generation type kinship system in the
Strance, Almi 1972 Role of women in Micronesia: Marshall Islands
Tobin, Jack A. 1952 Land tenure in the Marshall Islands.

Majuro
Milne, Carmen and Michael Steward 1967 The inheritance of land

Arno
Kiste, Robert C. and Michael A. Rynkiewich n.d. Incest and
Mason, Lecnard E. 1959 Space, the scarce commodity in atoll
Rynkiewich, Michael A. n.d. Adoption and land tenure among Arno

Social Organization

Rynkiewich, Michael A. 1972 Demography and social structure on
Rynkiewich, Michael A. 1972 Land tenure among Arno Marshallese.

Bikini
Kiste, Robert C. and Michael A. Rynkiewich n.d. Incest and

Namu
Pollock, Nancy J. 1974 Land tenure and land usage on Namu Atoll.

GUIDE TO TOPICS AND AREAS

Religion

Pacific Islands
Bornemann, Fritz 1956 P. W. Schmidt's Studien über den
Kennally, Most Rev. Vincent I., S.J. 1961 Oceania: A missionary

Micronesia (U.S.T.T.P.I.)
Cormack, Maribelle 1956 The Lady was a Skipper: The Story of
Crawford, David and Leona Crawford 1967 Missionary Adventures in
Damm, H. 1955 Micronesische Kultboote, Schwebealtäre und
Dunstan, J. L. 1947 Mission work in Micronesia.
Loomis, Albertine 1970 To All People.
Marshall, Mac and Leslie B. Marshall 1975 Holy and unholy
Maude, H. E. 1969 Review of David Crawford and Leona Crawford,
McGrath, Thomas B. 1964 The Micronesian Seminar.
Schmidt, P. W. 1953 Die Mythologien und Religionen der
Trifonovitch, Gregory J. 1973 Across cultures between Kuleanas.
Ushijima, Iwao 1967 The afterworld view and its underlying ideas
Walter, William J. 1952 Micronesian medicine Man.
Walter, William J. 1957 Witch Doctor.

Mariana Islands
Hynd, George W. 1974 Religion and magic among the ancient
Micronesian Seminar 1967 Translation of "Letter from the
Risco, A. and Msgr. O. L. Calvo, eds. 1970 The Apostle of the

Guam
McCall, Louis Edmund 1973 A study comparing scholastic
McGrath, Thomas B. 1973 Abortion: Some observations about Guam.
Micronesian Seminar 1966 Translation of "Letter of Fr. Cantova
Sanchez, Pedro C. 1975 The new Guam: A challenge to human Values.
Sullivan, Julius 1957 The Phoenix Rises: A Mission History of
Van der Poel, Cornelius J. 1973 Guam in Search of Its Own
Van der Poel, Cornelius J. 1975 Human and cultural values on Guam

Caroline Islands
Hezel, Francis X. 1971 Spanish Capuchins in the Carolines.
Hezel, Francis X. 1975 Indigenization as a missionary goal in the
Lessa, William A. 1959 Divining from knots in the Carolines.
Lopinot, Callistus, O.F.M. Cap. 1964 Die Karolinenmission der
Micronesian Seminar 1965 Translation of "Missions in the
Micronesian Seminar 1967 Translation of "Letter from the
Micronesian Seminar 1967 Translation of "The first missionary
Micronesian Seminar 1967 Translation of "The Capuchin Mission
Soucie, Edward 1963 Jesuit Brothers in the Caroline-Marshall

Palau Islands
Micronesian Seminar 1969 Translation of "Die religion der
Obak, Adalbert and Robert K. McKnight 1964 Mesubed Dingal: Patron
Stumpf, Margaret K. 1970 Palauan value orientation and Education.

GUIDE TO TOPICS AND AREAS

Religion

Tobi
Black, Peter 1975 Some vicissitudes of Roman Catholic dogma on

Yap Islands
Beauclair, Inez de 1963 Ueber Religion und Magie auf Yap.
Beauclair, Inez de 1967 Infant burial in earthenware pots and the
Beauclair, Inez de 1967 On religion and mythology of Yap Island,
Beauclair, Inez de 1968 On the religion of Yap Island,
Micronesian Seminar 1969 Translation of "Religious beliefs

Ulithi
Lessa, William A. n.d. The apotheosis of Marespa.
Walter, William J. 1951 My people of Ulithi.

Woleai
Alkire, William H. 1968 Porpoises and Taro.

Ifaluk
Beauclair, Inez de 1963 Black magic on Ifaluk.
Burrows, Edwin Grant 1952 From value to ethos on Ifaluk Atoll.
Lessa, William A. 1961 Sorcery on Ifaluk.
Spiro, Melford E. 1952 Ghosts, Ifaluk, and teleological
Spiro, Melford E. 1961 Sorcery, evil spirits and functional

Truk District
Rively, William E., S.J. 1953 The Story of the "Romance".

Truk Islands - Truk Lagoon
Caughey, John Lyon IV 1970 Cultural values in a Micronesian
Fischer, John L. 1957 Totemism on Truk and Ponape.
Fischer, John L. 1968 Microethnology: Small-Scale comparative
Goodenough, Ward H. 1955 Survival of the soul on Truk.
Goodenough, Ward H. 1966 Human purpose in Life.
Goodenough, Ward H. 1974 Toward an anthropologically useful
Kohl, Manfred Waldemar 1971 Lagoon in the Pacific.
Micronesian Seminar n.d. Translation of "Some remarks about

Etal
Nason, James D. 1975 Civilizing the heathen: Missionaries and

Ponape
Fischer, John L. 1957 Totemism on Truk and Ponape.
Fischer, John L. 1964 Semi-castration on Ponape.
Fischer, John L. 1968 Microethnology: Small-Scale comparative
McGrath, Thomas B. 1973 Sakau in tomw.
O'Brien, Ilma E. 1971 Missionaries on Ponape: Induced social and
Riesenberg, Saul H. 1948 Magic and medicine in Ponape.
Soucie, Edward 1964 Fr. Hugh Costigan, S.J. and Ponape, Caroline
Ward, Roger L. 1974 Ponapean apology rituals: Elaborations of the

Kusaie - Kusaie District

GUIDE TO TOPICS AND AREAS

Religion

Schaefer, Paul D. 1975 From "king" to pastor: The acquisition of

Marshall Islands District
Hezel, Francis X. 1975 Indigenization as a missionary goal in the
Micronesian Seminar 1965 Translation of "Missions in the
Soucie, Edward 1963 Jesuit Brothers in the Caroline-Marshall

Likiep
Feeney, T. J. 1952 Letters from Likiep.

GUIDE TO TOPICS AND AREAS

Political Organization

Pacific Islands

Barnett, Homer G. 1966 Review of Roland W. Force, ed., Induced
Force, Roland W., ed. 1965 Induced Political Change in the
Meller, Norman 1965 Political change in the Pacific.
Meller, Norman 1965 Three American legislative bodies in the

Micronesia (U.S.T.T.P.I.)

Force, Roland W. and Maryanne Force 1965 Political change in
Hughes, Daniel T. 1972 Traditional versus modern sources of
Hughes and Lingenfelter, eds. 1974 Political Development in
Hughes, Daniel T. and Douglas Mapou 1973 Structural variation of
Hughes, Daniel T. and James McLeod 1973 Typology of colonial
MacQuarrie, Alan M. 1969 The effects of political modernization
Mason, Leonard E. 1948 Micronesia: Isolation or Assimilation?
Mason, Leonard E. 1969 Popular participation in the development
Mason, Leonard E. 1972 Comments on political future of
Mason, Leonard E. 1974 Unity and disunity in Micronesia: Internal
McKnight, Robert K. 1969 Political leadership in Micronesia.
Micronesian Seminar 1973 Proceedings of a Seminar on Moral Issues
Oberem, Udo 1951 Die frühe Herrenkultur der Mikronesischen
Oberem, Udo 1953 Staatsaufbau in Mikronesien.
Singleton, John 1974 Education, planning and political

Mariana Islands

Carano, Paul 1972 Ancient Chamorro Leaders.
Solenberger, Robert R. 1964 Continuity of local political

Guam

Meller, Norman 1960 Political changes in American Pacific

Palau Islands

Barnett, Homer G. 1953 The Koror Community Center.
Force, Roland W. 1958 Leadership and cultural change in Palau.
Force, Roland W. 1961 Political change in Palau.
McKnight, Robert K. 1961 The mouth that explains: Mesaod Ngerel,
McKnight, Robert K. 1969 Rigid models and ridiculous boundaries:
McKnight, Robert K. 1974 Rigid models and ridiculous boundaries:
Useem, John 1950 Structure of power in Palau.
Useem, John 1952 Democracy in process: The development of
Vidich, Arthur J. 1949 Political Factionalism in Palau, Its Rise

Yap Islands

Lingenfelter, Sherwood G. 1971 The process of elite formation in
Lingenfelter, Sherwood G. 1971 Social structure and political
Lingenfelter, Sherwood G. 1974 Administrative officials, Peace
Lingenfelter, Sherwood G. 1975 Yap: Political Leadership and
Schneider, David M. 1957 Political organization, supernatural

Ulithi

GUIDE TO TOPICS AND AREAS

Political Organization

Lessa, William A. 1950 The place of Ulithi in the Yap Empire.

Truk District
Raken, Yokitaro and Robert Edmondson 1969 Representative

Truk Islands - Truk Lagoon
Pramuanradhakarn Thiravetya 1969 Current influence of traditional
Swartz, Marc J. 1959 Leadership and status conflict on Romonum,
Swartz, Marc J. 1965 Personality and structure: Political

Namoluk
Marshall, Mac 1975 The politics of prohibition on Namoluk Atoll.
Marshall, Mac and Mark Borthwick 1974 Consensus, dissensus, and

Etal
Nason, James D. 1972 Political change: An outer island

Ponape
Alkire, William H. 1968 Review of Saul H. Riesenberg, The Native
Bascom, Willard R. 1950 Ponape, the cycle of Empire.
Dahlquist, Paul A. 1974 Political development at the municipal
Fischer, John L. 1974 The role of the traditional chiefs on
Garvin, Paul L. and Saul H. Riesenberg 1952 Respect behavior on
Hughes, Daniel T. 1968 Democracy in a traditional society: A role
Hughes, Daniel T. 1969 Conflict and harmony: Roles of councilman
Hughes, Daniel T. 1969 Democracy in a traditional society: Two
Hughes, Daniel T. 1969 Reciprocal influence of traditional and
Hughes, Daniel T. 1970 Political Conflict and Harmony on Ponape.
Hughes, Daniel T. 1972 Integration of the role of territorial
Hughes, Daniel T. 1973 Democracy in the Philippines and on
Hughes, Daniel T. 1974 Changes in the value system associated
Hughes, Daniel T. 1974 Obstacles to the integration of the
Lieber, Michael D. 1970 Review of Saul H. Riesenberg, The Native
Maude, H. E. 1969 Review of Saul H. Riesenberg, The Native Polity
Riesenberg, Saul H. 1948 Ponapean Political and Social
Riesenberg, Saul H. 1968 The Native Polity of Ponape.
Soustelle, J. 1969 Review of Saul H. Riesenberg, The Native

Marshall Islands District
Meller, Norman 1960 Political changes in American Pacific

Majuro
Brum, Oscar de and Henry Rutz 1967 Political succession and
Kabua, Phillip and Nancy Pollock 1967 The ecological bases of

Arno
Rynkiewich, Michael A. 1974 The ossification of local politics:

Bikini
Mason, Leonard E. 1963 Changes in decision-making in a displaced

Political Organization

Kili
Mason, Leonard E. 1963 Changes in decision-making in a displaced

GUIDE TO TOPICS AND AREAS

Material Culture

Micronesia (U.S.T.T.P.I.)
Capell, Arthur 1954 Review of Erhard Schlesier, Die
Hagiwara, George and Max Mori 1965 Coir fiber-industry in
Klarwill, P. E. 1955 Review of Erhard Schlesier, Die
Lang, Werner 1951 Steinbauten in Mikronesien.
McKnight, Robert K. 1964 Handicrafts of the Trust Territory of
Montvel-Cchen, Marvin 1970 Canoes in Micronesia.
Riesenberg, Saul H. 1955 Review of Erhard Schlesier, Die
Schlesier, Erhard 1951 Die Erscheinungsformen des Männerhauses
Solheim, Wilhelm G., II 1952 Oceanic pottery Manufacture.

Mariana Islands
Johnston, Emilie G. 1972 Chamorro tools, implements and Utensils.
McGrath, Thomas B. 1972 The proas of the Marianas.

Guam
Baird, J. Henry 1954 The Guam Museum.
Glenn, Thelma H. 1975 The Guam Museum.

Caroline Islands
Riesenberg, Saul H. and A. H. Gayton 1952 Caroline Island belt

Palau Islands
Ashman, C. M. 1970 Native money of Palau.
Beauclair, Inez de 1963 Some ancient beads of Yap and Palau.
Beauclair, Inez de 1966 On pottery in Micronesia, Palauan lamps
Force, Roland W. and Maryanne Force 1959 Palauan money: Some
Hijikata, Hisakatsu 1956 Report on consecrated stone images and
Hijikata, Hisakatsu 1960 Ceramics with decoration found in the
McKnight, Robert K. 1964 Shell inlay: Art of Palau.
McKnight, Robert K. 1967 Palauan story Boards.
Obak, Adalbert and Robert K. McKnight 1964 Mesubed Dingal: Patron
Obak, Adalbert and Robert K. McKnight 1969 Kadam, the Palauan
Osborne, Carolyn and Douglas Osborne 1969 Construction of the
Owen, Hera W. 1974 A museum in Micronesia.
Ritzenthaler, Robert E. 1949 Native Money of Palau.
Schneider, David M. 1955 Review of Robert E. Ritzenthaler, Native
Simmons, D. R. 1970 Palau cave paintings on Aulong Island.
Smith, Allan H. 1957 Review of Robert E. Ritzenthaler, Native
Stumpf, Margaret K. 1972 Money of Palau.
Wypych, Konrad 1971 Native money of the Palau Islands.

Yap Islands
Beauclair, Inez de 1960 Notes on pottery of Yap, Micronesia.
Beauclair, Inez de 1961 Ken-Pai, a glass bracelet from Yap.
Beauclair, Inez de 1962 Addenda to "Ken-Pai": A glass bracelet
Beauclair, Inez de 1963 The stone money of Yap Island.
Beauclair, Inez de 1963 Some ancient beads of Yap and Palau.

GUIDE TO TOPICS AND AREAS

Material Culture

Woleai

Alkire, William H. 1970 Systems of measurement on Woleai Atoll,

Truk Islands - Truk Lagoon

Goodenough, Ward H. 1968 Arts and crafts in Truk.
LeBar, Frank M. 1951 Trukese material culture, a study in
LeBar, Frank M. 1963 Some aspects of canoe and house construction
LeBar, Frank M. 1964 A household survey of economic goods on
Moore, D. R. 1967 Review of Frank LeBar, The Material Culture of

Puluwat

Doran, Edwin, Jr. 1972 Wa, vinta, and Trimaran.

Etal

Nason, James D. n.d. The effects of social change on marine

Nukuoro

Davidson, Janet M. 1968 A wooden image from Nukuoro in the
Volprecht, Klaus 1968 Nukuoro, zur Sammlung Kapitän Jeschke in

Kapingamarangi

Blackwood, Beatrice 1951 Review of Te Rangi Hiroa, Material
Hiroa, Te Rangi [Peter H. Buck] 1950 The Material Culture of

Marshall Islands District

Ittel, W. H. 1949 Sailing canoes of the Marshall Islands.
Jenkins, W. S. 1946 Wartime canoe building in the Marshall
Riesenberg, Saul H. 1959 A New Guinea canoe prow found in the
Sinoto, Yosihiko H. 1959 Drifting canoe Prows.
Tinker, Spencer 1950 Some Marshall Islands fish Traps.
Wright, Rear Admiral Carleton H. 1948 Sailing canoes of the

Bikini

Kiste, Robert C. 1972 Relocation and technological change in

Kili

Kiste, Robert C. 1972 Relocation and technological change in

GUIDE TO TOPICS AND AREAS

Cultural Ecology

Pacific Islands
Mason, Leonard E. 1951 Man in the culture-environment
Mason, Leonard E. 1962 Habitat, man and Culture.
Murdock, George P. 1963 Human influences on the ecosystems cf

Micronesia (U.S.T.T.P.I.)
Knudson, Kenneth E. 1970 Resource fluctuation, productivity, and
Nason, James D. 1967 Ecological aspects of cultural stability and
Tobin, Jack A., et al. 1957 Notes on the present regulations and
Wilson, Erika 1974 Seabirds and Micronesians.

Caroline Islands
Alkire, William H. 1959 Residence, economy, and habitat in the
Alkire, William H. 1960 Cultural adaptation in the Caroline

The Woleai
McCoy, Michael A. 1973 Fish--something Old.
McCoy, Michael A. 1974 Man and turtle in the Central Carolines.

Etal
Nason, James D. 1975 The strength of the land--community

Arno
Mason, Leonard E. 1959 Space, the scarce commodity in atoll
Mason, Leonard E. and Harry Uyehara 1953 A quantitative study of

GUIDE TO TOPICS AND AREAS

Culture and Personality

Pacific Islands
Gladwin, Thomas 1961 Oceania.

Micronesia (U.S.T.T.P.I.)
Brislin, Richard W. and Walter Scott Wilson 1971 Perception of
Jordheim, G. D. and Inger A. Olsen 1963 The use of a non-verbal
Kearney, G. E. 1964 Comment on 'The use of a non-verbal test of
King, A. R. 1964 Comments on Jordheim and Olsen's use of a
Levy, Robert I. 1969 Personality Studies in Polynesia and
McGrath, Thomas B. 1968 Anxiety and conformity in traditional
Spoehr, Alexander 1952 Time perspective in Micronesia and

Saipan
Beaglehole, Ernest 1952 Review of Alice Joseph and Veronica
Joseph, Alice and Veronica F. Murray 1951 Chamorros and
Joseph, Alice and Veronica F. Murray 1957 Rorschachs of 100

Caroline Islands
Joseph, Alice and Veronica F. Murray 1951 Chamorros and
Joseph, Alice and Veronica F. Murray 1957 Rorschachs of 100

Palau Islands
Mahoney, Francis B. 1950 Projective psychological findings in
Mahoney, Francis B. 1957 Rorschachs and Modified TATs of 120

Ulithi
Lessa, William A. 1957 Modified Thematic Apperception Tests of 99
Lessa, William A. and Marvin Spiegelman 1954 Ulithian Personality
Wallace, Anthony F. C. 1955 Review of William A. Lessa and Marvin

Ifaluk
Spiro, Melford E. 1950 The problem of aggression in a South Sea
Spiro, Melford E. 1950 A psychotic personality in the South Seas.
Spiro, Melford E. 1953 Ghosts: An anthropological inquiry into
Spiro, Melford E. 1957 156 Rorschachs, 126 Modified TATs, 83
Spiro, Melford E. 1959 Cultural heritage, personal tensions, and

Truk District
Fischer, John L. and Marc J. Swartz 1960 Socio-psychological
Gladwin, Thomas 1958 Canoe travel in the Truk area: Technology

Truk Islands - Truk Lagoon
Gladwin, Thomas 1952 Personality and development on Truk.
Gladwin, Thomas 1953 The role of man and woman on Truk: A problem
Gladwin, Thomas 1959 Culture and individual personality
Gladwin, Thomas 1964 Culture and logical Process.
Gladwin, Thomas and Seymour B. Sarason 1953 Truk: Man in
Goodenough, Ward H. 1965 Personal names and modes of address in
Goodenough, Ward H. 1966 Human purpose in Life.

-279-

GUIDE TO TOPICS AND AREAS

Culture and Personality

Henry, William E. 1954 Letter to the Editor: Trukese T.A.T.'s.
Masland, Richard L., et al. 1958 Mental Subnormality:
Schneider, David M. 1955 Review of Thomas Gladwin and Seymour
Swartz, Marc J. 1958 Sexuality and aggression on Romonum, Truk.
Swartz, Marc J. 1961 Negative Ethnocentrism.
Swartz, Marc J. 1965 Personality and structure: Political

Ponape

Fischer, John L. 1964 Semi-castration on Ponape.
Fischer, John L., et al. 1959 Totemism and Allergy.
Fischer, John L. and Marc J. Swartz 1960 Socio-psychological

Culture Change

Pacific Islands
Force, Roland W. and Maryanne Force 1975 Kith, kin, and fellow
Goodenough, Ward H. 1957 Oceania and the problem of controls in
Lieber, Michael D., ed. n.d. Exiles and Migrants in Oceania.
McKnight, Robert K. 1971 Past and future culture change: A quest
Meller, Norman 1959 Bilingualism in island legislatures of the
Spoehr, Alexander 1960 Port town and hinterland in the Pacific

Micronesia (U.S.T.T.P.I.)
Bowden, Elbert V. 1970 Micronesia--A laboratory model of grcwth
Boyer, David S. 1967 Micronesia: The Americanization of Eden.
Chutaro, Chuji 1971 Caught in the Squeeze.
Crocombe, Ron 1968 The Peace Corps in Micronesia.
Georgia Center for Continuing Education 1974 That Uncertain
Hatanaka, Sachiko 1967 The process of cultural change in
Hezel, Francis X. 1974 Unholy mackerel and the almighty Buck.
Mahoney, Francis B. 1974 Social and Cultural Factors Relating to
Marshall, Mac and Leslie B. Marshall 1975 Opening Pandora's
Mason, Leonard E. 1951 An interpretation of "native custom" in a
McKnight, Robert K. 1971 Two models of assimilation and change in
McLeod, James R. 1973 An analysis of Westernization: The new
Micronesian Seminar 1975 Developing Micronesia's People.
Mitchell, Roger E. 1972 Micronesian folklore and culture Change.
Oliver, Douglas L., ed. 1951 Planning Micronesia's Future, A
Pearse, Richard and Keith A. Bezanson 1970 Education and
Reed, Dwayne M. 1974 Modernization and health in Micronesia.
Reed, Dwayne M. 1975 Health effects of modernization in
Smith, Allan H. 1961 Review of John de Young, ed., Taro
Smith, Howard F. 1971 The forced-pace modernisation of
Solenberger, Robert R. 1968 Cultural conflict and language
Valle, Maria Teresa del 1971 Review of Douglas Oliver, ed.,
Yamashita, Antonio C. and Walter Scott Wilson 1971 Education and

Mariana Islands
Bowers, Neal M. 1950 Problems of resettlement on Saipan, Tinian,

Guam
Murphy, Joseph 1975 Life-Style on Guam: Communication and
Reed, Dwayne M., et al. 1970 Health effects of Westernization
Thompson, Laura 1946 Crisis on Guam.
Thompson, Laura 1947 Guam and Its People: A Study of Cultural
Van der Poel, Cornelius J. 1975 Human and cultural values on Guam
Yamashita, Antonio C. 1965 Attitudes and reactions toward Typhoon

Rota
Reed, Dwayne M., et al. 1970 Heal+h effects of Westernizaticn

Tinian
Spoehr, Alexander 1951 The Tinian Chamorros.

Culture Change

Palau Islands District
McGrath, William A. 1972 The effects of urban drift in the Palau
McKnight, Robert K. n.d. Commas in microcosm: The movement of

Palau Islands
Barnett, Homer G. 1960 Review of Roland W. Force, Leadership and
Beckett, Jeremy 1961 Review of Roland Force, Leadership and
Brown, Paula 1960 Review of Roland Force, Leadership and Cultural
Force, Roland W. 1957 Palau exhibit traces change in a Pacific
Force, Roland W. 1958 Leadership and cultural change in Palau.
Hankin, Jean H. and L. E. Dickenson 1972 Urbanization, diet and
Jacobs, Robert M. 1971 The effects of acculturation on the
Labarthe, Darwin, et al. 1972 Health effects of modernization
McKnight, Robert K. 1959 The Oyabun-Kobun in Palau, a
McKnight, Robert K. 1963 The changing face of Palauan Custom.
McKnight, Robert K. 1968 Palauan culture heroes as agents of
Smith, Allan H. 1961 Review of John de Young, ed., Taro
Useem, John 1945 The changing structure of a Micronesian Society.

Yap Islands
Labby, David 1973 Old Glory and the new Yap.
Lingenfelter, Sherwood G. 1971 The process of elite formation in
Lingenfelter, Sherwood G. 1974 Administrative officials, Peace
Lingenfelter, Sherwood G. 1975 Yap: Political Leadership and
Schneider, David M. 1957 Typhoons on Yap.

Ulithi
Lessa, William A. 1964 The social effects of Typhoon Ophelia

Truk Islands - Truk Lagoon
Goodenough, Ward H. 1971 A similarity in cultural and linguistic
Haser, Sachuo and Kibby White 1969 The problem of teenage boys on
Hezel, Francis X. 1972 The westernization of Truk: A backward
MacMeekin, Daniel H. 1975 Land law and change on Truk.

Puluwat
Duncan, Leith 1972 Review of Thomas Gladwin, East Is a Big
Gladwin, Thomas 1970 East is a big bird: Part I.
Gladwin, Thomas 1970 East is a Big Bird: Navigation and Logic on
Goodenough, Ward H. 1971 Review of Thomas Gladwin, East is a Big

Losap
Severance, Craig J. 1975 Becoming Ponapean: The accomodation of

Etal
Nason, Anita Kay 1970 An analysis of communicated social change
Nason, James D. n.d. The effects of social change on marine
Nason, James D. 1970 Clan and copra: Modernization on Etal
Nason, James D. 1975 Civilizing the heathen: Missionaries and
Nason, James D. 1975 Sardines and other fried fish: The

GUIDE TO TOPICS AND AREAS

Culture Change

Ponape

Coale, George L. 1951 A study of chieftainship, missionary
Dahlquist, Paul A. 1972 Kohdo mwenge: The food complex in a
Dahlquist, Paul A. 1974 Changes in Ponapean social identity: Food
Demory, Barbara 1974 The commercialization of sakau
Gillmar, Jack and Russell Weigel 1968 The Impact of an In-Country
Lieber, Michael D. n.d. The process of change: A relocated
Lieber, Michael D. 1968 Porakiet: A Kapingamarangi Colony on
Maude, H. E. 1969 Review of Michael D. Lieber, Porakiet: A
O'Brien, Ilma E. 1971 Missionaries on Ponape: Induced social and
Severance, Craig J. 1975 Becoming Ponapean: The accomodaticn of
Smith, Rcbert Clark 1970 Some prcblems of modernization in a
Sugimura, Kenichi 1953 Culture contact and culture change in

Mokil

Lord, Anthony S. 1974 Acculturatior and cultural identity: The

Kapingamarangi

Lieber, Michael D. n.d. The process of change: A relocated
Lieber, Michael D. 1968 Porakiet: A Kapingamarangi Colony cn
Maude, H. E. 1969 Review of Michael D. Lieber, Porakiet: A

Kusaie - Kusaie District

Lewis, J. L. n.d. Kusaien Acculturation.

Marshall Islands District

Chave, Margaret E. 1948 The changing position cf mixed-bloods in
Sugimura, Kenichi 1953 Culture contact and culture change in

Enewetck

Chambers, Anne 1971 A study cf the relocation of two Marshallese
Tobin, Jack A. 1967 The resettlement of the Eniwetck peeple: A

Ujelang

Tobin, Jack A. 1967 The resettlement of the Eniwetok people: A

Bikini

Chambers, Anne 1971 A study of the relocation of two Marshallese
Georgia Center for Continuing Education 1974 The Bikinians.
Kiste, Robert C. n.d. The relocation of the Bikinians.
Kiste, Robert C. 1967 Changing patterns of land tenure and social
Kiste, Robert C. 1968 Kili Island: A Study of the Relocation cf
Kiste, Robert C. 1972 Relocation and technological change in
Kiste, Robert C. 1974 The Bikinians: A Study in Forced Migration.
Mason, Lecnard E. 1950 The Bikinians: A transplanted Population.
Mason, Leonard E. 1950 Cultural adaptation of the Bikini
Mason, Leonard E. 1954 Relocation cf the Bikini Marshallese: A
Mason, Leonard E. 1957 Ecologic change and culture pattern in the
Mason, Leonard E. 1961 Changing family organization among
Riesenberg, Saul H. 1954 Modern atcmic Exiles.

Culture Change

Tobin, Jack A. 1970 Report on Bikini Atoll.

Jaluit
Mackenzie, J. Boyd 1961 Population and economy of Jaluit.

Kili
Georgia Center for Continuing Education 1974 The Bikinians.
Kiste, Robert C. n.d. The relocation of the Bikinians.
Kiste, Robert C. 1967 Changing patterns of land tenure and social
Kiste, Robert C. 1968 Kili Island: A Study of the Relocation of
Kiste, Robert C. 1972 Relocation and technological change in
Kiste, Robert C. 1974 The Bikinians: A Study in Forced Migration.
Leysne, Humphrey W. 1952 Food for Kili.
Mason, Leonard E. 1950 The Bikinians: A transplanted Population.
Mason, Leonard E. 1950 Cultural adaptation of the Bikini
Mason, Leonard E. 1954 Relocation of the Bikini Marshallese: A
Mason, Leonard E. 1957 Ecologic change and culture pattern in the
Mason, Leonard E. 1958 Habitat and social change on Kili Island.
Mason, Leonard E. 1958 Kili community in Transition.
Mason, Leonard E. 1961 Changing family organization among
Riesenberg, Saul H. 1954 Community development project at Kili.

GUIDE TO TOPICS AND AREAS

Applied Anthropology

Pacific Islands
Embree, John F. 1946 Anthropology and the War.

Micronesia (U.S.T.T.P.I.)
Barnett, Homer G. 1956 Anthropology in Administration.
Belshaw, Cyril S. 1957 Review of Homer Barnett, Anthropology in
Capell, Arthur 1957 Review of Homer Barnett, Anthropology in
Drucker, Philip 1951 Anthropology in Trust Territory
Embree, John F. 1950 Letter to the Editor: A note on
Fischer, John L. 1951 Letter to the Editor: Applied anthropology
Gladwin, Thomas 1956 Anthropology and administration in the Trust
Keesing, Felix M. 1949 Experiments in training overseas
Mahony, Frank J. 1959 Anthropology and public Health.
Mason, Leonard E. 1951 An interpretation of "native custom" in a
Mason, Leonard E. 1967 Research problems and ethics in
Mason, Leonard E. 1973 The anthropological presence in
Piddington, Ralph 1958 Review of Homer Barnett, Anthropology in
Useem, John 1945 Governing the occupied areas of the South
Useem, John 1947 Applied anthropology in Micronesia.

Palau Islands
Useem, John 1952 South Sea Island strike: Labor-Management

Truk Islands - Truk Lagoon
Gladwin, Thomas 1950 Civil administration on Truk, a Rejoinder.
Mahony, Frank J. 1957 The innovation of a savings institution on

Arno
Rynkiewich, Michael A. n.d. The underdevelopment of

Bikini
Mason, Leonard E. 1957 Ecologic change and culture pattern in the

Kili
Mason, Leonard E. 1957 Ecologic change and culture pattern in the

Ethnohistory

Pacific Islands
Dodge, Ernest S. 1968 The American sources for Pacific

Micronesia (U.S.T.T.P.I.)
Apple, Russell A. 1972 Historic Properties Policy and Program in
Mitchell, Roger E. 1970 Oral tradition and Micronesian history: A

Caroline Islands
Lessa, William A. 1962 An evaluation of early descriptions of
Lessa, William A. 1973 Review of Saul H. Riesenberg, ed., A

Palau Islands
Owen, Hera W. 1974 A museum in Micronesia.

Truk District
Mitchell, Roger E. 1970 Oral tradition and Micronesian history: A

Ponape
Dodge, Ernest S. 1974 Review of Saul H. Riesenberg, ed., A
Fischer, John L., et al., eds. n.d. The Book of Luelen:
Mikoletsky, Nikolaus 1972 Kulturhistorische Untersuchungen zum
Mikoletsky, Nikolaus 1972 Kulturhistorische Untersuchungen zum
Riesenberg, Saul H. 1972 Review of Sibley S. Morrill, Ponape:

Ngatik
Riesenberg, Saul H. 1966 The Ngatik Massacre.

Kusaie - Kusaie District
Mikoletsky, Nikolaus 1972 Kulturhistorische Untersuchungen zum
Mikoletsky, Nikolaus 1972 Kulturhistorische Untersuchungen zum

GUIDE TO TOPICS AND AREAS

Anthropological Economics

Pacific Islands
Reinman, Fred M. 1965 Maritime adaptation: An aspect of Oceanic

Micronesia (U.S.T.T.P.I.)
Wilson, Walter Scott 1953 The copra industry in the Trust

Rcta
Smith, James Jerome 1974 Household economic strategies on Rcta,

Palau Islands
Read, Kenneth R. H. 1971 Palauan tuna Fishing.

Truk Islands - Truk Lagoon
Berland, Joseph and Stephen Boggs 1969 The distribution of food
LeBar, Frank M. 1964 A household survey of economic goods on
Mahony, Frank J. 1957 The innovation of a savings instituticn on

Puluwat
Steager, Peter William 1972 Food in its social context on

Ponape
Bascom, Willard R. 1946 Ponape: A Pacific Economy in Transition.
Bascom, Willard R. 1948 Ponapean prestige Economy.
Dahlquist, Paul A. 1971 One pig, one yam, one sakau, and money:
Dahlquist, Paul A. 1972 The place of money in a ccntemporary
Dahlquist, Paul A. 1972 Kohdo mwenge: The food complex in a
Emerick, Richard G. 1967 Review of Willard R. Bascom, Ponape: A

Mokil
Murphy, Raymond E. 1950 The economic geography of a Micronesian

Kusaie - Kusaie District
Wilson, Walter Scott 1974 Elements of household economic

Marshall Islands District
Mason, Leonard E. 1953 Re-establishment of a copra industry in

Majuro
Domnick, Charles and Michael Seelye 1967 Subsistence patterns

Arno
Mason, Leonard E. and Harry Uyehara 1953 A quantitative study of

Namu
Pollock, Nancy J. 1970 Breadfruit and breadwinning cn Namu Atcll,
Pollock, Nancy J. 1974 Hcusehold economic strategies on Namu

Archaeology and Culture History

Pacific Islands

Davidson, Janet M. 1970 Polynesian outliers and the problem of
Emory, Kenneth P. and Yosihiko H. Sinoto 1959 Radiocarbon dates
Green, Roger C. and Marion Kelly, eds. 1970 Pacific Islands, COWA
Reinman, Fred M. 1965 Maritime adaptation: An aspect of Oceanic
Reinman, Fred M. 1967 Fishing: An Aspect of Oceanic Economy, An
Shutler, Richard, Jr. 1961 Peopling of the Pacific in the light
Yawata, Ichiro and Yosihiko H. Sinoto, eds. 1968 Prehistoric

Micronesia (U.S.T.T.P.I.)

Chapman, Peter Sherwood 1964 Micronesian archaeology: An
Chapman, Peter Sherwood 1967 Micronesia: 1960-1964.
Chapman, Peter Sherwood 1968 Japanese contributions to
Hanson, Lenore C. 1966 Archeological methods and problems in the
Hohnschopp, Henning 1971 Untersuchung zum
Lang, Werner 1951 Steinbauten in Mikronesien.
Marck, Jeffrey C. 1974 A lexico-statistical model for nuclear
Marck, Jeffrey C. 1975 The origin and dispersal of the Proto
Mason, Leonard E. 1960 Art forms and culture history in
Mason, Leonard E. 1966 Early Micronesian voyaging: A Comment.
Smith, Allan H. 1957 Report on research in Micronesian ethnology
Smith, Allan H. 1958 Report on research in Micronesian ethnology
Smith, Allan H. 1959 Micronesia.
Smith, Allan H. 1960 Micronesia.
Smith, Allan H. 1961 Micronesia.
Spoehr, Alexander 1950 Digging in Micronesia.
Spoehr, Alexander, et al. 1951 A program for Micronesian
Sykes, Egerton, ed. 1961 The archaeology of Micronesia.

Mariana Islands

Baird, J. Henry 1968 The purpose of the Mariana "Latte." Journal
Beaty, Janice J. 1962 Mystery of the Marianas latte Stones.
Dilatush, Donald 1945 Non-recent Chamorroan stone and pottery
Dilatush, Donald 1946 A further note on non-recent Chamorroan
Gifford, Edward W. 1958 Review of Alexander Spoehr, Marianas
Johnston, Emilie G. 1972 References to the latte of the Mariana
McCarthy, F. D. 1958 Review of Alexander Spoehr, Marianas
Plaza, Felicia 1973 Lattes of the Marianas.
Shutler, Richard, Jr. 1958 Review of Alexander Spoehr, Marianas
Spoehr, Alexander 1950 Exploring man's past in isles of the South
Spoehr, Alexander 1950 Notice on Marianas Archaeology.
Spoehr, Alexander 1951 Marianas expedition excavates ancient
Spoehr, Alexander 1957 Marianas Prehistory: Archeological Survey
Yawata, Ichiro 1944 Peculiar forms of the stone-piles on the
Yawata, Ichiro 1961 A burial type among the ancient Marianas
Yawata, Ichiro 1961 Burial systems of ancient Mariana Islanders.
Yawata, Ichiro 1963 Rice cultivation of the ancient Mariana

Guam

GUIDE TO TOPICS AND AREAS

Archaeology and Culture History

Berger, Rainer and W. F. Libby 1968 UCLA radiocarbon dates VIII.
Bryan, Edwin H., Jr. 1971 Notes on the ancient culture of Guam.
Bryan, Edwin H., Jr. 1972 Notes on the ancient culture of Guam
Bushnell, G. H. S. 1955 Review of Erik K. Reed, Archaeology and
Henrickson, Paul R. 1968 Two forms of primitive art in
Johnston, Emilie G. 1974 Spanish dikes in the Agana Swamp.
Osborne, Douglas 1947 Archeology of Guam: A progress Report.
Pettay, Louanna 1959 Racial affinity of prehistoric Guam.
Reed, Erik K. 1952 Archeology and History of Guam.
Reed, Erik K. 1954 Archeology in Guam, 1952: A status Report.
Reinman, Fred M. 1967 Notes on an archeological survey of Guam,
Reinman, Fred M. 1968 Guam prehistory: A preliminary field
Reinman, Fred M. 1968 Radiocarbon dates from Guam, Mariana
Reinman, Fred M. 1972 An Archaeological Survey and Preliminary
Stephenson, 1st Lt. F. A. 1971 Talofofo cave Writing.

Saipan

Dilatush, Donald 1950 Archaeological survey of Saipan Island,

Rota

Takayama, Jun 1973 The second excavation of Muchon on Rota.
Takayama, Jun and Tomoko Egami 1971 Archeology on Rota in the

Tinian

Libby, W. F. 1952 Chicago radiocarbon dates, III.
Pellett, Marcian, O.F.M., Cap. and Alexander Spoehr 1961 Marianas
Stewart, T. D. and Alexander Spoehr 1952 Evidence on the

Pagan

Egami, Tomoko and Fumiko Saito 1973 Archaeological excavation on

Caroline Islands

Sykes, Egerton, ed. 1960 The archaeology of the Caroline Islands.

Palau Islands

Davidson, Janet M. 1967 Review of Douglas Osborne, The
Gathercole, Peter W. 1967 Review of Douglas Osborne, The
Henrickson, Paul R. 1968 Two forms of primitive art in
Hijikata, Hisakatsu 1956 Report on consecrated stone images and
Hijikata, Hisakatsu 1960 Ceramics with decoration found in the
Narr, Karl J. 1970 Review of Douglas Osborne, The Archaeology of
Osborne, Douglas 1958 The Palau Islands: Stepping stones into the
Osborne, Douglas 1961 Archeology in Micronesia: Background, Palau
Osborne, Douglas 1966 The Archaeology of the Palau Islands, an
Reinman, Fred M. 1967 Review of Douglas Osborne, The Archaeology
Riesenfeld, Alphonse 1951 Some observations on the pottery of the
Sinder, Leon 1968 Review of Douglas Osborne, The Archaeology of

Yap Islands

Crane, H. R. and James B. Griffin 1958 University of Michigan
Crane, H. R. and James B. Griffin 1959 University of Michigan

GUIDE TO TOPICS AND AREAS

Archaeology and Culture History

Force, Roland W. 1960 Review of E. W. Gifford and D. S. Gifford,
Force, Roland W. 1961 Review of E.W. Gifford and D.S. Gifford,
Gifford, Edward W. and Delila S. Gifford 1959 Archeological
Solheim, Wilhelm G., II 1960 Review of E.W. Gifford and D.S.
Spoehr, Alexander 1960 Review of E.W. Gifford and D.S. Gifford,

Truk Islands - Truk Lagoon
Clune, Francis J. 1974 Archeological survey of Truk, Micronesia.
Takayama, Jun and Toshihiko Seki 1973 Preliminary Archaeological

Ponape District
Davidson, Janet M. 1967 Preliminary archeological investigaticns

Ponape
Alicata, Joseph E. 1947 Science spotlights mysteries of Ponape.
Brandt, John H. 1962 Nan Matol: Ancient Venice of Micronesia.
Fischer, John L. 1964 The abandonment of Nan Matol, ancient
Long, Austin 1965 Smithsonian Institution radiocarbon
Mikoletsky, Nikolaus 1972 Kulturhistorische Untersuchungen zum
Mikoletsky, Nikolaus 1972 Kulturhistorische Untersuchungen zum
Riesenberg, Saul H. 1948 Archeological remains in Ponape.

Nukuoro
Davidson, Janet M. 1966 Nukuoro--archeology on a Polynesian
Davidson, Janet M. 1967 An archeological assemblage of simple
Davidson, Janet M. 1967 Archeolcgy cn coral Atolls.
Davidson, Janet M. 1968 Nukuoro: Archeology on a Polynesian
Davidson, Janet M. 1971 Archeology on Nukuoro Atoll.
Garanger, Jose 1972 Review of Janet Davidson, Archaeology on
Garanger, Jose 1974 Review of Janet Davidson, Archaeology cn
Ray, Erwin R. 1973 Review of Janet Davidson, Archaeclogy on
Stuckenrath, Robert, Jr. 1967 University of Pennsylvania
Terrell, John 1973 Review of Janet M. Davidson, Archaeology on

Kusaie - Kusaie District
Davidson, Janet M. 1967 Preliminary archeological investigaticns
Mikoletsky, Nikolaus 1972 Kulturhistorische Untersuchungen zum
Mikoletsky, Nikolaus 1972 Kulturhistorische Untersuchungen zum

Art

Micronesia (U.S.T.T.P.I.)
Anonymous 1968 Notes on Micronesian Art.
Browning, Mary A. 1970 Micronesian Heritage.
Embree, John F. 1948 Kickball and some other parallels between
Griffing, Robert P., Jr. 1951 An exhibition of Micronesian art
Janssen, Roswitha 1971 Spiele in Mikronesien.
Mason, Leonard E. 1960 Art forms and culture history in
McKnight, Robert K. 1964 Handicrafts of the Trust Territory of
McLean, Mervyn 1972 Review of Mary A. Browning, Micronesian
Montvel-Cohen, Marvin 1974 The arts of Micronesia: A selective
Youd, Jean 1961 Notes on kickball in Micronesia.

Guam
Henrickson, Paul R. 1968 Two forms of primitive art in
McClain, E. G. and R. W. Clopton 1949 Guamanian Songs.

Palau Islands
Henrickson, Paul R. 1968 Two forms of primitive art in
Jernigan, Earl Wesley 1973 Lochukle: A Palauan art Tradition.
McKnight, Robert K. 1964 Orachl's drawings: Palauan rock
McKnight, Robert K. 1964 Shell inlay: Art of Palau.
McKnight, Robert K. 1967 Palauan story Boards.
Simmons, D. R. 1970 Palau cave paintings on Aulong Island.
Yamaguchi, Osamu 1967 The music of Palau: An ethnomusicological
Yamaguchi, Osamu 1968 The taxonomy of music in Palau.

Tobi
Yamaguchi, Osamu 1966 Some observations on music-language

Sonsorol
Yamaguchi, Osamu 1966 Some observations on music-language

Ifaluk
Burrows, Edwin Grant 1958 Music on Ifaluk Atoll in the Caroline

Truk Islands - Truk Lagoon
Murdock, George P. 1948 Waging baseball in Truk.

Puluwat
Steager, Peter William 1974 Where does art begin on Puluwat?

Kapingamarangi
Royce, Joseph and Ted Murray 1971 Work and play in

Marshall Islands District
Balos, Ataji 1965 Christmas song contest in the Marshalls.

GUIDE TO TOPICS AND AREAS

Botany

Pacific Islands
Barrau, Jacques 1965 Histoire et prehistoire horticoles de
Fosberg, F. Raymond 1963 Dynamics of atoll Vegetation.

Micronesia (U.S.T.T.P.I.)
Barrau, Jacques 1960 Plant exploration and introduction in
Embree, John F. 1946 University of Hawaii research in Micronesia.
Fosberg, F. Raymond 1946 Botanical Report on Micronesia.
Fosberg, F. Raymond 1948 Salinity and atoll Vegetation.
Fosberg, F. Raymond 1949 Atoll vegetation and Salinity.
Fosberg, F. Raymond 1959 The Vegetation of Micronesia.
Fosberg, F. Raymond 1960 The Vegetation of Micronesia I.
Hosaka, Edward Y. 1946 Botanical report on Micronesia.
Niering, William A. 1962 Review of F. Raymond Fosberg, The
Sachet, Marie-Helene and F. Raymond Fosberg 1955 Island
Sachet, Marie-Helene and F. Raymond Fosberg 1971 Island
Salcedo, Carl 1970 The search for medicinal plants in Micronesia.
Van Steenis, C. G. G. J. 1965 Man and plants in the tropics: An

Mariana Islands
Fosberg, F. Raymond 1960 The Vegetation of Micronesia I.

Guam
Bryan, Edwin H., Jr. 1975 Review of Benjamin C. Stone, The flora
Fletcher, Jack E. 1971 Notes on herb medicine in Guam.
Fosberg, F. Raymond 1960 The Vegetation of Micronesia I.
Inman, N. 1967 Notes on some poisonous plants of Guam.
Moore, Philip H. 1974 Familiar plants of Agana.
Souder, Paul B. 1963 Poisonous plants on Guam.
Stone, Benjamin C. 1971 The flora of Guam.

Pagan
Fosberg, F. Raymond 1958 Vascular flora of Pagan Island, Northern
Fosberg, F. Raymond and Gilbert Ccrwin 1958 A fossil flora from

Caroline Islands
Fosberg, F. Raymond 1947 Micronesian mangroves.
Fosberg, F. Raymond 1953 Vegetation of central Pacific atolls, a
Glassman, Sidney F. 1953 New plant records from Eastern Carcline
St. John, Harold 1948 Plant records from the Caroline Islands,
Stone, Benjamin C. 1961 Pandanus pistillaris in the Caroline

Fais
Fosberg, F. Raymond and Michael Evans 1969 A collection of plants

Woleai
Alkire, William H. 1974 Native classification of flcra on Wcleai

Satawal

GUIDE TO TOPICS AND AREAS

Botany

Fosberg, F. Raymond 1969 Plants of Satawal Island, Caroline

Gaferut
Niering, William A. 1961 Observations on Puluwat and Gaferut,

Truk Islands - Truk Lagoon
Hill, Peter J. R. and Benjamin C. Stone 1961 The vegetation of
Stone, Benjamin C. 1967 The flora of Romonum Island, Truk Lagoon,

Hall Islands
Stone, Benjamin C. 1959 The flora of Namonuito and the Hall
Stone, Benjamin C. 1960 Corrections and additions to the flora of

Namonuito
Stone, Benjamin C. 1959 The flora of Namonuito and the Hall

Puluwat
Niering, William A. 1961 Observations on Puluwat and Gaferut,

Namoluk
Marshall, Mac 1975 The natural history of Namoluk Atoll, Eastern

Ponape
Glassman, Sidney F. 1951 The flora of Ponape.
Glassman, Sidney F. 1957 The flora of Ponape and its
Sasuke, N. 1953 Breadfruit, yams and taros of Ponape Island.
Stone, Benjamin C. 1960 Corrections and additions to the flora of

Pingelap
St. John, Harold 1948 Report on the flora of Pingelap Atoll,

Nukucro
Stone, Benjamin C. 1966 Some vernacular names of plants from

Kapingamarangi
Stone, Benjamin C. 1966 Some vernacular names of plants from

Marshall Islands District
Fosberg, F. Raymond 1953 Vegetation of central Pacific atolls, a
Fosberg, F. Raymond 1957 Soils, vegetation, and agriculture on
St. John, Harold 1957 Adventive plants in the Marshalls before
Stone, Benjamin C. 1960 The wild and cultivated Pandanus of the
Stone, Benjamin C. 1963 Appendix: Marshallese cultivar index and
Taylor, William R. 1950 Plants of Bikini and other Northern

Aur
St. John, Harold 1951 Plant records from Aur Atoll and Majuro

Majuro
St. John, Harold 1951 Plant records from Aur Atoll and Majuro

-293-

GUIDE TO TOPICS AND AREAS

Economics

Pacific Islands
Pierard, Richard V. 1964 The German colonial society, 1882-1914.
Pieris, W. V. D. 1955 The manufacture of copra in the Pacific
Wenkam, Robert 1974 The Great Pacific Rip-Off: Corporate Rape in

Micronesia (U.S.T.T.P.I.)
Azuma, Aloysius Y. 1969 Survey and Development of Managerial
Bascom, Willard R. 1946 U.S. Commercial Company Survey on
Bowden, Elbert V., et al. 1966 Economic Development Plan for
Chapman, Wilbert McLeod 1946 Tuna in the Mandated Islands.
Foundation for the Peoples of the South Pacific 1971 A
Fox, Morris G. 1971 Strengthening the Contribution of Social
Hezel, Francis X. 1973 Reflections on Micronesia's Economy.
Houston, Neil T. 1954 Commercial Problems in the Trust Territory
Lyman, Richard, Jr. 1946 Report on the Marshalls, Carolines and
McClam, Virginia G. 1972 The Micronesian Islands: Economic
Nathan Associates, Inc., Robert R. 1967 Economic Development Plan
Nishi, Midori 1968 An evaluation of Japanese agricultural and
Oliver, Douglas L., ed. 1951 Planning Micronesia's Future, A
Skinner, Carlton 1972 The economic base and role of the private
Smith, Daniel C. 1972 Issues in the economic development of
Smith, Frances McReynolds, ed. 1972 Micronesian Realities:
Smith, Robert O. 1946 Survey of the Fisheries of the Former
Tabb, John R. 1966 Public Finance in Micronesia.
Toribiong, Johnson 1972 Micronesia, Economic trend, land and
Valle, Maria Teresa del 1971 Review of Douglas Oliver, ed.,
Weitzell, E. C. 1946 Resource development in the Pacific Mandated
Wiliander, Hans 1972 Economic realities of Independence.
Wilson, Peter T. 1966 Boatbuilding in the Trust Territory of the
Zachary, Wyman X. 1972 Micronesia: A viable economy, fact or

Mariana Islands
Gallahue, Edward E. 1946 The Economy of the Mariana Islands.

Guam
Duckstad, Eric E. 1956 Guam; Its Economy and Selected Development
Fages, Jean and Thomas B. McGrath 1975 Tourism development in
Gale, Roger 1974 Letter from Guam.
Gilliam, John D. 1975 Guam: Can the port be free when the economy
Sanchez, Gregorio C. 1975 Planning and its aftermath on Guam.
Unpingco, Norbert R. 1975 The realities facing Guam Today.

Palau Islands
McVey, Jim 1973 Fish--something New.

Truk District
Hall, Edward T., Jr. and Karl J. Pelzer 1946 The Economy of the

Truk Islands - Truk Lagoon

GUIDE TO TOPICS AND AREAS

Economics

Wilson, Peter T. 1971 Truk live-bait Survey.

Ponape
American Factors Associates 1970 Feasibility and Study for
Jackman, Harry H. 1969 Review of Willard R. Bascom, Ponape: A
Pelep, Stew 1960 Ponape fishermen set up successful Cooperative.

Marshall Islands District
Browning, Mary A. 1972 Traders in the Marshalls.
Mason, Leonard E. 1946 The economic organization of the Marshall

Education

Pacific Islands
Gladwin, Thomas 1960 The need: Better ways of teaching children

Micronesia (U.S.T.T.P.I.)
Anttila, Elizabeth K. 1965 A history of the people of the Trust
Capell, Arthur 1950 Education for Pacific People: Education in
Fink, T. Ross 1948 United States Naval policies on education in
Ford, C. Christopher 1974 Adult education in Micronesia: Problems
Gibson, Robert E. 1959 Education in the Trust Territory of the
Gutmann, James 1973 Micronesia: Politics and Education.
Hezel, Francis X. 1973 The school Industry.
Hezel, Francis X. 1973 Schools: Micronesia's biggest Industry.
Hezel, Francis X. 1974 Unholy mackerel and the almighty Buck.
Hezel, Francis X. and Charles Reafsnyder 1971 Micronesia: A
Hezel, Francis X. and Charles Reafsnyder 1972 Micronesia through
May, Walther 1957 Die Erziehung in Micronesien.
Micronesian Seminar 1974 Education for what? Proceedings of a
Peacock, Dan 1961 The new Pacific Islands Central School.
Peacock, Dan 1963 The Pacific Islands Central School Library.
Peacock, Dan 1965 Training island Librarians.
Pearse, Richard and Keith A. Bezanson 1970 Education and
Pickerill, Cicely P. 1954 Pacific Islands Central School.
Platt, William J. and Philip H. Sorensen 1967 Planning for
Ramarui, David 1975 Education in Micronesia: Practicalities and
Singleton, John 1972 Review of Francis X. Hezel and Charles B.
Singleton, John 1974 Education, planning and political
Smith, Alfred G. 1956 Literacy promotion in an underdeveloped
Smith, Allan H. 1961 Review of John de Young, ed., Taro
Smith, Donald F. 1968 Education of the Micronesian with emphasis
Smith, Donald F. 1969 American education in the Trust Territory
Smith, Donald F. 1971 A glimpse of German education in
U.S. Dept. of Health, Education and Welfare 1973 HEW/Interior
Yamashita, Antonio C. and Walter Scott Wilson 1971 Education and

Mariana Islands
Broadbent, William A. 1970 A Profile of Chamorro and Statesider
Heath, Laurel 1975 Education for confusion: A study of education

Guam
Johnson, Robert G. 1959 Recommendations for the administration of
Leon Guerrero, Wilfred P. and Robert Ota 1974 Implications of the
McCall, Louis Edmund 1973 A study comparing scholastic

Palau Islands
McKnight, Robert K. 1959 The Oyabun-Kobun in Palau, a
Smith, Allan H. 1961 Review of John de Young, ed., Taro
Smith, Donald F. 1970 The Micronesian Occupational Center (at
Stumpf, Margaret K. 1970 Palauan value orientation and Education.

Education

Truk District
Fischer, John L. 1961 The Japanese schools for the natives of

Truk Islands - Truk Lagoon
Fischer, Ann M. 1950 The role of the Trukese mother and its
Fischer, Ann M. 1957 The role of the Trukese mother and its
Halferty, Nancy 1974 Bilingual education in Truk.
Mirrer, Bonnie M. 1971 Educational change in Truk, Micronesia.
Nagao, Clarence M. and Masao Nakayama 1969 A study of
Pickerill, Cicely P. 1954 Pacific Islands Central School.

Ponape
Colletta, Nat Joseph 1972 American schools for the natives of
Peacock, Dan 1961 The new Pacific Islands Central School.
Peacock, Dan 1963 The Pacific Islands Central School Library.

Marshall Islands District
Horay, Patrick J. 1972 Education and acculturation in Marshall

GUIDE TO TOPICS AND AREAS

Folklore and Oral Literature

Pacific Islands
Poignant, Roslyn 1967 Oceanic Mythology.

Micronesia (U.S.T.T.P.I.)
Grey, Eve 1951 Legends of Micronesia.
Kirtley, Bacil F. 1955 A motif-index of Polynesian, Melanesian,
Lessa, William A. 1969 The Chinese trigrams in Micronesia.
Luomala, Katharine 1949 Micronesian Mythology.
Luomala, Katharine 1951 Micronesian informants as Collectors.
Luomala, Katharine 1966 Numskull clans and tales: Their structure
Mikoletsky, Nikolaus 1968 Mikronesische Eingeborenenliteratur.
Mitchell, Roger E. 1972 Micronesian folklore and culture Change.

Mariana Islands
Freeman, Lila L. 1972 Island Legends.

Guam
Van Peenan, Mavis W. 1971 Chamorro legends on the Island of Guam.
Van Peenan, Mavis W. 1972 Legends of Guam: Juan Malo and his

Caroline Islands
Mitchell, Roger E. 1968 Genre and function in Eastern Carolinian
Mitchell, Roger E. 1973 Micronesian Folktales.

Palau Islands
Jacobs, Robert M. 1971 The effects of acculturation on the
Kesolei, Katherine, ed. 1971 Cheldecheduck er Belau: Palauan
McKnight, Robert K. 1961 The mouth that explains: Mesaod Ngerel,
McKnight, Robert K. 1961 Mnemonics in preliterate Palau.
McKnight, Robert K. 1968 Proverbs of Palau.
Obak, Adalbert and Robert K. McKnight 1966 Palauan Proverbs.

Ulithi
Fischer, John L. 1963 Review of William Lessa, Tales from Ulithi
Lessa, William A. n.d. The apotheosis of Marespa.
Lessa, William A. 1956 Oedipus-type tales in Oceania.
Lessa, William A. 1961 Tales from Ulithi Atoll: A Comparative
Lessa, William A. 1962 The decreasing power of myth on Ulithi.
Lessa, William A. 1966 Discoverer-of-the-Sun, mythology as a
McKnight, Robert K. and Lester Hazell 1972 Folklore and culture

Satawal
Hijikata, Hisakatsu 1953 Dittilapal-Satewal.

Ifaluk
Burrows, Edwin Grant 1963 Flower in My Ear, Arts and Ethos of
Dodge, Ernest S. 1963 Review of Edwin G. Burrows, Flower in My
Elbert, Samuel H. 1964 Review of Edwin Grant Burrows, Flower in
Fischer, John L. 1964 Review of Edwin Grant Burrows, Flower in My

GUIDE TO TOPICS AND AREAS

Folklore and Oral Literature

Luomala, Katharine 1963 Review of Edwin G. Burrows, Flower in My
Spiro, Melford E. 1951 Some Ifaluk myths and folk Tales.

The Woleai
Lessa, William A. 1956 Myth and blackmail in the Western

Truk District
Fischer, John L. 1959 Meter in Eastern Carolinian oral
Fischer, John L. 1968 Folktale in the Eastern Carolines.

Truk Islands - Truk Lagoon
Fischer, John L. 1955 Language and folktale in Truk and Ponape: A
Fischer, John L. 1956 The position of men and women in Truk and
Fischer, John L. 1960 Sequence and structure in Folktales.
Goodenough, Ward H. 1966 The tale of Pupily-Eyeballs-Thing, A
Mitchell, Roger E. 1967 A study of the cultural, historical and
Mitchell, Roger E. 1968 The Oedipus myth and complex in Oceania

Puluwat
Elbert, Samuel H. 1971 Three Legends of Puluwat and a Bit of

Ponape District
Fischer, John L. 1959 Meter in Eastern Carolinian oral
Fischer, John L. 1968 Folktale in the Eastern Carolines.

Ponape
Blackburn, Thomas 1967 Some examples of Ponapean Folklore.
Fischer, John L. 1955 Language and folktale in Truk and Ponape: A
Fischer, John L. 1956 The position of men and women in Truk and
Fischer, John L. 1960 Sequence and structure in Folktales.
Fischer, John L. 1966 A Ponapean Oedipus tale, a structural and
Riesenberg, Saul H. 1951 Ponapean Omens.
Riesenberg, Saul H. and John L. Fischer 1955 Some Ponapean
Zan, Yigal 1971 A Ponapean Oedipus tale: An explanation of

Nukuoro
Fischer, John L. 1958 Folktales, social structure, and

Kapingamarangi
Alpers, Antony 1970 The eitu who went as a man's Wife.
Alpers, Antony 1970 The lobster and the Flounder.
Elbert, Samuel H. 1949 Utu-Matua and other tales of
Emory, Kenneth P. 1949 Myths and tales from Kapingamarangi, a
Fischer, John L. 1958 Folktales, social structure, and

Marshall Islands District
Chambers, Keith S. 1972 Tale traditions of Eastern Micronesia: A
Davenport, William H. 1952 Fourteen Marshallese Riddles.
Davenport, William H. 1953 Marshallese folklore Types.
Mitchell, Roger E. 1973 Micronesian Folktales.

GUIDE TO TOPICS AND AREAS

Folklore and Oral Literature

Majuro
Tobin, Jack A. 1970 The legend of Lijibake.

Namu
Pollock, Nancy J. n.d. The origin of clans on Namu, Marshall

GUIDE TO TOPICS AND AREAS

General and Popular Literature

Pacific Islands

Cammack, Floyd M. and Shiro Saito 1962 Pacific Island
Coolidge, Harold J. 1948 The Pacific Science Board.
Day, A. Grove 1971 Pacific Islands Literature: One Hundred Basic
Fosberg, F. Raymond and Marie-Helene Sachet, eds. 1953 Handbook
Green, Roger C. and Marion Kelly, eds. 1970 Pacific Islands, COWA
Hughes, Daniel T. 1971 A Bibliographic Resource for Demographic,
Keesing, Felix M. 1959 Field Guide to Oceania.
Marshall, Mac 1974 Research bibliography of alcohol and kava
Schneider, David M. 1966 Review of C.R.H. Taylor, A Pacific
Spoehr, Alexander 1955 Human background of Pacific Science.
Spoehr, Alexander (compiler) 1966 Bibliography of the
Taylor, Clyde Romer Hughes 1965 A Pacific Bibliography.
Ullman, James Ramsey 1963 Where the Bong Tree Grows.

Micronesia (U.S.T.T.P.I.)

Anonymous 1949 The Trust Territory: Its 2,130 islands form a new
Anonymous 1969 Micronesia--America's 'South Seas'.
Borden, Charles A. 1945 The far flung islands of Micronesia.
Bowen, R. N. (compiler) 1963 Bibliography of the Coordinated
Bowen, R. N. (compiler) 1964 Bibliography of the Scientific
Bryan, Edwin H., Jr. and staff 1970 Land in Micronesia and its
Caldwell, John C. 1969 Let's Visit Micronesia; Guam (USA) and the
Chapman, Peter Sherwood 1974 Micronesia 1965-1974: A
Clark, Eugenie 1951 Lady with a Spear.
Clark, LCdr. T. O. 1946 The administration of the former Japanese
Coolidge, Harold J., ed. 1966 Scientific Investigations in
Daeufer, Alice S. (compiler) 1969 Pathways to Micronesia.
Guam Recorder 1972 to present.
Halpern, Katherine Spencer 1973 Obituary of Ann Fisher.
Henning, Theodore F. 1961 Buritis in Paradise.
Hiatt, Robert W. (compiler) 1969 Contributions by the University
Hiatt, Robert W., et al. 1947 Uncle Sam's most primitive Wards.
Johnston, Emilie G. 1971 Micronesian nutrition Bibliography.
Johnston, Emilie G. 1973 Bibliography of Micronesian native
Kahn, E. J., Jr. 1966 A Reporter in Micronesia.
Kahn, E. J., Jr. 1971 A reporter at large: Micronesia Revisited.
Karig, Walter 1948 The Fortunate Islands, A Pacific Interlude; An
Kluge, P. F. 1968 Official Visitor's Guidebook to the Trust
Kluge, P. F. 1971 Micronesia: America's troubled Pacific Ward.
Marshall, Mac 1974 Review of Robert Wenkam and Byron Baker,
Mason, Leonard E. 1969 Anthropological research in Micronesia,
Micronesian Reporter 1951 to present.
Micronesian Seminar 1967 Bibliography of library materials:
Micronesian Seminar Bulletin 1965 to present.
Micronesica 1964 to present.
Mitchell, Roger E. 1971 Kubary: The first Micronesian Reporter.
Murphy, Robert T. 1974 A Postal History Cancellation Study of the
Nørlund, Mogens Christian 1966 Den forsvundne verden.

GUIDE TO TOPICS AND AREAS

General and Popular Literature

Owen, Hera W. 1973 Bat Soup, and Other Recipes From the South
Peace Corps 1969 The Story of Micronesia: With an Introductory
Price, Willard 1944 Japan's Islands of Mystery.
Price, Willard 1966 America's Paradise Lost.
Riesenberg, Saul H. 1951 People in Micronesia.
Riley, Frank 1969 Storm over Micronesia.
Spoehr, Alexander 1950 Report from Micronesia.
Suda, Akiyoshi 1952 Bibliography on physical anthropology of the
Tonkinson, Robert 1975 Review of Robert Wenkam and Byron Baker,
Toomin, Philip R. and Pauline M. Toomin 1963 Black Robe and Grass
Trumbell, Robert 1959 Paradise in Trust: A Report on Americans in
United States Department of the Army 1971 Pacific Islands and
U.S.T.T.P.I. 1967 to present. Highlights.
Utinomi, Huzio (compiler) 1950 Bibliography of Micronesia.
Vitarelli, William V. 1968 Twenty years in Micronesia.
Wenkam, Robert and Byron Baker 1972 Micronesia: The Breadfruit
Wright, Gordon (compiler) 1969 A Bibliography of Reports,
Wypych, Konrad 1969 W cieniu fe; sladami Jana Stanislawa

Mariana Islands
United States Department of the Navy 1944 Civil Affairs Handbook:

Guam
Beaty, Janice J. 1967 Discovering Guam: A Guide to Its Towns,
Caldwell, John C. 1969 Let's Visit Micronesia; Guam (USA) and the
Rainey, Mary C. and George L. Boughton 1975 The socialization of
Stevens, Russell L. 1953 Guam, U.S.A.: Birth of a Territory.
Vanatta, Jack 1947 Guam, the Gem of Micronesia.

Anatahan
Maruyama, Michiro 1954 Anatahan.

Palau Islands District
United States Department of the Navy 1944 Civil Affairs Handbook:

Palau Islands
Brower, Kenneth 1974 With Their Islands Around Them.
Clark, Eugenie 1953 Siakong--spear fisherman pre-eminent:
Read, Kenneth R. H. 1972 Kayangel Atoll.
Read, Kenneth R. H. 1974 The rock islands of Palau.
Stumpf, Margaret K. 1972 Palau--islands of Diversity.

Yap District
United States Department of the Navy 1944 Civil Affairs Handbook:

Yap Islands
Hiatt, Robert W., et al. 1947 Yap Re-discovered.
Klingman, Lawrence and Gerald Green 1950 His Majesty O'Keefe.
Moore, W. Robert 1952 Grass-skirted Yap.

Ulithi

GUIDE TO TOPICS AND AREAS

General and Popular Literature

Divine, David [Arthur Durham Divine] 1950 The King of
Walter, William J. 1955 Laughter on Ulithi.
Wees, Marshall Paul 1950 King-Doctor of Ulithi.

Ifaluk

Bates, Marston and Donald P. Abbott 1958 Coral Island, Portrait
Vayda, Andrew P. 1962 Review of Marston Bates and Donald P.
Walter, William J. 1957 Ifalik...changing Paradise.
Weckler, Joseph E. 1959 Review of Marston Bates and Donald P.

Truk District

Rively, William E., S.J. 1953 The Story of the "Romance".
United States Department of the Navy 1944 Civil Affairs Handbook:

Truk Islands - Truk Lagoon

Riley, Frank 1970 Micronesia...hotel on Truk kicks off a new

Pulap

Ullman, James Ramsey 1960 A strange tale of the South Seas.

Ponape District

United States Department of the Navy 1944 Civil Affairs Handbook:

Ponape

Price, Willard 1944 Ponape: A nut to Crack.
Zimbelman, Edward 1974 A night in "Venice": Nan Madol, ancient

Kapingamarangi

Emory, Kenneth P. 1947 South Seas diary; Report from the South
Hiroa, Te Rangi [Peter H. Buck] 1948 Bishop Museum Expedition
Hiroa, Te Rangi [Peter H. Buck] 1951 Kapingaramangi: A living

Kusaie - Kusaie District

United States Department of the Navy 1944 Civil Affairs Handbook:

Marshall Islands District

Duane, J. M. 1969 English-Marshallese Cookbook.
Fosberg, F. Raymond 1955 The Northern Marshall Islands
Spoehr, Alexander 1949 Life in the Marshall Islands.
United States Department of the Navy 1943 Military Government

Majuro

Spoehr, Alexander 1947 Micronesian Expedition completes Work

Arno

Hiatt, Robert W., Leonard E. Mason and D. Cox 1951 The Arno Atoll

Bikini

Markwith, Carl 1946 Farewell to Bikini.

GUIDE TO TOPICS AND AREAS

Geography

Pacific Islands
Bryan, Edwin H., Jr. 1950 Check list of Atolls.
Devita, Philip R. 1975 Review of David Lewis, We, the Navigators.
Fosberg, F. Raymond 1951 Coral atoll symposium: Basic information
Fosberg, F. Raymond, ed. 1963 Man's Place in the Island
Fosberg, F. Raymond 1975 Review of David Lewis, We, the
Freeman, Otis W., ed. 1951 Geography of the Pacific.
Friis, Herman R. 1967 The Pacific Basin.
Kennedy, T. F. 1966 A Descriptive Atlas of the Pacific Islands.
Lewis, David 1972 The Gospel according to St. Andrew.
Lewis, David 1972 We, the Navigators.
Lewthwaite, Gordon R. 1973 Review of David Lewis, We, the
Mason, Leonard E. 1962 Habitat, man and Culture.
Racule, Amani 1973 Review of David Lewis, We, The Navigators.
Richey, M. W. 1974 Review of David Lewis, We, The Navigators.
Sharp, Andrew 1972 David Lewis on indigenous Pacific Navigation.
Spoehr, Alexander 1957 Relation of humans to the atoll
Spoehr, Alexander 1964 Review of F. Raymond Fosberg, ed., Man's
Stoddart, D. R. 1968 Catastrophic human interference with coral
Wiens, Herold J. 1962 Atoll Environment and Ecology.

Micronesia (U.S.T.T.P.I.)
Akerblom, Kjell 1968 Astronomy and Navigation in Polynesia and
Apple, Russell A. 1972 Historic Properties Policy and Program in
Belknap, R. L. and Norma K. Lopes 1969 The United States Weather
Bryan, Edwin H., Jr. 1946 Geographic Summary of Micronesia.
Bryan, Edwin H., Jr. 1971 Guide to Place Names in the Trust
Cayford, Marilyn L. 1971 Transport strategy in Micronesia.
Coulter, John Wesley 1948 The United States Trust Territory of
Cox, Samuel Allen 1970 An analysis of geographical influences on
Duncan, Leith 1972 Review of Kjell Akerblom, Astronomy and
Embree, John F. 1946 University of Hawaii research in Micronesia.
Falanruw, M. V. C. 1971 Conservation in Micronesia.
Finney, Ben R. 1970 Review of Kjell Akerblom, Astronomy and
Fosberg, F. Raymond 1953 A conservation program for Micronesia.
Laubenfels, M. W. de 1950 Native Navigators.
Lewis, David 1969 Navigational techniques of the early
Lewis, David 1970 Polynesian and Micronesian navigational
McGrath, William A. and K. Aaron Mitchell (compilers) 1971 Trust
Otobed, Demei O. 1975 Conservation priorities in Micronesia.
Owen, Robert P. 1969 The status of conservation in the Trust
Riesenberg, Saul H. 1965 Table of voyages affecting Micronesian
Sachet, Marie-Helene 1966 Coral islands as ecological
Sachet, Marie-Helene and F. Raymond Fosberg 1955 Island
Sachet, Marie-Helene and F. Raymond Fosberg 1971 Island
Sahara, Tamotsu 1967 Land Classification Program Proposal for the
Sharp, Andrew 1966 Early Micronesian Voyaging.
Thompson, Laura 1949 The basic conservation Problem.
Tobin, Jack A., et al. 1957 Notes on the present regulations

Geography

United States Geographical Names Board 1955 Decisions on Names in
United States Hydrographic Office 1944 Caroline, Mariana,
United States Trust Territory of the Pacific Islands 1973 Maps of
Walter, William J. 1961 Typhoon in the Pacific.
Wenkam, Robert 1971 Micronesian parks: A Proposal.
Wenkam, Robert 1972 Parks for the Pacific.
Wenkam, Robert and Ken Brower 1975 Micronesia: Island Wilderness.
Wiens, Herold J. 1963 Some effects of geographic location upon

Mariana Islands
Bowers, Neal M. 1951 The Mariana, Volcano, and Bonin Islands.
McCoy, Michael A. 1973 A renaissance in Carolinian-Marianas

Guam
Karolle, Bruce G. 1973 A geography of Guam Island.
Perez, Gerald S. A. 1975 Guam conservation Priorities.
Taylor, John L. 1949 Guam: Focus of the Western Pacific.

Saipan
Taylor, John L. 1951 Saipan: A study in land Utilization.

Caroline Islands
Goodenough, Ward H. 1951 Native astronomy in Micronesia, a
Goodenough, Ward H. 1953 Native Astronomy in the Central
Manchester, Curtis A. 1951 The Caroline Islands.
McCoy, Michael A. 1973 A renaissance in Carolinian-Marianas
Stone, Benjamin C. 1961 Pandanus pistillaris in the Caroline

Palau Islands
Gressitt, J. L. 1952 Description of Kayangel Atoll, Palau
Gressitt, J. L. 1953 Notes on Ngaruangle and Kayangel Atolls,

Ulithi
Boykin, J. 1963 The voyage of the Ulithians.

Lamotrek
Alkire, William H. 1968 An atoll environment and Ethnogeography.

Gaferut
Niering, William A. 1961 Observations on Puluwat and Gaferut,

Truk Islands - Truk Lagoon
Carter, Jackson 1972 Truk: A land Problem.
Goodenough, Ward H. 1966 Notes on Truk's place Names.

Puluwat
Duncan, Leith 1972 Review of Thomas Gladwin, East Is a Big
Gladwin, Thomas 1970 East is a big bird: Part I.
Gladwin, Thomas 1970 East is a Big Bird: Navigation and Logic on
Goodenough, Ward H. 1971 Review of Thomas Gladwin, East is a Big
Lewis, David 1970 A return voyage between Puluwat and Saipan

GUIDE TO TOPICS AND AREAS

Geography

Lewis, David 1971 'Expanding' the target in indigenous
Lewis, David 1974 Wind, wave, star and Bird.
Niering, William A. 1961 Observations on Puluwat and Gaferut,
Riesenberg, Saul H. 1972 The organisation of navigational

Pulap
Ullman, James Ramsey 1960 A strange tale of the South Seas.

Etal
Nason, James D. 1975 Reconnaisance and plat mapping of coral

Ponape District
Murphy, Raymond E. 1949 'High' and 'Low' islands in the Eastern
Murphy, Raymond E. 1950 Geographic studies in the Easternmost

Nukucro
Carroll, Vern 1964 Place names on Nukuoro Atoll.

Kapingamarangi
McIntire, Elliot G. (compiler) 1960 A Library Brochure:
Niering, William A. 1956 Bioecology of Kapingamarangi Atoll,
Niering, William A. 1963 Terrestrial ecology of Kapingamarangi
Wiens, Herold J. 1955 The Geography of Kapingamarangi Atoll in

Kusaie - Kusaie District
Murphy, Raymond E. 1949 'High' and 'Low' islands in the Eastern
Murphy, Raymond E. 1950 Geographic studies in the Easternmost

Marshall Islands District
Brandt, John H. 1963 By dunung and bouj: Water movements,
Browning, Mary A. 1972 Walab im Medo: Canoes and navigation in
Browning, Mary A. 1973 Stick Charting.
Davenport, William H. 1960 Marshall Island navigation Charts.
Davenport, William H. 1964 Marshall Islands Cartography.
Davis, C. J. 1964 Stick charts of Micronesia.
Hines, Neal O. 1952 The secret of the Marshallese Sticks.
Hops, A. 1956 Ueber die Einmaligkeit der Marshall-Stabkarten im
Mason, Leonard E. 1951 Marshalls, Gilberts, Ocean Island, and
Milne, James 1953 Meto--Marshallese Navigation.
Playdon, Capt. George W., U.S.C.G. (Ret.) 1967 The significance
Spoehr, Alexander 1946 The Marshall Islands and Trans-Pacific
Street, Jchn M. (compiler) 1960 Eniwetok Atoll, Marshall Islands:
U.S. Dept. of the Army 1956 Military Geography of the Northern
Wiens, Herold J. 1957 Field notes on atolls visited in the

Majuro
Urguhart, Alvin W. (compiler) 1960 Majuro Atoll, Marshall

Arno
Mason, Leonard E., et al. 1950 Anthropology-Geography study of

GUIDE TO TOPICS AND AREAS

Geography

Enewetok
Blumenstock, David I. and Daniel F. Rex 1960 Microclimatic

Kwajalein
Bauer, F. H. 1960 Kwajalein Atoll Geography and Facilities.

Jaluit
Blumenstock, David I. 1958 Typhcon effects at Jaluit Atoll in the
Blumenstock, David I. 1958 Typhoon Ophelia at Jaluit Atoll.
Blumenstock, David I., ed. 1961 A report on typhoon effects upon
Blumenstock, David I., et al. 1961 The resurvey of typhoon effects
Mackenzie, J. Boyd 1961 Population and economy of Jaluit.

Taongi
Fosberg, F. Raymond 1957 Lonely Pckak [Taongi].
McIntire, Elliot G. (compiler) 1960 Taongi Atoll, Marshall

GUIDE TO TOPICS AND AREAS

Geology

Pacific Islands
U.S. Dept. of the Army 1956 Annotated Bibliography of Geologic

Micronesia (U.S.T.T.P.I.)
Bridge, Josiah and William D. Mark 1946 Mineral Resources of
Piper, Arthur M. 1946 Water Resources of Guam and the Ex-Japanese
Rogers, Oliver C. 1946 Report on Soils of Micronesia.
Stone, Earl L., Jr. 1953 Summary of information on atoll Soils.

Guam
Stensland, Carl H. 1957 The soils of Guam.
Tracey, Joshua I., Jr. 1957 Geological investigations on Guam.
Tracey, Joshua I., Jr. et al. 1959 Military Geology of Guam,
Tracey, Joshua I., Jr., et al. 1964 General Geology of Guam.

Saipan
Cloud, Preston E., Jr., et al. 1955 Military Geology of Saipan,
Davis, Dan 1958 Military Geology of Saipan, Mariana Islands.
McCracken, Ralph J. 1951 Soil geography of Palau and Saipan.
McCracken, Ralph J. 1953 A preliminary report on the soils of

Tinian
Doan, David B., et al. 1960 Military Geology of Tinian,

Pagan
Corwin, Gilbert, et al. 1957 Military Geology of Pagan,

Caroline Islands
Nugent, L. E., Jr. 1946 Coral reefs in the Gilbert, Marshall, and

Palau Islands
Mason, Arnold C., et al. 1956 Military Geology of Palau Islands,
McCracken, Ralph J. 1951 Soil geography of Palau and Saipan.
Vessel, A. V. and Roy W. Simonson 1958 Soils and agriculture of

Yap Islands
Johnson, Charles G., et al. 1960 Military Geology of Yap Islands,

Ifaluk
Tracey, Joshua I., Jr., et al. 1961 Natural History of Ifaluk

Truk Islands - Truk Lagoon
Stark, John T. and Richard L. Hay 1963 Geology and petrology of
Stark, John T., et al. 1958 Military Geology of Truk,
Valenciano, Santos and Kiyoshi J. Takasaki 1959 Military Geology

Kapingamarangi
McKee, Edwin D. 1956 Geology of Kapingamarangi Atoll, Caroline

GUIDE TO TOPICS AND AREAS

Geology

Marshall Islands District
Fosberg, F. Raymond 1954 Soils of the Northern Marshall atolls,
Fosberg, F. Raymond 1957 Soils, vegetation, and agriculture on
Fosberg, F. Raymond and Dorothy Carroll 1965 Terrestrial
Nugent, L. E., Jr. 1946 Coral reefs in the Gilbert, Marshall, and

Arno
Stone, Earl L., Jr. 1951 The soils of Arno Atoll, Marshall
Stone, Earl L., Jr. 1953 Summary of information on atoll Soils.
Wells, John W. 1950 Geology Study of Arno.

Bikini
Emery, Kenneth O., et al. 1954 Geology of Bikini and nearby

Rongelap
Kenady, Reid M., Jr. 1962 The soils of Rongelap Atoll, Marshall

History

Pacific Islands

Agthe, Johanna 1969 Die Abbildungen in Reiseberichten aus
Lingenfelter, Richard E. 1967 Presses of the Pacific Islands,
Mander-Jones, Phyllis 1967 A guide to manuscripts in the British
Nozikov, Nikolai N. 1946 Russian Voyages Round the World, M.A.
Purcell, David Campell, Jr. 1967 Japanese expansion in the South
Sharp, Andrew 1960 Discovery of the Pacific Islands.
Spoehr, Florence Mann 1963 White Falcon.

Micronesia (U.S.T.T.P.I.)

Alden, J. E. 1944 Press in paradise: The beginnings of printing
Anttila, Elizabeth K. 1965 A history of the people of the Trust
Ballendorf, Dirk 1974 The violent first Encounters.
Ballendorf, Dirk 1975 The Micronesian Ellis Mystery.
Bradley, W. P. 1967 The history of the Marianas, Caroline, Peleu
Cockrum, Emmett Erston 1970 The emergence of modern Micronesia.
Crawford, David and Leona Crawford 1967 Missionary Adventures in
Faivre, J. P. 1972 Review of Dorothy Shineberg, ed., The Trading
Hatanaka, Sachiko 1967 The process of cultural change in
Heine, Carl 1965 A historical study of political development and
Hezel, Francis X. 1972 Review of Dorothy Shineberg, ed., The
James, Roy E. 1949 The Trust Territory of the Pacific Islands.
Loomis, Albertine 1970 To All People.
Luomala, Katharine 1958 Review of Alfred Tetens, Among the
Marshall, Mac and Leslie B. Marshall 1975 Holy and unholy
Marshall, Mac and Leslie B. Marshall 1975 Opening Pandora's
Maude, H. E. 1969 Review of David Crawford and Leona Crawford,
McGrath, Thomas B. 1973 The Joachim deBrum Papers.
McGrath, William A. 1971 Resolving the land Dilemma.
McKinney, Robert Quentin 1947 Micronesia under German Rule
Murphy, Robert T. 1974 A Postal History Cancellation Study of the
Osborne, Douglas 1959 Review of Alfred Tetens, Among the Savages
Osborne, Douglas 1960 Review of Alfred Tetens, Among the Savages
Pla Carceles, Jose 1951 Espana en la Micronesia.
Purcell, David Campbell, Jr. 1971 Japanese entrepreneurs in the
Riesenberg, Saul H. 1965 Table of voyages affecting Micronesian
Shineberg, Dorothy, ed. 1971 The Trading Voyages of Andrew Cheyne
Tetens, Alfred 1958 Among the Savages of the South Seas, Memoirs
Ward, Herbert T. 1970 Flight of the Cormoran.

Mariana Islands

Carano, Paul 1972 Ancient Chamorro Leaders.
Haddock, Robert L. 1974 A hole full of History.
Heath, Laurel 1975 Education for confusion: A study of education
Lessa, William A. 1974 Drake in the Marianas? Micronesica,
Micronesian Seminar 1967 Translation of "The occupation of
Morton, Louis 1967 The Marianas.
Searles, P. J. 1974 Spanish Galleons.
Searles, P. J. 1975 Spanish Galleons.

GUIDE TO TOPICS AND AREAS

History

Wernhardt, Karl R. 1972 A pre-missionary manuscript record of the
Wiswell, Ella 1974 Translation frcm the Russian of V.M.

Guam

Beardsley, Charles 1964 Guam: Past and Present.
Carano, Paul 1974 British privateers visit Guam.
Carano, Paul 1975 Who's who--in Guam History.
Carano, Paul and Pedro C. Sanchez 1964 A Complete History of
Crofts, George D. and Emilie G. Johnston 1975 Governor Gregcrio
Doty, Richard G. 1972 Guam's role in the whaling Industry.
Dugan, Paul Fleming 1956 The early history of Guam 1521-1698.
Johnston, Emilie G. 1974 Spanish dikes in the Agana Swamp.
Mahone, Rene C. 1974 Biography of Guam's last Spaniard.
Maude, H. E. 1966 Review of Paul Carano and Pedro C. Sanchez, A
Sullivan, Julius 1957 The Phoenix Rises: A Mission History of
Walker, L. W. 1945 Guam's seizure by the United States in 1898.

Tinian

Graham, Robert 1974 Tinian, the history of an Island.

Caroline Islands

Hezel, Francis X. 1970 Catholic missions in the Carcline and
Hezel, Francis X. and Maria Teresa del Valle 1972 Early European
Micronesian Seminar 1967 Translation of "The occupation of
Quinn, P. E. 1945 Diplomatic struggle for the Carolines, 1898.
Riesenberg, Saul H. 1975 The ghcst islands of the Carolines.

Palau Islands District

Ballendorf, Dirk 1972 Americans/Palauans--their first Encounter.
Lessa, William A. 1975 The Portuguese discovery of the Iles of
Meredith, J. C. 1958 The Tatooed Man.

Palau Islands

Helfand, Harvey 1974 The pirate and Palau.
Lessa, William A. 1974 Francis Drake in Mindanao? Journal cf
Lessa, William A. 1975 Drake's Island of Thieves: Ethnological
Owen, Hera W., ed. 1973 Charles Gibbons: Visions of old Palau.

Yap District

Lessa, William A. 1975 The Portuguese discovery of the Iles of

Yap Islands

Duncan, David D. 1946 Yap meets the Yanks.
Hezel, Francis X. 1975 A Yankee trader in Yap: Crayton Philo
Rattan, Sumitra 1972 The Yap contrcversy and its Significance.

Ulithi

Micronesian Seminar 1965 Translation of "The discovery and

Truk District

Hezel, Francis X. n.d. Foreign ship contacts with Truk Islands.

GUIDE TO TOPICS AND AREAS

History

Truk Islands - Truk Lagoon

Clifton, James A. 1964 The acceptance of external political
Hezel, Francis X. 1972 Sailors Beware! Foreign contact with Truk
Hezel, Francis X. 1973 The beginnings of foreign contact with
Hezel, Francis X. 1973 The first European visit to Truk.
Hezel, Francis X. 1974 Dumont D'Urville on Truk.
Micronesian Seminar n.d. Translation of Jules Dumont d'Urville,
Micronesian Seminar n.d. Translation of Arellano's account
Mitchell, Roger E. 1967 A study of the cultural, historical and

Hall Islands

Schlesier, Erhard 1954 Eine alte Quelle über Lemarafat,

Ponape

Bascom, Willard R. 1950 Ponape, the tradition of Retaliation.
Brownell, Jean 1968 Papers of Ephraim and Myra Roberts of Ponape.
Clifton, James A. 1964 The acceptance of external political
Coale, George L. 1951 A study of chieftainship, missionary
Ehrlich, Paul 1974 Preliminary observations on the German times
Hempenstall, Peter John 1973 Indigenous resistance to German rule
Hempenstall, Peter John 1975 Resistance in the German Pacific
Riesenberg, Saul H. 1959 A Pacific voyager's Hoax.
Riesenberg, Saul H. 1968 The tatooed Irishman.
Riesenberg, Saul H., ed. 1972 A Residence of Eleven Years in New

Marshall Islands District

Browning, Mary A. 1968 The sailing of the Rurick.
Browning, Mary A. 1972 Traders in the Marshalls.
Hezel, Francis X. 1970 Catholic missions in the Caroline and
McGrath, Thomas B. 1973 The Joachim deBrum Papers.
Morison, Samuel E. 1944 Historical Notes on the Gilbert and

Mili

Ballendorf, Dirk 1970 Mutiny on the whaleship Globe.

Bikini

Gale, Roger 1974 Return to Bikini? The Progressive, 38:12-13.

Jaluit

Tobin, Jack A. 1970 Jabwor: Former capitol of the Marshall

Ebon

Ae'a, Hezekiah 1947 The history of Ebon, translated from the

GUIDE TO TOPICS AND AREAS

Linguistics

Pacific Islands

Capell, Arthur 1962 Oceanic linguistics Today.
Dyen, Isidore 1965 A Lexicostatistical Classification of the
Elbert, Samuel H. 1965 Phonological expansions in outlier
Grace, George W. 1959 The position of the Polynesian language
Grace, George W. 1970 Languages in Oceania.
Murdock, George P. 1964 Genetic classification of the
Pawley, Andrew 1967 The relationships of Polynesian outlier
Pawley, Andrew 1972 On the internal relationships of Eastern
Pawley, Andrew and Roger C. Green 1973 Dating the dispersal of

Micronesia (U.S.T.T.P.I.)

Bender, Byron W. 1971 Micronesian Languages.
Bender, Byron W. 1973 Parallelisms in the morphophonemics of
Cammack, Floyd M. and Donald M. Topping 1965 University of Hawaii
Capell, Arthur 1947 Review of, "Books on Micronesian
Capell, Arthur 1971 Review of Donald M. Topping, Spoken Chamorro,
Hall, Robert Anderson, Jr. 1945 English loan words in Micronesian
Harrison, Sheldon P. 1973 Reduplication in Micronesian Languages.
Hockett, Charles F. 1961 Recommendations on language policy in
Hollyman, K. J. (compiler) 1960 A Checklist of Oceanic Languages
Izui, Hisanosuke 1965 The languages of Micronesia: Their unity
Kaeppler, Adrienne 1967 Micronesia--Linguistics.
Marck, Jeffrey C. 1974 A lexico-statistical model for nuclear
Marck, Jeffrey C. 1975 The origin and dispersal of the Proto
Matthews, William K. 1950 Characteristics of Micronesian.
Sohn, Ho-min 1973 Relative clause formation in Micronesian
Solenberger, Robert R. 1968 Cultural conflict and language
Sugita, Hiroshi 1973 Comparison of verb-object relationships in
Trifonovitch, Gregory J. 1971 Language policy, language
Voegelin, Carl F. and Florence M. Voegelin 1964 Micronesia.

Mariana Islands

Burris, E. J. 1954 Sanvitores' grammar and catechism in the
Cruz, F. "Val" (compiler) 1967 Chamorro-English; English-Chamorro
Fischer, John L. 1961 The retention rate of Chamorro basic
Goo, Fannie and Albert H. Banner 1963 A preliminary compilation
Guam Business and Professional Women 1959 Learn Chamorro Quickly.
Kiste, Robert C. 1971 Review of Byron W. Bender, Spoken
Latta, F. Christian 1972 On stress and vowel harmony in Chamorro.
Mathiot, Madeline 1955 Chamorro phonemics with morphophonemic
Plaza, Felicia 1971 Origin of the word Chamorro.
Sanvitores, Diego Luis de 1954 Lingua Mariana.
Seiden, William 1960 Chamorro Phonemes.
Smith, James Jerome 1975 Review of Topping and Dungca, Chamorro
Solenberger, Robert R. 1953- Recent changes in Chamorro direction
Solenberger, Robert R. 1962 The social meaning of language choice
Topping, Donald M. 1962 Loanblends: A tool for Linguists.
Topping, Donald M. 1963 Chamorro structure and the teaching of

GUIDE TO TOPICS AND AREAS

Linguistics

Topping, Donald M. 1966 Lessons in Chamorro.
Topping, Donald M. 1968 Chamorro vowel Harmony.
Topping, Donald M. 1973 Spoken Chamorro Tomorrow.
Topping and Dungca 1973 Chamorro Reference Grammar.
Topping and Ogo 1969 Spoken Chamorro: An Intensive Language
Topping, Ogo and Dungca 1975 Chamorro-English Dictionary.
Voegelin, Carl F. and Florence M. Voegelin 1965 Chamorro in
Witucki, Jeannette 1973 Alternative analyses of Chamorro Vowels.

Guam

Garland, J. 1961 Chamorro text, Guam.
Hockett, Charles F. 1961 Recommendations on language policy in
Kehoe, Monika 1973 English on Guam.
Vesper, Don 1972 Guam as an example of U.S. Language policy.

Caroline Islands

Goo, Fannie and Albert H. Banner 1963 A preliminary compilation
Quackenbush, Edward M. 1968 From Sonsorol to Truk: A dialect
Quackenbush, Hiroko C. 1970 Studies in the phonology of some

Palau Islands

Capell, Arthur 1948 Palau-English Dictionary; English-Palau
Capell, Arthur 1957 Palau possessives and problems in morpheme
Carlson, Clayton H. 1967 Lessons in Palauan.
Carlson, Clayton H. 1968 Palauan Phonology.
Dyen, Isidore 1971 Review of Klaus Pätzold, Die Palau-Sprache
Flora, Marie Jo-Ann 1969 Analysis of the segmental phonemes of
Flora, Marie Jo-Ann 1974 Palauan phonology and Morphology.
Force, Roland W. and Maryanne Force 1961 Keys to cultural
Greenberg, Stephen, et al. 1969 The Palauan Verb.
Hsu, Robert W. 1960 Palauan Phonology.
Izui, Hisanosuke 1949 A propos d'une table de correspondances de
Josephs, Lewis S. n.d. Palauan Reference Grammar.
Mancill, Grace S. and Frances S. Woods 1969 Morphology and syntax
McManus, Edward n.d. Palauan-English Dictionary, Lewis S. Josephs
Pätzold, Klaus 1968 Die Palau-Sprache und ihre Stellung zu
Wilson, Helen Irene 1972 The phonology and syntax of Palauan verb

Tobi

Capell, Arthur 1950 Grammar and Vocabulary of the Language of
Haudricourt, A. G. 1969 Review of Arthur Capell, Grammar and
Z'graggen, J. A. 1971 Review of Arthur Capell, Grammar and

Sonsorol

Capell, Arthur 1950 Grammar and Vocabulary of the Language of
Haudricourt, A. G. 1969 Review of Arthur Capell, Grammar and
Z'graggen, J. A. 1971 Review of Arthur Capell, Grammar and

Yap Islands

Elbert, Samuel H. 1946 Yap-English and English-Yap Word Lists,
Hsu, Robert W. 1969 Phonology and morphophonemics of Yapese.

GUIDE TO TOPICS AND AREAS

Linguistics

Hsu, Robert W. 1969 Apocope and umlaut in Yapese.
Jensen, John T. n.d. Yapese Reference Grammar.
Jensen, John T. n.d. Yapese-English Dictionary.
Jensen, John T. 1966 Lessons in Yapese.
Lorrach, P. von 1953 Grammatik der Yap-Sprache in Mikronesien.

Ulithi
Elbert, Samuel H. 1947 Ulithi-English and English-Ulithi Word
Quackenbush, Edward M. 1966 Lessons in Ulithian.
Sohn, Ho-min 1969 An outline of Ulithian Grammar.
Sohn, Ho-min and Byron W. Bender 1973 A Ulithian Grammar.

Woleai
Smith, Alfred G. 1951 Gamwoelhaelhi Ishilh Weleeya.

The Woleai
Biggs, Bruce 1961 Review of Saul H. Riesenberg and Shigeru
Riesenberg, Saul H. and Shigeru Kaneshiro 1960 A Caroline Islands
Sohn, Ho-min 1971 a-raising in Woleaian.
Sohn, Ho-min 1975 A Reference Grammar of Woleaian.

Truk District
Benton, Richard A. 1968 Numeral and attributive classifiers in
Benton, Richard A. 1968 Substitutes and classifiers in Trukese.
Benton, Richard A., assisted by Sokichi Stephen 1967 Trukese; An
Dyen, Isidore 1949 On the history of Trukese Vowels.
Dyen, Isidore 1949 A Sketch of Trukese Grammar.
Elbert, Samuel H. 1947 Trukese-English and English-Trukese
Fischer, John L. 1965 The stylistic significance of consonantal
Goodenough, Ward H. and Hiroshi Sugita n.d. Trukese-English
Sugita, Hiroshi n.d. Trukese Reference Grammar.
Topping, Donald M. 1964 Contrastive analysis and sandhi

Truk Islands - Truk Lagoon
Biggs, Bruce 1961 Review of Saul H. Riesenberg and Shigeru
Fischer, John L. 1955 Language and folktale in Truk and Ponape: A
Fischer, John L. 1966 Syntax and social structure: Truk and
Goodenough, Ward H. 1963 The long or double consonants of
Goodenough, Ward H. 1964 Property and language on Truk: Some
Goodenough, Ward H. 1971 A similarity in cultural and linguistic
Riesenberg, Saul H. and Shigeru Kaneshiro 1960 A Caroline Islands
Sedwick, Ensign Benjamin Frank 1946 Puken Aueuen Fosun Ingnes

Puluwat
Elbert, Samuel H. 1970 Loan words in Puluwat.
Elbert, Samuel H. 1972 Puluwat Dictionary.
Elbert, Samuel H. 1974 Puluwat Grammar.

Pulap
Quackenbush, Hiroko C. 1966 Lessons in Pulapese.

GUIDE TO TOPICS AND AREAS

Linguistics

Ponape District
Fischer, John L. 1965 The stylistic significance of consonantal

Ponape
Fischer, John L. 1955 Language and folktale in Truk and Ponape: A
Fischer, John L. 1966 Interrogatives in Ponapean: Some semantic
Fischer, John L. 1966 Syntax and social structure: Truk and
Garvin, Paul L. 1949 Linguistic Study of Ponape.
Garvin, Paul L. 1954 Delimitation of syntactic Units.
Garvin, Paul L. 1954 Literacy as a problem in language and
Garvin, Paul L. 1958 Syntactic units and Operations.
Garvin, Paul L. 1959 The standard language problem: Concepts and
Garvin, Paul L. 1962 A study of inductive method in Syntax.
Garvin, Paul L. 1962 Ponapean Morphophonemics.
Garvin, Paul L. 1971 The sound pattern of Ponapean.
Garvin, Paul L. and Saul H. Riesenberg 1952 Respect behavior on
Lee, Kee-dong 1973 Verbal aspect in Kusaiean and Ponapean.
Lester, Mark 1966 Lessons in Ponapean.
McCauley, David P. 1967 Lessons in Ponapean.
Rehg, Kenneth L. n.d. Ponapean Reference Grammar.
Rehg, Kenneth L. 1973 On the history of Ponapean Phonology.
Rehg, Kenneth L. and Damien Sohl n.d. Ponapean-English

Mokil
Harrison, Sheldon P. n.d. A Reference Grammar of Mokilese.

Nukuoro
Carroll, Vern 1965 An outline of the structure of the language of
Carroll, Vern 1966 Generative elicitation techniques in
Carroll, Vern and Tobias Soulik 1973 Nukuoro Lexicon.
Elbert, Samuel H. 1946 Kapingamarangi and Nukuoro Word List, With
Pawley, Andrew 1967 The relationships of Polynesian outlier

Kapingamarangi
Elbert, Samuel H. 1946 Kapingamarangi and Nukuoro Word List, With
Elbert, Samuel H. 1948 Grammar and Comparative Study of the
Lieber, Michael D. and Kalio H. Dikepa 1974 Kapingamarangi Lexicon.
Pawley, Andrew 1967 The relationships of Polynesian outlier

Kusaie - Kusaie District
Lee, Kee-dong n.d. A Kusaien-English Dictionary.
Lee, Kee-dong n.d. A Reference Grammar of Kusaiean.
Lee, Kee-dong 1972 Some derivational rules of Kusaiean.
Lee, Kee-dong 1973 Verbal aspect in Kusaiean and Ponapean.
McCauley, David P. and H. E. S. George 1966 Lessons in Kusaiean.
Smith, Alfred G. 1951 Ki Luwn Specl Kosray.
Vesper, Ethel R. 1969 Grammatical and semantic classifiers as
Vesper, Ethel R. 1969 Phrase structures of Kusaien.
Vesper, Ethel R. 1970 A consideration of number in Kusaien.
Vesper, Ethel R. 1970 Kusaien possessives as relative clauses: A
Vesper, Ethel R. 1971 A semantic characterization of Kusaien

GUIDE TO TOPICS AND AREAS

Linguistics

Vesper, Ethel R. 1972 Kusaien reduplication: A lexical Problem.
Vesper, Ethel R. 1973 A consideration of derivation in Kusaien.
Vesper, Ethel R. 1973 Directional affixes: More evidence for

Marshall Islands District

Bailey, Charles-James N. 1967 Transformational outline of
Bargmann, A. 1955 A. Erdland's Grammatik und Wörterbuch der
Bender, Byron W. n.d. Marshallese Reference Grammar.
Bender, Byron W. 1963 A linguistic analysis of the place-names of
Bender, Byron W. 1963 Marshallese phonemics: Labialization or
Bender, Byron W. 1966 Towards a systematic phonemicization of
Bender, Byron W. 1968 Marshallese Phonology.
Bender, Byron W. 1969 An Oceanic place-name Study.
Bender, Byron W. 1969 Spoken Marshallese.
Bender, Byron W. 1969 Vowel dissimilation in Marshallese.
Bender, Byron W. and Tony de Brum 1966 Lessons in Marshallese.
Bender, Byron W., et al. n.d. Marshallese-English Dictionary.
Carr, Denzel 1945 Notes on Marshallese consonant Phonemes.
Elbert, Samuel H. 1952 Marshallese phonemes and Orthography.
Erdland, August 1955 Grammatik und Wörterbuch der
Fischer, John L. 1971 Review of Byron W. Bender, Spoken
Goo, Fannie and Albert H. Banner 1963 A preliminary compilation
Kiste, Robert C. 1971 Review of Byron W. Bender, Spoken
Ko, Young Kuk 1962 The segmental phonemes of Marshallese,
Koskinen, Aarne A. 1964 Review of Byron Bender, A Linguistic
Smith, Alfred G. 1951 Wahween Jibehhleh Kajin Marshall.
Tsuchida, Shigeru 1965 Velarization in Marshallese.
United States Department of the Navy 1945 Marshallese-English and

Pacific Islands
Banner, Albert H. 1961 Fish poisoning in the tropical Pacific.
Chan, George L. 1967 Health problems of coral atoll Populations.
Murai, Mary, et al. 1963 Nutritive value of coconut Sap.
Rosen, Leon, et al. 1967 Studies in eosinophilic meningitis 3.

Micronesia (U.S.T.T.P.I.)
Adels, B. R. and D. C. Gajdusek 1963 Survey of measles patterns
Alicata, Joseph E. 1965 Notes and observations on murine
Alpert, Elmer 1946 Nutrition and Dietary Patterns of Micronesia.
Anonymous 1947 Micronesian expedition of University of Hawaii
Brown, Paul, et al. 1965 Response to live attenuated measles
Crawford, H. E., et al. 1954 Ophthalmological survey of the
Cruetz, E. and R. Beken 1971 Air-Medec Micronesia.
Gould, K. L., et al. 1971 The epidemiology of measles in the
Greaves, F. C. 1948 The health services program in the Trust
Hankin, Jean H., et al. 1970 Dietary and disease patterns
Hartmann, Floyd W. 1947 Prevalence of dental caries in two groups
Hetzel, Alice M. 1959 Health survey of the Trust Territory of the
Jaffee, A. A. 1959 Dental Services in the United States Trust
Jardin, C. 1967 Food and dietary habits in Micronesia.
Johnston, Emilie G. 1971 Micronesian nutrition Bibliography.
Johnston, Emilie G. 1973 Bibliography of Micronesian native
Malcolm, Sheila 1955 Diet and Nutrition in the Trust Territory of
Maramba, Manuela G. 1960 The economics of food and nutrition in
Mulder, Donald W. and Leonard T. Kurland 1954 Amyotrophic lateral
Murai, Mary 1954 Nutrition study in Micronesia.
Peace Corps 1969 Peace Corps Health Program for the Trust
Reed, Dwayne M. 1974 Modernization and health in Micronesia.
Reed, Dwayne M. 1975 Health effects of modernization in
Reed, Dwayne M., et al. 1972 Epidemiologic studies of serum
Salcedo, Carl 1970 The search for medicinal plants in Micronesia.
Simmons, J. S., et al. 1944 Global Epidemiology:
Sloan, N. R., et al. 1972 Acedapsone in leprosy treatment:
U.S. Dept. of Health, Education and Welfare 1973 HEW/Interior
University of Hawaii 1967 Micronesian Health Monograph, No. 1.
Wolff, Robert J., et al. 1971 A study of knowledge, attitude

Mariana Islands
Elizan, Teresita S., et al. 1966 Amyotrophic lateral sclerosis
Kurland, Leonard T. 1957 Epidemiologic investigations of
Kurland, Leonard T. and Donald W. Mulder 1954 Epidemiologic
Kurland, Leonard T. and Donald W. Mulder 1955 Epidemiologic
Lessell, Simmons, et al. 1962 Parkinson-dementia complex.
Mathai, K. V. 1970 Amyotrophic lateral sclerosis and Parkinsonism
Plato, Chris C., et al. 1964 Frequency of glucose-6-phosphate

Guam
Anonymous 1966 The amyotrophic lateral sclerosis of Guam.

GUIDE TO TOPICS AND AREAS

Medical

Arnold, Arthur, et al. 1953 Amyotrophic lateral sclerosis:
Brody, Jacob A., et al. 1970 Catabolite levels in cerebrospinal
Brody, Jacob A. and Kwang-Ming Chen 1969 Changing epidemiology
Brody, Jacob A., et al. 1971 Recent neuropathologic observations
Brody, Jacob A. and Leonard T. Kurland 1973 Amyotrophic lateral
Eldridge, Roswell, et al. 1969 Amyotrophic lateral sclerosis
Elizan, Teresita S., et al. 1966 Amyotrophic lateral sclerosis
Fletcher, Jack E. 1971 Notes on herb medicine in Guam.
Gerry, Roger G., et al. 1952 The oral characteristics of
Gibbs, C. J., Jr. and D. C. Gajdusek 1972 Amyotrophic lateral
Glosser, J. W. and E. P. Yarnell 1970 Rabies control on Guam.
Haddock, Robert L. 1972 Guam declared rabies Free.
Hammon, W. McD. 1953 Japanese encephalitis and other related
Hammon, W. McD. and Gladys Sather 1953 Neutralization test survey
Hirano, Asao, et al. 1961 Parkinsonism-dementia complex,
Hirano, Asao, et al. 1966 Amyotrophic lateral sclerosis
Hirano, Asao, et al. 1961 Parkinsonism-dementia complex,
Koerner, D. R. 1952 Amyotrophic lateral sclerosis on Guam: A
Kurland, Leonard T. 1963 High incidence of neurological disease
Kurland, Leonard T., et al. 1961 Parkinsonism-dementia complex,
Lessell, Simmons, et al. 1962 Seizure disorders in a Guamanian
Malamud, Nathan, et al. 1961 Pathoanatomic changes in amyotrophic
Malcolm, Sheila 1958 The Diet of Mothers and Children on the
McGrath, Thomas B. 1973 Abortion: Some observations about Guam.
Mulder, Donald W., et al. 1954 Neurologic diseases on the island
Plato, Chris C., et al. 1969 Amyotrophic lateral sclerosis/
Plato, Chris C., et al. 1967 Amyotrophic lateral sclerosis/
Reed, Dwayne M. and Jacob A. Brody 1975 Amyotrophic lateral
Reed, Dwayne M., et al. 1970 Health effects of Westernization
Reed, Dwayne M., et al. 1966 The amyotrophic lateral sclerosis/
Reed, Dwayne M., et al. 1975 Amyotrophic lateral sclerosis and
Stanhope, John M., et al. 1972 Convulsions among the Chamorro
Stanhope, John M., et al. 1972 Convulsions among the Chamorro
Stanhope, John M., et al. 1972 Epidemiologic features of
Stewart, J. L. 1971 Rubella-Deafened children in Guam.
Torres, Jose M., et al. 1957 Amyotrophic lateral sclerosis among

Rota
Reed, Dwayne M., et al. 1970 Health effects of Westernization

Tinian
Stewart, T. D. and Alexander Spoehr 1952 Evidence on the

Caroline Islands
Blake, N. M., et al. 1973 Variation in red cell enzyme groups
Elizan, Teresita S., et al. 1966 Amyotrophic lateral sclerosis
Murai, Mary 1954 Food patterns in the Caroline and Marshall
Murai, Mary, et al. 1958 Some Tropical South Pacific Island Foods:

Palau Islands
Hankin, Jean H. and L. E. Dickenson 1972 Urbanization, diet and

GUIDE TO TOPICS AND AREAS

Medical

Labarthe, Darwin, et al. 1972 Health effects of modernization

Yap District
Brown, Paul and D. C. Gajdusek 1970 Disease patterns and
Brown, Paul, et al. 1966 Epidemic A2 influenza in isolated Pacific
McNair, Philip K., et al. 1949 Report of a medical survey of

Ulithi
Brown, Paul, et al. 1969 Persistance of measles antibody in the

The Woleai
Wallace, Gordon D. 1969 Serologic and epidemiologic observations
Wallace, Gordon D. 1969 Toxoplasmosis on Caroline Atolls.

Truk Islands - Truk Lagoon
Alicata, Joseph E. 1946 Helminthic infection among natives cf the
Darrell, Richard W., et al. 1964 Chorioretinopathy and
Fischer, Ann M. 1963 Reproduction in Truk.
Goodenough, Ward H. 1975 A terminal illness in Truk.
Mahony, Frank J. 1970 A Trukese theory of Medicine.
Walzer, Peter D., et al. 1973 Balantidiasis outbreak in Truk.

Namoluk
Marshall, Mac 1972 Of cats and rats and Toxoplasma gondii at
Wallace, Gordon D., et al. 1972 Cats, rats and Toxoplasmosis

Ponape
Alicata, Joseph E. 1946 Helminthic infection among natives of the
Demory, Barbara 1975 A look at malnutrition on Ponape.
Murrill, Rupert I. 1949 A blood pressure study of the natives of
Riesenberg, Saul H. 1948 Magic and medicine in Ponape.
Sloan, N. R., et al. 1972 Acedapsone in leprosy chemoprophylaxis:
Ward, Martha Coonfield 1974 Some anthropological methods for
Ward, Roger L. 1974 Sociocultural factors in the diagnosis cf
Ward, Roger L. 1975 Ponapean diagnosis: The role of symptoms in

Pingelap
Brody, Jacob A., et al. 1970 Hereditary blindness among
Carr, Ronald E., et al. 1971 Achromatopsia in Pingelap islanders:
Sloan, N. R., et al. 1972 Acedapsone in leprosy chemoprophylaxis:
Sloan, N. R., et al. 1972 Acedapsone in leprosy treatment:

Kapingamarangi
Miller, Ralph E. 1953 Health report at Kapingamarangi.

Marshall Islands District
Conard, Robert A., et al. 1957 Medical survey of Marshallese
Cronkite, E. P., et al., eds. 1956 Some Effects of Ionizing
Murai, Mary 1954 Food patterns in the Caroline and Marshall
Murai, Mary, et al. 1958 Some Tropical South Pacific Island Focds:
Peterson, Carl R., et al. 1965 Poliomyelitis in an isolated

-321-

GUIDE TO TOPICS AND AREAS

Medical

Sutow, W. W., et al. 1965 Growth status of children exposed to
Tate, Merze and Doris M. Hull 1964 Effects of nuclear explosions

Arno
Milhurn, J. D. 1959 Health and sanitation study of Arno Atoll.

Rongelap
Chakravarti, Diptiman and Edward E. Held 1963 Chemical and
Conard, Robert A., et al. 1960 Medical Survey of Rongelap People

Namu
Pollock, Nancy J. n.d. The risks of dietary change, a Pacific
Pollock, Nancy J. 1973 Breadfruit or rice: Dietary choice on a

GUIDE TO TOPICS AND AREAS

Military

Pacific Islands
Hough, Frank O. 1947 The Island War: The United States Marine
Isely, Jeter A. and Philip A. Crowl 1951 The U.S. Marines and
Lattimore, Eleanor 1945 Pacific Ocean or American Lake? Far

Micronesia (U.S.T.T.P.I.)
Adams, Col. Lawrence E. 1972 American involvement in Perspective.
Clark, LCdr. T. O. 1946 The administration of the former Japanese
Duke, Cdr. Marvin L. 1969 Micronesia: Western line of Defense.
Gale, Roger 1973 No one warned the Micronesians.
Haigwood, Col. Paul B. 1972 Japan and the Mandates.
Holbrook, Francis X. 1969 United States Naval defense and
Lane, Capt. Dwight A. 1972 Micronesia and Self-Determination.
Louis, William Roger, ed. 1972 National Security and
McPhetres, Sam 1975 Review of James C. Webb, Jr., Micronesia and
Millar, T. B. 1975 Review of William R. Louis, ed., National
Okumiya, Lt. Gen. Masatake 1968 For sugar boats or Submarines?
Peeke, C. E. B. 1968 For sugar boats or Submarines? U.S. Naval
Phillip, Alex 1971 Role of the U.S. Military in Micronesia.
Radford, Admiral Arthur 1951 The Navy in Micronesia.
Richard, LCdr. Dorothy 1957 U.S. Naval Administration of the
Stanford University 1948 Handbook of the Trust Territory of the
Useem, John 1945 The American pattern of military government in
Webb, James C., Jr. 1974 Micronesia and the United States'
Wilds, Thomas 1955 How Japan fortified the Mandated Islands.

Mariana Islands
Ballendorf, Dirk 1973 The confidential Micronesian Reporter.
Crowl, Philip A. 1960 Campaign in the Marianas.
Lincoln, Cdr. John R. 1972 The Mariana Islands.
Morton, Louis 1967 The Marianas.
United States Department of the Navy 1944 Civil Affairs Handbook:

Guam
James, Roy E. 1946 Military government: Guam.
Thompson, Laura 1944 Guam: Study in military Government.
Thompson, Laura 1947 Guam's bombed-out Capital.
Tweed, George and Blake Clark 1945 Robinson Crusoe, USN: The

Saipan
Feldkamp, Frederick 1945 Civil affairs on Saipan.
Moore, W. Robert 1945 South from Saipan.
Turner, Gordon B. 1950 The amphibious complex: A study of

Anatahan
Peter, Jim 1973 Odyssey on Anatahan.

Caroline Islands
Nystrom, Cdr. Frederic L. 1972 The Caroline Islands.

GUIDE TO TOPICS AND AREAS

Military

Palau Islands District
United States Department of the Navy 1944 Civil Affairs Handbook:

Yap District
United States Department of the Navy 1944 Civil Affairs Handbook:

Truk District
United States Department of the Navy 1944 Civil Affairs Handbook:

Truk Islands - Truk Lagoon
Bartlett, Cdr. D. 1970 Vice Admiral Chuichi Hara: Unforgettable
Hall, Edward T., Jr. 1950 Military government on Truk.
Murdock, George P. 1948 Waging baseball in Truk.

Ponape District
United States Department of the Navy 1944 Civil Affairs Handbook:

Ponape
Bascom, Willard R. 1950 Ponape, the tradition of Retaliation.

Kusaie - Kusaie District
United States Department of the Navy 1944 Civil Affairs Handbook:

Marshall Islands District
Bradley, David 1948 No Place to Hide.
Crowl, Philip A. and Edmund G. Love 1955 Seizure of the Gilberts
Hines, Neal O. 1962 Proving Ground: An Account of the
Hunter, Col. Clyde W. 1972 The Marshall Islands.
Moore, W. Robert 1945 Our new military wards, the Marshalls.
United States Department of the Navy 1943 Military Government

Enewetok
Kiste, Robert C. n.d. The people of Enewetak Atoll vs. the U.S.
Kiste, Robert C. 1975 Eniwetok resettlement project: Opinions

Bikini
Hines, Neal O. 1951 Bikini Report.
Kluge, P. F. 1947 Operation Crossroads.
Shurcliff, W. A. 1947 Bombs at Bikini: The Official Report of
Tobin, Jack A. 1970 Report on Bikini Atoll.

Rongelap
Holmes and Narver, Inc. n.d. Report of Repatriation of the

Physical Anthropology

Pacific Islands

Carroll, Vern, ed. 1975 Pacific Atoll Populations.
Howells, William W. 1970 Anthropometric grouping analysis of
Howells, William W. 1973 The Pacific Islanders.

Micronesia (U.S.T.T.P.I.)

Arai, Soji 1953 Anthropometric research on the Micronesians.
Hunt, Edward E., Jr. 1950 A view of somatology and serology in
Hunt, Edward E., Jr. 1951 Studies of physical anthropology in
Hunt, Edward E., Jr. 1966 Metrical variability and population
Imaizumi, Y. and Newton E. Morton 1970 Isolation by distance in
Kay, Alan 1974 Population growth in Micronesia.
Kidson, Cheviot S. 1967 Genetics of human populations; Studies in
Kidson, Cheviot S. and D. C. Gajdusek 1962 Glucose-6-phosphate
Morton, Newton E. 1973 Population structure of Micronesia.
Morton, Newton E. and J. M. Lalouel 1973 Bioassay of kinship in
Morton, Newton E. and J. M. Lalouel 1973 Topology of kinship in
Shapiro, Harry L. 1953 Physical anthropology of Micronesia:
Shinozaki, Nobuo 1953 Summary of the investigation on mixed-blood
Simmons, R. T. 1956 A report on blood group genetical surveys in
Simmons, R. T., et al. 1965 Blood group genetic variations in
Suda, Akiyoshi 1952 Bibliography on physical anthropology of the
Tauber, Irene and Chungnim C. Han 1950 Micronesian islands under
Underwood, Jane Hainline 1964 Human ecology in Micronesia:
Underwood, Jane Hainline 1965 Culture and biological Adaptation.
Underwood, Jane Hainline 1966 Population and genetic
U.S.T.T.P.I. 1975 1973 Population of the Trust Territory of the

Mariana Islands

Elizan, Teresita S., et al. 1966 Amyotrophic lateral sclerosis
Harris, Sarah Ellen 1953 Attempts to determine the blood group of
Kurland, Leonard T. 1957 Epidemiologic investigations of
Kurland, Leonard T. and Donald W. Mulder 1954 Epidemiologic
Kurland, Leonard T. and Donald W. Mulder 1955 Epidemiologic
Plato, Chris C., et al. 1964 Frequency of glucose-6-phosphate
Riesenberg, Saul H., et al. 1953 Blood groups of aboriginal
Solenberger, Robert R. 1960 Contrasting patterns of Carolinian

Guam

Brody, Jacob A. and Kwang-Ming Chen 1969 Changing epidemiology
Brody, Jacob A. and Leonard T. Kurland 1973 Amyotrophic lateral
Chung, Roy 1975 Fertility and the social structure of Guam.
Gavan, James A. 1952 Growth of Guamanian children--some
Greulich, William Walter 1951 The growth and development status
Kurland, Leonard T. 1963 High incidence of neurological disease
Kurland, Leonard T., et al. 1961 Parkinsonism-dementia complex,
McGrath, Thomas B. 1973 Abortion: Some observations about Guam.
Myrianthopoulos and Pieper 1959 The ABO and Rh blood groups
Plato, Chris C. and Manuel T. Cruz 1967 Blood group and

Physical Anthropology

Plato, Chris C., et al. 1969 Amyotrophic lateral sclerosis/
Plato, Chris C., et al. 1967 Amyotrophic lateral sclerosis/
Reed, Dwayne M. and Jacob A. Brody 1975 Amyotrophic lateral
Reed, Dwayne M., et al. 1975 Amyotrophic lateral sclerosis
Stanhope, John M., et al. 1972 Epidemiologic features of
Tashian, Richard E., et al. 1963 Inherited variant of
Torres, Jose M., et al. 1957 Amyotrophic lateral sclerosis
Underwood, Jane Hainline 1972 Report on a preliminary examination
Underwood, Jane Hainline 1973 Population history of Guam: Context

Saipan
Plato, Chris C., et al. 1966 Blood group investigations on
Tashian, Richard E., et al. 1963 Inherited variant of
Underwood, Jane Hainline 1965 Blood typing data, ABO and Rh(d),

Rota
Smith, James Jerome 1973 The population of Rota, May 1971.

Caroline Islands
Elizan, Teresita S., et al. 1966 Amyotrophic lateral sclerosis
Plato, Chris C., et al. 1966 Blood group investigations on
Simmons, R. T., et al. 1953 A blood group genetical survey in
Solenberger, Robert R. 1960 Contrasting patterns of Carolinian

Yap Islands
Clark, Peggy, et al. 1975 Serum proteins in people of the Yap
Goodenough, Ward H. 1972 Social implications of population
Hagaman, Roberta M. 1974 Divorce, remarriage, and fertility in a
Hunt, Edward E., Jr. 1951 Physique, social class and crime among
Hunt, Edward E., Jr. 1965 Polymorphisms of the ABO blood groups
Hunt, Edward E., Jr., et al. 1954 The depopulation of Yap.
Hunt, Edward E., Jr., et al. 1949 The Micronesians of Yap and
Hunt, Edward E., Jr., et al. 1965 The sex ratio of live births
Hunt, Edward E., Jr. and Jamshed Mavalwala 1964 Finger ridge
Mavalwala, Jamshed and Edward E. Hunt, Jr. 1964 Finger and palm
Plato, Chris C. and Jane Hainline Underwood 1969 Dermatoglyphics
Schneider, David M. 1955 Abortion and depopulation on a Pacific
Stevens, William D. 1949 A study of depopulation on Yap Island.
Underwood, Jane Hainline n.d. The Afghan caper, the Yapese
Underwood, Jane Hainline 1965 Blood typing data, ABO and Rh(d),
Underwood, Jane Hainline 1969 Ecological genetics of an island
Underwood, Jane Hainline 1969 Preliminary investigations of
Underwood, Jane Hainline 1973 The demography of a myth: Abortion
Underwood, Jane Hainline, et al. 1969 ABO, Rh, and MNS blood

Ulithi
Lessa, William A. 1955 Depopulation on Ulithi.
Lessa, William A. and Tracy Lay 1953 The somatology of Ulithi
Lessa, William A. and George C. Meyers 1962 Population dynamics

Woleai

GUIDE TO TOPICS AND AREAS

Physical Anthropology

Alkire, William H. 1972 Population dynamics of Woleai and

Lamotrek
Alkire, William H. 1972 Population dynamics of Woleai and

The Woleai
Plato, Chris C., et al. 1972 Dermatoglyphics of the Micronesians

Truk Islands - Truk Lagoon
Plato, Chris C. and Manuel T. Cruz 1966 Blood group and
Plato, Chris C. and Jerry D. Niswander 1967 Dermatoglyphics of

Namoluk
Marshall, Mac 1975 Changing patterns of marriage and migration on

Etal
Nason, James D. 1975 The strength of the land--community

Ponape District
Morton, Newton E. and Manabu Yamamoto 1973 Blood groups and
Steinberg, A. G. and Newton E. Morton 1973 Immunoglobulins in the
Yamamoto, Manabu and Linda Fu 1973 Red cell isozymes in the

Ponape
Murrill, Rupert I. 1950 Population, Physical Characteristics and
Murrill, Rupert I. 1950 Vital statistics of Ponape Island,

Mokil
Hussels, I. E. and Newton E. Morton 1972 Pingelap and Mokil
Morton, Newton E. and D. L. Greene 1972 Pingelap and Mokil
Morton, Newton E., et al. 1971 Pingelap and Mokil Atolls: Migration.
Morton, Newton E., et al. 1973 Pingelap and Mokil Atolls:
Morton, Newton E., et al. 1972 Pingelap and Mokil Atolls: Clans
Morton, Newton E., et al. 1972 Pingelap and Mokil Atolls: Historical
Morton, Newton E., et al. 1971 Pingelap and Mokil Atolls: Genealogy.

Pingelap
Carr, Ronald E., et al. 1971 Achromatopsia in Pingelap islanders:
Hussels, I. E. and Newton E. Morton 1972 Pingelap and Mokil
Morton, Newton E. and D. L. Greene 1972 Pingelap and Mokil
Morton, Newton E., et al. 1971 Pingelap and Mokil Atolls: Migration.
Morton, Newton E., et al. 1973 Pingelap and Mokil Atolls:
Morton, Newton E., et al. 1972 Pingelap and Mokil Atolls: Clans
Morton, Newton E., et al. 1972 Pingelap and Mokil Atolls: Historical
Morton, Newton E., et al. 1971 Pingelap and Mokil Atolls: Genealogy.

Nukucro
Carroll, Vern 1975 The population of Nukuoro in historical

Kusaie - Kusaie District
Morton, Newton E. and Manabu Yamamoto 1973 Blood groups and

GUIDE TO TOPICS AND AREAS

Physical Anthropology

Steinberg, A. G. and Newton E. Morton 1973 Immunoglobulins in the
Yamamoto, Manabu and Linda Fu 1973 Red cell isozymes in the

Marshall Islands District
Simmons, R. T., et al. 1952 A collaborative genetical survey in

Arno
Rynkiewich, Michael A. 1972 Demography and social structure on

Rongelap
Lisco, Herman and Robert Conard 1967 Chromosome studies on
Sussman, Leon N., et al. 1959 Blood groupings in Marshallese.

Namu
Pollock, Nancy J. 1972 Namu--an atoll population on the Move.
Pollock, Nancy J., et al. 1972 Kinship and inbreeding on Namu

GUIDE TO TOPICS AND AREAS

Political Science

Pacific Islands
Adam, Thomas R. 1967 Western Interests in the Pacific Realm.
Bailey, K. H. 1946 Dependent areas of the Pacific.
Brown, Bruce, ed. 1971 Asia and the Pacific in the 1970s: The
Cleveland, Harlan 1963 Reflections on the Pacific Community.
Davidson, James W. 1952 The changing political role of Pacific
Davidson, James W. 1971 The decolonization of Oceania.
Lattimore, Eleanor 1945 Pacific Ocean or American Lake? Far
Levi, Warner 1948 American attitudes toward Pacific Islands,
Meller, Norman 1958 Validity of records in the South Seas.
Meller, Norman 1959 Bilingualism in island legislatures of the
Meller, Norman 1965 Political change in the Pacific.
Meller, Norman 1965 Three American legislative bodies in the
Meller, Norman 1969 American legislatures in the Pacific.
Meller, Norman 1973 Legislative staff in Oceania as a focus for
Meller, Norman 1973 The Pacific legislature--spearhead for
Mihaly, Eugene B. 1974 Neutralization of Pacific Island states: A
Miller, William O. 1969 The United Nations and Oceania: New
Moos, Felix 1974 The old and the new: Japan and the United States
Perkins, Whitney T. 1962 Denial of Empire: The United States and
Pierard, Richard V. 1964 The German colonial society, 1882-1914.
Purcell, David Campell, Jr. 1967 Japanese expansion in the South
Robbins, Robert R. 1973 United States territories in Mid-Century.
Roucek, Joseph S. 1965 The Pacific in Geopolitics.
Sady, Emil J. 1950 The Department of the Interior and Pacific
Sady, Emil J. 1956 The United Nations and Dependent Peoples.
Sayre, Francis B. 1950 The Pacific islands we Hold.
Wainhouse, David W. 1964 U.S. dependencies: Decolonization begins
Weckler, Joseph E. 1958 Review of John Wesley Coulter, The

Micronesia (U.S.T.T.P.I.)
Adams, Col. Lawrence E. 1972 American involvement in Perspective.
Anonymous 1956 Modernizing without uprooting: The challenge of
Anonymous 1973 Micronesia: Strategic Trust Territory.
Arnold, Edwin G. 1947 Self government in United States
Bergbauer, Cdr. Harry W., Jr. 1970 A review of the political
Blaz, Vicente T. and Samuel S. H. Lee 1971 The Cross of
Bogan, Eugene F. 1950 Government of the Trust Territory of the
Boyd, Mary 1971 The southwest Pacific in the 1970s.
Brown, Carroll 1953 A survey of United States administration of
Burns, Richard D. 1968 Inspection of the Mandates, 1919-1941.
Cabranes, Jose A. 1973 The evolution of the 'American Empire'.
Carroll, Vern 1971 Review of Norman Meller with the assistance of
Clark, Roger 1973 The Trust Territory of the Pacific Islands:
Cockrum, Emmett Erston 1970 The emergence of modern Micronesia.
Collier, John 1946 Micronesia and trusteeship: Test for America
Collister, Cdr. Louis J. 1964 Trust Territory of the Pacific
Converse, Elizabeth 1949 The United States as Trustee--I.
Converse, Elizabeth 1949 The United States as Trustee--II.

GUIDE TO TOPICS AND AREAS

Political Science

Coolidge, Harold J. 1951 Science lends a hand.
Coulter, John Wesley 1957 The Pacific Dependencies of the United
Dean, Arthur 1947 Issues in Micronesia.
Dennett, Raymond 1945 U.S. Navy and dependent Areas.
Dobbs, James C. 1972 A macrostudy of Micronesia: The ending of a
Dybdal and Vasey 1973 Micronesia (United States Trust Territory
Embree, John F. 1946 Micronesia.
Embree, John F. 1949 American military Government.
Emerson, Rupert, et al. 1949 America's Pacific Dependencies.
Fifield, Russel H. 1946 Disposal of the Carolines, Marshalls, and
Fite, Jerry 1970 Cclonizing Paradise.
Gale, Roger 1973 No one warned the Micronesians.
Gilchrist, Huntington 1944 The Japanese Islands: Annexation or
Gilchrist, Huntington 1946 Trusteeship and the colonial System.
Goding, M. W. and T. Remengsau 1964 The Trust Territory of the
Goding, M. W. and V. N. Santos 1963 The Trust Territory of the
Gooding, Niles Russell 1962 The administration of the Trust
Grahlfs, Francis L., Jr. 1955 The effects of Japanese occupation
Grattan, C. Hartley 1944 Those Japanese Mandates.
Griswold, Lawrence 1972 Confusion in the confetti Islands.
Haigwood, Col. Paul B. 1972 Japan and the Mandates.
Hart, Thomas C. 1948 The United States and the Pacific Islands.
Hawaii Architects & Engineers, Inc. 1967 Goals and Policies,
Hawaii Architects & Engineers, Inc. 1968 Progress Report on
Hawkins, James 1969 Factors affecting Micronesian political
Hawkins, James 1969 Requirements for Micronesian political
Heine, Carl 1965 A historical study of political development and
Heine, Carl 1969 Micronesia's Future Political Status Commission:
Heine, Carl 1970 Micronesia is confused about what it Wants.
Heine, Carl 1970 Micronesia: Unification and the coming of
Heine, Carl 1974 Micronesia at the Crossroads: A Reappraisal of
Hempenstall, Peter John 1975 Review of Carl Heine, Micronesia at
Hitch, Thomas K. 1946 The administration of America's Pacific
Hitchcock, David I., Jr. 1974 Information and Education for
Hobbs, William H. 1945 The Fortress Islands of the Pacific.
Hopkins, J. W. 1964 Toward self-government in the Trust
Jackman, Harry H. 1967 America in the West Pacific: Integrating
Jacobson, Harold K. 1960 Our "colcnial" problem in the Pacific.
James, Roy E. 1949 The Trust Territory of the Pacific Islands.
Johnson, Donald D. 1970 The Trust Territory of the Pacific
Johnston, William J. 1970 The United States as a Pacific Power.
Jones, Garth Nelson 1954 Administration of the Trust Territcry of
Kahn, E. J., Jr. 1966 The small islands: America and its
Kanost, R. F. 1970 Localization in the Trust Territory of the
Keesing, Felix M. 1945 The former Japanese Mandated Islands.
Keesing, Felix M. 1947 Administration in Pacific Islands.
King, Norma N. 1975 Review of Carl Heine, Micronesia at the
Kiste, Robert C. 1975 Micronesia: The politics of the Colonized.
Kostelnik, Mary B. 1971 Democracy in Micronesia: An examination
Lane, Capt. Dwight A. 1972 Micronesia and Self-Determination.
Logan-Smith, Nat 1962 A descriptive analysis of the personnel

Political Science

Louis, William Roger, ed. 1972 National Security and
Maki, Jchn M. 1947 US strategic area or UN Trusteeship? Far
Mander, Linden A. 1956 The U.N. Mission's 1956 survey of the
Marston, Geoffrey 1969 Termination cf Trusteeship.
Mason, Leonard E. 1948 Trusteeship in Micronesia.
McClam, Virginia G. 1971 United States public policy and its
McDonald, Hugh 1949 Trusteeship in the Pacific.
McPhetres, Sam 1975 Review of James C. Webb, Jr., Micronesia and
Meller, Norman 1966 The identification and classification of
Meller, Norman 1967 Districting a new legislature in Micronesia.
Meller, Norman 1967 Representational role types: A research Note.
Meller, Norman 1968 American Pacific outposts: Guam, Samoa, and
Meller, Norman 1969 The Congress of Micronesia--A unifying and
Meller, Norman 1970 Indigenous leadership in the Trust Territory
Meller, Norman 1974 Micronesian political change in Perspective.
Meller and Meller 1969 The Congress of Micronesia.
Metelski, John B. 1974 Micronesia and free association: Can
Micronesian Seminar 1973 Proceedings of a Seminar on Moral Issues
Midkiff, Frank E. 1953 Administering the Pacific Trust Territory.
Midkiff, Frank E. 1953 Problems in the administration of the
Midkiff, Frank E. 1954 Problems of the Pacific Trust.
Midkiff, Frank E. 1954 United States Administration of the Trust
Mihaly, Eugene B. 1970 United States strategy in the Western
Mihaly, Eugene B. 1973 Micronesia: A U.S. strategic pawn of 2000
Mihaly, Eugene B. 1974 Tremors in the Western Pacific.
Millar, T. B. 1975 Review of William R. Louis, ed., National
Milner, George 1956 Political progress in Micronesia.
Mink, Patsy T. 1971 Micronesia: Our bungled Trust.
Moore, W. Robert 1948 Pacific wards of Uncle Sam? National
Moos, Felix 1972 Strategy and occupation: The U.S. and Japan in
Morgan, H. Wayne 1965 Making Peace with Spain: The Diary of
Morgiewicz, Cdr. Daniel J. 1968 Micronesia: Especial Trust.
Murdock, George P. 1953 Administrative needs and objectives in
Newlon, Robert Edward 1949 Evolution of the United States'
O'Connor, LCdr. Edward C. 1969 Micronesia--America's Western
Oberdorfer, Don 1964 America's neglected colonial Paradise.
Pelzer, Karl J. 1950 Micronesia--a changing Frontier.
Pomeroy, Earl Spencer 1948 American policy respecting the
Pomeroy, Earl Spencer 1951 Pacific Outpost.
Porter, Catherine 1944 The Japanese Mandates.
Powells, Guy 1970 Political alternatives in Micronesia.
Quigg, Philip W. 1969 Coming of age in Micronesia.
Rappaport, Michael D. 1972 The constitution of Micronesia:
Robbins, Robert R. 1947 United States Trusteeship for the
Robbins, Robert R. 1968 Law Note.
Robbins, Robert R. 1969 Political future of Micronesia and the
Rowley, Charles D. 1972 Transition to independence: Some New
Sahir, Abul Hasan 1966 United States' Trust Territory in the
Salii, Lazarus E. 1972 Liberation and conquest in Micronesia.
Sayre, Francis B. 1948 American trusteeship in the Pacific.
Sayre, Francis B. 1951 Trust Territories' progress toward

Political Science

Shahan, James Buhl 1951 American colonial administration in the
Sheridan, Francis P. 1954 Why strategic areas? A study of the
Sigler, Jay A. 1960 American administration of the Pacific
Silk, Ekpap 1969 Creation of the Future Political Status
Singleton, John 1974 The U.S. Trust Territory in the Pacific.
Smith, Allan H. 1956 Attitudes and relationships
Smith, Donald F. 1971 The political evolution of Micronesia
Smith, Donald F. 1973 Diversity in Micronesia.
Smith, Frances McReynolds 1972 From Trust Territory to
Smith, Frances McReynolds, ed. 1972 Micronesian Realities:
Smith, Stanley A. de 1969 Options for Micronesia: A potential
Smith, Stanley A. de 1970 Microstates and Micronesia: Problems of
Stanford University 1948 Handbook of the Trust Territory of the
Taylor, Theodore W., et al. 1951 Management Survey of the
Thomas, Theodore Hubert 1957 The aims and organization of the
Thompson, Laura 1948 A model trusteeship for Micronesia.
Toomin, Philip R. and Pauline M. Toomin 1963 Black Robe and Grass
Udui, Kaleb 1972 America's dilemmas in carrying out its
Udui, Kaleb 1972 Free Association--A political status option of
Uherbelau, Victorio 1972 Does a "domestic" Micronesia really
Uludong, Francisco T. 1969 A review of some aspects of
Uludong, Francisco T. 1969 Whither Micronesia? IN Political
Uludong, Francisco T. 1972 Comments on political future of
Useem, John 1946 Americans as governors of natives in the
Useem, John 1946 Social reconstruction in Micronesia.
Valentine, Charles A. 1963 Social status, political power, and
Valle, Maria Teresa del 1971 The Congress of Micronesia.
Webb, James C., Jr. 1974 Micronesia and the United States'
Wiens, Herold J. 1962 Pacific Island Bastions of the United
Wiliander, Hans 1972 Independence as a political Alternative.
Wilson, James 1973 The applicability of the principle of
Wright, Rear Admiral Carleton H. 1948 Trust Territory of the
Wyttenbach, Richard Harrington 1971 Micronesia and strategic
Yinug, Martin 1972 Leadership requirements in Micronesia.
Yotopoulos, Pan A. 1972 The hard realities of developing a new

Mariana Islands
Lincoln, Cdr. John R. 1972 The Mariana Islands.

Guam
Carano, Paul 1972 Development of representative self-government
Force, Roland W. 1973 The Guam experiment: Beginning of a new
Meller, Norman 1960 Political changes in American Pacific
Meller, Norman 1968 American Pacific outposts: Guam, Samoa, and
Munoz, Ben G. 1975 Law enforcement in Guam.
Pomeroy, Earl Spencer 1951 Pacific Outpost.
Porter, Catherine 1944 Guam.
San Agustin, Joe T. 1965 United States guaranteed municipal
Stevens, Russell L. 1953 Guam, U.S.A.: Birth of a Territory.
Tansill, William Raymond 1951 Guam and Its Administration.
Thompson, Laura 1946 Crisis on Guam.

GUIDE TO TOPICS AND AREAS

Political Science

Saipan
Embree, John F. 1946 Military government on Saipan and Tinian.
Feldkamp, Frederick 1945 Civil affairs on Saipan.
Hawaii Architects & Engineers, Inc. 1968 Saipan, Mariana Islands
Williams, John Z. 1946 Administration of the natives of Saipan.

Rota
Hawaii Architects & Engineers, Inc. 1972 Rota, Mariana Islands.

Tinian
Embree, John F. 1946 Military government on Saipan and Tinian.
Gale, Roger 1974 Tinian: New base in Asia.

Caroline Islands
Bieber, Patricia 1973 Translation from the Spanish of Rafael
Nystrom, Cdr. Frederic L. 1972 The Caroline Islands.

Palau Islands
Hawaii Architects & Engineers, Inc. 1968 Koror, Palau District.
Hawaii Architects & Engineers, Inc. 1973 Babelthuap, Palau
Vidich, Arthur J. 1953 The political impact of colonial

Yap Islands
Hawaii Architects & Engineers, Inc. 1968 Yap, Yap District.

Truk Islands - Truk Lagoon
Clifton, James A. 1964 The acceptance of external political
Hawaii Architects & Engineers, Inc. 1968 Moen Island, Truk
Hawaii Architects & Engineers, Inc. 1972 Tol, Truk District.

Ponape
Clifton, James A. 1964 The acceptance of external political
Hawaii Architects & Engineers, Inc. 1968 Ponape Island, Ponape
Jackman, Harry H. 1964 Co-operative housing at Metalanim, Ponape,

Kusaie - Kusaie District
Abraham, Isamu 1974 Kusaie's quest for separate district status.

Marshall Islands District
Anonymous 1954 Islanders appeal to the United Nations on bomb
Hunter, Col. Clyde W. 1972 The Marshall Islands.
Mason, Leonard E. 1949 The Marshallese lock to Uncle Sam.
Meller, Norman 1960 Political changes in American Pacific
Tate, Merze and Doris M. Hull 1964 Effects of nuclear explosions

Wotje
Hawaii Architects & Engineers, Inc. 1972 Wotje, Marshall Islands.

Majuro
Hawaii Architects & Engineers, Inc. 1968 Majuro, Marshall Islands

GUIDE TO TOPICS AND AREAS

Political Science

Enewetok
Kiste, Robert C. n.d. The people of Enewetak Atoll vs. the U.S.
Kiste, Robert C. 1975 Eniwetok resettlement project: Opinions

Kwajalein
Hawaii Architects & Engineers, Inc. 1968 Ebeye and Carlson

Kili
Riesenberg, Saul H. 1954 Community development project at Kili.

GUIDE TO TOPICS AND AREAS

Psychology

Micronesia (U.S.T.T.P.I.)
Brislin, Richard W. 1970 Back-translation for cross-cultural
Brislin, Richard W. 1974 The Ponzo illusion: Additional cues,

Guam
Paler, Abraham D. 1975 Draw-a-man: The IQ test for Guam Children.
Rainey, Mary C. and George L. Boughton 1975 The socialization of
Womack, William W., et al. 1969 Adolescent psychiatry in Guam.

Truk Islands - Truk Lagoon
Masland, Richard L., et al. 1958 Mental Subnormality:

GUIDE TO TOPICS AND AREAS

Zoology

Pacific Islands
Banner, Albert H. 1961 Fish poisoning in the tropical Pacific.

Micronesia (U.S.T.T.P.I.)
Anonymous 1947 Micronesian expedition of University of Hawaii
Baker, Rollin H. 1946 Some effects of the war on the wildlife of
Baker, Rollin H. 1951 The Avifauna of Micronesia, Its Origin,
Embree, John F. 1946 University of Hawaii research in Micronesia.
Fischer, John L. 1969 Letter: "Starfish infestation: Hypothesis."
Mayr, Ernst 1945 The land and fresh-water birds of Micronesia.
Oakley, Richard G. 1946 Entomological Observations in the
Paszkowski, Lech 1971 John Stanislaw Kubary-naturalist and
Sachet, Marie-Helene and F. Raymond Fosberg 1955 Island
Sachet, Marie-Helene and F. Raymond Fosberg 1971 Island
Townes, Henry K. 1946 Results of an Entomological Inspection Tour
Wilson, Erika 1974 Seabirds and Micronesians.

Mariana Islands
Schultz, Leonard P., et al. 1953 Fishes of the Marshall and
Schultz, Leonard P., et al. 1960 Fishes of the Marshall and
Schultz, Leonard P., et al. 1966 Fishes of the Marshall and

Saipan
Elameto, Jesus M. 1975 Carolinian names of common fishes in

Caroline Islands
Elameto, Jesus M. 1975 Carolinian names of common fishes in

Palau Islands
Clark, Eugenie 1953 Siakong--spear fisherman pre-eminent:
Helfman, Gene S. and John E. Randall 1973 Palauan fish Names.

Truk Islands - Truk Lagoon
Brandt, John H. 1962 Nests and eggs of the birds of the Truk
Wilson, Peter T. 1971 Truk live-bait Survey.

Namoluk
Marshall, Mac 1971 Notes on birds from Namoluk Atoll.
Marshall, Mac 1975 The natural history of Namoluk Atoll, Eastern

Marshall Islands District
Amerson, A. Binion, Jr. 1969 Ornithology of the Marshall and
Fosberg, F. Raymond 1966 Northern Marshall Islands land biota:
Fosberg, F. Raymond 1969 Observations on the green turtle in the
Schultz, Leonard P., et al. 1953 Fishes of the Marshall and
Schultz, Leonard P., et al. 1960 Fishes of the Marshall and
Schultz, Leonard P., et al. 1966 Fishes of the Marshall and

Arno

GUIDE TO TOPICS AND AREAS

Zoology

Marshall, J. T., Jr. 1951 Vertebrate ecology of Arno Atoll,

Enewetok
Richardson, Frank 1960 Preliminary report on the birds of

Bikini
Hines, Neal O. 1951 Bikini Report.

Rongelap
Richardson, Frank 1960 Preliminary report on the birds of

o Farallon De Pajaros

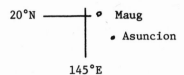

20°N ——————|o Maug

           • Asuncion

145°E

       o Agrihan

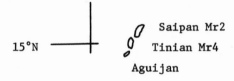

0 Pagan Mr5

    o Alamagan

    • Guguan

    . Sarigan

    ⌐ Anatahan Mr6

     • Farallon De Medinilla

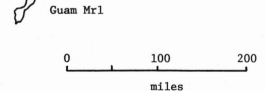

         Saipan Mr2

15°N ——————| Tinian Mr4

     Aguijan

   ⌐ Rota Mr3

    Guam Mr1

0   100   200

miles

MARIANA DISTRICT AND GUAM

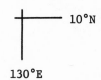

10°N

130°E

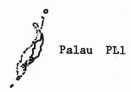

Palau PL1

Sonsorol PL4

Pulo Anna PL2

Merir PL5

Tobi PL3

Helen

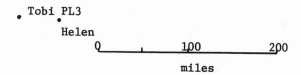

0 100 200

miles

0°

PALAU DISTRICT

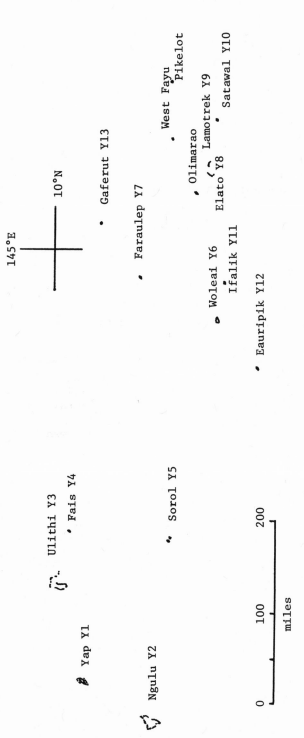

145°E

10°N

Gaferut Y13

West Fayu
· Pikelot

· Faraulep Y7

· Olimarao
Lamotrek Y9
Elato Y8 · Satawal Y10

Woleai Y6
Ifalik Y11

Eauripik Y12

Ulithi Y3
· Fais Y4

· Sorol Y5

Yap Y1

Ngulu Y2

0   100   200
         miles

YAP DISTRICT

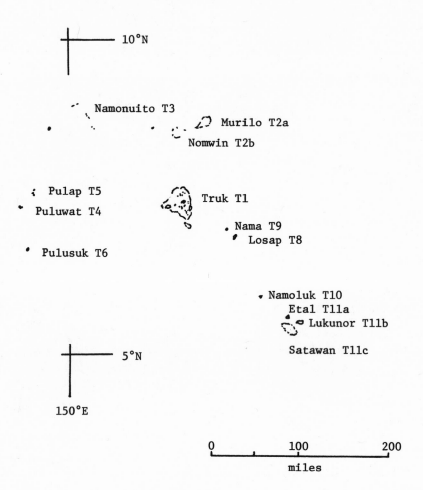

10°N

Namonuito T3

Murilo T2a
Nomwin T2b

Pulap T5
Puluwat T4

Truk T1

Nama T9
Losap T8

Pulusuk T6

Namoluk T10
Etal T11a
Lukunor T11b

Satawan T11c

5°N

150°E

0   100   200
miles

TRUK DISTRICT

ᘓ Oroluk Pn2

. Pakin Pn3
ᕬ Ponape Pn1
Ant Pn4 • Mokil Pn6

• Pingelap Pn7

ᕬ Ngatik Pn5

┼──— 5°N

160°E

ᕬ
Kusaie K

ᕬ Nukuoro Pn8

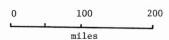

```
0          100         200
├─────────┼─────────────┤
         miles
```

ᕬ Kapingamarangi Pn9

PONAPE DISTRICT AND KUSAIE

15°N

165°E

Taongi Ms27

Bikar

Eniwetok Ms11

Bikini Ms13

Rongelap Ms15
Rongerik Ms14
Ailinginae

Utirik Ms1
Taka

Ailuk Ms3

Mejit Ms2

Wotho Ms16

Likiep Ms4

Jemo

Wotje Ms5
Erikub

Maloelap Ms6

Aur Ms7

Majuro Ms8
Arno Ms9

Mili Ms10

Ujae Ms17
Lae Ms18

Kwajalein Ms19

Lib Ms20

Namu Ms21

Ailinglapalap Ms22

Jaluit Ms23

Kili Ms24

Namorik Ms25

Ebon Ms26

Ujelang Ms12

0   100   200
        miles

5°N

MARSHALL DISTRICT